ADOLESCENT SEX ROLES AND SOCIAL CHANGE

ADOLESCENT SEX ROLES AND SOCIAL CHANGE

LLOYD B. LUEPTOW

COLUMBIA UNIVERSITY PRESS
NEW YORK   1984

Library of Congress Cataloging in Publication Data

Lueptow, Lloyd B.
  Adolescent sex roles and social change.

  Bibliography: p.
  Includes index.
  1. Youth—United States—Longitudinal studies.
2. Adolescent psychology—United States—Longitudinal
studies. 3. Sex role—United States—Longitudinal
studies. 4. Sex differences (Psychology)—
Longitudinal studies. 5. Personality—Longitudinal
studies. I. Title.
HQ796.L79   1984   305.2′35′0973   83-7842
ISBN 0-231-05712-1

Columbia University Press
New York Guildford, Surrey

Clothbound editions of Columbia University Press books are Smyth-
sewn and printed on permanent and durable acid-free paper.

To my wife
Jean

And our children
Diana and Steven

CONTENTS

PREFACE

This book is concerned with changing sex roles and with some aspects of the changing society that contains them.

As in the recent studies by Duncan and Duncan (1978) and Veroff, Douvan, and Kulka (1981), it uses an earlier survey as baseline data for the examination of change or stability revealed by later replication of the instrument in the same social context. In the present case, the baseline data were created by a 1964 survey carried out by a curriculum study council made up of twenty Wisconsin high schools. The purpose of the council was to carry out applied research within the member schools directed toward curriculum improvement and development. The goal of the 1964 survey was to develop data on the characteristics related to the post-high school experience of the students, especially the noncollege-bound student. I was lucky enough to be involved in this enterprise as a research associate serving a university urban studies team that provided resources to the council, and thus was able to suggest variables especially pertinent to achievement and occupational goals, in addition to the items on educational experiences and evaluations. The overall cluster of variables plus transcript information resulting from that effort are the baseline data for the present examination of sex role change and social change.

In the early 1970s it occurred to me that the 1964 baseline data were well suited to the study of sex difference and change among the adolescent seniors and proposed the research to the now latent study council. In spite of the numerous surveys being conducted in the high schools that spring, the real concerns at that time about invasion of privacy and the problems associated with the intense advocacy of the protection of human subjects, even in survey research, the administrations of seventeen of the original high schools agreed to the survey (delayed one year because of funding problems). The result was to establish a rich cluster of variables on adolescent experience, goals, values, and behavior.

In preparing the research proposal for the 1975 replication I was surprised to discover that in the early 1970s there was relatively little published empirical evidence documenting the revolution in sex roles so many writers were addressing. Interestingly enough, the literature very clearly revealed major value shifts between the 1960s and the 1970s as well as important differences between the sexes on many personal and social variables. With some notable exceptions, that picture has not changed greatly in the ensuing period, as the literature reviews presented below and the major replication studies of Duncan and Duncan (1978) and Veroff, Douvan, and Kulka (1981) reveal.

This study addresses three questions: the amount of sex role differentiation in the personal, social, and educational characteristics of these high school adolescents, the amount of change in these characteristics over the time period, and the change in the amount of difference between the sexes, i.e., sex role change. In meeting these issues, the study has been broadly inclusive. In addition to the many variables whose "sex typing" has been established in previous literature, I have operationalized sex roles as any statistically significant difference between the sexes. Social change is change in the level of each variable, while sex role change is a change, usually reduction, in the differences between the sexes across the years. Given the breadth of the information and its close tie to the reality of these student's lives, it seems unlikely that many important aspects of sex role change could go unobserved in this research.

To establish the significance of the variables of this study to the field of sex roles, the empirical report has been embedded in a reasonably comprehensive review of the literature on sex differences and on changing sex roles. The predictions or implications of this literature have been detailed and what seemed to be interesting linkages between various bodies of literature have been stated, at times in somewhat speculative terms. I have attempted, however, to provide a full, summary treatment of the empirical evidence in each relevant area and have tried to show how specific variables of this study bear upon substantive and theoretical issues emerging in the study of sex roles. For the reader thoroughly immersed in the entire literature of sex roles, much of this will be redundant and such readers may wish to skim some of these sections.

However, even these readers may find an occasional feature of interest because of two aspects of the treatment. In the first place, I have attempted to provide a broad social and psychological perspective for interpreting these results. This social psychological perspective seems especially important for the understanding of sex role phenomena, encompassing as they do cultural, structural, and personal elements. Second, here and there I have taken a critical and skeptical view of some "congenial truths" and have tried to hold an objective, data-oriented approach to these interpretations. This will result in an occasional departure from our conventional understandings.

This book also contains analysis using a number of variables viewed as facilitating variables, in an attempt to test the possibility that change may be greater in some groups (children of working mothers, for example) than in others. This analysis is performed for nearly every major cluster of dependent variables, and reported section by section throughout the book. While my conclusion is that these variables have little to do with the amount of change observed in this study, it is true that this analysis consistently returns results that approach statistical significance, in some cases, high significance. Those readers agreeing with my conclusion may wish to start skipping those sections as they read through the report. However, for those interested in pursuing the possibility that my conclusion is erroneous, the discussions of outcomes are presented throughout the book in the sections where the relevant sex role characteristics are presented and discussed.

Overall, this work differs from previous work in the extensiveness of the personal information, the focus on educational factors and the systematic testing of the proposition of sex role change across a full set of variables concurrently rather than selectively. The result is a picture of sex-differentiated adolescent experience that reveals some instances of sex role change but which for the larger part shows stable sex differences within a context of social change.

ACKNOWLEDGMENTS

This research was made possible by the dedicated and concerned high school administrators and counselors who fielded the 1964 survey, made the data available to me, and cooperated in the 1975 replication. Without their initial interest and continuing support, this study could never have been carried out. It was also made possible by the thousands of high school seniors who were willing to take the time to provide the questionnaire information and who agreed to the use of their transcript data.

Thus, I would like to acknowledge my deep appreciation to the superintendents, principals, counselors, student participants, and others who assisted me in the 1975 data gathering in the following Wisconsin high schools: Appleton East, Appleton West, Berlin, Bonduel, Brillion, Depere, Fond du Lac Goodrich, Green Bay Preble, Kimberly, New London, Omro, Oshkosh North, Oshkosh West, Reedsville, Ripon, Southern Door, Wild Rose, Winneconne, and Wittenburg-Birnamwood.

I would also like to express my appreciation for the assistance and courtesy provided by the dean's office of the School of Education at the University of Wisconsin-Oshkosh. The endorsement of the 1975 replication by the dean of that college and the toleration of my working presence in the dean's office and the Department of Counseling during the spring and summer of 1975 made the replication possible. I should especially like to thank Richard Hammes and Larry Masters for their assistance in the field aspects of the study. As the last executive secretary of the Fox Valley Curriculum Study Council, Dr. Masters was especially critical in helping me organize the survey administration and in sponsoring me in visits to participating schools. I remain deeply in his debt.

The 1975 survey was supported by a grant from the University of Akron Faculty Research Committee and by a major grant from the National Institute of Mental Health that provided resources for the 1975 coding and the processing of the substantial data files from the two surveys. The supplementary data gathering carried out in the summer of 1975 to examine response bias was made possible by a contract with the Department of Health, Education and Welfare. Reduced teaching loads to work on this manuscript were provided by the University of Akron in the fall semesters of 1979 and 1980. I appreciate the responsiveness of Dean Claibourne Griffin and Professor Richard Gigliotti, Head of the Sociology Department, to requests for reduced loads during this period.

The computer center at the University of Akron has provided the very large amounts of time and storage required by this project. I am appreciative of this crucial contribution by the director of the center, Frank Thomas, and by members of his staff, notably Marge Duffalo, who helped me master new systems and approaches. Both suffered my demanding and complaining presence until the tremendous processing advantage of remote terminal access removed me from their scene. Dean Griffin further facilitated this analysis by acquiring portable terminals for the college, which vastly increased my analysis speed while also enabling me to occasionally see my wife and children.

Over the years my friend and colleague McKee McClendon has served as a sounding board and provided more statistical and methodological advice than the scattered acknowledgments in the text indicate, or than I was always able to absorb. McKee of course has no responsibility for my use or misuse of his advice.

Mary Minard Moynihan, my research assistant on the 1975 replication, supervised the coding and processing of the data. The accuracy of these data owe much to her tireless efforts in this phase of the study.

Production of a research monograph also prompts me to acknowledge a long-standing debt to William H. Sewell, whose classes, personal contacts, and research example have had a considerable and lasting influence on my work and my values.

Finally, I appreciate the contribution of Irene Fort, who did a lot of the typing and a great deal of organizing the communications and procedures necessary to the 1975 replication as well as the present manuscript. Her cheerful, zestful competence and ability to catch my mistakes and recoup my lost deadlines have saved many of my efforts throughout this long project. I should also like to thank Beverly Riggin and Patricia Conely for their help and for their patience with my endless corrections and revisions, and Julia Charek, who has had the unenviable task of producing the final copy of all the tables of this report.

ADOLESCENT SEX ROLES AND SOCIAL CHANGE

CHAPTER 1

SOCIAL CHANGE AND SEX ROLE CHANGE: AN OVERVIEW

The study reported in this book is about change in a variety of sex-related aspects of personality and experience. It draws on the records and responses of seniors in seventeen high schools in a midwestern state, half of whom graduated in 1964 and half in 1975. As the same information and opinions were collected in both years, the study provides a range of information about change in personality and circumstance over that decade. As the decade from the mid-1960s to the mid-1970s was an especially critical period for changes in the roles of women and men, these data constitute pertinent information about the amount of change or stability in sex-related aspects of personality and experience. As we shall see, these data encompass a broader range of variables and characteristics relevant to issues of changing sex roles than previous studies have yet reported, and in that regard, the information to be described in the following pages is relatively unique.[1]

SEX ROLES

In considering change and stability of characteristics and experiences over the study decade, I use the concept of sex roles, notwithstanding the substantial terminological problems associated with this and with related concepts. In this research sex roles are used to refer to all of the differences between the socialized boys and girls who are the subject of this research.

There is general agreement in the literature that men and women are distinguished by social norms and customs and that in all societies, the behavior of women and men is differentiated, even though not every society assigns exactly the same behavior to the same sex (Daly and Wilson 1978; Chafetz 1978). Women and men are expected to hold different positions, exhibit different behaviors, and manifest different traits of personality. In all of these aspects, there are social norms and conventions specifying the assigned characteristics and positions. The conceptual problems emerge when origins of the characteristics are considered and when the relevance of the traditional assignments is assessed in conjunction with the variability and freedom of contemporary societies, with their extensive potentials for alternative forms and arrangements. It is obviously one thing if all assignments of personal characteristics are totally arbitrary social outcomes that can be modified over time through the demands of sociocultural systems; it is something else again if the characteristics are largely or partially the result of clear and obvious physical differences between the sexes. Unfortunately, at the present time, these questions are unanswerable, and in some cases, as in the linkages between biological and psychological levels, not even clearly formulated as meaningful and testable theoretical propositions. The terminology reflects this confusion. Traditional social scientific formulations turn out to be less than adequate for the tasks at hand.

Sex role is the term originally used to refer to the different positions and behaviors of women and men. In social science, role refers to the behavior expected of the occupant of a position in society. Positions are viewed as locations in social space, placed and operationally defined in terms of their interrelationships with each other and with the institutions that contain them. Assignment to these positions is made variously, on the basis of either the *qualities* a person manifests, or on the basis of some *performance* capability that the person exhibits or is presumed to be able to exhibit. The assignment on the basis of some quality such as age, sex, or biological relatedness is described as *ascription,* while attainment of a position through some effort and qualification by the individual is described as *achievement.* The traditional assignment of clusters of role behaviors on the basis of sex has been an ascribed process.[2] The contemporary movement toward individual freedom and choice in social roles irregardless of sex is a fundamental shift in social allocation from ascription to achievement. At the same time, such change robs the concept of sex roles of much of its original meaning. If sex or gender has nothing to do with role assignment, there would be no differentiation on that basis and no utility whatsoever in the concept.

There is currently some argument among students of sex roles about the appropriateness of the concepts of sex roles versus gender roles. For some, gender role is preferable because it emphasizes the presumed arbitrariness of sex role assignment. Because gender is more clearly social than sex, it conveys an additional emphasis on arbitrary assignment as compared to more deterministic implications of assignment on the basis of sex.[3] In this the concept of gender roles suggests an arbitrariness in assignment that future research evidence may or may not sustain. As the bulk of the relative literature uses the concept of sex role, that concept is used throughout this study, although with the recognition that the majority, but probably not all, of the sex-typed differences are arbitrary social assignments not necessarily tied to sexual categories, and that sex role and gender role are essentially equivalent concepts. Both gender role and sex role will become empty concepts if future societies find no socially important differences in the underlying physiology of women and men. At present, however, this seems an unlikely possibility.

Sex role differentiations are clearest in traditional social structures where the fact of sexuality underlies important differences in the cluster of behaviors assigned to either men or women in the family. Generally speaking, these are the patterns referred to by Parsons and Bales (1955) as the instrumental-expressive distinction and documented to one degree or another from Zelditch (1955) to Weitz (1977) as basic sociocultural differences in the roles of women and men. In general, and almost universally, women have been assigned responsibility for childbearing, child rearing, and related household behaviors, while men have been assigned roles having to do with external relations, hunting, and warfare.

At the level of personality, the concept of sex role has been used to refer to differential expectations of general behavioral and temperamental characteristics associated with sterotypes of men and women (Broverman et al. 1972). While this aspect overlaps considerably with the structural usage of sex roles, the intersex consensus and persistence over time of sex role stereotypes (Lueptow 1980c) suggests utility of the concept beyond the specific application to family role differentiations. The differentiation of expected behavior and personality characteristics of women and men is reflected at the individual level in conceptions of gender identity that are related to portrayal of masculine and feminine behaviors within and outside of specific role contexts.

This study consequently uses sex role as an imperfect but useful concept to refer to those differences between women and men that are socially recognized and defined by appropriate normative role expectations. Whether these expectations are derived from social circumstances such as traditional role differentiation with the family, or from the needs of the sexes in interpersonal relations, or from some aspect of biological difference, is not a substantial issue in this research. My concern is with demonstrated differences between the sexes that will be taken as indicators of sex role differentiation. The greater the difference the stronger the role differentiation is assumed to be. From this perspective, change in sex roles appears as change in the differences between the sexes.

SEX ROLE CHANGE AND SOCIAL CHANGE

Throughout the analysis to follow, an effort is made to distinguish change in sex roles from general social change. As it turns out, this is considerably easier to accomplish at the empirical operational level than at the conceptual level. At the conceptual level, the distinctiveness but also the ubiquity of women as a social category creates special problems of definition.[4] In the sense that women as a category are distinct from men as a category, distinctions between sex role change and social change are relatively simple. However, as women and men together make up society, obviously important aspects of change experienced by women are also experienced by men and are not, consequently, processes of sex role change per se, but rather of social change. The overlaying of social roles with sex roles precludes a precise and generally applicable conceptual distinction between these two forms of change. They can be distinguished, nevertheless, most usefully by conceptualizing the nature of the empirical operations used later in the examination of the results of the study.

Social Change

Social change consists of those alterations of social institutions, interpersonal relations, cultural values, and personal experience and orientation that are broadly manifest in the society as a whole. Obviously, in this general formulation, sex role change is encompassed within social change, and in fact represents one of the striking and significant varieties of change occurring at the present time. However, other changes occur irrespective of sex role effects and represent social change rather than sex role change. Still other changes are ambiguous, reflecting some aspect of general change, but involving differential effects on the sex roles of men and women.

For example, the increasing affluence of these times affects both men and women, but the differential gains experienced by men and women in income, status, and prestige over recent decades reflect sex role processes. Similarly, increased longevity, introduction of labor-saving devices within the home, and reduction in size of family, and fertility rates are all changes experienced by women and men, although in some aspects experienced differently in terms of the components of sex role patterns and identities.

While it is impossible to satisfactorily disentangle these concepts, it is useful to distinguish at least the extreme manifestations of general social change from those of sex role change. By making this distinction, even while accepting the ambiguities between the two concepts, we are prepared for instances where examination of only one role might indicate occurrence of sex role change, when in fact general social changes were unfolding. As we examine the evidence on change over the period, social change will be described as those changes occurring equally for women and men without altering their relative positions along the dimension of change. This operationalization is relatively clear-cut and simple to utilize in a study such as this.

Sex Role Change

Sex role change as distinct from general social change involves change in the relative differences between the sexes on any aspect under consideration. While this formulation leaves much to be desired, it follows from the treatment of sex roles and is a consequence of the difficulty of clearly distinguishing sex role across all levels. The concept is clearest in considering changes in family roles, from patriarchy to equality to alternative life styles, but has application also at levels of personality, where increased assertiveness of women or increased compassion of men might be involved. The central point is change in relation to the other sex. In the final analysis, and consistent with sociological formulations of status and role, sex roles are meaningful only in terms of opposite sex comparisons and contrasts. Masculinity has no meaning independent of femininity.

Theoretically, change in the degree of differentiation between women and men could occur by either increasing or decreasing the original differences. However, with some notable exceptions, such as Phyllis Schlafly, no one seriously considers the possibility of sex role change involving *increased* differentiation. Except in discussions or analysis of profeminist goals or antiabortion or an ERA event, students of sex roles do not even consider the possibility of increasing differentiation, either in family roles or in interpersonal relations.

The overwhelming expectation, in some cases the clear goal, of writers on changing sex roles is the reduction of differentiation in the roles of women and men in family, work and community, and to some degree also in interpersonal relations. At the latter level, however, unexplored linkages between biological determinants of sexuality and traditional interactions between men and women leave open the possibility that at the level of sexuality and interpersonal relations change may not involve important reduction in the degree of differentiation currently existing. In all other respects there is an expectation that sex differences in personality, family roles, kinds of work, and community and political participation will decline, if not disappear. The only real issue along these lines in today's sex role literature is the manner in which dedifferentiation is expected to occur.

As Wesley and Wesley (1977) have observed, reduction in sex role differentiation can occur through increasing masculinization of the woman's role, through feminization of the man's role, or jointly through a convergence in both roles through reduction in stereotypic patterns and adoption of characteristics of the opposite role. While masculinization is the overwhelming interpretation of contemporary sex role change, the other themes are also represented in the literature.

Masculinization

Masculinization is the central theme in discussions of changing sex roles, both as a description of the assumed nature of contemporary sex role change and, from a feminist perspective, as the desired outcome of contemporary change and feminist activity. The pervasiveness of the masculinization theme is apparent to anyone who has read a number of the textbook treatments written to service the increasing number of courses in the sociology or psychology of sex roles and in women's studies programs. These works tend to be written from the perspective of women's roles (see Freize et al. 1978 for one illustration), an understandable perspective considering that this curriculum and these writings are a reaction to a previously male social science in which generic man very imperfectly embraced the distaff side of humanity. The emphasis on women's roles, rather than men's roles, results in attention to masculinization rather than feminization when discussion of change is undertaken. Men enter, but are understandably not central to the discussions in this literature; thus the only empirical and theoretical possibility is to emphasize change in the role of the women, i.e., masculinization.

Masculinization, both as a goal and as a description, is consistent with the assumption common in this literature that sex differences are the result of arbitrary socialization experiences in which girls are taught to exhibit characteristics that later maintain their subordination to male power and dominance. While interpretations vary considerably, the most common theme in this literature emphasizes arbitrariness over biological or functional determinism. Consequently, there is an assumption that the removal of these arbitrary learnings (Hoffman 1977) will result in the elimination of many of the characteristics of the feminine stereotype, that women will become more like men in their ability to achieve, their feelings of self-confidence, their assertiveness, and the community and occupational roles they play. From this perspective, sex differences are taken as evidence of stability, and reduction of difference through feminine assumption of previously masculine roles or behaviors is viewed as change.

Feminization

Feminization of masculine roles emerges in this literature as a corollary to the concern about limitations imposed by the content of sex role stereotypes. While this concern is overwhelmingly for the restrictions and constraints imposed on women, there is some attention paid to the penalties imposed on men. This attention is generally limited to two central themes: the stresses of competitive achievement and the advantages of expressive release. This often takes the form of noting the benefits to men of letting down and being able to cry. On the whole, however, this theme of change in the male role is not fully developed, and is normally advanced more as a goal than as a description of contemporary change in sex roles.

For the most part, there is no clear expectation that men will in fact be undergoing change in characteristic masculine patterns toward the direction of increased feminization. If anything, the literature on socialization of sex role characteristics reiterates the theme that male characteristics are more important and are of greater concern to socializing agents than are female characteristics. Implications of this view are, of course, that men are even more constrained by their roles than are women. Thus, the feminization of men is a conceptual, perhaps an ideal, possibility that is not fully explored and probably not actually anticipated by students of sex roles.

Role Convergence

Role convergence involves men and women adopting patterns of behavior and exhibiting personality characteristics traditionally associated with the opposite sex.

One application of this theme is in the sense of reciprocity in sex roles, especially regarding family and work. As Scanzoni (1972), Bernard (1975), and others have noted, traditional sex roles in recent times have involved a division of labor between women and men along lines of family and work. Men have been predominant in extrafamilial roles, especially in careers, and have held the responsibility for occupational success and family support, while women have had primary responsibility for the home and child rearing and expressive sexual gratification. The significant point of these arrangements is that men have been supported in their career endeavors while women's work has been viewed as only supplementary. Consequently, assumption of equivalent career patterns and opportunities by women will necessarily require changes in role patterns between individual pairs of men and women. The ideas advanced center on greater assumption by men of housekeeping and parenting duties as well as emotional support for women entering career training or higher education. Other aspects involve men and women sharing jobs, taking less demanding jobs, or assuming single parenthood. In any event, convergence in family roles involves the crossing over and the assumption of role responsibilities and opportunities previously held by the opposite sex, primarily in the areas of work and family.

The other application of the convergence theme is at the level of personality and is expressed in the concept of androgyny, which refers to the combination of masculine and feminine characteristics in the personality, developed recently in the work of Bem (1977) and Spence and Helmreich (1978). In this research, androgynous individuals have been shown to exhibit characteristics appropriate to the situation, being nurturing and expressive when that was called for and being more independent and instrumental when those characteristics were required. As a concept, androgyny reflects an underlying shift in conceptualization from trait personality formulations to situational determinants along the lines of an early classic paper by Brimm (1960). Androgyny also is a long-standing feminist goal, as it suggests freedom for both women and men through convergence of characteristics without some of the negative (from the masculine perspective) connotations of feminization. However, in spite of substantial work in the area, androgyny remains more of a conceptual development than an actual description of the form being taken in the change of contemporary sex roles.

The nature of this study permits observation of convergence in the former sense through similarity of family and career orientations of women and men, for example, but not in the latter sense of androgyny. I do not have, from either records or survey, the type of information on situationally specific behavior that would permit examination of change in levels of androgyny.

SOURCES OF CHANGE

The sources of changing sex roles can be viewed at several levels: in the context of broad historical or cultural change, in the immediate pressures emanating from collective behavior and ferment, and in new patterns transmitted through socialization. While the purpose of this research study is to document change or stability rather than to test alternative explanations of change, such explanations represent the sociocultural and social psychological framework within which my interpretation is made. In addition, while the study is directly concerned with alternative models of change, much of the data and interpretation is relevant to selected issues and propositions based on these various themes. Consequently, I will take a brief look at some of the critical aspects of change at cultural, social, and personal levels.

Cultural Trends

The major cultural trends in the background of the important changes assumed to be occurring at present are the historical processes of secularization and rationalization. These processes are significant because their emergence established cognitively rational approaches to understanding and to the development of social forms that were sharp departures from those based on unquestioned acceptance of sacred, traditional patterns. The overwhelming significance of this shift is described by Berger:

Rationalization, in the sense that Weber understood this term, is the leading motif of modern history. It is the initially slow but nonetheless revolutionary force by which the traditional structures and conventions of society have been transformed, one by one, to give way to patterns of conduct in which means and ends are conjoined with rational consistency. . . . The overall effect of rationalization on the modern West has thus been as complete a metamorphosis of society as may be found in all human history. (1973:320).

The specific and critical outcome of this process was the development of modern bureaucratic forms of organization and the deliberate control of behavior by authorized individuals in terms of the instrumental significance the behavior had for anticipated outcomes, rather than by sacred traditional principles. More broadly formulated, the shift from traditional to modern forms of social organization has been a central concern in both classical and contemporary social science. Thus, Tönnies (1940) distinguished between *Gemeinschaft* and *Gesellschaft* forms of social organization, the one involving shared values, unformulated commitments, and the natural spontaneity (expressiveness) of behavior based on deeply internalized norms about which there was strong consensus, the other involving individual purposes and conscious, rationally calculated choices based upon considerations of the (instrumental) benefits of specific outcomes and relationships. This change involved a switch from treating others as ends in themselves to treating them as means to ends. In systems of social exchange involving specialization of activities and functional interdependence, people relate to each other in terms of their instrumental utility rather than in terms of their ultimate worth or value as unique individuals experienced as ends. The difference, of course, is the difference between the interactions in the formal spheres of society, between salespeople and customers, teachers and students, and those in the informal relationships between intimate friends, relatives, and lovers.

Finally, these distinctions were succinctly formalized by Parsons (1951) in the pattern variable dichotomies, where the patterns of traditional society and primary relations were characterized as particularistic, ascriptive, collectivity-oriented, affective, and diffuse as contrasted to the universalistic, affectively neutral, achievement, individualistic, and specific relationships in modern urban industrial society. The central distinguishing pattern variables describing these shifts are those of universalism and particularism and achievement and ascription. The first pair describes relationships based on general rules and norms that apply to all members of a category, such as teachers or students, versus those based on personal knowledge and experience in a unique relationship between named persons, friends, or relatives. The second describes the basis for status assignment or attainment, either ascribed on the basis of some characteristic such as sex or age, or achieved through instrumental processes and the demonstration of competence. The first reflects qualities, the second performance.

Feminine sex roles have been located in a *Gemeinschaft* system characterized by particularism and ascription (Bernard 1975, 1981), while all other major statuses reflect elements of the *Gesellschaft* pattern—universalism and achievement. Interestingly enough, there is no mechanism in a universalistic-achievement society for providing universal status recognition to a role that is enacted within the particularistic context of the family as a primary group. The woman occupying this role in a modern society does not have a clear status but must draw upon the achieved status of the husband. Feminists have recognized the significance of this circumstance and understandably take issue with the sociological formulations documenting these circumstances. Contemporary moves to reformulate the role through monetary recognition of the economic value of housekeeping in the economy (Giele 1978) effectively shift the role from ascription to achievement. Paying a friend for friendship violates the traditional particularistic patterns just as paying a wife to housekeep does. The unmodified sacredness of the traditional patterns in the other central aspects of the woman's role has largely precluded serious discussion of secularization of motherhood and parenting, although the current argument over abortion clearly introduces the dilemma between traditional values of procreation emphasizing the interest of the collectivity in the birth and the modern individualistic values espoused by feminists regarding the individual woman's control of her body and of birth. To my knowledge, there is as yet, however, no serious discussion of the ultimate processes of rationalization in terms of payment for childbearing and for sexual relations based on individual contracts rather than traditional values and prescriptions.[5]

Social Forces

Contemporary social forces operating within the broad historical context constitute a more immediate and more widely recognized cause of change in sex roles. These forces involve both structural change and collective behavior. Structural factors important to the changes assumed to have occurred consist of increased labor force participation by women and weakening of aspects of family structure. Collective behaviors of significance involve the general ferment and rejection of tradition in the 1960s, the civil rights movement, and the resurgent women's movement.

The employment of married as well as single women in World War II, as they have been involved in emergency situations (Rossi 1964) historically, is assumed to have started the alteration in public conceptions of the acceptability of married women working outside the home (Chafe 1977). Even though women in nontraditional jobs were soon replaced by returning GIs and the innovative patterns of the 1940s crises replaced by the intensification of sharply differentiated family sex role patterns through the 1950s and early 1960s, there was at least a public demonstration of the potential in female employment and of the arbitrariness of traditional occupational role assignments.

Of more direct significance are the demographic changes that have occurred recently, with implications for traditional family roles versus employment outside the home. As Oppenheimer (1973) has noted, the postwar period was a period of rapid economic expansion requiring large numbers of workers beyond those traditionally available in the labor force. The significance for sex roles was that the greatest increase in demand occurred in the clerical jobs traditionally filled by women. The confluence of the economic expansion and the demand for clerical workers occurred in the face of the declining pool of young, single women that resulted from the reduced birth rate of the 1930s. These circumstances created a demand for female workers that could not be met by the pool of traditional unmarried women. This demand was first filled by married women past the child-rearing age and later, and most dramatically, by women with young school-age and even preschool children. All of these processes were facilitated by other changes that were occurring in the family and life experience themselves. Family size began to decline and longevity continued to increase, as did age of marriage and age at first birth. These pressures all worked in concert toward employment of women outside of the home, although, as we shall see subsequently, not necessarily in nontraditional jobs.

Other causes of change, especially those related to the resurgence of the latent woman's movement, occurred in the 1960s. The two major relevant themes in the 1960s were the marked ideological changes and the strength of the civil rights movement.

The ideological changes that occurred between 1960 and 1970 can best be described as liberating. Between these dates, and probably most clearly in the late 1960s, American youth rejected traditional values and institutions for individualistic goals and orientations (Morris and Small 1971; Goertzel 1972; Yankelovich 1974, Farley, Brewer, and Fine 1977; Duncan and Duncan 1978; Veroff, Douvan, and Kulka 1981). Partly as a result of the Vietnam War, but probably also reflecting broader social processes associated with modernization and secularization, youth in the 1960s sharply decreased their valuation of traditional institutions such as religion, family, government, and work and increased their valuation of personal, reflective, sensual, and hedonistic goals. Interestingly enough, these youths became liberated from tradition but not from each other. Values of interpersonal relation, friendship, and obligation persisted and even strengthened, but outside of, rather than within traditional institutional constraint. Morris and Small note in describing their results,

While there was much stress on the social in the sense of the interpersonal, there was very little reference to "society" as such. . . . The favoring of "freedom to live as one wants" was strong, as the favoring of pleasure, enjoyment, and sensibility. . . . Self-development in a framework of interpersonal sensitivity—this is perhaps the main impression which these replies convey. (1971:259)

The rejection of traditional values was clearest in religion, which showed an important decline in commitment and recognition, rejection of convention in its various forms, and rejection of patriotism as a special type of conventional orientation. College youth in the 1960s and perhaps noncollege youth in the 1970s (as Yankelovich's data suggest) deemphasized, if not rejected, the conventional virtues of organized society for freedom and personal experience and development. In this regard, Morris and Small's (1971) research results are especially interesting in that the major change from the 1950s was in views about a way of life having to do with "preserving the best man has attained." In 1950 this was the second most important of the thirteen ways of life for both men and women. By 1970 it was ranked *seventh by men* and *eleventh by women*. Only "controlling the self stoically," and "obeying the cosmic purpose" were less valued by female college students in 1970, a dramatic illustration of Chafe's contention that "the women's liberation movement was both drawing upon and reinforcing changes taking place in the society" (1977:122).

The other major relevant force in the 1960s was the civil rights movement and the related radical politics overlapping both the civil rights movement and the Vietnam protest actions. The collective behavior promoting these ends involved large numbers of women who would become active in the women's movement. While Chafe (1977) and other writers have drawn parallels between the circumstances of black Americans and of American women, both of whom were assigned to ascribed statuses by white males, Rossi (1964) has emphasized the fact that women are the only subordinate group living in closer proximity with the members of the superordinate group than with each other. She notes that one consequence of this has been that collective action in the women's movement has generally been successful only when tied to other movements, such as abolition and social welfare, where male support could be obtained. The civil rights protest behavior of the 1960s appeared to provide such a tie-in to obtain male support against traditional constraints, inequalities, and discriminations. In this regard it was similar to the previous movements in the nineteenth and early twentieth century (Chafe 1977).

While the ferment of the 1960s provided substantial numbers of women the experience of protest and activism, the underlying machismo of the male leadership, especially in the civil rights movement, prevented the full integration of the women's movement and the civil rights movement (Freeman 1973), a pattern intensified by the special differences in the orientations of black and white women regarding the issues of racial and sexual discrimination and inequality (Chafe 1977).

The other energizing force was the establishment of President Kennedy's national and state commissions on the status of women. These actions established networks of communication and interaction relating concerned and articulate women to one another and to establishment structures important to change. While the younger activistists from the civil rights and protest movements and the older, more established women in the state commission networks reflected different approaches and goals with respect to the nature of the establishment and uses of power, the movement was energized and structured by these two concerns as well as by the public reaction to *The Feminine Mystique* when it appeared in 1963. In all of these ramifications, the movement in the 1960s had more vitality and significance than in previous periods, and differed from previous periods of manifest action by being considerably more diverse and broader in its purposes. Not since the Seneca Falls Conference in 1848 had the women's movement pursued the women's issues across such a broad and comprehensive front (Chafe 1977). Unlike the Seneca Conference, the important goals of the contemporary movement have been realized in national legislation and in public consciousness. Women have been included in civil rights legislation and, after some struggle, in the enactment of civil rights and equal opportunity programs, and the Equal Rights Amendment was nearly successful.[6] It is difficult, of course, to relate these successes directly to change in women's roles, and there appears to be no clearly formulated, generally accepted theory of change in sex roles resulting directly from these events. In this regard it is worth noting that Mason, Czajka, and Arber (1976) do not find support for the proposition that changes in women's role attitudes between 1964 and 1974 were caused by the women's movement.

At the level of personality, these social and historical forces operate through learning and socialization. We will return to this question in some detail in chapter 6. At that point we will note that change processes in socialization can theoretically be said to operate through four important mediums: (1) the portrayal of sex role models in the mass media, where change would result from portrayal of more nontraditional roles; (2) socialization by parents who have changing, nontraditional conceptions of the roles their daughters will be playing; (3) family socialization where the mother herself is a nontraditional role model, the only one of these four possibilities for which there is a substantial body of empirical evidence; and (4) educational experiences with nontraditional models in textbooks, curricula, and especially in such clearly sex-typed activities as athletics, shop, and home economics.

THE PICTURE OF CHANGE: OVERVIEW OF THE EVIDENCE

The detailed evidence on change in sex roles will be examined in the following chapters as the evidence from this study is presented. For now, it is worth noting that the empirical research evidence up to the early 1980s does not support the pattern of overwhelming and pervasive change that appears in the theoretical, speculative, and polemic literature of this area. In addition, the evidence to date has been limited to documentation of change and stability in a relatively few specific patterns. Studies dealing with the change across the full range of sex-typed experiences at social, interpersonal, and personal levels have yet to appear in any substantial number, and those that have (Duncan and Duncan 1978; Veroff, Douvan, and Kulka 1981) return a picture of sex role stability rather than of sex role change. Thus, the evidence that exists at the present time is somewhat incomplete as a representation of the scope of change being discussed in the literature, and uneven in its conclusions about the amount of change that is actually occurring, our public conception of overwhelming change notwithstanding.

As of the early 1980s, the major evidence of sex role change has accumulated for labor force participation, family, and sexuality. There is almost no evidence of change in the various dimensions of personality and interpersonal relations that differentiate the sexes and that constitute the focus of much of the theoretical speculation and argument in the sex role literature.

While we will be returning to these points in greater detail and with reference to the specific sources in the literature as well as the relevance of this research to questions raised by research and theoretical speculation in each substantive area, this chapter concludes with an overview of the current evidence.

The clearest and most significant evidence to date is on the change in patterns of female employment. Since 1950 the proportion of all women who are in the labor force has increased from about one-third to one-half. However, of even greater significance is the pattern of the increase. The greatest increases have occurred among younger, married women with school-age and even preschool children. This increase in working mothers is the most dramatic substantive change that has been observed. The majority of married women now work outside of the home. Home is woman's place for only a substantial minority of all married women. The implication of these changes may, however, be somewhat mitigated by the stability in the nature of work. To a very large degree this increased employment has been in traditional occupations that emphasize social factors and support over cognitive and task performance. Outside work as a secretary or a nurse may not represent as much of a departure from traditional sex role patterns as the employment statistics might suggest.

The other major body of evidence relates to selected aspects of family role patterns and circumstances. Here there is clear demographic and attitudinal evidence of change. Birth rates have continued to decline, divorce rates continue to rise, and marriage is being postponed to later years. In addition, increasing numbers of families consist of single parents, the great majority women. In the broad historical view, contemporary family relations are also more characterized by equalitarianism than patriarchy, although there is some question as to the completeness of this shift.

Perhaps the greatest change consistently observed has been attitudes about woman's place. The American public, but especially American women, now accept the idea of equality inherent in women's employment and interests outside of the home and equal qualifications for public office. In terms of what people say, the feminine mystique is most certainly on the wane. The limited evidence on what people do, however, shows a different picture. Studies of change in detailed aspects of family relationships over these periods find some small changes in role arrangements, but no substantial change in the roles of husbands and wives. The basic relations between women and men in families do not appear to have changed in the recent past.

The final area of change is sexuality. Here two patterns seem to have occurred. Most directly relevant to changing sex roles is the pattern of masculinization. Women's attitudes and behavior regarding premarital intercourse and other sexual behavior have changed to become more similar to those of men, perhaps even surpassing men in some respects. The double standard, like the feminine mystique, is also disappearing. The other aspect of change in sexuality has to do with increasing correspondence between attitudes and behavior. Attitudes appear to be shifting toward behavior that has been exhibited but not acknowledged all along, a fact that may have exaggerated earlier differences between the sexual behavior of women and men.

Apart from these major changes, evidence is either missing or very weak and inconsistent. There is almost no evidence of change in sex roles across the numerous dimensions of personality and interpersonal behavior that differentiate the sexes. The variables of this study provide new evidence on change and stability that goes beyond the customary dimensions just reviewed.

CHAPTER 2

THE 1964 – 1975 SURVEYS: DATA AND ANALYSIS

The central concept of this research study was the use of a 1964 survey of high school seniors as baseline information for the study of changing sex roles. Consequently, in 1975[1] an identical instrument was administered in most of the same high schools to provide the terminal information for the study of change. As in any study of this type, the information available depends on the content of the baseline study. Fortunately, the 1964 survey was unusually comprehensive, having been originally conceived as baseline data for a longitudinal study of the graduating class.

THE 1964—1975 SURVEYS

The 1964 survey was initiated by a group of twenty high schools who had organized a curriculum study council for the purpose of doing cooperative research on curriculum and program improvement. The 1964 survey was intended to provide information useful in appraising the value of the high school program to the noncollege-bound student. Consequently, the information included in the survey was intended to be relevant to both an analysis of the student's school experience and the relation of that experience to postgraduate success. To provide elaboration and control, a number of personality variables were added. These included achievement orientations and patterns as well as the student's educational and occupational aspirations and work orientations and life goals. The comprehensiveness of the 1964 survey and the focus on work and achievement has of course proven fortuitous for research on change in sex roles over that period. The content of the 1964 survey ranges over a substantial number of dimensions that mirror key elements in the life of high school seniors about to enter the workforce or go on to advanced education. In this respect, the baseline materials provide data that to the present time have not been generally examined in published research on changing sex roles. As in the Duncan and Duncan (1978) and Veroff, Douvan, and Kulka (1981) studies, which are similar in concept, the data enable the consideration of change and stability across a full range of experiences from the perspectives and circumstances of the individuals involved. As these students were in typical real-life circumstances at the time of the surveys, and were being asked about vital goals and important personality characteristics, the data seem closer to actual, ongoing social reality than do those resulting from the typical laboratory study or survey of college freshmen, often in classes on sex roles or marriage and the family.

Although some of the material collected in the baseline survey is more relevant than others, considering the pervasiveness of the women's movement and the breadth of goals and issues being advanced, it is difficult to find indicators of experience, personality, or aspiration that are totally irrelevant to current issues about changing sex roles. In any event, this study draws on the following categories of information, listed roughly in the order they appear in the questionnaire.

1. The *rating of perceived usefulness* of twenty-four vocational and ten academic courses to the respondent's future occupation was obtained. Each course the respondent had taken was rated as either "very helpful," "somewhat helpful," or "not at all helpful" to the future occupation. While the original purpose of these items was to provide an evaluation of the curriculum that could be used for planning, the items are also useful for examining sex differences and change related to sex role stereotyping and performance. Various contemporary writers stress the significance of perceived utility and appropriateness of courses by girls and boys as one explanation for sex-related performance differences. These items turn out to be appropriate to that interest as well as to questions of the relevance of vocational and academic curriculum to both sexes.

2. *Number of semesters of vocational and academic courses* taken between grades 10 and 12 were obtained from respondents' self-reports and from student records. The self-reports provide information from the perspective of the student on course taking in the relatively general categories of major subject areas. Information on course taking from school records is more detailed and is of course a more accurate representation than self-reports relying on recall. The coding categories established in the 1964 analysis for the transcript information included eighteen vocational and twenty academic courses. Course taking is another explanation recently advanced for differences in sex-typed achievement areas such as mathematics, English, and science (Fox, Fennema, and Sherman 1977).

Apart from the relevance to possible sex-typed achievement differences, course taking also bears upon sex-typed curriculum patterns, especially in the vocational program, where separate sex-related sequences have been common.[2] Because of the strong emphasis on shop for boys and clerical for girls, patterns strongly criticized in today's literature, course enrollments turn out to be an important dimension for a study of change or stability in sex-role patterns.

3. *Grades in academic and vocational courses* are included for sophomore, junior, and senior years. They of course provide relatively hard evidence of differential performance between the sexes and over the years relative to well-documented differences in areas of achievement. These differences are attributed to stereotyping and to biological predispositions and determinants. Differential change observed among students in the same schools over the period would be significant evidence of sociocultural influences.

4. *Participation in extracurricular activities* was noted, including students' reports of the number of years of participation in each of seventeen athletic and nonathletic activities. This information is relevant to contemporary concerns about participation in competitive athletic programs and especially in team sports. Sex differences in extracurricular activities have been pronounced in the past. Consequently, some of the changes in community and occupational roles might be observed first in changing patterns of extracurricular participation.

5. *Evaluation and rating of extracurricular activities* were also obtained. Students indicated their perception of "how helpful the activity will prove to be . . . in later life," on the same three-point scale as in the rating of courses: "very," "somewhat," and "not at all helpful." They also indicated the most helpful activities and the activities they wished they had participated in and the activities they would drop if given a second chance. While this supplementary information is more relevant to school program development than to sex roles, it does provide subjective views of activities to supplement the self-reported behavior. These evaluations have the further advantage of permitting observation of changes in sex-related preference and desire that might precede change in patterns of actual participation.

6. *Study patterns and hours* provide another view of sex-relevant differences in these adolescents' behavior. Respondents were asked to report the number of hours of study per week in five designated and one open location: library, study hall, home, bus, classroom, and other. They also reported the years of most intense study and the courses they most enjoyed studying. Evidence on these study patterns provides us with two useful kinds of infor-

mation. It serves as an indicator of possible (probably likely) differences in the academic habits of boys and girls that might underlie some of the female achievement superiority during these years. In addition, this information can be used as a control in analyzing and interpreting the differential performance of girls and boys in the sex-typed courses to see if differences are primarily a function of study patterns rather than sex.

7. *Occupational values* were obtained using the items from Rosenberg (1957). These items reflect three important aspects of work: intrinsic satisfaction with work itself, extrinsic satisfaction in such concomitants of work as money and security, and satisfaction in the interpersonal aspects of the occupational role. While men and women are equally oriented toward intrinsic aspects of work, they differ in their orientations toward extrinsic rewards and especially in their orientations toward working with and helping people. As these orientations are highly sex-typed, change or stability in these patterns has important implications for occupational segregation and the sex typing of work.

8. Fairly extensive responses on *occupational preferences, aspirations, and expectations* were obtained in the original research because of the concern with post-high school success of noncollege-bound youth. The most directly useful responses for the present purpose are those indicating an ideal preference and those indicating an actual plan or expectation. The former was elicited by the item "If I were absolutely free to go into any kind of work I wanted, my choice would be _____," the latter by the item "The occupation I plan to follow is _____." Considering the centrality of occupational orientations to many of the issues surrounding sex role stereotypes and sex role change, these responses will provide the basis for several analyses and interpretations. Analyzed in terms of the situs dimension (Morris and Murphy 1959), they enable examination of the degree of potential occupational sex typing and segregation and of change or stability in such patterns. In addition, the difference between the expected and the preferred occupations can be used to examine the subjective perception of obstacles or discrimination in occupational attainment processes, between what the student really wants and what the student expects. Reduction in discrimination and sex typing of work should be reflected in reduction in sex-related differentials in these discrepancies.

Examination of these responses in terms of occupational status permits examination of sex differences in occupational aspiration. While the sexes are unexpectedly similar in overall status attainment (McClendon 1976; Treiman and Terrell 1975a; but see Sewell, Hauser, and Wolf 1980), feminist emphasis on professional and managerial advancement and opportunity might be reflected in differential change in levels of expected and preferred occupation.

9. *Educational aspirations*, both in terms of college and in terms of vocational or technical education, were obtained from items on postgraduate plans. The item "Do you plan to enter college after you graduate from high school?" used response categories of "Yes, I *definitely will* enter college," I have *tentative plans* to enter college," and "No, I *definitely will not* enter college." This formulation permits the clear delineation of those who unequivocally plan on college from those with vaguely formulated plans.

10. *Persons consulted about post-high school plans* were designated by providing the students with a checklist of thirteen persons from mother and father to employer, preceded by the items "Have you talked to any of the following about your plans after high school? Indicate by checking the blank following the group(s) that you have talked to about post-high school plans." Students also responded to items asking them to designate the three most influential consultants. While these responses do not relate as closely to important sex role issues, they do bear on the question of the origins of change and the idea that change forces emanate from outside the family (Bandura, 1969; Lueptow, 1975). From this perspective, change in the number and importance of outside consultants is an important dimension of the general process of sex role change, especially that change viewed as masculinization.

11. Description of the *amount and the value of high school counseling* was generated by several items dealing with (a) awareness of counseling service; (b) number of visits during and before the senior year; (c) whether or not a vocational choice was discussed and if so, whether potential ability, test scores, and the nature of the occupation were discussed; and (d) evaluation of the helpfulness of the counselor in making educational and occupational post-high school plans.

Responses to these items are relevant to sex role issues, as they bear on the view that school counseling and advisement have been forces for stability and traditionalism rather than liberating influences breaking the restraints of sex role stereotypes. From this perspective, both sex-related differences and also the change in the counseling experience provide crucial information on the existence and possibly the process of sex role change.

12. The *achievement value items* used in this study were taken from the achievement value scales used by Rosen (1956, 1959) and Strodtbeck (1958). These items have consistently related to other important variables both in

the earlier work of Strodtbeck and Rosen and in more recent research (Schwartz 1971; Lueptow 1975; and Anderson and Evans 1976). They also exhibit relatively high internal consistency (alpha = .66).

These items tap a central conflict in the literature on sex roles, that of achievement patterns versus the affiliation patterns more traditional of women (Komorovsky 1946; Hoffman 1972). It is generally assumed that women face special problems in affiliation, dependency, and expressiveness that contradict necessary achievement learning and performances (Kluckhohn 1969). Thus, sex differences and change in these items tap a central feature of contemporary sex roles.

13. Ten *life goal* items presented as "a list of objectives that different people have in life" were each evaluated as being "highly important," of "medium importance," or of "little importance" to the respondent. These items were originally developed from the categorization of open-ended responses to a question about goals in life from several hundred entering college freshmen from the same general geographic area as that of the present study. The wording of each item was intended to reflect the content of one of the life goal categories. Consequently, the items cover the range of important goals named spontaneously by college-bound adolescents only four months older than the respondents of this study.

The content of the goals reflects one of the central role conflicts experienced by women—career versus family. Other goals include such components of the feminine stereotype as being religious and making a contribution to society and helping other people. Evidence of sex differences, change, and stability along these dimensions is central to sex role research. Phrased as they are as individual goals rather than as general attitudes about women's roles, these items have a relevance to life experience not always present in responses to abstract items on women's appropriate roles more commonly used in sex role research (see Mason Czajka, and Arber 1976).

14. *Family background information* was obtained from the student respondents and includes most of the customary information gathered in survey research. The number of older and younger siblings was given separately, permitting analysis of family size and birth-order effects. Unfortunately for this research, sex of siblings was not determined, so analysis of the effects of sex composition on sex-typed personality patterns is impossible.

Parental education, residence, and family income were obtained in categorical responses that seem adequate for residence and for education but somewhat inadequate for family income because the appreciable increase in family income over the decade produced a severely truncated distribution in 1975. Parents' occupation was obtained from the student respondents and categorized by status and situs. On that basis, effects of parental, especially maternal, occupation on both aspirations and on sex-typed expectations can be examined.

The most important omission in the family background data is religion. School administrators in 1964 thought this too sensitive a variable. Consequently, there were no questions on family or respondent religious affiliations in either 1964 or 1975.

15. Student views about *functions of the high school* were obtained by providing respondents with a list of sixteen possible educational, cultural, and developmental purposes of the high school and having each item rated by the student as "very important," "fairly important," and "unimportant." In addition, students designated the "most important" functions. While these items have more relevance to the student role than to sex roles, questions of sex differences, stability, and change in student values about high school may add further dimensions to our view of sex-typed patterns within the student subculture. Furthermore, some of the items, such as those dealing with personal skills, morality, and physical development have obvious sex-related components.

16. *Peer status ratings* were obtained by having each respondent name the three students who were the "best athlete," "best student," "most important," "most popular girl," and "most popular boy." Status scores for each student in the survey consist of the number of choices received by the respondent. Sex difference and change in the status of students, especially in the first three categories, where females and males essentially compete for the nominations, should be of special interest. The question of popularity and achievement, especially for adolescent girls, has of course been an important theme from Coleman (1961) to the present.

While these different dimensions vary in their direct relevance to this research, review of the total set does indicate that the 1964 baseline data have provided a valuable set of variables for the study of sex role change. By studying the extensive set of responses and record information ranging over the attitudes, behavior, and experiences so represented, we can evaluate sex differences and change from the perspective of adolescents actually involved in real-life experiences and looking beyond to post-high school goals and aspirations. Overall, we have a set of indicators that touch, in varying degree, on a large share of the total set of life experiences and orientations of these adolescent youths. Sex-typed behavior and, most importantly, change in sex roles that escape the broad range of these variables are probably peripheral and unimportant.

Time Period

The time period encompassed by the 1964–1975 survey appears to be equally valuable for study of changing sex roles. The dramatic changes in the labor force participation of married women had begun to occur just prior to this decade (Bednarzick and Klein 1977). Married women beyond child-rearing years who had children had entered (or reentered) the labor force in record numbers, and the substantial increases in labor force participation among women in the childbearing ages who had children were starting and would accelerate throughout the 1960s, increasing from 39.0% in 1960 to 50.2% in 1972, while employment of mothers with preschool children would increase from 18.6% in 1960 to 30.1% in 1972 (Hoffman and Nye 1974:5).

The 1964 survey occurred one year after the publication of *The Feminine Mystique* and three years after the establishment by President Kennedy of a National Commission on the Status of Women. The National Organization of Women (NOW) was formed two years after the 1964 baseline survey and entered its strongly active period midway through the study period.

The 1960s were times of considerable ferment and agitation on the national scene in rebellion against the Vietnam War, in support of civil rights, and in opposition to many traditional patterns and institutions. As Freeman (1973) observes, this period of public activism in the civil rights and protest movements involved large numbers of younger feminists who carried a strong liberation theme into the women's movement. All of these activities appear to have been coalesced in varying degrees to produce major shifts at the end of the 1960s in general values and personal orientation (Yankelovich 1974; Veroff, Douvan, and Kulka 1981), female president responses (Ferree 1974; Schreiber 1978), sexuality (Schmidt and Sigusch 1972) and sex typing of children's tasks (Duncan and Duncan, 1978). In fact, interpreting female president responses led Duncan and Duncan to conclude that their 1971 survey was carried out "just at the point of 'take off' in acceptance of new roles for men and women" (1978:5).

The 1964 respondents were born in the immediate postwar years of 1946–1947. They experienced a childhood characterized by traditional feminine roles and demographically evidenced by the postwar baby boom. They were entering their teens at the end of the 1950s, "the turning point that marked the end of the era of the feminine mystique" (Bernard 1975:76), as the birth rate resumed its historical downward trend. Thus, while they reached high school just as change was beginning to occur, the bulk of their lives had been spent in the traditional milieu. Furthermore, while the changes were starting to percolate in the early 1960s, they would not gather full steam until the mid-1960s and attitudinally not until the end of the 1960s. Fortunately for this research, and possibly also for continuing historical interest in the results of this study, the baseline cohort appears to be the last one to have grown up totally within the traditional milieu.

On the other hand, the 1975 respondents were born in 1957–1958, just at the end of the traditional milieu. They are one of the first two or three cohorts born as observable social changes occurred. Speaking of this cohort, Bernard observes:

They are among the first adolescents to be exposed to the new feminist movement of the late 1960s and early 1970s . . .

They are the first generation of adolescents to find their textbooks challenged for the sexism of their contents, their school boards challenged for the disparity in funds expended on boys' and girls' athletic programs, their schools challenged for not permitting girls to take shop courses. . . .

During the lifetime of these adolescents, new styles have been adopted by their mothers as well as by their peers. . . .

They are the first adolescents to arrive on the scene at a time when there is a rebellion in process against motherhood as we institutionalize it in our society. . . .

They are the first adolescent generations to vote for a president; see abortion as a political issue; confront a drug culture; . . . have free access to contraceptives; learn of zero population growth. (1975:69–71)

And of special implication for the substantive concerns of the present study:

A great deal of the research on which our knowledge of adolescence rests does not, therefore, fit this new generation. (1975:69–71)

Thus, the circumstances of the baseline survey and the following decade of change have provided us with an unusually appropriate pair of cohorts for the study of change in contemporary sex roles: one of the last, if not *the* last group of traditional experience and one of the first groups exposed to the winds of change in the 1960s. If these forces have produced change in contemporary sex roles, we should observe it in these groups.

STUDY POPULATION

As previously stated, the basic concept of this study is the readministration of a questionnaire in 1975 that had been previously administered to graduating seniors in twenty high schools in 1964. Because three of the original school systems declined to participate in the 1975 replication, the study is based on the 1964 responses of only those students in the seventeen systems for which both sets of data were available: 2,773 in 1964, 2,827 in 1975, with almost exactly equal numbers of females and males.

The high schools involved range from very small schools of fewer than 100 graduating seniors to a very large school of over 500 graduating seniors.[3]

The schools are scattered over nine contiguous counties of a midwestern state. The counties range from heavy industrial to open farmland, with urban places ranging from small towns to moderately large cities. However, while the range of school size, urbanization, and density is substantial, the study area does not include any major metropolitan county of 500,000 or more.

Although the participating systems are spread over a nine-county area, nine schools with about two-thirds of the students in the 1964 survey were located within the three central counties of the area. Comparison of change in population composition with the rest of the state indicates the counties are generally typical of the state as a whole. The rural-urban balance in these counties is slightly more urban than the state as a whole, although the three counties bracket the state proportion with percentage urban in 1970 of 57.1, 68.6, and 77.8%, compared to the overall state percentage of 65.9. Percentage nonwhite ranges from 0.4 to 1.1 in these counties compared to the state 3.6%.[4] School enrollment of 16 to 17-year-olds was within 1% of the state total in 1964, but in 1970 the reported enrollments were 95.0, 99.9, 95.6% compared to the state total of 94.0%. Median years of education in the counties in 1970 was within 0.3 years of the state median for both males and females. The critical variable of female employment was very representative in this area, with 40.8% of women 14 and over employed statewide, while 41.4, 40.7, and 42.2% were employed in the three counties. These values reflect somewhat different rates of increase, as the state increase in female employment was 40.2%, while the three counties increased 40.0, 53.4, and 46.5%, respectively. Finally, the status distributions of occupations within the counties were very similar to the state as a whole. Thus, while the population of this study is not a probability sample of the state population, it is heterogeneous and broadly representative.

Given the regional variation in the United States, no single state can be taken as generally representative, but a midwestern state may serve as a reasonable median for a nation that ranges from the high liberalism of the northeast to the more traditional south and conservative southwest. Alexander, Eckland, and Griffen's (1975) nationwide replication of Sewell's Wisconsin model provides some support for this position.

INFORMED CONSENT, RESPONSE RATE, AND BIAS*

The 1964 survey was administered by the counselors in each of the participating high schools. In 1964, students were assembled and instructed to fill out the questionnaires, which were accurately presented as attempts by the school systems to gather information to be used in the future for curriculum planning. The face sheets of the questionnaires had lines for student name and address accompanied by promises of confidentiality and the pledge that the answers would be seen only by the research study group, a pledge that was kept through the ensuing years. After an identification number was assigned to the questionnaire, the face sheet was removed and stored separately. Ironically, in the face of what was to come in the 1975 administration, not a single piece of individual information was ever made available, nor were there any complaints from the 3,461 participating students or their parents.

In 1975, the questionnaires were administered under a different research climate. While there has never been, to my knowledge, any evidence of harmful disclosure of confidential survey information by social scientists, the post-Watergate public was very sensitive about invasion of privacy, a concern that became law in the Buckley Amendment to the Family and Educational Privacy Act of 1974, which treats the unauthorized use of questionnaire and archival data about students as invasion of privacy (Davis 1975). The liability of school administrations inherent in that act raised numerous questions for administrators (Chase 1975; Cutler 1975), and as Davis (1975) notes, increases the difficulty of conducting research requiring the use of student records.

The other concern impinging on this research had to do with harm to research subjects that was being revealed in examination of some medical

---

*Analysis and formulation in this section draw heavily on a prior collaboration with Samuel A. Mueller, "The Impact of Informed Consent Regulations on Response Rate and Response Bias," *Sociological Methods and Research* (November 1977), 6:183–204.

research practice (Katz 1972). Notwithstanding the substantial differences between research studies in which poverty stricken, uninformed syphillis victims were left untreated to serve as controls, and such innocuous surveys as those used in this study, procedures established by the Department of Health, Education and Welfare in 1974 and amended in 1975 (45 C.F.R. Part 46) could be interpreted by local review committees to embrace survey administration. The central concept of the new procedures was that of informed consent. Persons with majority status (including students 18 and over in most jurisdictions) had to verify, through a signed statement, that they have been informed of possible risks involved in the research and had consented to participate. A parent's signature on such a form was necessary for students under 18.

In this research preparation, the local review board charged with protecting the public from harm and, perhaps of even more importance, ensuring that the sponsoring institution did not incur liability, consisted for the most part of people who were not social scientists. They understandably took a conservative and cautious view of possible harm and invasion of privacy.

Because of the confusion and ambiguity surrounding the problem at the time the 1975 survey was being planned, the research effort faced two problems. The first had to do with informed consent and privacy. The local university review committee decided that student respondents in the 1975 survey must be volunteers and must give signed consent. The problem of volunteer assemblies and administrations, troublesome as it was, was further complicated by the fact that about half the students were under 18 and thus minors who could not give informed consent, even if they agreed, but had to have parental consent (this for a survey that had deleted "religion" as too sensitive an item!).

The other problem had to do with school administrator's uncertainty and apprehension about privacy and school records. The confusion about liability on this point was so great that some administrators were speaking of destroying aptitude and evaluation materials, not to mention limiting access of outside researchers conducting a study of sex role change. These complicated procedures and official concern all added to the normal difficulties of organizing such a research and were in part responsible for the delay in conducting the survey and, later on, in conducting the data file preparation and collations for the 1975 survey.

The procedural resolution for the 1975 survey was an informed consent statement on the face of the questionnaire to be filled out and signed by the adult student 18 or over or detached to be taken home for parents' signature for those under eighteen. In addition, and representing what hindsight showed to be an important error of judgment, students were asked to write a nine-digit random number on the questionnaire and on the face sheet of the questionnaire. This number was to be used to collate the two parts and to enable 17-year-olds to fill out a voluntary questionnaire that would remain unidentified without the matching face sheet. In a wonderful demonstration of the unpredictability of human behavior, I assumed that minor students, having spent an hour completing the questionnaire, would be ego-involved enough to take the consent form home for parental signature and return it to the school.

In two schools, all of this was complicated further because the school board required signature of its own consent form to permit access to the student records.

Response Rate

Thus, the 1975 survey proceeded on a voluntary basis under mechanisms that complicated the administration and increased the problems of data organization and preparation. These procedures reduced the overall response rate to 63.2% a reasonable rate for surveys but well below the 100% of the 1964 survey.[5] Because of concern about the possible bias this might produce, and because the study constituted a natural field experiment on the effects of the new informed consent procedures, a supplementary data gathering and analysis was proposed in the weeks following the 1975 survey and was supported by an additional contract award from HEW. The central question of the supplementary analysis was whether the grades, intelligence, and grade-intelligence correlations were different for the participants than for the nonparticipants.[6]

Other research on the factors influencing voluntary consent and participation has shown that more intelligent people, girls, and achieving students are more likely to volunteer (Wicker 1968; Rosenthal and Rosnow 1975), and that is generally what we also find in tables 2.1, 2.2. In both consent (age) groups, but especially in the parental consent group, girls were more likely to volunteer to participate than boys. Similarly, more intelligent students and students with higher grades were more likely to participate. However, the greatest effect by far is produced by type of consent. About 70% of the student consent group participated (i.e., gave their formal signed consent) compared to only 42% of the parental group. As it turned out, student motivation to take the consent forms home for parental signature and return

Table 2.1.

Study Participation by Type of Consent,
Grade Point, Sex, and Intelligence

| | | Male | | | | Female | | | | Total | | | |
| | | Parental Consent | | Student Consent | | Parental Consent | | Student Consent | | Parental Consent | | Student Consent | |
Intell	GPA	% Part	Tot. Cases	% Part	Tot. Cases	% Part	Tot. Cases	% Part	Tot. Cases	% Part	Tot. Cases	% Part	Tot. Cases
low	low	32.0	(122)	63.2	(367)	37.0	(108)	68.2	(255)	34.3	(230)	65.3	(622)
	med	35.7	(28)	65.2	(112)	47.2	(72)	72.7	(143)	44.0	(100)	69.4	(255)
	high	40.0	(10)	63.6	(22)	36.4	(33)	68.3	(63)	37.2	(43)	67.1	(85)
med	low	33.7	(98)	63.2	(193)	35.8	(67)	55.6	(99)	34.5	(165)	60.6	(292)
	med	40.8	(71)	66.0	(153)	45.0	(100)	63.9	(147)	43.3	(171)	65.0	(300)
	high	49.0	(51)	81.0	(100)	53.7	(149)	73.6	(178)	52.5	(200)	76.3	(278)
high	low	20.0	(45)	70.3	(74)	38.5	(13)	71.4	(21)	24.1	(58)	70.5	(95)
	med	38.3	(81)	72.5	(131)	55.6	(45)	67.2	(61)	44.4	(126)	70.8	(192)
	high	47.7	(172)	82.6	(235)	52.2	(247)	79.9	(289)	50.4	(419)	81.1	(524)
Total		37.4	(729)	68.9	(1509)	46.4	(883)	70.5	(1349)	42.4	(1612)	69.7	(2858)

Table 2.2.

Discriminant Function
Analysis of Participation*

Variable	Standardized Discriminant Function Coefficient	Canonical Correlation
Intelligence	-.005	
Grade Point	.438	
Type of Consent	.943	
Sex	.044	
		.293

*Using statistical procedures in Nie et al., (1975).

them to school was comparatively weak, notwithstanding that these students had actually completed the questionnaires and detached the identifying face sheet. As I have noted, taking the questionnaire did not prove to be ego-involving enough to overcome the obstacle of carrying the consent sheet home and returning it.

Careful examination of the percentages in table 2.1 reveals some complex interactions that alter slightly the general findings on intelligence, sex, and grade point.[7] The sex differences largely disappear under parental consent, except for the highest intelligence group. Grade point, however, remains an important factor even when other variables are controlled, although it is more important in the parental consent group among the more intelligent students.

These patterns suggest that student nonparticipation was due more to apathy and irresponsibility than to objection to the study or concern about harm or invasion of privacy. Thus, high participation rates occurred among students who could give formal consent at the time of the survey and among younger students whose grades suggest that they were the more motivated, conscientious students. The stronger effect of grades among the more intelligent, especially male students, is consistent with this concept. For parental consent boys with high ability external constraints on personal volition are minimized. These students have the ability to obtain whatever grades they choose, they play a sex role that permits independence and autonomy, and they are beyond the immediate control of the school regarding the return of the consent forms. The stronger relations between grades and participation in the more intelligent male groups is thus consistent with a motivational explanation of participation. Viewing grades as an index of motivation also provides an explanation for the failure of the expected sex differences to occur when grades are included in the analysis. Grades are probably a better and more direct index of such conformity to school programs and purposes than sex is.

The relative effects of these variables are summarized in the discriminant function analysis presented in table 2.2. As we have observed, type of consent and grade point are the most important linear determinants of participation, with type of consent being twice the size of the coefficient for grade point, while the coefficient for sex is negligible and that of intelligence essentially zero.

Thus, in 1975, even though the survey was sponsored and scheduled by each high school administration, only 63.2% of the graduating seniors in these eighteen high schools were included in the research. While various unobserved changes in the school circumstances between 1964 and 1975 were certainly involved in these differences, it seems likely that a large portion of the reduction in participation from 1964 to 1975 was due to the factor of voluntary participation, complicated by the procedures of informed consent.

Response rates varied considerably across the schools. School size, type of survey administration, and student consent group all had effects on response rate.

Because of the logistics of assembling students, variation in the mechanics of administration were related to school size. In the smallest three schools, the surveys were administered under voluntary circumstances, but in courses that were required of the entire senior class. The majority of administrations were conducted in medium-sized schools where assembly halls, cafeterias, and libraries were used to administer the questionnaires to the class assembled as a group. While the survey participation was always announced as voluntary, student freedom to attend these assemblies varied from school to school, in some cases being clearly optional, in others required. Finally, in the three largest schools, the surveys were administered in the first-period homerooms, by the homeroom teachers.

Assuming participation is more a matter of motivation and volition than of deliberate objection to the research itself, we should find that school size and administrative procedure have more to do with the participation of the student consent group, affected primarily by the circumstances of administration and the ability of the school to influence or control its students. The parental consent group would be influenced by these same factors, but in addition by motivation, commitment, and family and community circumstances related to the distribution and return of the parental consent forms.

Because there was no real objection to the survey, for the 18-year-olds the major circumstance was their attendance at the survey administration assembly, and secondly their willingness to complete the questionnaire.

Figures 2.1 and 2.2 are scatter diagrams of the response or participation rate by size of school class for student and parental consent groups treated separately with type of administration designated. These diagrams reveal two interesting patterns: school size has a nonlinear effect on participation and, as expected, the effect of school size is much stronger for the student than for the parental consent group.

The nonlinear effect for the student consent group (figure 2.1) is impressive. The curve generated by a polynomial of the second order explains 81% of the variance in school participation rates when the markedly discrepant school is treated as an outlier.[8] Even with that school included, 64% of the variation in participation is accounted for. Figure 2.2 shows that, as expected, school circumstances are less effective in accounting for response

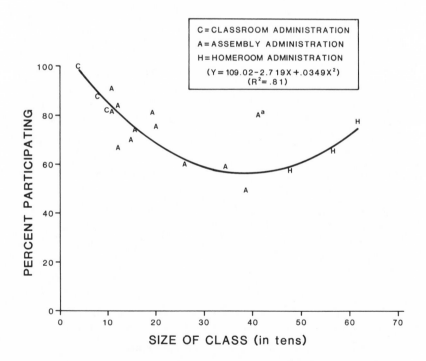

C = CLASSROOM ADMINISTRATION
A = ASSEMBLY ADMINISTRATION
H = HOMEROOM ADMINISTRATION
$(Y = 109.02 - 2.719X + .0349X^2)$
$(R^2 = .81)$

Figure 2.1 Percentage Participating by Size of Class: Student Consent Group

[a] School treated as an outlier. Not included in regression.

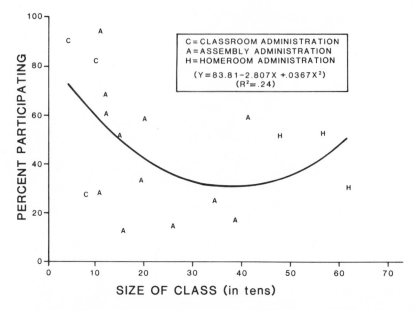

Figure 2.2 Percentage Participating by Size of Class: Parental Consent Group

rate among the minor students under parental consent. Even so, a second-order polynomial accounts for about one-quarter of the variance in the parental group also.

While the nonlinear effect was not expected, it is consistent with the idea that school control processes are most effective in smaller schools where students are known and accountable even without attendance lists, but that as size increases, so does anonymity and loss of control. The increased participation in the three largest schools suggests that at some point different approaches involving smaller groups and accountability restore some of the school control. Although size and administration are confounded, within each type of administration size is important. For example, in figure 2.1 the drop in response rate in the three smallest schools is almost completely explained by the school size ($r = -.9997, p < .01$). A linear regression also fits the schools using assembly administration ($r = -.8370, p < .01$). Thus, within type of administration, increasing size means increasing inability of the school administration to elicit cooperation and participation from its students. These findings are consistent with the classic concept (Wirth 1938) that size produces anonymity, which reduces the effectiveness of social control efforts.

The higher participation in the larger schools using homeroom administrations is also consistent with the idea of identifiability, since homeroom sizes are between twenty and thirty-five students. The increasing participation over the three schools requires some other explanation. However, since this relationship is weak enough to have occurred by chance in a linear test ($r = .9680$, $p < .10$), I will not speculate about it.

Bias

Response rate is important because of the possibility that the respondents will be different from the nonrespondents in ways related to the variables under study and will consequently produce a bias in the estimates of the population based on values in the participant group only.[9]

To answer those questions, additional data gathering of overall grade point and aptitude scores was carried out in the summer following the survey administration using records of the entire classes with nonparticipants' identification removed. Grades and intelligence are appropriate variables for this purpose as they index a wide range of social and educational circumstances. The correlation between them represents the application of student ability to the academic purposes of the school, and consequently provides an index of the orientation of the student toward the academic programs (see Coleman 1961:263–264, for a classic application of this principle). In addition, accumulating research findings (see Sewell and Hauser 1975; and Alexander, Eckland, and Griffen 1975 for illustrations and citations) have shown that intelligence also serves to mediate the effect of socioeconomic status on grades and to independently affect teacher and parent encouragement for boys to attend college. Rosenthal and Rosnow (1975) have shown bias in intelligence and in grades, but it appears that no one has yet examined the bias in correlation between these variables.

Two questions can be answered with this analysis. The first is whether the bias (or the difference—the tests in each case are equivalent, though the values of the descriptive parameters are not) is statistically significant. Second, regardless of the answer to that question, I am interested in the *amount* of the bias, most often expressed in standardized terms as the proportion of a standard deviation it represents, in a fashion similar to Rosenthal and Rosnow (1975) and Cohen (1969). The coefficients of determination for the regression of the criterion variables on participation will also be presented as another indicator of the magnitude of the bias introduced through nonparticipation.

Since several different intelligence tests were used in the several schools, and since there were some school-to-school differences in the way grade-

Table 2.3.

Bias in Grade Point and Intelligence

Participation Group	Males					
	Parental Consent			Student Consent		
	X	SD	N	X	SD	N
	(Grade Point)					
Participants	.099	.981	(273)	-.176	.977	(1038)
Nonparticipants	-.213	1.001	(453)	-.469	.916	(466)
Total	-.095	1.004	(726)	-.267	.968	(1504)
Difference (P-NP)	.312**	-.020		.293**	.061	
Bias (P-Total)	.194	-.023		.091	.009	
Standardized Bias (Bias/SD)	.193			.094		
r^2	.023**			.020**		
	(Intelligence)					
Participants	.270	.914	(262)	-.005	1.059	(964)
Nonparticipants	.158	.962	(418)	-.274	1.030	(426)
Total	.201	.945	(680)	-.088	1.057	(1390)
Difference (P-NP)	.112	-.048		.269**	.029	
Bias (P-Total)	.069	-.031		.083	.002	
Standardized Bias (Bias/SD)	.073			.078		
r^2	.003			.014**		

point average was represented, these two variables are expressed throughout the balance of this discussion as standard scores within each school.

Table 2.3 presents the different measures of bias for individual students in the total population and for the several consent subgroups. Of these ten comparisons, eight of the differences between participant and nonparticipant means are statistically significant. The differences, however, are very small, and the biases, of course, are even smaller. The overall bias in grades is only .084 of a standard deviation and that of intelligence .032 of a standard deviation. Neither of these values is substantial, and both are much smaller than the value of .20 that Cohen (1969:23–24) designates as a small effect. The coefficients of determination at the bottom of each panel of table 2.3 throw further substantive meaning onto the bias values. In no case does the fact of participation or nonparticipation account for more than 2.3% of the variance in the variables of interest, and it accounts for only 1.1% of the variance in the total population for grade point and for only 0.2% of the variance in the total population for intelligence score. These values are surprisingly small given the overall participation rate of only 63.2%. (See note 5.)

Table 2.3 also shows that there is neither substantively nor statistically significant bias in the variances of either variable in the total population. Among the consent subgroups, the two-tailed F tests for homogeneity of variance show only one of the eight comparisons to be statistically significant, and even this difference is quite small.

Table 2.3. (continued)

Participation Group	Females								
	Parental Consent			Student Consent			Total		
	X	SD	N	X	SD	N	X	SD	N
	(Grade Point)								
Participants	.469	.844	(410)	.198	.988	(950)	.084	.989	(2671)
Nonparticipants	.235	.973	(473)	-.054	.967	(395)	-.126	.999	(1787)
Total	.343	.922	(883)	.124	.988	(1345)	.000	.998	(4458)
Difference (P-NP)	.234**	-.129**		.252**	.021		.210**	-.010	
Bias (P-Total)	.126	-.078		.074	.000		.084	-.009	
Standardized Bias (Bias/SD)	.137			.075			.084		
r^2		.016**			.013**			.011**	
	(Intelligence)								
Participants	.228	.888	(394)	-.084	1.005	(888)	.032	1.008	(2508)
Nonparticipants	.068	.940	(440)	-.164	.925	(369)	-.049	.981	(1653)
Total	.144	.919	(834)	-.107	.982	(1257)	.000	.998	(4161)
Difference (P-NP)	.150*	-.052		.080	.090		.081**	.027	
Bias (P-Total)	.084	-.031		.023	.023		.032	.010	
Standardized Bias (Bias/SD)	.091			.023			.032		
r^2		.008**			.001			.002**	

* p .05
** p .01

Table 2.4 presents the results of the analysis of the relation between intelligence scores and grades, which are taken as indicators of unspecified but general student orientations toward school. Bias in the correlation coefficients in table 2.4 is the differences between Fisher's logarithmic transformations of the correlations for the participants and those of the population. Cohen (1969:75–76) argues that this difference is conceptually equivalent to the bias values of the means in table 2.3. If that is so, the data in table 2.4 are encouraging. The biases (in terms of Fisher's z) are of the same small orders of magnitude as the biases in the means. Only two of the five differences between participation and nonparticipant correlations are statistically significant. However, none of the differences between the unstandardized regression coefficients of grade-point average on intelligence scores for the participants and nonparticipants is significant, despite the fact that the values of the standardized and unstandardized coefficients are very close to each other. Clearly then, the amount of bias in the grade-point-intelligence correlation introduced by the informed-consent procedures is minor. Insofar as these correlations actually do index general student orientations toward the school program, these results have positive implications for the representativeness of the participant group on other educationally relevant variables not directly examined in this analysis, but of concern in this research.

Table 2.4.

Bias in Correlation and Regression Between Intelligence Score and Grade Point Average

Participation Group	Males Parental Consent			Males Student Consent			Females Parental Consent			Females Student Consent			Total		
	r	b	N	r	b	N	r	b	N	r	b	N	r	b	N
Participants	.67	.72	(262)	.60	.57	(964)	.60	.57	(394)	.64	.62	(888)	.61	.60	(2508)
Nonparticipants	.58	.60	(416)	.67	.49	(423)	.67	.69	(440)	.55	.57	(368)	.58	.59	(1647)
Total	.62	.65	(678)	.64	.55	(1387)	.64	.69	(834)	.61	.62	(1256)	.60	.60	(4155)
Difference (P-NP)[a]	.16*	.12		-.11	.08		-.11	-.12		.14*	.05		.05	.01	
Bias (P-Total)[a]	.10	.07		-.04	.02		-.04	-.12		.04	.00		.02	.00	

*p < .05, two-tailed test
[a]Difference and bias of r's expressed in Fisher's z-units

ANALYSIS

Empirical analysis of the data of this study uses regression wherever the data permit. The strategy is to locate sex-typed variables by examining sex differences. Conducted over the substantial range of information available in this research, this analysis will enable us to locate those dimensions that empirically define sex roles. As a practical matter, this approach enables us to evaluate the content of sex roles from numerous perspectives and relate that to the current literature. The concept of sex roles is questioned by failure to observe sex differences or by inconsistencies between differences observed in these data and differences described in the sex role literature. Because a satisfactory theory of sex roles has yet to be advanced, this inclusive view of sex roles is necessary, as is my empirical foundation for the conceptualization. Nevertheless, and even in the absence of good integrative theory, patterns of observed differences should be internally consistent with general expectations and with various ad hoc formulations of pertinent features of sex roles.

Differences between the sexes across the years reflect social change. Again, the strength of the observed differences and their relevance to known patterns of change over this period are taken into account. As with the role patterns, patterns of change should be coherent at least with the ad hoc and empirical literature on change across the decades. As with sex roles, sociology lacks generally accepted theories of change embracing the range of variables to be examined. Nevertheless, I expect that, analogous to sex differences, differences across the years will manifest an internal coherence consistent with other research and writing about social change and sex role change.

Sex role change is reflected in *change in the amount of sex difference over the study period*. Sex role change in the form of masculinization would be observed as a reduction in sex differences between 1964 and 1975 as a result of change in the levels of the variable among females. Feminization, on the other hand, would be reflected by a reduction in sex difference over the period due to change in the level of the variable among males. Finally, role convergence would be observed as reduction in sex differences over the period as a result of change in the levels of both males and females. Sex role change involving intensification of sex-typed patterns is not expected, but would involve an increase in observed sex differences.

In these analyses, sex and year are treated as dummy variables[10] with male = 0, female = 1 and 1964 = 0, 1975 = 1. Thus, regression coefficients describe the change in variables of interest attributable to being a female compared to being a male and being of the 1975 cohort compared to the 1964. Obviously, the former reflects sex difference, the later, social change.

As described above, sex role change involves the interaction of sex and year on the variable of interest. Empirically, this is treated as the product of (sex × year). This coefficient expresses the difference of the differences between the sexes at the two points in time. What this amounts to is that the amount of difference between the sexes depends on the time. Whether this reflects masculinization, feminization, or convergence depends upon the sign and strength of the interaction term. However, this effect is more easily comprehended from examination of the average values in the four basic cells created by the two dummy variables. Consequently, in presenting the results, I report tables of mean values along with the regression coefficients.

Facilitating Conditions

The analysis is carried one step further by considering whether sex role change is greater in some subgroups than in others. Certain conditions that establish distinctive groups have been treated in the literature as important to change processes. I would expect change to appear first among certain groups whose life experience makes them receptive to the themes of change or places them in special relationships to change agents or experience. A number of these circumstances are included in the analysis to determine if change is greater in these expected groups and to examine the possibility that while there may be no observable change in the overall general population, there may be change in some of these selected subpopulations.

While there is no generally accepted, integrated theory of sex role change, three general processes linking individual personality with broader social forces have been advanced in different treatments of both social change and sex role change. These processes reflect variation in socialization content and experience, differences in receptivity and awareness of contemporary change, and personal flexibility and adaptability in accepting new patterns and meanings. A number of variables in the data of this study serve to tap these three themes.

Variation in Socialization Subgroups

Variation in socialization subgroups has been extensively treated in the literature on changing sex roles. The basic idea is that nontraditional socialization experience is introduced by changing public conceptions about women's role and by consequences of work on the image of the woman and on her actual personality characteristics.

The mother's work status has special significance in this respect for two slightly different reasons. In the first place, the working mother is viewed as a nontraditional role model for the daughter, both because she performs work outside the home and thus has independence and autonomy from patriarchal control, and because her income and work status increase her power and influence within the family.[11] From a second perspective, work could be seen as important because it represents a context within which the mother may acquire nontraditional values and orientations related to work, but carried into the family socialization experience and especially significant for the daughter.

Another aspect of family socialization is the traditionalism of the family value systems—especially with regard to patriarchy and sacred, traditional views of women's role. Assuming that Lois Hoffman (1977) and other writers are correct in believing that families train daughters for what the parents assume to be the traditional women's role based on homemaking and childbearing, the degree to which family value systems are in fact so organized necessarily becomes an important issue in locating groups within which change would most likely occur. Because traditional family roles are anchored in religious belief systems, commitment to fundamentalist religions should retard change compared to those having no religious affiliation or who are affiliated with nonfundamentalist religion (Monteiro 1978; Thornton and Freedman 1979). From this perspective, the absence of an indicator of religious orientation is an unfortunate ommission for this study. In the absence of information about parental religious values, I am forced to use a substitute indicator of family traditionalism.

Because of the relation between religion, modern values, and attitudes about fertility (Scanzoni 1976) and abortion (Monteiro 1978), I assume that larger families are more traditional and use number of siblings as an indicator of traditional family orientation. This indicator is unfortunately flawed by the lack of information on parental age. Consequently, while large families unequivocally reflect the variable, in small families, secular orientation and parents' age are confounded. Nevertheless, size is used as one relatively weak indicator of family traditionalism.

A corollary to the proposition about family traditionalism and stability is the proposition that change would be generally facilitated by significant contact with extrafamilial individuals, especially such secular others as teachers and counselors located in universalistic contexts (Bandura 1969:250–251; Lueptow 1975). Thus, number of extrafamilial others consulted about postgraduate plans is used as a facilitating variable intended to explore this dimension.

Aware and Informed Subgroups

Highly aware and informed subgroups constitute the second major approach to change. While this theme has not been developed as extensively by students of sex roles, there are some relatively clear-cut applications of the proposition that certain groups are more attentive to and aware of media presentation of the themes of social change.

This thesis was advanced in an early, classic paper by Bronfenbrenner (1958), who explained previously conflicting findings about permissiveness in child training by time ordering the researches and showing that middle-class families were responding first, followed later by working-class families, to media communication of "expert" child-care procedures that changed from restrictive to permissive and then back again. More recently and more relevant to my concern is Schreiber's (1978) research showing close relations between media coverage of women (*Reader's Guide* column inches) and marked shifts in attitude about a female president. Schreiber concluded that the relation between education and nontraditional attitudes (Hyman, Wright, and Reed 1975; Yankelovich 1974; Ferree 1974; but see Mason, Czajka, and Arber 1976) was caused by the greater attention more educated people pay to the message of the media. Thus, he argued, education is important, not simply because it socializes new values, but because it creates an awareness in people and a receptiveness to media themes.

One item in this survey dealt with daily reading of a newspaper and is taken as a rough indicator of the respondent's "awareness of what the current 'fashion' on that issue [sex role change] is" (Schreiber 1978:176).

Whether education is important because it promotes greater awareness of current media content or because it represents greater liberalism and receptiveness to nontraditional ideas, it seems likely that youths raised by more highly educated parents will have been exposed to more liberal views and be more informed about current fashions. Thus, parental education will be used as a facilitating variable on the assumption that sex role change will be more likely to occur among students from families with higher levels of education and awareness of current issues.

Finally, Bronfenbrenner (1965) and Sewell (1965) have suggested that urban experience, independent of education, will have exposed the student to a greater range of alternatives. Even though contemporary communication and transportation have eliminated most of the significance of the rural-urban distinction, urban residence is also used as a subgroup in which somewhat greater change might be expected.

Flexible Personalities

Flexible and adaptive personalities and the context within which they occur are described by several lines of theory and findings. These contexts are ones that produce personalities that are flexible and adaptive and, for one reason or another, more prone to adopt new modes of values and behavior. Social class, occupation, and education have long been viewed as major parameters of these social contexts, from Riessman's (1950) flexible, almost selfless, other-directed person, attuned to the winds of change, to the more formal arguments recently advanced by Bernstein.

Bernstein (1971) argues that social classes represent different socialization contexts with respect to the acquisition of linguistic forms and cognitive styles, and that predictable interactions organized around positional relationships result in a restricted linguistic code and particularistic meanings tied to localized contexts. These are more common in working-class contexts. Middle-class socialization occurs in person-oriented contexts where meanings are not implicit but must be made explicit, where the individual must formulate and express his or her own understandings, and where the general meanings are universalistic, not particularistic. This latter context utilizes an elaborated linguistic code that is capable of making the discriminations and carrying the burden of communication such unfamiliar interactions require. Relevance to change occurs in that middle-class socialization involves both codes, thus providing the ability to shift roles. Bernstein argues that the ability to shift codes is the ability to shift roles. Bernstein's arguments are consistent with the idea that change will occur first in the educated middle class.

In a related formulation, Fullan and Loubser (1972) have developed the argument that modern society requires adaptive capacity and that education is a means, not presently fully realized, for developing such capacity in individuals. Adaptive capacity involves both the generation of new patterns and forms and the selective retention of certain patterns or elements from the total store of elements. In cognitive functioning it means such things as flexibility in redefining information, openness to new experience, sense of control, empathy, and the ability to "analyze, abstract and recombine new elements in terms of their logical interrelations" (1972:275). These are essentially the components of creativity and intelligence.

Empirical evidence very closely related to these conceptions has been obtained in research on the relations between social structure and personality, especially between occupational experience and cognitive variables. Schooler (1972) has found that intellectual flexibility is related to socialization in a multifaceted environment indexed by youth, father's high level of education, urban residence, regions with industry and high educational expenditures, and "modernist" religions. Kohn and Schooler (1978) found that intellectual flexibility was a result of occupancy of occupations characterized by self-direction (closeness of supervision, routinization of work, and substantive complexity of the job). More recently, these same relationships between conditions of work and cognitive processes have been observed for women (Miller et al. 1979). Most of the variables just discussed can also be seen as indicators of intellectual flexibility and adaptability. However, of special interest for this analysis are the Rosenberg items that deal with creative and self-expressive orientations. These two items are used in this study as in the research by Boyle (1969) as crude indicators of the psychological factors of creativity and flexibility. Greater change is expected among those groups high on these creative and self-expressive value orientations. Finally, while intelligence does not necessarily imply flexibility, its relevance to information and the adaptive factor of selective retention (Fullan and Loubser 1972) indicates its significance for the subgroup analysis.

A summary listing of the full set of facilitating variables is given in table 2.5. They cover a broad range of circumstances thought to facilitate change in sex roles, especially along the dimension of masculinization, which is assumed to be the most likely form this change will take. In the analysis to follow, the full set is used in some of the preliminary analysis, but a reduced set is used in the bulk of the analysis because the lack of effect among the facilitating variables did not warrant the substantial computer costs of running the full set of interactions for each of the variables of this study. The reduced set are viewed as reasonable proxies for the full set and used to examine the possibility that facilitating effects might be observed at some point in the analysis. They consist of mother's work, number of consultants, father's education, reading a newspaper, and intelligence, and are designated in table 2.5.

In the regression analysis, the facilitating variables are constructed as products of two- and three-way interactions. A facilitating effect appears in

Table 2.5.

Variables Facilitating Change in Sex Roles

Facilitating Variables	Likely Relevance of the Facilitating Variable		
	Socialization Influence	Awareness of Change	Personal Flexibility and Adaptability
Personal			
A. Intelligence			x a
B. Creativity			x
Family			
C. Father's Education		x a	x
D. Mothers Education		x	x
E. Moth–Fath Education Difference		x	
F. Mother Working	x a		
H. Number of Sibs	x		
I. Eldest Child			x
Extra-Familial Consultation			
J. Number	x a		
K. Teacher, Counselor	x		
L. Visits to Counselor	x		
M. Received Occup. Inform.	x		
N. Value of College Counselling	x		
O. Value of Occup. Counselling	x		
Community			
P. Urban Residence		x	
Q. Newspaper Reading		x a	

a Variables selected as representative of the set for truncated analysis used throughout the main body of the study.

the three-way interaction of sex times year times facilitating variable, net of all other direct and interactive terms in the equation. A significant three-way interaction means that the sex role change appearing as a significant two-way interaction is more pronounced at some levels of the facilitating variable than at others. While greater than three-way interactions can be generated by direct extension of this approach, Cohen and Cohen point out that they "are most difficult to conceptualize, not likely to exist and are costly in statistical inference (1975:296). I do not carry interpretation beyond the three-way analysis of sex by year by facilitator.

CHAPTER 3

PERSONALITY, SEX DIFFERENCES, AND CHANGE: REVIEW OF THE EVIDENCE

The issue of sex differences in personality lies at the heart of most issues on sex roles, whether empirical, conceptual, or ideological. In the final analysis, it is the differences in personal characteristics and life orientations between the sexes, institutionalized in stereotypes and manifest in values about women's proper place, that constitute the elemental features of the contemporary interest in sex roles. Sex roles are important only as they constitute a unique pattern of differentiation not reducible to other lines of demarcation such as class, race, and age. Insofar as there are differences, either real or assumed, sex roles represent a viable area of study and concern. Without differences between the sexes in personality characteristics, orientations, and expectations, the area reduces to the study of other dimensions of social process. Consequently, the initial question in research of changing sex roles is the strength of sex as a variable in explaining variation in personality and experience.

Evaluation of sex differences in personality is compounded by problems and issues at empirical, conceptual, and ideological levels. At the empirical level there are problems of measurement, design, and strategy that plague the collection of data and that rest on prior neglect of women in the study of "man" (Maccoby and Jacklin 1974; Block 1976). It is difficult to assess sex differences accurately in the face of stereotypic conceptions held by both subject and observer. This difficulty is accentuated by the fact that much of the evidence on sex difference comes from research in which sex was a control variable and not the direct variable of interest, and by the fact that social science has not been strongly interested in feminine characteristics and dimensions, but rather has tended to be a science of male behavior developed by males (Hochshild 1973; Kirschner 1973; Bernard 1975).

At the conceptual level, the major problem is the lack of an adequate theory of sex roles to permit interpretation and evaluation of significant and insignificant variables and dimensions. Apart from variables embedded in such limited formulations as occupation, achievement, and aggression, it is difficult to delineate the specific variables constituting the critical tests. For example, in their list of myths about sex differences, Maccoby and Jacklin treat each trait equivalently, regardless of the substantial differences in the behavioral implications of such traits as tactile sensitivity, aggression, and empathy. The possibility that aggressiveness-assertiveness might constitute an important underlying, general trait serving as the foundation for other traits could not be easily handled in the absence of integrating, elucidating theory.

Because of these problems, I adopt an inclusive perspective and consider all variables for which sex differences have been shown, including some variables that remain equivocal. This approach generates a reasonably comprehensive cluster of traits and circumstances that will serve as background for my empirical analysis. Such an approach provides the full range of potential change dimensions as they appear in today's research and speculation. It also serves as a review of the evidence to date.

An additional conceptual problem arises in the appraisal of the importance of difference. In considering sex differences, most writers are clear in their recognition that each sex is to some degree heterogeneous on nearly all variables of interest, and with overlap, sometimes considerable, of the distributions of women and men. With one or two exceptions,[1] the issue of sex difference is essentially one of degree rather than kind. In a very literal sense, sex differences of importance are those that are largely explained by sex, in the sense of explained variance in regression and analysis of variance conceptions. Unimportant differences are those exhibiting more variance within each sex than between. As these formulations describe differences of degree rather than of kind, conceptual interpretation of the empirical reality is necessarily equivocal. It becomes a question of whether the writer wishes to emphasize the overlap in the distributions or their distinctiveness.[2]

Finally, there are legitimate, as well as self-interested, ideological concerns involved in the interpretation of this evidence. Because sex differences can be (and have been) used as rationales for the maintenance of traditional, restrictive, inequitable role arrangements, feminist writers are trying to avoid the Type I error of erroneously rejecting the hypothesis of no difference. Similar concerns have emerged in the analysis of social class and poverty, race and intelligence. In each of these areas, as in sex roles, conceptual interpretation of equivocal evidence leans strongly toward the humanitarian alternative. In practice this has meant discounting evidence on class and genetic causes of poverty and low achievement and minimizing the significance of sex differences and emphasizing environmental explanations. The "congenial truths" (Mackie 1977) supporting these perspectives tend to be uncritically accepted while the contrary evidence is subjected to rigorous critique or is explained away. While understandable, this approach leads to understating sex differences, especially those differences that are critical pillars of sex-typed role assignments.

In this chapter I will review the evidence on sex differences in personality. Some sense of the differences, as the current evidence reveals them, is important for delineating central dimensions of contemporary sex roles along which change could be expected and where it would have special significance. With evidence on sex differences in hand, we will then examine the evidence to date on sex role change, although it will become clear that the evidence on change does not yet bear directly on some of the most important sex differences.

SEX DIFFERENCES

The literature on sex differences consists of four relatively clear-cut bodies of work on (1) sex-role stereotypes, (2) sex differences in personality, (3) sex differences in achievement orientations, and (4) sex differences in attitudes about family and career, although the evidence on *change* and innovation in family roles is much more extensive than that on attitudinal *difference* between the sexes about family role divisions.

Sex Role Stereotypes

Sex role stereotypes consist of orientations and values about the typical and appropriate personal characteristics of women and men. As such they are viewed both as public beliefs about the nature of men and women and also as the individual perception of what one is to be—and do. They are viewed as self-fulfilling, providing components of self-concept and identity as well as of role expectations of appropriate sex-typed behavior.

The nature of sex role stereotypes has been clearly delineated in extensive studies, from early work by Brim (1958) and McKee and Sherriffs (1959), through early examination of the content by Broverman et al. (1972) and

Block (1973), and more recent and methodologically advanced work on stereotypes by Williams and his associates (Williams and Bennett 1975; Williams and Best 1977; Williams et al. 1977), to the contemporary concern with androgyny (Bem 1977; Spence and Helmreich 1978). Through all of this research, the agreement on the basic characteristics of typical women and men has been striking. Without exception, these studies generate a picture of the public conception of male and female personality that sharply distinguishes the two sexes.

Examination of the content of the stereotypes and of the interpretations of the various students of sex role stereotyping reveals two major dimensions running through the formulations. The first of these is the instrumental-expressive distinction first advanced by Parsons, Bales, and Olds (1955) and by Zelditch (1955) and used by Brim (1958) in his early research on the effects of sibling gender composition on stereotypic traits of young children. The early formulations derived the instrumental-expressive distinction from patterns of leadership observed by Bales and his colleagues in studies of small groups. It turned out that in these small groups, two types of leaders emerged: one who was recognized as the top person for task concerns involving ideas, guidance, and direction, and another who was best liked and who had more to do with tension release than with task success. While these roles were not always held by different individuals, the pattern of differentiation occurred enough and was related to other empirical evidence on phasing of group concerns between task and emotional interests to warrant the view that groups had two central problems: task accomplishment, and personal satisfaction and group morale or integration.

While the subjects in Bales' Harvard groups were all men, the generalization by Parsons and Bales of this pattern to the nuclear family as a small group resulted in the classic sex typing of the father as the instrumental leader and the mother as the socioemotional or expressive leader. As the instrumental leader, the father would need the personality characteristics related to objective appraisal of reality, evaluation of alternative approaches, willingness to guide, pressure, and control the other members, and the independence to be unaffected by the absence of affectivity and love resulting from his emphasis on these task concerns. The mother, on the other hand, would necessarily manifest higher levels of emotional involvement, sensitivity to the feelings of others, and personal warmth and concern leading to supportive, integrated actions.

As Zelditch's (1955) research applications of these ideas reveal, the family has one clear distinction as a small group in addition to the sex differentiation. The father as instrumental leader of the group has also a leadership role as representative of the group to the broader society. He must be concerned with the external boundaries of the group. Thus, the mother's expressive leadership is related to her integrative role performed within the family and even within the household, where the hearth was the symbol of her function, but the father's role has an important external component symbolized by the hunt, war, and the council in which he represents the (his) family.[3]

The other major dimension of sex role content has to do with strength and weakness. While this dimension is related to the concept of the male as leader, representative, and defender of the group to the broader society, the full range of masculine and feminine characteristics has not been, to my knowledge, related to structural demands, as have the instrumental-expressive characteristics. Rather, the characteristics of male strength and female weakness or dependency seem to be more an idealization or exaggeration of the basic physical differences between women and men.

These two dimensions, the instrumental-expressive and strength-weakness are reflected in contemporary formulations of the basic elements of sex role stereotypes. Thus, Broverman et al. (1972) concluded that the central factors in the ratings of their ad hoc set of items described a ''competency cluster'' for the male stereotype and a ''warmth-expressiveness'' cluster for the female. More recently, Bem (1974:156) has described the difference as one in which ''masculinity has been associated with an instrumental orientation, a cognitive focus on 'getting the job done,' and feminity has been associated with an expressive orientation, an affective concern for the welfare of others.''

In their work on androgyny, Bem, Martyna, and Watson (1976) contrasted masculine independence with feminine nurturance. Spence and Helmreich (1978) have also used the instrumental-expressive distinction with reference to the fundamental dimension distinguishing masculinity-feminity concepts and have equated those dimensions with the agentic-communal distinction, as does Block. ''Agency is concerned with the organism as an individual and manifests itself in self-protection, self assertion, and self-expression. Communion, according to Bakan, is descriptive of the individual organism as it exists in some larger organism of which it is a part and manifest itself in the sense of being at one with other organisms (1973:515).'' Finally, Ward and Balswick (1978) recently found that the first, and most important, factor in the analysis of responses of high school students describing the typical woman or typical man were strong-dominant for males and interpersonal virtues for females.

These themes are readily apparent in the traits most often presented in seven representative published studies on sex role stereotypes. Traits that have appeared in at least two of these studies are listed in tables 3.1 and

Table 3.1.

Content of the Male Stereotype

Adjective Content	Source of Adjective or Phrase									
	Bem (1974)	Block (1973)	Brim (1958)	Broverman et al. (1972)	Burns (1977)	Lueptow (1980)	Sherriffs and McKee (1957)	Spence and Helmreich (1978)	Ward and Balsnick (1978)	Williams and Bennett (1975)
STRENGTH AND AGGRESSIVENESS										
active				x				x		
acts as a leader	x			x						
adventurous		x		x			x	x		x
aggressive	x		x	x	x	x	x		x	x
ambitious	x	x	x	x			x			x
assertive	x	x								x
boastful							x			x
competitive	x	x	x	x	x	x		x		
courageous							x			x
daring							x			x
dominant	x	x		x	x	x	x	x	x	x
feelings not easily hurt				x				x		
forceful	x						x			x
little need for security				x				x		
loud				x						x
never cries				x	x			x		
stern							x			x
strong									x	x
tenacity	x		x							
tough							x			x
SELF SUFFICIENCY										
independent	x	x		x	x		x	x		x
individualistic	x						x			
makes decisions easily	x		x	x		x		x		
not easily influenced				x				x		
responsible		x	x						x	
self confident			x	x		x	x	x		x
OBJECTIVITY										
likes math and science				x						x
logical				x	x		x			
rational		x							x	x
stable					x					x
steady							x			x
unemotional				x					x	x
objective				x	x					

Table 3.2.

Content of the Female Stereotype

Adjective Content	Source of Adjective or Phrase									
	Bem (1974)	Block (1973)	Brim (1958)	Broverman, et al. (1972)	Burns (1977)	Lueptow (1980)	Sheriffs and McKee (1957)	Spence and Helmreich (1978)	Ward and Balsnick (1978)	Williams and Bennett (1975)
EXPRESSIVE										
affectionate	x	x	x		x	x	x			x
cheerful	x	x	x							
emotional, feeling				x			x		x	x
kind			x				x			
sensitive		x					x			x
sentimental							x			x
sympathetic	x	x				x	x			
tactful					x		x			
talkative		x			x	x				x
understanding	x						x			
warm	x				x		x			
WEAKNESS AND DEPENDENCY										
cries easily				x	x					
dependent					x					x
gentle	x			x	x		x			x
obedient			x		x					
passive				x	x					
shy	x	x					x			
submissive				x	x		x		x	x
weak					x				x	x
EMOTIONALITY										
dreamy							x			x
excitable				x			x			x
frivolous							x			x
fussy							x			x
high-strung							x			x
OTHER										
artistic		x					x			
attractive									x	x
curious		x				x				
does not use harsh language	x				x					
idealistic		x			x					
religious					x		x			
sophisticated							x			x

3.2, although close synonyms have not been counted. Only the literal wording in each study has been tabulated. Even so, there is a fair amount of repetition in these studies, even at this relatively specific level.

It is apparent that the predominant clusters of traits that have emerged in these studies and about which there is the greatest repetition are masculine strength and female expressiveness or warmth, quite consistent with the Ward and Balswick (1978) formulation, "strong men and virtuous women." To a considerable degree, men are seen as assertive, dominant, and competitive, while women in these studies are described in expressive terms heavily loaded with nurturant and supporting warmth and affection.

In addition to the strength-assertiveness dimension, the male stereotypes also reveal two reasonably long, often repeated clusters of traits, one centering on independence and self-sufficiency and the other on cognitively organized task orientations, both consistent with the instrumental formulation. Men are seen as oriented toward an empirical, task-relevant reality where logic, rationality, and objectivity are the important features of the personality. The relevance of these characteristics to modern occupational roles is apparent and suggests that this perception of male personality may have emerged through recognition of the nature of economic activity in modern society, where rationalization of work and secular, empirical patterns predominate.

The other aspect of the male stereotype has to do with independence and self-sufficiency. Men are perceived as autonomous persons, making their own decisions, being self-reliant and self-confident. The parallel to the individualism, self-orientation theme of modernization is again striking. As contrasted to collectivity orientation of traditional societies and primary group contexts, the stereotype of the male is in many respects the picture of modern man.[4]

The expressive theme in the perception of the "typical female" is clearly represented in these studies (table 3.2), where such attributes as affectionate, sensitive, sympathetic, understanding, and talkative reflect maternal, expressive role demands. Feminine weakness and dependency are also repeated in the stereotypic content of these studies and again reflect the complement of the male stereotypic pattern of assertiveness and independence. Finally, the female stereotype contains a cluster of characteristics reflecting negative, at times almost neurotic, aspects of expressive, self-centered emotionality and defensiveness. While less often repeated in the various studies, these traits describe an emotionality that complements the logic and objectivity of the male, instrumental theme.

Thus, for whatever historical or systemic reasons, women are seen in these studies as interpersonal specialists behaving with the affective concern appropriate to those occupying a particularistic, ascribed role within the family and in deference to male strength and autonomy. These personality characteristics are consistent with the demands of family roles emphasizing expressive concerns involving personalized relations with members of the primary group rather than to the more extended role demands of the broader society, especially those related to the universalistic-achievement patterns of the occupational role system. They are also consistent with conventional and traditional patterns of interpersonal sexuality organized around male strength and assertiveness and female weakness and submissiveness.[5]

The consistency of the stereotypic content that appears in these several research formulations also appears in the correlations between the sexes and across the cultures. Thus, Broverman et al. (1972) found correlations of $r = .95$ for average "adult male" responses of men and women and $r = .95$ for average "adult female" responses. Williams et al. (1977) report correlations of $r = .90, .75, .89$ between the percentage of males and females assigning each of 300 traits to the typical male in England, Ireland, and the United States, respectively, and $r = .90, .78, .89$ between the sexes in the assignment of the 300 traits to females.

My own (1980c) analysis showed similar patterns. Correlations between the average ratings of twenty traits showed correlations of .98 in both 1974 and 1977 between male and female ratings of typical male and $r = .95$ in both years between male and female ratings of typical female.

Thus, for whatever the reason, conceptions of the typical personalities of men and women are clear, consistent, and consensual.[6] Further, these conceptions clearly relate to the differing roles women and men have played in work, family, and community.

Personality Differences

Personality differences between the sexes remains a controversial and inconclusive issue, although the evidence on some characteristics related to the stereotype is relatively clear-cut. However, evidence on these differences is complicated by the absence of an integrated theory of sex roles. As it stands now, this research has accumulated largely as an extension of incidental findings, many resulting from the inclusion of sex as a control variable in research on other variables of interest.

Lacking an adequate theory of sex roles and in the absence of unequivocal comprehensive empirical evidence, I use the revealed stereotypic content as a frame of reference for the consideration of sex differences. While this will appear to some a questionable stance to take, one could argue that the highly consensual, internally consistent formulations of characteristics might well be a good gender starting point in the absence of sex role theory pointing toward the most significant dimensions. Without other formulations, the public conception of the nature of women and men might be a reasonable point of departure—sort of a naive psychology of sex roles.

While there has not yet been definitive research designed to assess all of these particular dimensions, the Maccoby and Jacklin (1974) review remains the most comprehensive and useful review of the evidence on sex differences. I use this work as the primary source, aware that it has been severely criticized by Block's (1976) exhaustive review. However, for my present purpose of summarizing revealed differences between the sexes, this may not be such a serious limitation. The gist of Block's criticism is that the research designs being summarized, the weak power of the small sample size, and Maccoby and Jacklin's own faulty scholarship have all operated to seriously *understate* the real difference between women and men, a conclusion shared by Hoffman (1977).

While the content of the tables in Maccoby and Jacklin does not correspond exactly to the content of the stereotype, it does provide points of contact for several of the key dimensions of the stereotypes as they have been formulated in the research just reviewed. In summarizing the Maccoby and Jacklin results, I use a shorthand notation based on Block's formulation of the number of studies being summarized, the proportion of them showing boys and men to be higher on the characteristic and the proportion showing girls and women to be higher (N, M $= p$, F $= p$).[7] In twelve of the summaries, Block (1977) located omissions, sixty-three in all. In nearly every case, the inclusion of omitted cases increased the observed differences in the stereotypic direction. These additional studies are incorporated into the following summary.

The major characteristic of the male stereotype is aggressiveness-assertiveness. Consistent with both the stereotype and general conclusions in the literature (see Weitz 1977:11–22), the research evidence shows boys and men to be much more aggressive than girls and women. Of the ninety-four studies reviewed by Maccoby and Jacklin, fifty-two, or 0.55 of them, show men to be more aggressive, while only four, or 0.05 show women to be more aggressive (94, M $= .55$, F $= .05$). The remainder show no sex difference at the .05 level of significance.[8] Similar differences occur also for dominance. The summary of studies show men considerably more likely to attempt to direct group activities, influence peers, or control adults than women (47, M $= .42$, F $= .04$). Men were also more competitive (26, M $= .31$, F $= .11$), although in this case the differences were not as extreme. Finally, evidence is clear that men are more active, and the differences in this case are quite substantial (60, M = .41, F = .05). Thus, and somewhat surprisingly given the assumption that sex role sterotypes do not reflect actual circumstances, research evidence provides strong support for the central masculine stereotypic pattern of aggressiveness and assertiveness.

The dominant female stereotypic patterns of sensitivity to the needs of others, nurturance, sympathy, and support are not as directly evident in these summaries as the male patterns were, possibly because these patterns become more clearly manifest in adult years rather than in the early years, the ages of subjects in many of the samples reviewed. Nevertheless L. Hoffman (1977) has argued that affiliation needs become predominant in adolescence. She notes also that the review by M. Hoffman (1977) of studies on sex differences in empathy showed that in all sixteen studies, girls were found to be more empathetic, a stronger conclusion than Maccoby and Jacklin's summary on sensitivity to social cues (31, F = .23, M = .10). Maccoby and Jacklin also found that girls exhibit greater tactile (13, F = .38, M = .00) and auditory (26, F = .23, M = .08) sensitivity, differences relevant to greater interpersonal sensitivity.

While there are no direct measures of talkativeness, the differences in verbal memory (22, F = .45, M = .00) and verbal skills generally are quite dramatic. I will return to this issue in the following chapters on academic achievement, but in several different aspects, verbal skills, either tested (131, F = .28, M = .09) or spontaneous (29, F = .28, M = .07), were higher for girls and woman. This was especially true in large sample studies of hundreds or thousands of students, where the power of large sample size produced a more clear-cut difference (26, F = .85, M = .15).

There is somewhat stronger support in the Maccoby and Jacklin review for the stereotypic factors of dependency and submissiveness. The research summaries showed that girls and women are considerably more fearful and timid (25, F = .40, M = .00) and more anxious on either general anxiety measures (23, F = .56, M = .00) or test anxiety (9, F = .62, M = .00). However, dependency per se is only partially supported by indirect evidence on proximity-seeking toward friends (23, F = .52, M = .09), but not toward parents (48, F = .17, M = .15). Girls are also much more likely to comply with adult requests (24, F = .54, M = .04), girls and women more often conform to peer pressures (59, F = .32, M = .07), and girls more often engage in spontaneous imitations (13, F = .32, M = .00). Finally, in thirteen other studies of dependency not tabled in Maccoby and Jacklin, Block (1976:Table 1) reports overwhelming evidence of female dependency (13, F = 1.00, M = .00).

The male instrumental characteristics are not so clearly demonstrated, although as task accomplishment overlaps with achievement orientations there is some evidence from Maccoby and Jacklin that will be discussed in the following section on achievement.

There are male intellectual characteristics that are consistent with orientation to empirical aspects of the external world. Males have much higher spatial and quantitative scores than females, especially after puberty. For the samples with subjects over ten years of age, spatial analytic (35, M = .54, F = .00) and nonanalytic scores (11, M = .73, F = .00) strongly favor boys and men, as do quantitative scores (24, M = .67, F = .04). Whether these actually represent cognitive skills central to instrumental task orientation of course cannot be determined. Furthermore, at the ages examined in these studies, there is general lack of evidence and support for the greater objectivity, emotional control, and logic attributed to males in the stereotypic content. In fact, the one piece of evidence reported is contrary to the stereotype, as boys are clearly more impulsive than girls (43, M = .33, F = .07).

Thus along the major dimensions of masculine aggressiveness and assertiveness, and along lines of female anxiety and compliance, the empirical evidence is consistent with the stereotypic content. Evidence on female nurturance and support is generally lacking, however, as is evidence of greater male objectivity. However, overall it appears that there are sex differences in personality that are generally of the sort described by the stereotypes.

Achievement Orientations

Achievement orientations are the personal reflections of a predominant distinction in the stereotypic roles of men and women, that between the accomplishment of tasks and the reaching of goals (the instrumental theme) versus the affiliative orientations of women (the expressive theme). This distinction appears at several levels—culture, social structure, and personality.

At the cultural level, the relevance of achievement is set by the shift from ascription to achievement as the major mechanism for status assignment and recognition. Modern urban-industrial societies organized on the principles of universalistic-achievement differ profoundly from the traditional systems organized on the basis of particularistic ascription. In the latter, all members are accepted into the society and recognized by the ascriptive roles to which they are assigned. In such systems, human capabilities must necessarily be viewed in terms of the common, if not the lowest, denominator of the characteristics within the population. In this situation the major responsibility of the individual is conformity to the necessarily limited expectations of the society. Under these circumstances the major problem is deviation, not accomplishment, and the major psychological mechanism is guilt and anxiety as the failure to meet the expectations directed toward the ascribed role results in negative evaluations and sanctions.

The achieved role, on the other hand, requires an active pursuit of the position or instrumental goals. Individuals in a universalistic-achievement society must mobilize their personal resources and exhibit overt and empirically validated accomplishments and qualifications. This situation is one in which the social agents attend to performance, which, depending on the position, can be defined in very demanding and exclusive terms. The universalistic system rewards attainment and performance but it does not directly punish failure.[9] Indirectly, of course, individuals are punished as they fail to attain those social positions containing the major social rewards and prerogatives.[10] The unsuccessful executive or job candidate loses the potential for gains and personally desirable profit, but is not directly punished. Obviously, achievement has quite different implications and significance in these two systems of status assignment.

A second relevant formulation at the cultural level involves value orientations related to Weber's formulation of the Protestant ethic. These values, which Weber originally viewed as components of the religious beliefs and circumstances of Calvinists, later were seen as the central components of middle-class society, especially for patterns of activism and passivity, individualism and collectivity orientation, and future orientation rather than orientation toward the past (Strodtbeck 1958; Rosen 1956, 1959). Kluckhohn (1969) related these patterns to culturally based sex differences, arguing that the dominant American culture of activism, future orientation, and individualism was not shared by women, who instead functioned within a substitute culture of passivity, present orientation, and collectivity orientation. According to Kluckhohn, the dominant male culture emphasized *doing,* the female culture *being.*

At the social level these alternatives appear in the instrumental-expressive distinction previously discussed as an important component of the sex role sterotype. The instrumental role supposes achievement and accomplishment, the expressive role, affiliation and attraction, sets of demands that are generally viewed as incompatible (see Komorovsky 1946; Horner 1975; L. Hoffman 1972, 1977). Thus, girls face a unique crisis regarding achievement, in that achievement represents the masculine instrumental role rather than the feminine expressive-affiliation role. In her classic and widely cited paper, Komorovsky held that college women faced this conflict between the achievement demands of college and the affiliative demands of dating and popularity, a conflict that appeared to produce psychological stress. Horner argued that this conflict created special concerns for highly motivated women for whom the conflict was expecially severe. L. Hoffman (1977) asserted that girls are trained to be wives and mothers, thus taught the essentials of the expressive, affiliative role, while boys are taught the instrumental, achieving role.

Plausible and engaging as these formulations are, they have not fared well in empirical research support. Careful replication and analysis of Komorovsky's (1946) study by Dean (1975) indicates that the presumed conflict was less than severe, that competence and achievement were necessarily subjugated only occasionally by women and that men experienced much the same conflict between achievement and competency and affiliation. Horner's (1975) central conclusion has been largely discounted by the consistent finding of Levine and Crumrine (1975) and others that the incidence of fear of success was as great for men as for women.[11]

The course of these studies suggests that students of women's roles, in focusing only on the circumstances of one sex, may have misinterpreted a general social group process as unique to one sex. The finding of equivalency in more recent research including both sexes reminds us that the original work on the differentiation of instrumental and expressive roles was carried out in all-male groups. Thus, it appears likely that the underlying factor in this area is the inherent inconsistency of affectively neutral task requirements with affective expressive and affiliative demands. Being warm and friendly and cold and calculating are incompatible stances. The best liked man was not the best idea man in Bales' research on leadership in small groups (Parsons and Bales 1955). Competence and the exhibition of superior intellect may degrade interpersonal attraction for both men and women. Calculating, assertive, affectively neutral task-oriented behavior by intimate role players may be unwelcome in either sex, even though the same characteristics may be valued in occupational roles previously sex typed as masculine.

At the level of personality, evidence on sex-related aspects of achievement processes is unusually confused and convoluted. In this area the contemporary weakness in the conduct of social and behavioral research is confounded with the marked emphasis on male rather than female personality in the origin and development of the central concepts and measures,[12] and finally, by the unfortunate gulf between the literatures of sociology and psychology.

The three important dimensions of achievement orientations at the level of personality are achievement motivation, achievement values and educational-occupational aspirations, and the cluster of affective and cognitive factors that Rosen (1956, 1959) termed the achievement syndrome. Achievement motivation is a readiness to be affectively aroused under achievement cues to pursue goals involving standards of excellence. Achievement value orientations are viewed as cognitive and affective conceptions enabling choices among alternatives and serving to channel the diffuse motivational forces into socially appropriate activities leading to high levels of educational and occupational aspiration and attainment.

While there was considerable cross-fertilization in the early study of these patterns,[13] in the succeeding years, and certainly in the recent past, these areas have greatly diverged. The great bulk of research has been on the concept of achievement motivation, carried out by the McClelland TAT measure which I discuss shortly. Work on level of educational and occupational aspiration has been subsumed under the general status attainment model currently receiving so much attention in sociology and education. The achievement value-orientations as defined by Rosen (1956, 1959) have rarely been studied, except, as their content is subsumed in the modernization research or, in a related concern with beliefs about fatalism and control of the environment. These historical branchings have diminished the interesting social-psychological integration suggested by Rosen's early label.

The area taken as a whole is a good illustration of male-oriented social science, since all the components of the achievement syndrome were originally studied only in males.

Achievement Motivation

Achievement motivation has been defined as a "need to excel in competition with a standard of excellence" (McClelland et al., 1953). This standard could be personal and the competition a matter of improving over past performances (every day in every way . . .) or it could reflect competitive performance levels and involve winning out over others. The empirical validation was the evidence of affective arousal measured by the presence of achievement imagery in TAT protocols following presentation of achievement cues. These cues involved the conceptions of high intellectual and leadership potential. Included in test instructions given to male subjects, these cues produced an increase in imagery compared to protocols written with more neutral instructions that did not mention leadership or intelligence. One of the early surprises in this research was the finding that women's scores on achievement did not vary according to the cues.

While the whole line of research has been plagued by validity problems and contradictory findings, there has been an overall accumulation of consistent evidence and, as Spence and Helmreich (1978:74) note in their summary of this literature, "the corpus of the research taken as a whole provides considerable evidence for validity of the formulation, and for the existence of stable, measureable individual differences." This outcome was true primarily for males, as the measure appeared to be less adequate in predicting feminine achievement. For example, in his review of thirty-two studies, Klinger (1966) found significant relationships between achievement motivation and academic performance in 64% of the twenty-two studies involving males, but in only three of the ten studies involving females.

Given the sex differences in arousal and predictability, coupled with the centrality of achievement in sex role convergence, much attention has been directed toward explaining why the measure holds better for males than for females.

The sex differences in affective arousal following achievement cues have been treated in two distinct ways. One of these is reflected in Maccoby and Jacklin's (1974:138) interpretation that the constant high level of girls's achievement imagery means that boys' levels of achievement motivation have to be aroused, whereas girls' levels are high all of the time. The other more common interpretation is that the achievement arousing instructions and the original TAT cues have been inappropriate for girls. Thus, French and Lesser (1964) found that women who were oriented toward traditional women's roles exhibited increased achievement imagery when the arousing instructions stressed social skills rather than leadership or intellectual skill. Similarly, Hoffman (1972) has argued that the tests have failed to adequately measure women's achievement through affiliation rather than through task accomplishment. Finally, Horner (1975) used the achievement-affiliation conflict to explain the failure of achievement motivation to adequately predict feminine achievement. She argued that the traditional stereotype of women's roles made success an unsettling, even fearful prospect for women and posited the motive, fear of success. The Catch 22 of that formulation was that the higher the achievement motive, the more important and likely the success, and consequently, the more relevant the fear of success and the less likely the real level of achievement motivation would be reflected in actual performance. As I have noted, the problem with fear of success is that it is equally common in men (Levine and Crumrine 1975) and appears to be more reflective of role expectations than of motivational dynamics (Deaux 1976). Consequently, it cannot seriously be advanced as a explanation for the differential achievement processes of women.

Another interesting and potentially informative line of explanation for sex differences in achievement patterns is based on expectancy and attributional aspects of the actor's definition of the achievement situation. The actor's subjective expectation of success is important because of the manner in which the expectation of success interacts with the stable level of achievement motivation. Atkinson's (1964) model treats the total motivation to succeed as $(T_s = M_s \times I_s \times P_s)$, where T_s is the total motive to succeed, M_s is the motive to succeed, (i.e., n achievement), P_s is the probability of success, and I_s is the incentive value of success. Simple calculation of $I_s \times P_s$ shows that the tendency to approach success is maximized at any level of M_s when the probability of success is .50, the level of intermediate or moderate risk. The idea of moderate risk taking is consistent both with McClelland's (1961) conception of the entrepreneur as a moderate risk taker and with studies showing that people with a high need for achievement (and low fear of failure) choose tasks, even occupations, with moderate levels of risk (Weiner 1972:205–226).

The other aspect of Atkinson's formulation is the motive to avoid failure, operationally defined as test anxiety. Anxious people afraid of failing will be motivated to avoid the task in exactly the same degree as people motivated to approach success, for any given probability of success and need. Overall motivation is seen as an outcome of the differences between motivation to succeed minus motivation to avoid failure.

The relevance of these formulations for the issues of women's achievement is fairly direct. As we have observed, clear sex differences appear in self-confidence and in fear and anxiety, two factors directly involved in determining subjective levels of expected success and fear of failure. At any given ability level, males generally expect to do better than females; consequently, the range of moderate risk taking is subjectively different for men and women. Placed in an academic context, this would mean that the average aptitude female would have expectations of success below those of the average male. This would mean that the $(I_s \times P_s)$ multiplier would be greater for average males but for only the high aptitude females. This interesting formulation relating affective and cognitive interactions to dimensions of sex roles has considerable indirect support in male-female differences in expectancies (Frieze 1972; Deaux 1979), but only one study, to my knowledge, focused on the significance of this for explaining sex differences in predicting achievement behavior with the motive to achieve. In that research, Gjesme (1975) found that correlations between achievement and grades were in fact higher for high aptitude than for low aptitude girls, a result not observed in my earlier analysis of such a pattern in a population of college men (Lueptow 1973).

The other important effect has to do with the consequences of sex differences in the attribution of causality (Deaux 1976). The actor can consider the cause of behavior to be something internal, such as ability or effort, or can consider the causes to be something external such as luck or such obstacles as task difficulty.[14] Maccoby and Jacklin (1974) report no sex difference on internal or external attribution, although age does interact with these differences. In the nine studies they reviewed of children between 6 and 11 years, girls were more likely to make an internal attribution (9, F = .22, M = .11) while for adolescents and young adults in college, boys were more likely to make internal attributions (8, M = .38, F = .12), although in neither case were the results overwhelming. Of somewhat more direct interest is the interaction of sex role stereotypes with these processes (Feather and Simon 1975). Men are assumed to be more competent. When they succeed their success is attributed to skill or effort, internal attributions consistent with the initial stereotypic assumptions. On the other hand, women are assumed to be less competent. When they succeed, causes are more likely to be attributed to luck or ease of the task (Weiner 1972; Feather and Simon 1975; Deaux 1976, 1979), again consistent with the sterotypic assumptions. Of special interest in these respects are the findings that women choose games of luck and chance over men's choice of games of skill (Deaux, White, and Farris 1975).

The implications of the attribution research for achievement motivation are fairly direct. The goal of the achievement motive is a personal accomplishment. Consequently, it can be satisfied only through individual accomplishment, not through luck, chance, or other agencies. If these formulations are correct, then attribution, like expectancy, would explain the failure of achievement motivation scores of women to predict achievement behavior as well as those of men. While the answers are far from in, this line of work provides one of the strongest illustrations of how our understanding of general human behavior is facilitated by interest in sex roles. It also suggests that important gains in female achievement could be accomplished by changing women's perceptions of task success and themselves.

The final concern in this extended discussion of achievement and sex roles has to do with socialization. The general model holds that achievement motivation is produced by early emphasis on independence and mastery training (Winterbottom 1958) that is apparently more effective in egalitarian families (Rosen and D'Andrade 1959; Rehberg and Sinclair 1970) where fathers exert less direct power on their sons.[15]

The basic instrumental-expressive distinction applied to sex roles as well as the content of the sex role sterotypes suggests that socialization of boys would include emphasis on independence and mastery training, but that parents would emphasize the opposite patterns for girls. Various students of sex roles have argued that such differential socialization accounts for the differences in achievement patterns between girls and boys (Block 1973; L. Hoffman, 1972, 1977). Hoffman has made an especially strong case for this position, arguing that boys are socialized for achievement and accomplishment while girls are socialized in the expressive-affiliative patterns that parents assume will be required for their adult assumptions of the maternal role.

These formulations are directly questioned by Maccoby and Jacklin's (1974) review, which fails to provide any support at all for the differential socialization of males and females. Regarding the restrictions of independence and action, they find essentially no difference in parental restrictiveness of play area, or child's initiative, or in protectiveness and setting of limiting rules (38, M = .26, F = .21). They also fail to observe important differences in the rewarding or punishing of dependency (19, F = .22, M = .17). Similarly, achievement demands that include pressures for college education are only slightly more prevalent in male background (15, M = .33, F = .20). None of these summaries approaches the differences observed in the previously mentioned studies along the sterotypic patterns. They are also consistent with the findings of Anderson and Evans (1976) showing that females receive more independence training than males, especially in the Mexican-American subculture.

Achievement Value Orientations

Achievement value orientations were introduced by Strodtbeck (1958) and Rosen (1956, 1959) and were derived from a generalized interpretation of Weber's conceptions of the Protestant ethic and Kluckhohn's (1969) formulations of dominant and substitute cultural profiles. From that perspective, the three dimensions of special significance were activistic-passivistic, present-future, and familistic-individualistic orientations. As we have noted, activism, future orientation, and individualism are cultural themes distinguishing modern societies, middle classes, and upwardly mobile ethnic groups from traditional societies, working classes, and less mobile ethnic groups.

These orientations were measured by a series of items having to do with striving for success versus fatalism, the acceptance of present circumstances with planning for the future versus living for today, and separation from parents. As in the early work in achievement motivation, the populations of these early studies were males.

Within these male populations, achievement values were related to grades, educational aspirations, social class, and ethnicity (Rosen 1956, 1959). They were also related to paternal and maternal power in ways suggesting that boys needed maternal support to develop achievement orientations in the face of paternal power (Strodtbeck 1958), and that traditional patriarchal family structure suppressed the acquisition of achievement orientations in boys (Rehberg and Sinclair 1970; Rosen 1973). In analysis closely paralleling mine, Kerckhoff (1974) found measures of achievement values (termed fatalism in his report) intervened between family background, school success, and educational expectations.

The implications of these culturally based value orientations for sex roles were made explicit by Kluckhohn (1969), who argued then as L. Hoffman (1977) has more recently, that the dominant profile in American society (activism, future orientation, individualism) was held by men. Women, on the other hand, carried a substitute profile involving passivism, present orientation, and collectivity orientation. From this perspective, the substitute profiles of women's culture are

markedly at variance with the dominant American values which are much better and more often expressed in the role of the man. The [woman's] role is a variant role, patterned in accord with variant values, whereas the masculine role, mainly an occupational one, is a dominant role expressing dominant values. (Kluckhohn 1969:457)

Kluckhohn further suggested that the gap between the two cultures was becoming more extreme with each passing year, a prescient background formulation of the situation more specifically addressed in *The Feminine Mystique*. Part of the surprise and intensity conveyed by the content and the reaction to *The Feminine Mystique* could be accounted for by the implications of this thesis. Women and men were not different and equal in a complementary way described by a division of labor; rather the domestic role of the wife was organized on a fundamentally different schema than the occupational role of the husband, creating a value conflict embedded in the cultural patterns, one necessarily divisive and derogatory of the carriers of the substitute profile.

Although the thesis is provocative, few writers have attempted to explicate this bifurcated and sex-differentiated concept of a separate women's culture having direct relevance to achievemant orientations.[16] At lower levels of abstraction, however, the issue is clearly raised. Rossi (1965) used related ideas to explain why women were not successful in scientific fields. More recently, as we have noted, L. Hoffman (1972, 1977) has focused on two components of these general patterns, affiliation and achievement, while Block (1973) and others have drawn on the equally general orientations of agency and communion, which tap aspects of these themes. However, apart from the study of values about women's roles, usually formulated in terms of career versus homemaking, there has been almost no research on sex differences along these dimensions. Nevertheless, the consistency of discursive writings and the content of the sex role stereotypes that are congruent with the cultural patterns being described clearly suggest that an important component in the sex differences on achievement orientations must derive from differences in these basic profiles. Given all this, it comes as some surprise to discover that in the few studies that have been carried out, the results are inconsistent with the Kluckhohn formulations.

In research drawing on some of these themes, Schwartz (1971) failed to find clear-cut differences between ninth- and twelfth-grade girls and boys in either Anglo-American or Mexican-American populations on a number of similar value orientations, including a universalistic measure, future orientation, and independence from family. Furthermore, there were no sex differences in the relations between the values and academic achievement in either subculture, results that Shcwartz (1971:459) considered unexpected in veiw of the "usual assumptions about sex-linked differences in child-rearing practices, especially in the Mexican-American subculture." Even more unexpected was the finding in an earlier analysis of the baseline data used in this book, that girls actually scored higher than boys on the Rosen-Strodtbeck achievement value items (Lueptow 1975). This was especially true for the activism and future orientations, although even in individualism, girls exhibited more willingness than boys to make the sacrifice of leaving parents. Furthermore, the effect of achievement values on college plan with parental education and student intelligence controlled was about the same for both sexes, although the values had an effect only on boys' grades when parental education and student intelligence were controlled. The only finding in that analysis at all consistent with Kluckhohn's formulation was the fact that family background characteristics, and especially same-sex modeling, were better and more consistent predictors of boys' than of girls' level of achievement value orientations, a finding consistent with the idea that socialization in nontraditional patterns such as these achievement value orientations would occur more often outside of the family, perhaps through the agency of more universalistic counselors and employers (see Bandura 1969:250–252). In any event, contrary to general concerns and assumptions in the literature, girls appear to have higher levels of achievement orientations than boys do.

Educational and Occupational Aspirations

Educational and occupational aspirations constitute the final component of the achievement syndrome. While Rosen (1956, 1959) originally studied differences in educational and occupational aspiration as important dependent variables in their own right, these orientations have since been subsumed under the broader analytic concept of status attainment.[17] Especially as developed in the work of Sewell and his associates (Sewell and Hauser 1975), the level of aspiration, perhaps more correctly described as an expectation, is treated as an intervening variable between family background factors and educational and occupational attainment. The early work of Blau and Duncan (1967) was the classic point of departure for this line of research, a classic notable in our present context also by its focus on males only. Nevertheless, Blau and Duncan demonstrated that male occupational status attainment was a result of educational attainment, which in turn was a function of level of family socioeconomic status and ability. Thus a model was established describing the main lines of the status attainment process, a model significant because it demonstrated that class position (as measured by the occupation) was not ascribed, that is, directly transmitted from parent to child, but rather reflected achievement and competence publicly certified by degree attainments.

The basic status attainment model was extended by Sewell and Hauser (1975) to include the social psychological variables of encouragement by parents, teachers, and peers to go on to college and by the student's plan (aspiration) to attend college (Sewell and Shah 1968). Thus the Wisconsin model describes a process in which family background factors are important in determining ability and the encouragement received from significant others. Ability largely determines grades, which, together with family background, results in encouragement by significant others. Encouragement in turn is the most important factor determining aspiration, although ability and grades also remain important. Aspiration, then, determines educational attainment, which in turn largely determines occupational status attainment.

When these models are examined from the perspective of sex differences they reveal both expected and unexpected patterns. As expected, the early studies revealed higher overall educational and occupational aspirations and attainment for men than for women (Sewell 1971), although the differences were not overwhelming, even in the early 1960s. Furthermore, boys received greater encouragement to attend college from their parents than girls did, although no sex differences were observed in families where either parent had received at least some college education (Sewell and Shah 1968).

The unexpected findings, considering concerns about differential achievement processes and sex discrimination, are that the overall occupational status distributions of women and men are similar and that the process of status attainment is essentially the same for both sexes (McClendon 1976).[18] Contrary to views that women are overqualified for their jobs, it turns out that except for family size, family backgound factors predict equally the educational and occupational attainment of men and women in the national labor force (see Rehberg and Rosenthal 1978). Furthermore, the effect of education on occupational status is essentially the same for women and men (Treiman and Terrell 1975a; McClendon 1976).

However, these similarities conceal differences in type of work and income return. While men and women receive the same increment of status for each additional year of education, women's positions tend to be in the middle ranges of the distribution, neither extremely high nor low. Even within limited ranges there are some differences, in that the female semiprofessions of teaching, nursing, and social work are lower than male managerial, medical, and legal professions. Furthermore, the similarity observed for status does not hold for income, as the coefficient of the effect of status on income for women is about two-thirds as large as the coefficient for men (Treiman and Terrell 1975b). Women with the same educational qualifications receive equivalent status but less economic return than men, although this difference is due more to sex typing of work than to overt job discrimination.

Finally, there are sex differences in the effects of parental characteristics on the expectation-attainment process. While the results are not especially strong, there do appear to be some like-sex effects in that mother's occupational status adds some explanation to daughter's occupational attainment (Rosenfeld 1978) beyond that of father's occupation. Similarly, father's education has more effect on son's educational expectations while mother's education has more effect on daughter's (Rosen and Aneshensel 1978).

Other research on status attainment provides some support for the pattern of vicarious status attainment by women. For instance, Turner (1964) found that women's education was related to their career goals, but not to their extrinsic status goals. In an analogous study, Tyree and Treas (1974) discovered that vicarious status attainment of women was more similar to men than the direct status attainment of women who entered the labor force. In other words, status attainment through marriage and affiliation was more similar to male patterns than direct achievement was. These two studies suggest an interesting feminine advantage in occupational attainment—it can be free of concern for money and other extrinsic rewards that can be obtained through marriage. On the other hand, this pattern probably lies behind income inequality.

Discussion and Interpretation

Taken as a whole, the empirical evidence on sex difference in achievement orientations is suggestive and voluminious, but far from definitive. Furthermore, it is not exactly consistent with the current writing and interpretation of achievement processes. While L. Hoffman's (1972, 1977) view of female disadvantage due to training for marriage and affiliation is accepted by most students, that position is not clearly supported by the evidence.

As we have seen, the main evidence on sex differences in achievement has to do with differences in the way achievement imagery is aroused in women and men and in the way scores based on that imagery predict achieving performance. To account for those sex differences, various writers have developed some interesting and provocative interpretations having to do with the implications of sex role characteristics and sterotypes for expectancy and attribution factors that interact with achievement motivation to produce total levels of motivation for success. Notwithstanding the interest and elegance of some of these models, a number of important inconsistencies point toward substantially different conclusions and outcomes.

In the first place, the basic difference in arousal has been interpreted to mean that female achievement motivation is actually more internalized and constant than male. Second, regardless of the issue of predictability of achieving performances by achievement motivation scores, the fact is that females perform at higher levels in nearly all courses in high school and college (Hoffman 1972). Third, the plausible arguments that activism, future orientation, and individualism are characteristics of male but not female culture and experience are not supported by empirical evidence on sex differences in achievement value orientations derived from that perspective. In several different samples of college and high school youths, results show either no sex difference, or show females to have a more activistic, future-oriented, and individualistic orientation than males do. This is a surprising and important finding considering the widespread assumptions about cultural definitions of males and females. Finally, in spite of assumptions of inequality and discrimination in occupational attainment, it turns out that the status attainment porcesses of women and men are remarkably similar. In the achievement of occupational status, educational qualifications of women and men are equally recognized even though both men and women in predominatly female jobs receive less income.

All of these contradictions are consistent with the finding that, surprising as it appears, the evidence does not support the conventional wisdom regarding sex differences in socialization for achievement and affiliation. Neither in reinforcement nor in modeling studies is there yet any substantial empirical support for differential socialization of males and females (Maccoby and Jacklin 1974).

It is not easy to reach a sound conclusion in this complicated and somewhat confused body of material, but taking the area as a whole, one must conclude that the sex differences in achievement orientations are greatly overstated, if they are not actually incorrect. In fact, the full range of findings, especially considering the substantial performance differences of girls, suggests feminine advantage rather than disadvantage. This is especially clear in the socially more realistic and relevant areas of achievement values, academic performance, and adult status attainment than in the less realistic TAT measures of need for achievement.

There is another possibility, accounting especially for the sharp inconsistency between the literature on sex differences in achievement motivation and the findings on achievement value orientations. The measure of need for achievement takes into account excellence both in terms of personal task accomplishment, i.e., doing something well, reaching a significant goal, and also in terms of winning in competition with others. The difference between intrinsic and competitive achievement (Lipman-Blumen and Leavitt 1976) in the list of sex role stereotypes suggests one possible explanation: *women may be high achievers but weak competitors.* They may have equal or greater needs to perform, have internalized the norms of universalistic achievement even better than their male contemporaries, but may not seek direct competitive success. Beating another person may not be the goal of females operating within the patterns I have just summarized. Recalling the strong sex typing of aggressiveness, assertiveness, and competitiveness in the sterotypes along with similar empirical evidence on sex differences in personality leads us to consider the possibility that part of the confusion in this area may be due to inaccurate formation of the key variables achievement and competition. They may be quite different things, especially as they relate to the content of sex role stereotypes and sex-typed personality characteristics. It might be fruitful in future work to sort out these effects in examining sex differences in achievement and accomplishment.[19]

For this study, I have assumed that the evidence indicates women to actually be higher achievers than men, that the concept of parental socialization for dependency and mediocrity has been considerably overstated, and that on the record women do better than men except when aggressive, competitive success is the goal.

Attitudes About Family and Career

Differences in attitudes and values about family and career are more generally assumed than measured. The common viewpoint in the writing about sex roles holds that the modern family has been organized asymmetrically, that women's roles have been defined primarily in family terms while men's roles reflect both occupational and family concerns, with primacy often given to the former. Because of this accepted, and in some respects, obvious view, there has been less interest in describing the nature of sex differences in these orientations than in delineating the nature of the conflict posed by the asymmetrical demands on the woman's roles.

Career Versus Family

Career versus family is viewed as the central concern for contemporary women involved in the ongoing changes in roles and relationships. While success-oriented men in demanding careers have at times faced this conflict, the "work-intoxicated father" (Bernard 1975) has been viewed as a somewhat variant pattern, one that could only be sustained because the wife played a supporting role within the family, leaving the husband free to concentrate fully on the demands of the occupational role. In the nature of such asymmetry, similar choices for the woman are generally precluded by the lack of equivalent support and release from family responsibilities. Without important change in the organization of work and family even at the professional level, wives have continued to be responsible for home *and* children (Poloma and Garland 1971).

This conflict between demands of career and family is addressed in several ways in the literature. At younger ages, during courtship years, the conflict between affiliation and achievement has been advanced as one explanation for the differences in achievement between boys and girls (Komorovsky 1946; Horner 1975; Hoffman 1972). During adult years the significance of work and family on each other has been addressed from the perspectives of both work and family. The concern that work would detrimentally affect the maternal parenting role was severe enough to lead to extensive research that has demonstrated that with the possible exception of male academic achievement (Hoffman 1980), mothers' work does not seriously affect the development of the child (Hoffman and Nye 1974). The reciprocal concern about the effect of family role obligations on work is currently under study. It appears that the asymmetry of family obligations results in corresponding difference in career success. Male career success seems to be facilitated by the marital state, female career success appears to be limited by marriage. This pattern has now been observed in graduate training (Feldman 1973), in college faculties (Astin and Bayer 1975), and in the general labor force (Treiman and Terrell 1975a, 1975b).

The relation between work and family has been viewed from another perspective as well, Work is seen as a psychologically desirable alternative to the stultifying, low-status homemaker role. There are several aspects to this comparison, the most important of which relate to the very nature of role assignment either through ascription or achievement. As a traditional, ascribed position, buttressed by religious and humanistic values, the homemaker status is a uniquely ambiguous feature in the concern about contemporary sex roles. Occupancy of a particularistic-ascribed position cannot be easily given recognition in a universalistic-achievement system. There is no important clear-cut mechanism in contemporary society for awarding status to a person related primarily to a particular set of others who serve as the link between the occupant of the ascribed position and the broader society. Success in motherhood, wifedom, and homemaking cannot be recognized beyond the family and even if it were, the nature of ascription precludes emphasis on uniqueness and high accomplishment. "Mother of the year" is a symbolic, not an empirically verifiable, achievement. A good deal of the argument between profeminists and antifeminists about homemaking reflects the overlapping of these two bases of assigning status to women. In any event, the lack of recognition accorded homemaker status, the isolation and invisibility of the homemaker from the broader universalistic system of relationships and influences are the serious problems of occupants of such an anachronistic role form in contemporary society.

The consequences of this for the individual woman were of course recognized by Freidan (1963) and remain the underlying theme of the women's movement. From this perspective, the traditional motherhood role in modern society is viewed as pathogenic (Bernard 1975:217–220) and as a source of psychological stress (Gove and Tudor 1973).

Scholarly and feminist reactions to this circumstance are varied, but they all in one way or another involve mitigating the consequences of particularism-ascription by altering the nature of the role toward the universalistic-achievement pole. Thus, Bernard (1973:267), noting that the universalistic system operates as an exchange system (a "cash nexus" compared to a status system), argues for new societal forms enabling diversion of economic resources directly to the mother. Feminists have of course also recognized the significance of money as status recognition in this kind of society, as has Giele (1978) in her discussion of the rationalization of the family.

Notwithstanding these interesting and provocative interpretations, the most common solution to the problem of women in the ascribed family role is the emphasis on the occupational role as an important alternative or supplement to the marital role. Generally, the occupation is seen as self-fulfilling and self-rewarding (Ferree 1976), as well as providing resources that give the employed woman greater power and influence within the family (Blood and Wolfe 1960).

However, as Wright (1978) has noted, this view that work is ennobling and self-fulfilling is a relatively new theme in social science. Except those involved in intrinsically satisfying career and higher status occupations, male jobs have been analyzed more often in terms of alienation and anomie than in terms of self-fulfillment. It has been assumed that most men worked for money, not for intrinsic, self-actualizing work experience. Duncan and Duncan's (1978) analysis shows that the general public holds this view for women also. The great majority of men and women think women work for money. Only negligible percentages of respondents think women work solely for independence or to get out of the home, although women are considerably more likely to give the latter reason than men are. When money is discounted by dealing with the sizable proportion of women and men who would wish to work even if they did not need the income, the most common reason is filling time, avoiding boredom. Only 8% of women in 1976 would work primarily to get out of the home (Veroff, Douvan, and Kulka 1981).

Attitudes About Women's Roles

Attitudes about women's roles vary across the sexes in predictable ways. Women tend to be more liberal, to view the sexes equally, and to sanction working outside of the home to a greater degree. However, while consistent, these patterns are qualified by sample and by question.

Among samples of college students, women are generally more liberal about women's working outside the family, receiving equal pay, and possessing the ability to function effectively in community and political leadership roles (Bayer 1975; Scanzoni 1976; Lueptow 1980c). However, among general populations, there is less difference in the views of women and men about the appropriate role of women. Thus, while several studies to be discussed subsequently show changes in attitudes about women's roles, they fail to show much sex difference in attitudes about a female president (Ferree 1974; Schreiber 1978) or about the reasons women work (Duncan and Duncan 1978). Perhaps some of the reported difference in the college samples reflect the unique emphasis placed on changing women's roles in the college milieu as compared to the general population, where cultural similarity is perhaps greater than sex differences.[20]

Generally, men and women differ in their views about sex roles, but the differences are not extreme, and they do not represent fundamental conflicts in basic orientations. For example in my (1980c) analysis of attitudes about women's roles, I found clear sex differences but almost perfect correlation between the average scores of women and men across twenty women's role items. I interpreted this to mean that while the sexes differed on the traditional-modern conception of women's roles, they were in substantial agreement about which role aspects were more traditional and which were not. A similar result was obtained by Duncan and Duncan (1978:138–139) regarding sex differences in the ratings of institutions, a finding they took as a reminder that the focus on sex differences sometimes obscures the fact that "women and men live in the same world."

Other findings in Duncan and Duncan's (1978) study of roles of husbands and wives revealed differences between men and women that were generally stereotypic. Thus, women were less active politically and less knowledgeable in giving informative responses, were generally more likely to give "don't know" or no opinion responses. Women had the major housekeeping responsibility, with a clear division of labor along stereotypic lines. These patterns were modified by the wife's work status in that working wives received more help in housekeeping than did nonworking wives. Women were also more religious than men and maintained different patterns of participation related to church, PTA, and card groups.

Occupational Preferences and Values

The major theme in sex differences in occupational preference and orientation is the sex typing of work. Women and men have held sharply differentiated occupational roles that have reflected both the asymmetrical family circumstance and consequent restrictions marriage has traditionally placed on women (Oppenheimer 1968; Treiman and Terrell 1975b) and the components of sex role stereotypes. By and large, women who worked have been expected to enter one of a limited set of occupations that have reflected public conceptions of appropriate female behavior. Thus, "In 1970, about half of all working women were in only 20 occupations and no less than 30 percent were either elementary school teachers, retail sales clerks, bookkeepers, waitresses or stenographers, typists and secretaries" (Treiman and Terrell 1975b:158). These jobs are characterized by their people orientation and their deemphasis of mental skill and physical strength (McLaughlin 1978). They also tend to be occupations without authority over other adults, especially adult males, and reflect traditional stereotypic patterns of deference, nurturance, and service or support. The highly sex-typed roles of elementary school teacher, nurse, and social worker involve family-like patterns of mothering and expressiveness, as Parsons (1959) has observed in his classic article on the classroom and the elementary school teacher as a universalistic mother surrogate. Public conceptions of appropriate sex-typed occupations are relatively clear-cut and consistent with sex role stereotypes. In fact, Albrecht, Bahr, and Chadwick (1977) found more sex stereotyping of occupations than of personality in a statewide sample of Utah households.

Given the consensus and clarity in both sex role stereotypes and in the sex typing of occupations, sex differences in occupational preference have been, if anything, overdetermined by the institutionalized expectations of appropriate occupational goals. The main question under these circumstances becomes how soon the patterns impinge on the orientations of boys and girls. Research summarized by Safilios-Rothschild (1979) indicates that recognition of appropriate occupational orientations occurs very early in the child's development and is maintained as a constant pressure toward sex-typed work through the years of education by the content of sex role stereotypes and ideology. Boys' and girls' choices of both expected and aspired occupations are concentrated in appropriate sex-typed positions (Marini and Greenberger 1978). Furthermore, the choices of girls show a tendency to shift from inappropriate to appropriate occupations between the seventh and twelfth grades (Rosen and Aneshensel 1978). Thus, the consistency and control embodied in the stereotypes of men's and women's personalities carries over to the choice of occupational roles as well. In fact, sex-typed occupational assignment is but one aspect of general sex role stereotyping.

Turning to the meaning of work as represented by occupational value orientations, we find that the traditional, stereotypic views of women and work also appear in sex-related differences in occupational values. These orientations also reflect traditional sex role differentiation with perhaps somewhat more direct emphasis on the instrumental-expressive dimension. Women tend to value working with and helping people, while men tend to value money, security, and advancement possibilities (Rosenberg 1957; Flanagan and Jung 1971). While there are some contradictions in research findings on occupational values, they appear to be related to the way components of jobs are categorized and grouped.

There is a tendency to distinguish between *intrinsic* job satisfactions, related to work, personal accomplishment, and self-expression, and *extrinsic* satisfactions related to working conditions, such fringe benefits as security and prestige, and associations with co-workers. When this distinction is used, sex differences are not consistent (see Herzberg et al. 1957; Centers and Bugental 1966), primarily because such sex-related factors as pay, pleasant co-workers, and advancement may be lumped together as extrinsic factors, or differentially categorized as intrinsic or extrinsic. However, when the discrete components are examined separately, the pattern is clear and consistent. Women always place a higher value on people in terms of valuing co-workers, helping others or rating pleasant co-workers as an important aspect of the job, while men always give greater emphasis to advancement and promotion possibilities and to such extrinsic factors as money and security (Centers and Bugental 1966; Manhardt 1972; Schuler 1975; Rosenberg 1957; Flanagan and Jung 1971; Veroff, Douvan, and Kulka 1981). Interestingly enough, considering my conclusions about feminine achievement, when promotion, leadership, and influence are separated from the intrinsic satisfactions of self-expression, challenging work, and recognition for work, there are no important sex differences in the intrinsic work values.[21] These results are consistent with my suggestion that women are interested in achievement and task accomplishment, but are less concerned about competitive success or beating someone else.

Generally, men and women view occupations in ways consistent with sex role stereotypes and with the sex typing of work along the lines of family role differentiation. In this regard, problems in the work on developing vocational interest measures is suggestive. Even within the same occupation, there are differences in the interest scores between the sexes (Johnson 1977). This principle is illustrated in a study of male and female nursing students in which Auster (1978) found clear and stereotypic differences between the sexes. Male nursing students rated security, leadership, money, social status, and freedom from supervisors more highly, while female nursing students rated being helpful to others and working with people much more highly. The intrinsic factor of using special abilities and aptitudes was rated equally highly by both sexes, although men rated the other intrinsic factor of "creative and original" significantly higher.[22] Interestingly enough, the male and female students did not differ on evaluation of adventure, although this was one of the least important of the ten occupational values.

Overall, then, occupational preferences have occurred within a highly sex-typed context that has channeled the majority of men and women into sex-segregated occupational roles where they have not been in direct competition with each other. Personal orientations toward work are consistent with this sex typing and suggest that whatever the origins turn out to be, men and women are motivated to obtain the differentiated rewards embedded in sex-typed occupations and consistent with the main lines of sex role stereotypes.

CHANGE AND STABILITY IN SEX ROLES

In this section I examine the current empirical evidence on sex role change. For the most part I focus on evidence relating to change in the relative differences in male and female roles or personalities. As I noted in the opening chapter, there is no comprehensive and integrated theory of sex roles and sex role change to use as a framework for this empirical review. Nevertheless, the accumulation of research evidence and theoretical and speculative discussion essentially rests on the idea that in family, occupation, and community the roles of women and men have been differentiated, essentially along instrumental and expressive lines reflecting the asymmetrical organization of sex roles in the family. The widespread assumption of change is essentially masculinization and convergence. It is assumed that women will increasingly adopt role contexts and role stances previously masculine, and that, at least in family relations and parenting, men will adopt previously feminine behavior.

With the exception of important recent work by Veroff and his colleagues (Veroff et al. 1980; Veroff, Douvan, and Kulka 1981), and theoretical discussion by L. Hoffman (1977), few writers seriously address the question of change in sex-related aspects of personality. By far the bulk of the literature focuses on change in attitudes about women's roles and stereotypic conceptions rather than on changes in sex-related personality itself.

While the following literature review cannot claim comprehensiveness, it is advanced as a reasonably complete evaluation of the current literature on sex role change.

Sex Role Stereotypes

Sex role stereotypes involve two distinct components: (1) public perceptions of the typical personality traits of women and men, and (2) attitudes about sex role behaviors, almost always treated as attitudes about women's roles. In spite of McKee and Sherriffs' (1959:356) early assertion that "we accept without hesitation two basic assumptions made by nearly every writer in this field: that the roles of the two sex groups are changing today and that the relationship between the groups is in disequilibrium," the evidence after two decades of research on the changing roles of women and men supports their viewpoint only in attitudes about women's roles, not in perceptions of personality differences.

Perceptions of Personality Traits

Public perceptions of the personality traits of women and men have remained clear and constant, as my examination of the content of the stereotypes has shown. From the early research by McKee and Sherriffs (Sherriffs and McKee 1957; McKee and Sheriffs 1959) through the widely cited work of Broverman et al. (Rosenkrantz et al. 1968; Broverman et al. 1972) to the more recent work of Williams and colleagues (Williams and Bennett 1975; Williams and Best 1977, 1982; Williams et al. 1977) and my studies of college students (Lueptow 1980c; Lueptow and Clough n.d.), there has been a remarkable stability in the stereotypic responses to items about the personal characteristics of women and men.

Longitudinal studies of change in the perceptions of the typical male and female in the same population (students in the same college, for example), are almost nonexistent, but the one or two that have been carried out also fail to show change. My (1980c) study of stereotypic conceptions of students in introductory sociology sections between 1974 and 1977 showed surprising stability in attitudes. Correlations between the average ratings across twenty-one personality traits in 1974 and again in 1977 was .99 for typical male and .99 for typical female, whether rated by male or female respondents. These patterns continued through 1980. The correlations between the 1974–1980 ratings were .99 for typical male, as rated by either sex, and .98 for typical female when rated by males, .99 when rated by females (Lueptow and Clough n.d.). These nearly perfect correlations indicate that stereotypic perceptions of sex-related personality traits held remarkably constant among these university students through the last half of the 1970s. Research by Neufeld, Langmeyer, and Seeman (1974) is the only other pertinent longitudinal research, and while it is somewhat limited by design weaknesses, the direction of the findings provides strong support for the present interpretation in that Neufeld and associates reported a heightening of stereotyping between 1948 and 1970.

It is difficult to account for this stability according to any of the sociocultural models of change previously described. Rather, the continued observations of consensus and stability in conventional sex-role stereotypes will eventually require consideration of alternative explanations, possibly involving significant biological differences between the sexes and the importance of maintaining those differences within contexts of interpersonal sexuality. While it is too early to know, the constancy of the stereotype suggests either that men and women actually are fundamentally different or that it is important for them to perceive such difference, possibly for affective purposes and motivations relevant to sexual relations.

Another possibility is that conceptual and methodological considerations underlying the use of typical man and typical woman or ideal man and ideal woman necessarily require respondents to think in terms of broadly accepted sociocultural definitions of sex differences in personality. Typical man and typical woman are general concepts akin to average man formulations of national character or average personality that may not have applicability to actual personality differences. The fact that ratings of self by men and women are correlated .85 in 1974, .77 in 1977 and 1980 in my study and fall between the masculine-feminine poles in other studies indicates that while these respondents can conceptualize the typical man or woman as highly consensual constructs, their own self-conceptions are considerably less stereotypic. Still, when one compares self-ratings on each personality characteristic individually, an approach that heightens the differences observed, men and women apply the stereotypic ratings to themselves. Female respondents in my study differed significantly from men in rating themselves as more talkative, friendly, sympathetic, creative, responsible, romantic, and affectionate then men rated themselves, while male respondents rated themselves as more aggressive, athletic, timid!, decisive, adventurous, cynical, competitive, authoritative, domineering, and self-confident than women rated themselves.[23]

Attitudes About Women's Roles

Attitudes about women's roles reveal a markedly different picture from that shown by evidence on perceived personalities of women and men. When considering the appropriate role behaviors of women and men, the research evidence is generally consistent in showing substantial change, especially between the 1960s and 1970s.

The central theme in attitudes about women's roles is the choice between motherhood and career. As I have noted, this is the central issue in the evaluation of change. As Scanzoni (1976:43 fn) remarks, citing Bumbass, "Motherhood has been the last major vestige of ascribed status in modern society." The inherent conflict between the unlimited, familistic demands of the mother or parent role and the individualistic, success-oriented purposes of the occupational role has been seen as central to the whole issue of sex role change. Other, less critical, dimensions have to do with the issue of the division of labor within the family and general equality between the sexes in role requirements and opportunities within the general community. All of these involve issues of ascription versus achievement. Ascribed roles assume underlying differences justifying the elements of ascribed status—in the present instance, sex differences. Whether or not these assumptions are justified is the central concern in evaluating the legitimacy of these views. From this perspective it is not surprising that one of the critical restraints on the public conception of changing women's roles is the demands imposed on mothers by the very young child. Nevertheless, the overall sense of the findings on attitudes about women's roles, viewed in a longitudinal perspective, is nicely captured by the enthusiastic blurb of the Institute for Social Research's Newsletter (Winter 1980, 8:3). "Fifteen-Year Study Documents Tremendous Change In Women's Sex-Role Attitudes."

While there may be differences of opinion about the ultimate scope of the change, that there has been change is abundantly clear. Within the past two or three decades, the general public, but especially women and college students, have begun to accept the view of women's roles defined more by the universalistic-achievement than by the particularistic-ascription standard. With the possible exceptions of the view that the child has legitimate ascriptively based demands upon its mother, and the related issue of ascription and collectivity orientation in societies taking precedence over the individual woman in abortion concerns, the public has accepted the idea that women should have essentially the same rights and privileges as men.

Not surprisingly, these patterns are clearest among women, and especially among women in college who are most directly exposed to the influences of feminist and liberation themes. Thus, Parelius (1975) found substantial changes over a very short time period, between 1969 and 1973, in attitudes about family and careers of women in a liberal women's college. Over this period, the proportion of women doubled who believed that women's careers were equally important, that husbands and wives should equally share housework, and that there were other satisfactions in life besides having children and being married. Smaller, but quite substantial shifts were observed by Bayer (1975) in national samples of college freshmen, 1970–1973. The percentage who agreed that "the activities of married women are best confined to the home and family" decreased from 57.0% to 40.9% of the men and from 36.7% to 18.8% of the women, sex differences that appear to varying degrees in other studies of changing attitudes toward women's roles (Boyd 1974). In a study of the responses of women in the general population to attitudes about women's roles in surveys between 1964 and 1974, Mason, Czajka, and Arber (1976) found substantial, if not dramatic, change between the various three- and four-year comparison intervals across a number of dimensions of the woman's role. Finally, Thornton and Freedman (1979) found substantial increases between 1962 and 1977 in the percentage of a Detroit area panel who agreed with egalitarian family role items. These changes reflect an overall increase from less than 50% in three of the four items in 1962 to over 60% in all four items by 1977. This may not be "tremendous," but it is certainly significant.

While the changes in these studies are substantial, they are qualified by two or three specific factors that are suggestive of the underlying conflicts between the ascriptive and achievement views. In the first place, there is no overall rejection of family and motherhood roles in favor of occupational or career roles. Thus, even in the liberal feminist atmosphere of Douglas College, only a small, albeit increasing, minority of women would sacrifice marriage or childbearing if it interfered with their career (Parelius 1975b). Similarly, as late as 1974, Mason, Czajka, and Arber found that less than half of the women disagreed that "it is much better for everyone involved if the man is the achiever outside the home and the woman takes care of the home and family" (1976:594), although this represented an increase of almost 16% over the 1970 survey on that item. Similar patterns prevail among college freshmen. In his national sample, Bayer found that in 1973, about 41% of the men but only about 19% of the women agreed that "the activities of married women are best confined to the home and family" (1975:392), levels of agreement that represented substantial decreases from those only four years before when 57% of the men and 37% of the women agreed with the item.

The only study to show stability in these attitudes may have reflected the relatively unique characteristics of the population samples, and the important qualifier of young children in the household. Thus, Monteiro (1978) found only negligible changes between 1970 and 1975 in the small percentage of women who agreed that it was "all right for a woman to work away from home if she has small children," changes that only increased from 13.4% to 14.5% agreed. The significance of young children in the public conception of women's obligations can be seen by the almost universal agreements of these same women; 94.9% in 1970 and 96.6% in 1975 said that it was "all right for a married woman to have a job outside the home if she has no small children" (1978:table 1). Intermediate evidence on change was obtained by Boyd (1974) in her analysis of Canadian public opinion polls, where changes of about 10% from traditional toward more liberal attitudes were observed between 1960 and 1970.

Attitudes tend to be most liberal in equality of opportunity and expectation in the broader community. Generally, there has been increased acceptance of feminine competence and authority, and willingness to grant equal rewards for equal job performances. In his national sample of college students, Bayer (1975) found near consensus on the proposition that the same work should produce the same salary and advancement possibilities. In 1970, 81% agreed, by 1973, this had increased to 92%. Even in comparisons between the 1950s and the 1960s, Boyd (1974) had observed a small (about 10%) increase in the proportions who expressed confidence in women professionals, although Boyd did not observe any change in the percentage who preferred a male boss. This remained at around 64% and reflected a 7% increase between 1953 and 1964 in the proportion of women who stated a preference for a male boss over a female boss. Interestingly enough, the proportion favoring a male boss increased with education, although at each level of education, the level of the preference remained constant between 1953 and 1964. These contrary patterns may reflect uniqueness in the Canadian population or they may reflect outcomes of personal experience and circumstance, given that more women had had work experience in 1964 than in 1953. As Kanter (1976) has observed, women are perceived as less able to function in positions of power and authority, although this may be due more to the limitations of the sex-typed positions they occupy than to underlying sex differences. In such positions, both sexes exhibit leadership inadequacies according to Kanter (1976).

There have been substantial changes in acceptance of female authority at a more abstract level. Public opinion polls show a substantial increase in the proportion of respondents who would accept a woman as president (Ferree 1974; Schreiber 1978). Men were originally more accepting of the proposition in 1958 and 1967 than women were. Not until 1972 did women become more liberal, and then the effect appeared primarily among college graduates. Schreiber argues that this occurred among the educated because they are more attuned to the liberation and feminist message of the media, and not because the educational experience itself was more liberalizing.

While the evidence has been consistent in showing liberalization of attitudes about women's roles, some recent work suggests that the process may be slowing. In my own analysis (Lueptow 1980c), attitudes about the effects of the Equal Rights Amendment on the family became more traditional between 1974 and 1977 among men. This has been followed by a similar shift among women, who also became more traditional between 1977 and 1980 (unpublished analysis). More significantly, recent analysis by Cherlin and Walters (1981) of the General Social Survey data showed a similar pattern in samples of the national population. While attitudes about women working outside the home and running for president became more liberal between 1972 and 1975, there was no further liberalization between 1975 and 1978. In fact, consistent with my own local observations, Cherlin and Walters found that college-educated women actually became considerably more *traditional* in the latter period. Thus, as of the early 1980s, there is some qualification to the picture of constant liberalization of attitudes about women's roles. This will bear watching.

For now, however, there is substantial evidence of changes in attitudes about women's roles, and this change seems to have occurred primarily near the end of the 1960s and continued on into the 1970s, probably because of the influence of media attention given to changing roles and women's liberation. In that conjunction it is worth recalling that the end of the 1960s was a period of intense questioning and rejection of established institutions and arrangements. There is considerable evidence that social institutions such as religion and citizenship were being devalued and replaced by an interpersonal morality based on conceptions of fairness, personal rights, independence, and reciprocity (Morris and Small 1971; Goertzel 1972; Yankelovich 1974; Farley, Brewer, and Fine 1977; Duncan and Duncan 1978; Veroff, Douvan, and Kulka 1981). While there has been little systematic treatment of the specific linkages between the general social changes of the 1960s and the women's movement ideology, it seems likely that they represent two sides of the same coin, that of freedom from traditional, institutionalized constraints.

Personality Differences

Personality differences between the sexes constitute one of the anomalies in the study of sex role change. For while there is an overwhelming assumption of sex role change, there has been almost no developed research or even serious discussion about changing personality. With the notable exception of recent work by Veroff and his colleagues, nearly all of the research has focused on either the perception of personality embodied in the stereotype or on the changes in the role aspects. Since there is not yet full agreement as to the nature of sex differences in personality, this may not be surprising. Until the nature of the differences is established, change is obviously going to be difficult to observe, except in those areas such as cognitive abilities, where hard measurement and recordkeeping will provide continuing evidence of sex difference or change in aspects of personality. (We will return to that specific aspect of personality in chapter 5.) In other aspects of the stereotype, however, it will be extremely difficult to document change, as distinct from reformulation and reinterpretation, except where, as in this study, some baseline data have been established and subsequently replicated.

The major psychological interest in the area of sex role change has to do with the concept of androgyny. This focus tends to beg the issue of sex role change in an interesting way. Androgyny involves the situationally specific exhibition of traits by men and women that makes the overriding question of change in sex-related aspects of personality generally moot. Androgyny not only views change as convergence, it tends to defuse the significance of sex-related personality characteristics viewed as general traits. Posited as a goal for future development, androgyny evokes an image of psychological and sociological completeness independent of sex differences in which the best of the male and female stereotype is combined, or available to both men and women, and in which the instrumental and expressive roles are modified and intermingled (Giele 1978). However, so far these formulations represent beginnings and speculations, not empirical evidence of change in sex-related aspects of personality.

At present, about the only research effort other than this one actually directed toward change in sex-related aspects of personality is that of Veroff and his colleagues in *The Inner American* and related publications.

The strategy of *The Inner American*, like that of my research and of Duncan and Duncan (1978), involves the replication (in 1975) of an earlier (1957) survey that served as the baseline for analysis of change in the variables of interest, in this case including, but not limited to, sex roles.[24] The study is of special interest because the terminal date coincides with that of my research and the baseline extends the period nearly a decade.

The variables of immediate interest are those having to do with well-being and self-perceptions.

The analysis of *The Inner American* revealed expected sex differences in feelings of well-being. While there is no significant sex difference in overall happiness, women reported being more worried, having more nervous breakdowns, needing help from others at some time to solve a problem, and being more frequently overwhelmed. While these differences are small, they are also stable over the period.

Stereotypic patterns also appear in the sources of well-being. Men tend to attribute their levels of happiness to economic and occupational circumstances, women to their children, their family, and their personal characteristics, a fairly straightforward demarcation along the lines of the instrumental-expressive, or Gemeinschaft-Gesellschaft distinctions. Sources of unhappiness show the same bifurcation. Job, world, and community problems are seen by men as the source of their unhappiness, while women more often list children, marriage, and family health as the sources of their unhappiness. Interestingly enough, the only evidence of sex role change in this particular analysis occurred with respect to jobs. Women with at least high school education, but especially those with college degrees, gave the job as source of unhappiness much more often in 1976 than in 1957. This is an interesting finding, since it is these college-educated women who became less liberal on women's role items in the last half of the 1970s (Cherlin and Walters 1981).

Findings on self-perception also revealed stereotypic patterns, although at some variance with Maccoby and Jacklin's (1974) conclusion that females had lower self-confidence but not lower self-esteem. Veroff, Douvan, and Kulka (1981) found that males had a more positive conception of themselves, had higher self-esteem, and saw their uniqueness more often reflecting internal aspects of personality. While there was an observable shift in this analysis away from normative and role criteria toward more individualistic bases for defining self, there was no evidence of sex role change.

Thus, in personal well-being and in self-perceptions, Veroff, Douvan, and Kulka (1981) find evidence for sex differences, for social change toward more individualistic patterns, but not any substantial evidence of sex role change.

The 1957 and 1975 surveys are relatively unique in their inclusion of projective measures to assess levels of motivation. Results of comparisons of achievement, affiliation, and power motives were reported by Veroff et al. (1980). I will return to achievement motivation later, but can note here that scores on affiliation motivation revealed a strong sex-by-year interaction that was not explicitly analyzed. Percentages showed, however, that female scores remained constant, but male scores declined substantially. Thus, while men scored higher on the affilation motive in 1957 and were consequently nonstereotypic, by 1975 women had stronger affiliation motives. Both sexes increased in power, viewed as fear of weakness, but men also increased in power defined as the hope of power.

With one or two exceptions, this evidence on sex-related personality differences reveals relatively small but generally stereotypic differences between the sexes, differences that tended to remain constant over the 1957–1975 period.

Achievement Orientations

A decline in achievement orientations would be consistent with evidence from attitude and value surveys in the 1960s showing a deemphasis of personal responsibility, institutional commitment, and success striving and an increasing emphasis on hedonism, interpersonal relations, and individualism. While there does seem to have been a change in national character from the 1960s to the 1970s, the implication of this for sex role change has only been suggested. Thus, Frieze et al. (1978) in attempting to account for the divergent findings on fear of success, suggests that men are becoming less achievement-oriented and more fearful of success.

This idea receives support from the analysis of Veroff et al. (1980), who found that women's achievement motivation, but not men's, increased between 1957 and 1975. Furthermore, the greatest increase in female scores occurred with a picture showing a woman upholstering a chair, suggesting to the authors that women's achievement motivation was not limited to performance in the workplace, but was more general, an interpretation consistent with Maccoby and Jacklin's (1974) view of the continuing salience of female achievement motivation. Veroff et al. (1980) attributed the male patterns to the decline in normative responsiveness and derogation of achievement by the counterculture of the 1960s, but argued that women have responded to the increased achievement press of the women's movement. These causal propositions could not be tested with their data.

Another important pattern of change in sex-related achievement differences has to do with the increased educational attainment levels of women over the past decade. These increased levels of attainment have reduced considerably the sex differences noted in early research (Rehberg and Rosenthal 1978). Comparing earlier findings by Sewell and Shah (1968) and by Alexander, Eckland, and Griffen (1975) with their own results, Rehberg and Rosenthal conclude that there also appears to be change reflected by the decreased importance of family background in the educational attainment of women. The increased effect of ability that they observe is consistent with rationalization of women's roles. However, other school processes remain sex differentiated and the ascribed characteristics of sex and social class account for more of the variance in all but four school outcomes than does ability.

Family and Career

Family and career have been the locus for substantial changes in the actual roles of women over the past several decades. In fact, the change in the working experience of women with young children has been both the symbol and the essence of the major change in sex roles.

Four aspects of changing family and career roles are reviewed here. (1) the dramatic increases in the participation of women in the labor force; (2) changes in family and career goals of women; (3) change and stability in family sex roles; and (4) change in levels of sex segregation in occupations.

Women in the Labor Force

The number of women in the labor force has increased dramatically, in what Waite refers to as "probably the single most dramatic and pervasive trend in the status of women since 1940" (1976:65 see also Bednarzik and Klein 1977; Hoffman and Nye 1974; Miller 1978).

While women traditionally had been employed, female employment in this society over the past hundred years had been largely premarital employment of young, unmarried women during the period preceding their family role assumptions. This employment, while not uncommon, involved only about one-fourth of all women from 1850 through 1940 (Hoffman and Nye 1974), but never involved more than 15% of married women during this whole period. Thus, the traditional sex role pattern in this society was organized around fairly common early employment of about one-fifth of all women, primarily from rural and working class families (Smuts 1971). However, these women left employment upon marriage and most certainly upon the birth of children.

This traditional pattern changed with the employment pressures of the Second World War. During that period, middle-class and employer prejudices against women in the labor force were overridden by the need for, and employment of, large numbers of women in the war effort.

Following the Second World War, a number of circumstances appear to have altered the expectation that married women would return to the home and reinstate the traditional pattern of female employment. Oppenheimer (1973) notes three important circumstances that operated to promote female employment, an employment that was nontraditional in its emphasis on married rather than single women. The first of these was the heavy demand for workers resulting from the increased manufacturing and economic expansion of the war years that continued into the 1950s. Second, there was a strong relative increase in white-collar jobs disproportionately filled by women, and third, during the 1950s there was a reduced cohort of younger unmarried women who had traditionally filled these jobs, due to the large reduction in fecundity during the 1930s. Oppenheimer argued that all of these coalesced to produce a substantial, unmet demand that could only be filled by older, married women. Faced with the need to fill white-collar positions in that climate, employers reduced their traditional resistance to employing older, married women and, in fact, age became less of a factor in determining female employment (Waite 1976). Other social forces, such as the effect of modernity on fertility (Scanzoni 1976) and the effect of wife's earning potential and past experience, have increased over the period, while inhibiting factors such as presence of young children have decreased (Waite 1976).

The net effect of these processes was to bring large numbers of married women over 40 whose children were largely grown back into the labor force. This change was followed by increased participation of married women in their childbearing years, followed finally by the most dramatic change of all, the greatly increased employment of younger married women with children under 6 years of age. By 1975, these patterns had transformed the nature of female employment. Over half of all women were now employed, but even more significantly, the proportions of women with children between 6 and 17 who were employed had increased from 26% in 1948 to 52% in 1975, while the proportion of women with children under 6 who were employed increased from 11% in 1948 to 37% in 1975 (Miller 1978). In the space of two decades, the traditional pattern of women in the home, men on the job was substantially altered. While far from unanimity (a point often overlooked in interpretations of these trends), the working woman with children was no longer the normative and statistical rarity that she had been before the 1950s.

Work is now an accepted and viable alternative to homemaking and child rearing. While I am aware of no detailed analysis at this point, it appears that changes in employment predated the popular perception of changes in women's roles that I have examined in the preceding section. Here as in the area of sexuality, the major function of the attitudinal and value changes appears to have been to create correspondence between the behaviors actually being carried out and the public perception of those behaviors expressed in values and opinions. By the 1970s the public conception of women's role alternatives had apparently caught up with the actual role performances themselves.

Family and Career Goals

Personal attitudes about family and career have also changed drastically over these periods. In studies, largely of college women, the consistent finding is that educated women no longer plan to channel their talents completely to the internal workings of the family, in socialization of children and support of the career-oriented husband. Rather, they intend increasingly to pursue careers outside of the family, although as Parelius notes, "these women remain basically positive about both marriage and motherhood. They reject neither men nor children. Their goals imply a restructuring of the family, but not its dissolution (1975b:152), " a finding also observed by Bronzaft (1974).

Nevertheless, the acceptance of both family and career represents a substantial shift in postgraduate plans for the typical graduate who in the 1950s planned on a concentration in marriage and the family and did not anticipate the combination of career and family that is the contemporary pattern. These shifts were substantial. For example, Cross (1971) reported that in 1964, 64% of entering freshmen women hoped to be housewives when they finished their education. By 1970 this had dropped to 31% who hoped to be a housewife only. The sex differences and change in orientations toward family and career are illustrated by the 1952–1974 comparisons of Cornell students reported in Farley, Brewer, and Fine (1977). In 1952, 87% of Cornell women expected to obtain their greatest satisfaction from family life while only 6% expected to obtain the greatest satisfactions from occupations. By 1974 almost four times the 1952 proportion expected to obtain their greatest satisfactions from occupations.

Veroff, Douvan, and Kulka (1981) observed similar patterns in the general American population. The proportion of women indicating they would work even if they didn't need the money increased from 58% in 1957 to 77% in 1975, while men's proportions stayed about 84%. In addition, their research shows work to be an increasingly important source of unhappiness for women and to a lesser degree an increasing source of happiness, especially at higher status levels where personal involvement is highest. Clearly, work has acquired a different relevance for women in 1975 than it had in 1957.

The increasing emphasis on work was associated with a deemphasis on family. Farley, Brewer, and Fine (1977) observed a large drop from 87% to 57% of college women saying family life would be the source of their greatest satisfaction. Males also decreased their valuation of family from 60% to 48%. Veroff, Douvan, and Kulka (1981) found similar shifts, but with sex role change limited to the youngest, unmarried group only. Both sexes increased their acceptance of unmarried life and their view that marriage is restrictive. For unmarried, thus generally younger, women, this represented a very sharp reversal of their more idealized version of marriage held in 1957.

While these patterns show an increase in the valuation of work by women and a decrease in the valuation of family as important life goals, neither sex disavows family. Women now have two goals instead of the earlier exclusive focus on marriage and the family.

Family Roles

Family roles, as the basis for important sex role differentiation, appear surprisingly stable. In spite of the important changes in the extrafamilial employment of women, the significant demographic changes surrounding marriage, fertility, and alternative life styles, and the liberalization of attitudes about "woman's place," there is not much evidence of change in the actual relationships of women and men in the most traditional sex-related context. The paradoxical nature of this circumstance is apparent in the discussion of family in two recent works on sex role change.

Mandle reviews the evidence on demographic changes surrounding marital relations and the effect of female employment on socialization and power within the family and concludes that with regard to sex role change,

available studies seem to indicate that the structural change represented by increased labor force participation of married women has had only a minor effect on the quality of marital relationships after 1960. . . . [T]he evidence on the effect of increased wives' employment indicates that it is only a potential generator of redefinitions of roles, power, and relationships. (1979:128)

Similarly, Giele (1978) discusses at some length the transition to symmetrical, egalitarian families that she sees as a major change but notes that major cross-cultural research shows that the two sexes continue to maintain traditional differences in actual duties and behaviors within the family.

Probably the most significant data on change and stability in contemporary family roles have been obtained in the earlier analysis by Duncan, Schuman, and Duncan (1973), *Social Change in a Metropolitan Commu-*

nity, and the more recent and most directly relevant work by Duncan and Duncan (1978), *Sex Typing and Social Roles.* The earlier work, on social change, was concerned with various social, religious, political, and family behaviors and attitudes in the Detroit area between the 1950s and 1971. The conclusion on changing family roles in the early study was that "small adjustments are being made without altering the general principles upon which couples work out their respective roles" (1973:17), and while there were some small changes in the division of labor between husbands and wives, "Overall, however, there is not important change in the organization of functions in the household since 1950" (1973:19).

The more recent study by Duncan and Duncan (1978) was based largely on a more intensive analysis of the data of the earlier study, but with more sophisticated analytic techniques and with the examination of facilitating variables, such as education and religion, that could be viewed as influencing the amount of change. This study is especially interesting in the present context because it is similar to my work in the logic of the design and approach to social change and sex role change. Like this study it deals with sex role change across a decade by examining the actual responses of men and women reporting on their own behavior, circumstances, values, and goals. As such it provides a body of evidence that goes considerably beyond the current demographic summations and the repeated studies of college students on women's roles and typical personality. In addressing the relevance of discrete, empirical data as compared to speculation about changing sex roles, Duncan and Duncan's comment applies to both studies.

Explanations of the positions of women and men in the social structure and prescriptions for change now seem to outnumber careful descriptions of those positions and the respects, if any, in which they have changed since the 1950's. Our objective is simply to contribute some reliable observations on the sexual differentiation of social roles in a contemporary community. (1978:20–21)

Duncan and Duncan found evidence of sex difference and social change, but they did not find much evidence of fundamental and important change in sex roles within the family. Interestingly enough, with one or two exceptions, they found that social change and sex differences often occurred together. While both sexes changed in various characteristics, the difference between the sexes remained the same, a pattern also observed repeatedly by Veroff, Douvan, and Kulka (1981).

To briefly summarize some of the relevant findings from Duncan and Duncan (1978), while there were more women working in 1971 than in 1956, the reasons for working remained the same although there was an interesting liberation theme in the one difference that changed. In 1971 women were more likely to give "get out of home" as a reason for working. However, in both years the overwhelming reason given by both husbands and wives was money. The combination of money and escape from homemaking suggests a theme of liberation coupled with the advantages of extra income. There is no sense in these responses of the theme so often treated in discussions of changing sex roles from a college-level perspective, of work as self-fulfilling and important in its own right.[25]

Social change but not sex role change was observed in several areas in the Duncan and Duncan research. There was substantial change in attitudes about women working, consistent with the national changes already discussed. Thare was also a liberalization of types of work seen as acceptable, although in both respects men were more conservative, and this difference was maintained over the time period. Similarly, there was increased political participation and rating of social institutions, but sex differences persisted; religious participation and commitment declined, but sex differences persisted; and both sexes changed attitudes about divorce, but sex differences prevailed.

Evidence of sex role change was clear-cut in only one or two instances. Women became relatively less trusting than men in 1971. There was also some indirect support in the reduced participation of women in church-connected groups, and in the somewhat tenuous conclusion that religious commitments were decreasing more rapidly between the female respondents and their mothers than between the male respondents and their fathers, although this was not a totally clear finding.

Change *was* observed in several of the housekeeping and decision variables. Men in 1971 were more likely to make their own breakfast, while women were more likely to do the grocery shopping and make repairs around the house. Women were also more likely to do the evening dishes in 1971 than in 1955, but they were also more likely to make the final decision about the husband's job. The authors conclude that these patterns had more to do with appropriateness of the assignments than with changing sex roles.

The closest thing to clear evidence on sex role change appeared in the data on socialization. Parents revealed a strong shift away from sex typing of children's tasks over the 1953–1971 time period. Whereas in 1953 girls were assigned dusting and making beds while boys washed the car and shoveled walks, by 1971 making beds and washing the car were not as sex typed, shoveling walks was considerably less sex typed, but dusting remained largely the girl's chore. Considering the time intervals of the Duncan and Duncan and this study, it is of some interest that more recent (1976) data showed a dramatic increase in the change on these values. The odds on "both" nearly trebled for all four chores and the sex typing for dusting was greatly reduced.

Evidence on attitudes and practices of child training and socialization is less clear-cut. In the first place, Duncan and Duncan failed to find important sex differences in child-rearing techniques, sanctions, and with one or two exceptions age norms. They conclude: "Like Maccoby and Jacklin (1974), though, we mostly find 'a remarkable degree of uniformity in the socialization of the two sexes' " (1978:260). Parental values regarding conformity versus independent thought show surprising lack of sex differentiation and no sex role change, although there is a change away from conformity to traditional rules and an increased acceptance of independent judgment. The authors observe that these results do not support the conception of sex typing analogous to the traditional-modern distinction that I have already discussed.[26]

Thus, the data from the Detroit area studies do not support the concept of important changes in sex roles within the family between the 1950s and 1971. They observe sex difference and social change, but not sex role change. The significant structural changes in women's work and the important social processes surrounding the women's movement appear not to have produced measurable change in various elements of family roles.

Occupational Sex Segregation

Occupational Sex segregation of work, like the evidence on family roles, qualifies the picture of substantial sex role change produced by the increased participation of married women with children and by the increasing acceptance of the legitimacy of women's career orientations. To a considerable degree, women are involved in greater numbers in the labor force but are doing more or less what they have traditionally been doing.

The sex segregation of work rests on differing views of the personalities and social circumstances of women as compared to men. From the perspective of the stereotype, it is clear that the traditional roles of teacher, nurse, social worker, secretary, and household worker reflect the characteristics of women as described by the family-based sex role stereotype. McLaughlin (1978) finds some support for this pattern in his analysis of sex differences in status determinants. In analyzing the characteristics of occupationa predominantly male, predominantly female, and mixed, McLaughlin found stereotypic differences. Male occupations were high on work with data, low on people, high on work with things and strength, and median on mental skill. Female occupations were characterized by work with people and low mental skill requirements. Of some interest from the standpoint of androgyny, the mixed occupations were characterized by work with data and people but not things, and were lower than female occupations on strength but by far the highest on mental skill. This is consistent with the idea that androgynous personalities are best equipped for the intellectually and expressively demanding contemporary occupations.

Occupational sex segregation is also seen to emerge from the characteristics of women in the marketplace, especially the limitations that family life and childbearing and child rearing place on occupational commitment and career development. As Oppenheimer (1968) has observed, the female occupations are those involving discontinuity, which in turn requires the prejob training characteristic of women's jobs and male professions, but quite different from the career development within the organization resting on advancement and investment in a single organization. Because of the breaks in employment for childbearing as well as the geographic mobility traditionally associated with husband's career, women's jobs have been of the type where the training and qualifications are brought to the job, and of course can be taken off the job without great loss to the employee. These jobs result in a flat career line (McClendon 1976), where years of service do not result in increased status or income, but also where people can drop out of the labor force and reenter without any serious loss of employable qualification, although without any gain either (Wolf and Rosenfeld 1978). Women in sex-typed jobs leave and enter at the same level, women who reenter the labor force in male jobs are much more likely to be upwardly mobile. Thus, the unique characteristics of women's jobs have a two-sided value: on the one hand they are generally closed to the type of mobility generated by advancement within organizational structures, but on the other hand they provide insurance of employability for people who drop out and reenter the labor force.

Whatever the advantage or disadvantage, the evidence on occupational segregation is clear—it has continued. While Gross' (1968) conclusion about the continuation of sex segregation of occupations from the turn of the century to 1960 has been questioned by Williams (1976) as inadequate because of the change in the occupational categories, it is clear that at least for the year-by-year comparisons, the overall index of dissimilarity remained constant. More recent work has shown continuation of sex segregation. Treiman and Terrell (1975b), analyzing just the eleven major occupational categories, found no change at all in the segregation of white men and women between 1940 and 1970, although the nonwhite segregation index did decline from .58 to .49 over the period. Using 441 occupational categories for 1960–1970–1976 comparisons, the United States Commission on Civil Rights (1978) found that occupational segregation of white men and women *increased* from 62.4 to 66.1, levels of segregation that are consistent with Gross' analysis for 1960. The Commission analysis also showed a decline in segregation for black women both in comparison with majority men and with majority women.

Thus, while there has been a great increase in the numbers of women entering the labor force, with all the implications for sex role change that entails, the analysis of segregation and dual labor markets indicates that traditional role performances are still the norm, that sex role change involving different personality and circumstantial factors has not yet occurred to any great degree.

While there has not been important change in actual occupational distributions through the mid-1970s, other research indicates that change may be in the offing. Recent research on the occupational preferences of high school seniors in Virginia shows a convergence in level of occupational aspiration between 1970 and 1976 due to male increases in blue-collar preferences and female increases in professional choices, resulting in a decline in the index of dissimilarity (seven categories) from 43.6 to 38.2 (Garrison 1979). A somewhat greater decline in the index of dissimilarity was observed by Herzog (1982) between 1976 and 1980 in a national sample of high school seniors, although the only occupational level out of fourteen showing a significant sex-by-year interaction was clerical worker. On the other hand, Herzog observed no change in the occupational value orientations of these seniors, which would suggest continuing sex-typed work preferences, a pattern that could be disguised by the broad occupational categories used in research on the level of occupational aspiration.

CHAPTER 4

SOCIAL CHANGE AND SEX ROLE CHANGE IN ORIENTATIONS TOWARD LIFE, WORK, AND ACHIEVEMENT

In the preceding chapter I reviewed the main issues and evidence on sex differences and sex role change. This literature reveals a general consistency of content in personality, in stereotype, and in sex and family role patterns. There is public consensus about the personality characteristics differentiating "typical" men and women. These characteristics are partially documented in research on personality differences and they reflect some of the fundamental differences in family role assignments conceptualized roughly along the instrumental-expressive dimension. There is also consistent evidence on the dimensions along which change is occurring, especially in labor force participation and attitudes about women's family and community roles.

In this chapter I examine the orientations of the high school seniors toward several dimensions central to these contemporary concerns about changing sex roles: life, work, and achievement orientations. This analysis of change differs from much of that already reported in that it involves the actual orientations and expectations of students toward their own personal circumstances. In this regard it has a relevance not found in typical survey evidence on attitudes about women's roles or sex role stereotypes.

The range of variables examined in this chapter does not encompass the full set of concerns described in the preceding chapter, especially regarding sex role stereotypes and family role arrangements. Chapter 3 must be viewed as describing a background of traits, characteristics, and plans against which

Portions of this chapter have appeared as "Social Change and Sex-Role Change in Adolescent Orientations Toward Life, Work, and Achievement, 1964–1975," *Social Psychology Quarterly* (March 1980), 43:48–59 and "Sex-Typing and Change in the Occupational Choices of High School Seniors, 1964–1975," *Sociology of Education* (January 1981), 54:16–24.

this evidence will be appraised. Some of the evidence presented here, such as family versus career in the life goals and achievement orientations and aspirations, bears directly on the central issues. Other evidence, such as the occupational values of leadership, working with and helping people, and adventure, obviously taps central dimensions of sex role stereotypes even though it was not developed expressly for that purpose.

As previously noted, the basic approach to the questions of sex difference and change is through regression analysis. Each of the life goal, occupational values, and achievement value items is regressed on sex, year, and year-by-sex interaction. A similar approach is taken to the analysis of occupational and educational aspiration levels. In each case the regression coefficient for sex reflects sex difference, that for year reflects social change, and the interaction of sex by year represents differential change, my operational definition of sex role change.

Analysis of sex differences and change in occupational preferences is handled differently. As differences in preference independent of occupational status level basically require comparison of occupational situs dimensions, analysis of preferences will be carried out by comparing the distributions of choices of males and females and by examination of the amount of sex typing in the choices over the two time periods.

Life Goals

Life goals tap one of the important themes in the literature on changing sex roles, that of the shift from women's role as one of homemaking and motherhood to a role that also includes increasing participation in and commitment to occupational and community roles outside the family. As we have seen, there is substantial evidence that public attitudes have changed markedly in the acceptance of extrafamilial role involvement by the wife and increasing internal involvement of the husband in the domestic affairs of the family. The final state toward which this change appears to be heading is the symmetrical family structure in which both wives and husbands have equal internal and external commitments.

The picture of change emerging from attitude surveys of the general public is also reflected in the personal orientations of college women, who show substantial change in emphasis from homemaking, which was the predominant concentration in the 1950s and 1960s, to joint orientations emphasizing both family and career goals. However, comparable data on more heterogeneous and representative high school samples has to this point not been presented.

Table 4.1.

Life Goals

1.	Live up to other's expectations, SHOW my parents, teachers, and friends that I can make good.
2.	Obtain money and LUXURY, a very substantial income and have expensive and luxurious things.
3.	Obtain the kind of work or OCCUPATION that I want to be in, avoid just having a job.
4.	Be RELIGIOUS, live a deeply religious life, live for God.
5.	Have travel, ADVENTURE and excitement, avoid living a routine life, be creative and do different things.
6.	Make a CONTRIBUTION to society, be of service in helping other people, do something to make this a better world.
7.	Have SECURITY and comfort, a secure job with enough money to buy a home and care and live comfortably.
8.	Have STATUS and prestige, be respected and accepted by others, have others look up to me, be proud of myself.
9.	Find the right person to marry, enjoy married life, raise and care for a FAMILY.
10.	Be a SUCCESS in life.

Results

The content of the ten life goal items is presented in table 4.1.[1] Because of the general assumptions about changing sex roles as well as the demographic data on labor force participation and the changing orientations of college women, we would expect to see a marked devaluation of family over the period and an increase in the valuation of occupational goals. Evidence on change in values between the 1960s and 1970s (Morris and Small 1971; Goertzel 1972; Yankelovich 1974; Farley, Brewer, and Fine 1977; Duncan and Duncan 1978) would suggest change from traditional values regarding religion and contribution toward new emphasis on such hedonistic goals as luxury, adventure, and security. Females specifically might be expected to increase their values of occupation, success, and luxury more than males while decreasing such traditional values as religion and making a contribution.

Male and female responses to the life goal items are stereotypic [2] (table 4.2). Girls value religion, making a contribution to society, and family, while boys stress showing others, luxury, security, status, and success. Interestingly enough, there is no sex difference in the importance of occupation as a life goal in either 1964 or 1975. Contrary to some of the assumptions about sex differences, both boys and girls value occupation as the most

Table 4.2.

Life Goals by Sex, Year, and Sex by Year
(N=5420)

Goal	Average Life Goal Score 1964		1975		Metric Regression Coefficients[a]			
	M	F	M	F	Sex	Year	Inter	R^2
Show	2.45	2.34	2.17	2.01	-.11	-.28		.06
Luxury	1.79	1.49	1.92	1.58	-.30	.12		.07
Occupation	2.84	2.84	2.77	2.73		-.07		.01
Religion	2.31	2.46	1.89	1.88	.15	-.42	-.17	.14
Adventure	2.28	2.26	2.44	2.48		.16		.02
Contribution	2.42	2.62	2.33	2.52	.20	-.08		.03
Security	2.62	2.56	2.49	2.43	-.13	-.06		.01
Status	2.21	2.09	2.15	1.98	-.12	-.06		.02
Family	2.63	2.74	2.48	2.59	.11	-.15		.02
Success	2.82	2.76	2.74	2.62	-.06	-.08	-.05	.02

[a]Only the coefficients twice the standard error are reported.

important goal and success as the second most important goal, followed by family, security, and adventure. Thus, while the sex differences observed are stereotypic, the similar emphasis on occupation by the two sexes questions somewhat the image in the sex role literature of female lack of concern with work for its own sake. In anticipation of the section on occupational values, it is worth noting that the phrasing of the occupational item in table 4.1 treats it as an intrinsic oreintation, i.e., wanting to have a self-satisfying position, not just a job.

The coefficients for year in table 4.2 reveal a fair amount of change in life orientations, for the most part consistent with the evidence on social change previously described. These students increased their valuation of only two goals—luxury and adventure, both hedonistic goals. Somewhat contrary to the dependency theme in the feminine stereotype, attaining expensive and luxurious things is the goal that most sharply distinguishes the sexes, while adventure, which is clearly a component of the masculine stereotype, does not.

The other changes were also consistent with the evidence on changing popular culture from the 1960s to the 1970s. For the most part these students reject controls, both at the institutional and at the interpersonal levels. For example, the greatest change by far is the devaluation of religion as a life goal. This change in orientation is great enough so that along with the sex difference and the interaction to be discussed later, 14% of the variance in religion as a life goal is accounted for. Living a deeply religious life became one of the least important goals by 1975. While not as dramatic, there is also a deemphasis of family as a life goal. At the interpersonal level, these students show a marked rejection of showing others they can make good, making a contribution, and being a success. In various ways these patterns confirm the evidence on the changes in the past decade involving increasing individuation and hedonism and decreasing acceptance of traditional institutions, values, and social obligations.

Turning to the central question of this research, changing sex roles, we find religion the only definite instance of predicted change. Between 1964 and 1975 girls decreased their valuation of religion even more than boys did. Whereas in 1964, the female/male values were 2.46/2.31, by 1975 they were low and almost identical, 1.87/1.89. This is clearly in the expected direction and provides us with the only case in table 4.2 where either masculinization or convergence occurs. Over this time period, girls considerably more than boys reject the traditional control of institutional religion.

That the religion effect is limited to religion and not the general feminine stereotypic pattern of nurturance and support is apparent in the absence of significant interaction coefficients in table 4.2. While girls have drastically reduced the emphasis on religion, there is no significant interaction for making a contribution. While both sexes change along this dimension, the sex difference is maintained. Thus, girls appear to be rejecting the institutionalized, perhaps organized, aspects of religion, but have not become masculinized in terms of rejecting nurturant and conforming goals. It seems that religious beliefs and practices, not to mention male control of organized religion, are anathema to many of these girls who at the same time continue to accept traditional altruistic and supportive feminine orientations.

The only other significant interaction in table 4.2 is the weak effect for success. Here the pattern involves an intensification of traditional distinctions as girls became relatively less concerned about success than they were in 1964. While the statistically significant effect is so weak it is essentially trivial, it is interesting that among this relatively heterogeneous high school sample, females were slightly less concerned about being a success in 1975 than in 1964. This is contrary to general themes about increasing emphasis on professions and careers that run through the sex role literature on college women.

The analysis of life goals does not provide much support for expected sex role changes involving feminine life orientations toward achievement and success in careers rather than toward interpersonal satisfaction in family and homemaking. The change that did occur reflected the general social change from commitment to traditional institutions and arrangements toward individualized, hedonistic, and sensual goals that various observers have documented as occurring between the 1960s and 1970s. Within these broad changes, sex differences are substantially maintained.[3]

The dramatic change in the importance of religion as a life goal, combined with the continued female acceptance of making a contribution to society, suggests that the rejection of religion has more to do with the rejection of adult, traditional, probably masculine authority in organized religion than with the rejection of traditionally feminine patterns of altruism and compliance. Absence of additional information on religion precludes further analysis bearing on this interpretation, although I will return to this theme of the rejection of adult institutions in following sections.

Facilitating Conditions

Facilitating conditions for sex role change were extensively examined in the analysis of change in life goals. As discussed in chapter 2, a number of circumstances have been advanced that could produce initial change from traditional sex role patterns (see table 2.5). As the evidence on the consequences of these various circumstances is not yet clear, the analysis of possible facilitating conditions was approached in a broadly inclusive manner. The analysis just described was repeated sixteen times, each time including one of the facilitating variables to determine whether the interaction of sex and year, which I took as the indicator of sex role change, was itself affected by the level of the facilitating variable.[4] The specific indication of a facilitating effect was taken to be a sex-by-year-by-facilitator coefficient at least twice the standard error.

The most striking thing about this analysis is the relative absence of significant three-way effects. In spite of the plausibility of many of the arguments developed in chapter 2 and in other sources in the sex role literature, in only 8 of the 160 regressions did a facilitating variable have significant effects on the pattern of sex role change. This is exactly the number expected by chance at the .05 level of significance. Furthermore, two of the significant interactions (the effect of mother's education on security and newspaper reading on status) are contrary to prediction and two interactions (the effect of teacher's and counselor's influence on luxury and urban residence on security) are ambiguous. Thus, the picture of stability in sex differences in life goals is not altered in the analysis of the full range of facilitating variables. There do not appear to be subgroups among whom sex role change in life goals is more advanced. This somewhat surprising finding strengthens the conclusion that, with the exception of religion, there has been little sex-differentiated change in life goal orientations across the decade.

While the facilitating analysis resulted in findings easily attributable to chance, two of the ten analyses involving the theoretically important variable of mother's work did produce third-order regression coefficients over two standard errors. While both sexes decreased their valuation of occupation as a life goal, this decrease was most pronounced among daughters whose mothers did not work. Another very minor, but provocative, effect was observed in making a contribution. Daughters of working mothers declined slightly more in life goal values (–.13 to –.08) than daughters of nonworking mothers.

Although these interactions are interesting, they do not basically alter the conclusion of chance findings. Nevertheless, the regression equations for the eight significant facilitating variables are presented in appendix A, panel 1, for the interested reader.

Because of the absence of substantial effects in the preceding analysis and the cost of running sixteen regressions for each dependent variable, analysis of facilitating conditions is somewhat truncated in the following sections, with the number of facilitating variables reduced to just the major indicators. Thus, as described in chapter 2, mother's work status and number of consultants will be included as important indicators of nontraditional socialization, father's education and newspaper reading as indicators of attention to change processes, and intelligence as an important indicator of personality and adaptability. Any strong facilitating conditions should be revealed by these variables.

Summary and Conclusion

The analysis of life goals revealed clear-cut sex differences that were for the most part stereotypic. Males and females differ in life orientations in ways that reflect sex role stereotypes.

On the other hand, there are two important exceptions in the findings—that the sexes do not differ at all in their emphasis on occupation as a life goal and on valuation of adventure and excitement. Even in 1964, these important exceptions to the stereotypes appear. The stereotypic patterns in other regards juxtaposed with this similarity in occupational orientations points toward the possibility that work and career may not be perceived as such a strong conflict by these students. In any event, somewhat traditional female personalities in this study also place stress on occupation and adventure to the same degree as males.

There was appreciable social change observed in these responses, almost all of it consistent with the proposition that the values of youth are shifting away from traditional, institutionalized, adult patterns toward more hedonistic and sensual individualism.

Finally, and most significantly, what there did not appear to be in these responses was evidence of sex role change. The life goals of these students, while sex-differentiated and changing, did not change in ways reducing sex-differentiated life orientations. Both sexes changed, but the sex differences were maintained. The two significant sex-by-year interactions did not contradict these interpretations. Women became less success-oriented and dramatically less religious. However, persistence of sex differences in altruistic goals suggests that the striking decline in religion may have reflected disavowal of organized institutional aspects of the church, and not the altruistic, compliant, and supporting characteristics encompassed within the feminine stereotype.

Analysis of the facilitating variables failed to show any important subgroup effects beyond chance. With the possible exception of mother's work, none of the facilitating factors were important to the amount of sex role changes.

WORK ORIENTATIONS

Orientations toward work have been treated from three perspectives: the meaning of work, that is the aspects of work most valued, the type of work preferred, and the status level of the occupation aspired to or expected. In this section the meaning of work and the sex typing of occupational preferences are examined. Level of educational and occupational aspiration will be examined in the final section in this chapter.

Occupational Values

Occupational values used in this study were taken from Rosenberg (1957) and were obtained through the use of a question asking the student respondents to rate each item as a requirement of a job they would consider ideal.

Table 4.3.

Occupational Values

1.	Provide an opportunity to use my special ABILITIES and aptitudes.
2.	Provide me with a chance to earn a good deal of MONEY.
3.	Permit me to be CREATIVE and original.
4.	Give me social STATUS and prestige.
5.	Give me an opportunity to work with PEOPLE rather than things.
6.	Enable me to look forward to a stable, SECURE future.
7.	Leave me relatively FREE of supervision by others.
8.	Give me a chance to exercise LEADERSHIP.
9.	Provide me with ADVENTURE.
10.	Give me an opportunity to be HELPFUL to others.

These items are listed in table 4.3. As originally interpreted by Rosenberg, seven of the items formed three dimensions often treated in the literature on occupational motivation and choice. These are people-oriented (Items 5 and 10), intrinsic work orientation (Items 1 and 3), and extrinsic rewards (Items 2, 4, and 6). The research evidence on values is consistent with some aspects of the stereotype in that females consistently rate interpersonal aspects as more important while males rate the extrinsic aspects of money, status, and security as more important. Evidence on intrinsic orientations is not quite so consistent, as women have generally valued the intrinsic aspects of work as highly as men have, notwithstanding the implications of both stereotypic distinctions and the instrumental-expressive pattern.

Results

The patterns just described for the life goals also appear in the sex-differentiated responses to the occupational values (table 4.4). By far the strongest effect in table 4.4 appears in the sex differences on working with people, a highly stereotypic value. The second strongest effect appears in the other "people-oriented" value, being helpful to others. Girls in this study clearly reflected the central components of the stereotype in their orientations toward work. Responses of these students are also consistent with the stereotype in the greater importance boys place on the extrinsic factors of money and status, although not on security. Boys also place much greater importance on freedom from supervision, adventure, and to a lesser degree, leadership.[5]

There is one clear and important departure from the stereotype in that girls

Table 4.4.

Occupational Values by Sex, Year, and Sex by Year
(N=5507)

Occupational Value	Average Occupational Value				Metric Regression Coefficients[a]			
	1964		1975					
	M	F	M	F	Sex	Year	Inter	R2
Abilities	2.81	2.88	2.74	2.81	.07	-.07		.02
Money	2.46	2.24	2.54	2.34	-.22	.09		.04
Creative	2.36	2.42	2.40	2.50	.08	.06		.01
Status	1.95	1.79	1.91	1.76	-.15			.01
People	2.16	2.63	2.26	2.66	.47	.10	-.07	.10
Security	2.83	2.81	2.77	2.70	-.04	-.09		.01
Freedom	2.07	1.86	2.28	2.08	-.20	.21		.05
Leadership	2.07	1.99	2.18	1.95	-.08	.11	-.15	.02
Adventure	2.14	1.98	2.29	2.34	-.16	.15	.21	.04
Helpful	2.52	2.81	2.50	2.77	.28			.07

[a]Only the coefficients twice the standard error are reported.

are somewhat more likely to view the intrinsic aspects of work as more important than boys are. While this effect is weak compared to the patterns just described, it is, nevertheless, contrary to traditional distinctions emphasizing male instrumental roles. It also qualifies the assumption underlying some of the sex typing of work, that women are less interested in work or career, but are in the labor force primarily to supplement their husband's earnings. These data show that girls place more, not less, importance on the intrinsic factors of using abilities and aptitudes and having a chance to be creative and original. This is especially interesting when we consider that these are high school students, not specially selected college women, who express these orientations. These orientations toward the intrinsic aspects of work may of course represent interest in the affiliative or service functions that characterize women's work. In this respect, these orientations toward the intrinsic aspects of such jobs would be analogous to the achievement motivation patterns in which feminine achievement motivation is seen as directed toward affiliative, not task, success ((Stein and Bailey 1975). In any event, and depending on the interpretation of the intrinsic orientations, the differences observed in table 4.4 are traditional and stereotypic and are essentially the differences observed by Rosenberg (1957) in his study of college students.

The changes between 1964 and 1975 can be interpreted, as I have the life goals, as reflections of the broader value changes from commitment to traditional social institutions and values toward increased liberty, hedonism, and individualistic striving. Money and creativity become more important while the work ethic theme in abilities and aptitudes declines slightly, as does the valuing of security. On the other hand, freedom, leadership, and adventure become substantially more important. The shift from institutions to relationships is reflected in the increasing importance of working with people, although this interpersonal orientatinn is not selfless—i.e., there is essentially no change in valuing helping others. Thus, the interpersonal theme appearing in these data seems restricted to potentially self-rewarding interactions in work rather than to generalized altruism or social consciousness.

There is very little evidence of sex role change in table 4.4, and the changes that are observed are somewhat contradictory. The clearest and somewhat surprising evidence of change occurs in adventure. The female change in this value is so great that by 1975, girls rate adventure even more highly than boys do, a definite reversal of the 1964 difference. This dramatic shift in a pattern associated with the masculine stereotype could reflect masculinization, or it could reflect a hedonistic liberation theme. Considering the change in leadership lends some strength to the latter interpretation. Girls in these schools were less interested in leadership in occupations in 1975 than they were in 1964, even after several years of feminist activism and publicity about equal opportunity and attainment of higher level managerial and executive positions. When viewed from the perspective of these heterogeneous samples of high school seniors, these appear to be less important concerns than they might be among more consciously aware groups of college women. The other change, people orientation, is due to the fact that the male increase in this value was greater than the female increase, thus producing one of the few illustrations of convergence through feminization of male patterns in this study.

These several patterns are strikingly similar to uninterpreted value orientations reported by Flanagan and Jung (1971) in their 1960–1970 replication of the original Project Talent survey in 134 of the original schools. They found that girls rated "work that seems important to me" as a more important job factor than did boys, and the difference was maintained over the decade. They also found substantial differences, constant over the decade, in the rating of "meeting and working with sociable, friendly people," that favored girls. Finally, in an item related to the issue of leadership, ''opportunity for promotion and advancement,'' Flanagan and Jung observed an 8% decline in percentage of boys rating this as extremely or very important, but a decline of 15% among the girls. In 1960, 69.0% of the boys and 61.7% of the girls rated this as very or extremely important, but by 1970, the comparable percentages were 60.6% and 46.6%. There clearly appear to be sex-related processes involved in these orientations and while they include the unexpected intrinsic orientations of females, they do not reflect interest in leadership and advancement. In fact, the activism and publicity of the later 1960s seems to have produced just the opposite result. These high school girls want satisfaction in work, excitement, and adventure but they do not increasingly seek leadership and competitive advancement possibilities.

Facilitating Variables

Results for the five facilitating variables—intelligence, father's education, mother's work status, number of consultants, and reading a daily newspaper—upon sex role change in occupational value orientations were consistent with those of the more extensive analysis of the sixteen facilitating variables reported in the life goal analysis.[6] Only two of the fifty three-way regression coefficients were greater than twice their standard error, again about the number that would be expected by chance alone. Thus, as in the analysis of life goals, there is no real evidence for the effect of the facilitating conditions on sex role change over the years. At the same time, both of the significant interactions are in the predicted direction and are theoretically meaningful. The surprising decline in valuation of leadership by girls observed in table 4.4 occurs only among girls below the mean in measured intelligence, while the increase in valuation of adventure is greatest among girls who read a newspaper. In fact, in 1964 girls who read a newspaper had lower scores on adventure than those who did not, suggesting that the message of the media may well have changed across the decade. The leadership finding suggests that the challenges of full occupational equality may appear imposing to girls of lower aptitude.

Interesting and provocative as these two findings are, they do not alter the fact that these results could easily be chance findings. Nevertheless, the two significant equations are presented in appendix A, panel 2.

Summary and Conclusion

Analysis of occupational value-orientations has revealed substantial sex difference (for the most part stereotypic) and appreciable social change, but no consistent pattern of sex-by-year interactions describing sex role change along lines of masculinization or convergence.

Orientations toward work show a substantial and traditional sex difference in the female valuation of working with and helping people. These differences were large and reflect the basic dimension of sex role differentiation along the instrumental-expressive distinction. They are also consistent with the characteristics of traditional sex-typed occupations.

Other orientations, much less extreme, show predicted emphasis of boys on extrinsic factors and on leadership and adventure. A somewhat unexpected (although not new) finding emerged in the slightly greater female orientation toward intrinsic aspects of work. These girls expressed commitment to the intrinsic aspects of work, as did the Project Talent girls (Flanagan and Jung 1971). This is an emphasis often overlooked in discussions of sex typing and work or of women's achievement orientations.

Social change comparable to that of the life goals was observed. Generally, there was a decrease in intrinsic value of work and an increase in freedom and personal satisfaction in work. There was also an increased valuation of working with people. Overall, these changes in work orientations were consistent with the well-documented changes in values between the 1960s and 1970s.

There did not appear to be consistent evidence of changing sex roles in the occupational orientations. Differential change was observed in three items, but they reflected complex patterns. Girls increased valuation of adventure, but they also decreased their valuation of leadership, while boys became relatively more people-oriented. Thus, there was evidence for convergence but also for intensification of traditional patterns.

Facilitating variables again failed to reveal any significant effect on these interactions, for the observed pattern was again almost exactly what would have been expected on the basis of chance alone.

Occupational Preferences

Occupational preferences are ordinarily analyzed from either of two perspectives: (1) the content and nature of the job and its duties, sometimes referred to as occupational situs, or (2) the status or prestige level publicly awarded to the position. The second of these approaches really describes status attainment or mobility, or, as in this study, when formulated as an orientation, an occupational aspiration. I will return to the aspirational theme later. In this section I consider the content of the occupational expectations and preferences, with the major focus on the sex typing of the preferences. As I have noted, there is ample evidence that at least until the very recent past, there has been substantial sex segregation of work. Women have traditionally occupied a handful of occupations that reflect the characteristics of sex role stereotypes and family role assignments.

Because preferences for named occupations constitute nominal data when examined separately from occupational status levels, the analysis in this section is different from the regression analysis used in the remainder of the chapter. In this section I compare distributions, using the index of dissimilarity and the actual proportions within sex-typed occupations.[7]

I examine the stability of sex typing itself in two ways, first by comparing the distributions of boys and girls using the index of dissimilarity and second by observing the proportions of girls and boys in jobs chosen predominantly (by at least 70%) by members of the opposite sex.

Finally, dissimilarity in the occupation expected and the occupation desired if the student were completely free to select any occupation he or she wished is taken as a reflection of perceived obstacles to attainment of true occupational preferences. Considering that much of the writing on occupational choice and experience emphasizes the limitations placed on female occupational selection by sex-typed and appropriateness factors, discrimination and conflicts between marital and career goals, the ideal-expected discrepancy is expected to be greater for girls but to show a relatively greater reduction over the period. It is possible that reductions in the constraints of sex-typing may also reduce the ideal-expected discrepancy for boys, although probably to a lesser degree, considering the broader options boys originally had.[8]

Because of the nature of the data and measures used in this section (see note 7), analysis by facilitating groups would be unwieldy and inherently inconclusive. Consequently, in this section I dispense with the five measures used previously and present data only on the effect of college plan, which stands in one way or another as a proxy for each of the other five.

Results

As expected, table 4.5 reveals convergence in the occupational preferences of boys and girls over the period. Male-female dissimilarity scores for both

Table 4.5.

Dissimilarity of Male–Female Occupational Orientation
Distribution by Sex

Occupational Orientation	1964		1975	
	Index of Dissim.	Number of Occup.	Index of Dissim.	Number of Occup.
Expected	71.0	87	63.2	102
Ideal	68.3	87	59.0	103

expected and ideal occupations decreased by around 8% over this time period. However, this reduction in sex-based dissimilarity is relatively small compared to the overall dissimilarity of the male and female distributions. Even in 1975, about 60% of one sex would have to change occupational preference or expectation to eliminate sex-based differentiation, just slightly less than the segregation index of 68.4 reported by Gross (1968) for the 1960 American labor force. Thus, while we clearly observe change, it is merely the beginning of the process. The occupational orientations of the sexes were still clearly differentiated in 1975.

Also as expected, sex-based dissimilarity is greater for both years in the expected occupations than in the ideal occupations (table 4.5), consistent with the idea that a portion of occupational sex typing is due to the perception of situational constraints. However, the small differences between expected and ideal indicate that the greatest effects in sex-typed preferences are internal results of socialization or basic sex differences.

A more direct view of sex typing can be obtained by shifting attention from the overall distributions to the concentration of male and female choices in predominately male or female occupations (tables 4.6, 4.7).

In 1964, concentration of female preferences in sex-typed occupations was very high (table 4.6). Four-fifths of all girls expected to enter one of twelve occupations in which the percentage female was 88%, while three-quarters stated ideal preferences for occupations in which the percentage female was 89.2%. By 1975 considerable but somewhat complex change had occurred in this pattern. In the first place, the twelve expected and seventeen ideal occupations that were sex typed in 1964 remained sex typed in 1975, with female choice concentrations of near 90%. However, while these occupations remained strongly sex typed, far fewer girls planned to enter them. This change is especially marked in the expected occupations, where the proportion of girls planning to enter occupations predominantly female in 1964 dropped from 79.7% to 49.8%. By 1975, one-half of these

Table 4.6.

Concentration of Choices in Predominantly Female[a] Occupations: 1964-1975

	1964			1975		
Expected Occupations	Male	Female	% Female	Male	Female	% Female
Plan to enter 12 occupations predominantly Female in 1964	128	937	88.0	68	559	89.2
Plan to enter 15 occupations predominantly Female in 1975	-	-	-	76	712	90.4
Total Responding	1124	1175		1093	1122	
% in (12) 1964 Female Occup.	11.4	79.7		6.2	49.8	
% in (15) 1975 Female Occup.	-	-		7.0	63.5	
Ideal Occupations						
Preference for 17 occupations predominantly Female in 1964	116	955	89.2	90	576	86.5
Preference for 18 occupations predominantly Female in 1975	-	-	-	86	713	89.2
Total Responding	1240	1259		1174	1201	
% in (17) 1964 Female Occup.	9.4	75.9		7.7	47.9	
% in (18) 1975 Female Occup.	-	-		7.3	59.4	

[a] Predominantly female occupations are those chosen by at least five respondents, at least 70% of whom were female.

girls expected to enter occupations that were preferred by one-third or more of their male peers in 1964. This is an appreciable change, consistent with our contemporary conceptions of changing sex role patterns.

However, table 4.6 also reveals a countertrend. While fewer girls expected to, or hoped to, enter occupations that were predominately female in 1964, by 1975 choices for a number of new sex-typed occupations[9] had emerged, which mitigated somewhat the female shift from the traditional sex-typed occupations. By 1975, 712, or 63.5%, of all girls expected to enter fifteen occupations that were predominantly female and that had a percentage female of 90.4%. The result of this is to reduce by only 16.2% the proportion of girls expecting to enter occupations predominantly female. The fact that only 7.0% of the boys expected to enter one of these predominantly female jobs in 1975 underscores the segregated nature of these new expectations and indicates that substantial pressures of sex-typed choice continued to exist in 1975.

That these pressures are not totally situational is revealed by the substantial percentage of girls (59.4%) who stated a preference for a predominantly female job in 1975. While this proportion is 4.1% less than the proportion

Table 4.7.

Concentration of Choices in Predominantly Male[a] Occupations: 1964-1975

Expected Occupation	1964			1975		
	Male	Female	% Male	Male	Female	% Male
Plan to enter 30 occupations						
predominantly Male in 1964	766	49	94.0	772	203	79.2
18 White Collar	469	45	91.2	390	191	67.1
12 Blue Collar	297	4	98.7	382	12	97.0
Plan to enter 24 occupations						
predominantly Male in 1975	-	-	-	644	67	90.6
11 White Collar	-	-	-	245	55	81.2
13 Blue Collar	-	-	-	399	12	97.1
Total Responding	1124	1175		1093	1122	
% in (30) 1964 Male Occup.	68.1	4.2		70.6	18.1	
% in (18) WC Male Occup.	41.7	3.8		35.7	17.0	
% in (12) BC Male Occup.	26.4	0.3		34.9	1.1	
% in (24) 1975 Male Occup.	-	-		58.9	6.0	
% in (11) WC Male Occup.	-	-		22.4	4.9	
% in (13) BC Male Occup.	-	-		36.5	1.1	
Ideal Occupation						
Preference for 30 occupations						
predominantly Male in 1964	885	118	88.2	815	239	77.3
20 White Collar	598	109	84.6	490	220	69.0
10 Blue Collar	-	-	-	350	20	94.6
Preference for 23 occupations						
predominantly Male in 1975	-	-	-	688	87	88.8
10 White Collar	-	-	-	338	67	83.5
13 Blue Collar	-	-	-	350	20	94.6
Total Responding	1240	1259		1174	1201	
% in (30) 1964 Male Occup.	71.4	9.4		69.4	19.9	
% in (20) WC Male Occup.	48.2	8.7		41.7	18.3	
% in (10) BC Male Occup.	23.1	0.7		27.7	1.6	
% in (23) 1975 Male Occup.	-	-		58.6	7.2	
% in (10) WC Male Occup.	-	-		28.8	5.6	
% in (13) BC Male Occup.	-	-		29.8	1.7	

[a]Predominantly male occupations are those chosen by at least five respondents, at least 70% of whom were male.

expecting a predominantly female occupation, the difference is small and does not support the idea that the substantial segregation exhibited in the 1975 choices reflects situational pressures running counter to the subjective preferences of these students. It appears that there are forces for continuation of occupational segregation that exist in the values and motivations of these students as well as in situations, and that they mitigate substantially the declining choice of traditional 1964 sex-typed occupations.

Concentration of preferences for occupations that are predominantly male reveals patterns that are different and even more complex than those of females (table 4.7).

In the first place, whereas female sex-typed occupations were almost all white collar, male sex-typed jobs are both white collar and blue collar, and as table 4.7 reveals, the patterns of change and stability are sharply differentiated by level of work. Change in the sex typing of predominantly male jobs occurs in the white-collar but not the blue-collar jobs. The proportion male in eighteen expected white-collar jobs dropped from 91.2% in 1964 to 67.1% in 1975, a change that reduced by exactly one-half the number of expected white-collar jobs predominantly male. On the other hand, the proportion male in twelve expected blue-collar jobs remained essentially constant: 98.7% in 1964 and 97.0% in 1975. Similar patterns appeared in the ideal occupational responses, where the sex typing of 1964 blue-collar occupations slightly increased from 97.0% to 97.3% in 1975.

The differentiation of change by level of occupation is a result of two reinforcing patterns: female entrance into the previously sex-typed white-collar occupations, and male shift from the white-collar occupations to the blue-collar jobs.

Table 4.7 shows that nearly all of the increased female preference for traditionally male occupations occurred among the white-collar jobs. Thus, in 1964, only 3.8% of the girls expected to enter one of the eighteen predominantly male white-collar occupations, but by 1975, 17.0% of the girls expected to enter one of those jobs, a substantial invasion of these originally segregated positions. However, the corresponding increase for blue-collar jobs was only from .3% to 1.1%. Similar, but less pronounced, patterns are observed in the ideal occupation responses. Girls expected to enter and preferred male white-collar but not blue-collar occupations. As in the other findings, this pattern is only slightly greater in the ideal than in the expected occupations, and does not support the idea of significant situational barriers to female choices of occupations they would ideally prefer.

The change in male orientations between 1964 and 1975 involves a reduction in the level of occupational expectations, and to a lesser degree in occupational preferences. The proportion of boys expecting or desiring to enter a sex-typed white-collar occupation declined between 1964 and 1975 while the proportion increased for the sex-typed blue-collar jobs.[10] The results of these shifts is that by 1975 substantially higher percentages of boys expected to and hoped to enter highly sex-typed blue-collar occupations in which, as we have observed, the proportion of males approaches 100%, but decreased proportions of boys expected or preferred to occupy predominantly male white-collar jobs. Overall, this results in a slight decrease in the proportion of males in predominantly male jobs.

The combined result of these patterns is a rough equivalency between the sexes. Whereas around 80% of the girls, but only about 70% of the boys, were in same-sex occupations in 1964, by 1975 roughly 60% of both sexes expected or preferred occupations predominantly chosen by members of their own sex. Thus, while the patterns are complex, by 1975 girls were not any more segregated than boys, although most of these students remained oriented toward occupations that are highly sex typed.

While this analysis has shown a reduction in sex typing of occupational orientations, the patterns are complex and do not reflect a simple convergence of male and female orientations. The stability of sex typing in the 1964 female jobs, the shift of female choice to the predominantly male white-collar jobs coupled with the shift of male choices out of those occupations into blue-collar jobs that remain highly sex typed, all indicate that insofar as these choices are eventually articulated in adult careers, it appears that female opportunity will increase, but that sex-typed and segregated occupational distributions may well persist, nevertheless.

Turning to the final analysis, table 4.8 presents the findings on the expected-ideal dissimilarity. These findings are consistent with the previous analysis in not indicating a strong sex-based difference between the occupations these students expected to go into and the occupations they would ideally prefer. Only about one-fifth of the boys and one-fourth of the girls would have to change their preferred occupations to produce harmony between preference and expectations. Difference between male and female dissimilarity scores is in the predicted direction in that females experience a somewhat greater discrepancy than males do, but the differences are small, 6.2% in 1964, 2.9% in 1975, and provide only limited support for the assumption that girls would seek a much broader range of occupational positions were consciously perceived situational constraints and barriers eliminated. Furthermore, the negligible shift from 1964 to 1975 in female expected-ideal dissimilarity scores does not suggest consciousness of improving options in attaining ideally desired occupations over this period.

The increasing variability in the options of both boys and girls appears in the number of occupations named in table 4.8. Both sexes, but especially girls, showed an increase in the number of occupations actually named. The result of this is to reduce the male-famale discrepancy in number of possible jobs. In 1964 girls named only 66% as many occupations as boys did, but

Table 4.8.

Dissimilarity of Expected-Ideal Occupational
Orientation Distributions by Sex and Year

	Males		Females	
Year	Index of Dissim.	Number of Occup.	Index of Dissim.	Number of Occup.
1964	20.4	83	26.6	55
1975	22.3	97	25.2	79

by 1975 this had increased to 81%. Thus, the overall patterns of table 4.8 support the proposition that change, reflecting increased female opportunity, is under way, although the magnitude of the effects is relatively small.

The Facilitating Variable, College Plan

Sex typing of choice, as expressed in the male-female dissimilarity scores, is considerably affected by college plan (table 4.9). The occupational choices of college-bound boys and girls are considerably more similar than the choices of noncollege-bound youth. This is true for both expected and ideal choices, although dissimilarity is lower in the distribution of ideal than expected, consistent with my original interpretations of the meaning of the ideal, expected terms. Not surprisingly, it appears that convergence in occupational choice has occurred primarily among college-bound youth. While there has

Table 4.9.

Dissimilarity Scores by College Plan

Dissimilarity Distribution		Dissimilarity Scores			Number of Occupations		
		No College Plan	College Tentative	College Definite	No College Plan	College Tentative	College Definite
Male-Female							
Expected	1964	84.3	76.7	61.4	68	58	51
	1975	79.1	66.1	50.6	80	64	66
Ideal	1964	84.7	68.4	55.6	70	65	58
	1975	74.7	58.4	48.0	90	61	66
Expected-Ideal							
male	1964	24.8	26.7	23.8	70	60	55
	1975	24.1	28.7	25.0	79	59	62
female	1964	30.0	34.1	23.7	38	34	43
	1975	31.0	36.1	22.0	70	49	51

been some noticeable improvement between 1964 and 1975, especially in the ideal patterns, nearly 80% of the expected choices of noncollege-bound boys or girls would have to be changed to produce comparable distributions. The choices of these students are certainly more segregated than integrated, even in 1975. For that matter the college-bound dissimilarity values of 50.6 and 48.0 still represent a substantial, albeit reduced, amount of segregation of occupational choice.

College plan has some small effect on the expected-ideal dissimilarity scores of girls (table 4.9). College-bound girls with definite plans are more likely to have occupational expectations in line with their preferences than are other girls, although there is little change in this pattern over the time period. The stability of these scores suggests that the benefit of college may lie more in the nature of jobs and perhaps the greater desirability of the college-qualified jobs than in college as the leading edge of sex role change in relating ideal and expected occupational orientations.

Summary and Conclusions

This analysis has observed change in the occupational orientations of high school girls between 1964 and 1975 that is consistent with general assumptions about changing sex roles involving increased opportunity and choice and resulting in convergence in the choices of boys and girls. We have also observed countervailing patterns pointing toward continued occupational segregation.

The changes in the choices and expectations of female students were generally consistent with propositions about changing sex roles formulated in terms of liberation and masculinization or convergence. Girls changed their orientations more between 1964 and 1975 than boys did, and these changes resulted in convergence in the distributions of occupational choice and preference of boys and girls as reflected by decreasing male-female dissimilarity scores. Girls also showed a greatly decreased orientation toward a limited number of traditionally female occupations, resulting in a reduction in the proportion of girls planning to enter sex-typed occupations. The potential size of this reduction was reduced by the emergence of new, predominantly female occupations, highly sex typed and involving relatively large numbers. Thus, changing patterns of female occupational choice suggested continued development of sex-typed occupations.

The changes in male orientations between 1964 and 1975 were considerably different from the female changes just described. The predominant change in orientation for male choice was from white-collar to blue-collar occupations, resulting in increased proportions of boys choosing highly sex-typed blue-collar occupations and a reduction in the proportion of those choosing sex-typed white-collar jobs. Furthermore, there was absolutely no movement of male preference and expectation toward the small number of occupations that had been sex-typed as female in 1964. While fewer students expected or desired to enter those jobs, the jobs themselves remained as sex-typed in 1975 as they had been in 1964. Finally, the skilled blue-collar jobs sex typed as male in 1964 remained almost totally male in 1975. Few girls expected to or desired to enter one of the predominantly male skilled blue-collar occupations.

The lack of movement into previously female occupations suggests a male resistance to processes of feminization, as does the male shift from previously male white-collar occupations being sought by girls in 1975 to the skilled blue-collar occupations that remain steadfastly masculine.

A number of circumstances could have accounted for these shifts: the war ended, as did the draft, making college less important to many of the boys; blue-collar crafts continued to become increasingly desirable occupations; and traditional patterns of apprenticeship operate to perpetuate masculine predominance in these occupations more effectively than in white-collar occupations reached through education and formal training in public schools.[11] However, and for whatever the reasons, male choices are shifting from the occupations being increasingly sought by women to those jobs their female peers have not yet chosen to any large degree.

Notwithstanding these somewhat complicated patterns and speculations, the result of the changes described was to reduce the sex typing of occupational orientations. By 1975, about 60% of both sexes expected to enter and preferred sex-typed occupations, a decline from 1964 levels of 20% for the girls and 10% for the boys. While these changes describe a pattern of role convergence, they also reveal a persisting substantial orientation toward sex-typed jobs. In 1975, the majority of these students expected to enter and prefer jobs in which over 70% of the incumbents were members of the same sex.

Finally, the analysis of differences between expected and ideal orientations provided some weak support for the proposition that girls experience more constraint on their occupational choices than boys do. Furthermore, the analysis revealed reduction in these differences consistent with the idea that liberating change is occurring and reducing the barriers that women, compared to men, faced. Overall, however, these effects were very weak, almost negligible. They certainly did not suggest important sex differences in the perception of contemporary situational constraints or limitations on ideal occupational preferences. Whatever constraints exist on choice appear to be in the socialization experiences themselves, not in the perception of contemporary obstacles as barriers between the conscious desires of these students and their expected attainments.

The effect of college plan reinforced some of these distinctions. Segregation of choice was least among the college bound, as was the discrepancy between ideal and expected. It appears that choices and options are less constrained for the college bound, as may be their underlying values and orientations.

ACHIEVEMENT

As I noted in the preceding chapter, the distinction between ascription and achievement and their ramifications in culture, society, and personality is one of the most important and widely discussed issues in the contemporary literature on sex roles and sex differences. In the most literal sense, the contemporary change in women's roles is a change from ascribed to achieved status, which might be expected to create the role conflicts and invidious comparisons between the sexes that are so common in the sex role literature. Men are seen as emerging from a sociocultural tradition reflecting long concerns with instrumental achievement patterns that women are just now developing. Consequently, female emphasis on achievement is seen as both nontraditional and conflicted.

Given these views, it is surprising that the empirical literature fails to provide strong support for male superiority in achievement patterns or achievement orientations. In fact, we have seen that many of the central ideas, such as the ahievement-affliative conflict, fear of success, differential achievement socialization, achievement orientations, and differences in status attainment appear not to be true. I have suggested that careful reading of this literature leads to quite different conclusions—that the sexes are equivalent or that women are even stronger achievers than men, excepting such themes as competitive strivings to win out over others. While competition is contrary to the supportive, nurturant elements in the sex role stereotypes, achievement, especially achievement channeled into helping and benefiting others, is not.

In this section I report the results of the analysis of achievement value orientations and briefly examine academic achievement as reflected by grade point. In the following section I consider sex differences and sex role change in educational and occupational attainment processes.[12]

Achievement Value Orientations

Achievement value orientations used in this study are presented in table 4.10. The items used in this research are taken from Rosen (1959) and reflect themes discussed by Kluckhohn (1969) as characteristics of modern American society. They are also seen as distinguishing male and female orientations because men have participated in and acquired the dominant values of individualism, activism, and future orientation while women have

Table 4.10.
Achievement Values by Sex, Year, and Sex by Year
(N=5334)

Achievement Value Items[a]	Average Achievement Value				Metric Regression Coefficients[b]			R²
	M	F	M	F	Sex	Year	Inter	
All a man should want out of life in the way of a career is a <u>secure</u>, not too difficult job, with enough pay to afford a nice car and eventually a home of his own.[c]	2.97	3.25	2.87	3.11	.28			.03
When a man is born the success he is going to have is already in the cards, so he might just as well <u>accept</u> it and not fight against it.[c]	3.53	3.69	3.30	3.51	.16	-.29		.04
The secret of happiness is not expecting too much out of life and being <u>content</u> with what comes your way.	2.74	2.77	2.67	2.66				.00
Nothing is worth the sacrifice of moving away from one's <u>parents</u>.	3.21	3.31	3.14	3.30	.09	-.15		.01
The best kind of a job to have is one where you are part of an <u>organization</u> all working together even if you don't get individual credit.	2.61	2.55	2.58	2.68	-.06	-.19	.16	.00
<u>Planning</u> only makes a person unhappy since your plans hardly ever work out anyway.	3.24	3.34	3.03	3.20	.10	-.29	.08	.03
Nowadays with world conditions the way they are, the wise person lives for <u>today</u> and lets tomorrow take care of itself.	3.21	3.23	2.80	2.79		-.37		.06
Total Score	21.5	22.1	20.4	21.2	.61	-1.40		.04

[a]High Scores represent disagreement and high achievement.

[b]Only the coefficients twice the standard error are reported.

[c]See Footnote 15 for discussion of the use of generic "man" in these items.

been socialized in the variant, substitute patterns of collectivism, passivism, and present orientation. The former are the characteristics of universalistic-achievement societies, the latter of particularistic-ascriptive societies.

In table 4.10, the first three items reflect passivistic orientations, the fourth and fifth, collectivistic, and the sixth and seventh, present orientation.

Results

Results of the analysis of sex differences and change in achievement value orientations are presented in table 4.10. Consistent with findings and inter-pretations about social changes between the 1960s and 1970s, the strongest effects in table 4.10 are due to time. Students in 1975 were considerably more passivistic and present-oriented and somewhat more collectivistic.

The observed sex differences are contrary to the Kluckhohn (1969) inter-pretations and to general views on sex differences in achievement. Girls showed an advantage over boys in five of the seven individual items and in the total score.[13] Surprising as it appears in the face of the literature on sex differences in achievement and success, girls were less passivistic, less con-cerned about maintaining contact with parents, and more oriented toward planning for the future. While the differences are not great, their presence in both of these large samples will require some reappraisal of assumptions about achievement orientations resulting from parental differentiation in the socialization of the sexes.[14]

Persistence of these differences over the 1964–1975 time period is shown in the lack of significant interactions and in the content of the two interac-tions that are statistically significant. While the 1964 values were stereotypic regarding working in an organization, by 1975 a reversal had occurred. Boys became slightly more accepting of organizational jobs, but girls markedly decreased their acceptance of such an achievement context. This shift is interesting considering the contrary patterns just observed with people ori-entation in the occupational values. Girls became somewhat more people-oriented over this period with respect to jobs, but less accepting of organi-zational achievement. People, but not organization, suggests the same sort of liberating, noninstitutional pattern observed in religion and contribution in the life goals. One theme of women's liberation may have taken root here—that social institutions and social organizations have been formulated by men and constrain female experience and success. Whether this is a cor-rect interpretation, the fact is clear enough that there is an intensification of the female advantage on the organization achievement value item.

The other significant interaction also intensified the female advantage, through the greater decline of male scores. Both sexes rejected planning more in 1975, but boys changed more, almost doubling the difference by 1975.

These findings are very similar to those of Veroff et al. (1980), showing that females, but not males, increased in achievement motivation between 1957 and 1975. While the present results show the decline in achievement orientations that would be expected by the value shifts of the late 1960s, the fact that girls had a significantly smaller decline in planning and actually increased on the organization item is consistent with the idea advanced by Veroff et al. that the women's movement exerted a press for feminine achievement that counteracted the declining emphasis on achievement and success in the late 1960s.

On the other hand, the higher score of girls in 1964 and the persistence of the differences in five of the seven value items suggest that higher achievement orientations may in fact be integral to the feminine sex role. It seems likely that "process achievement" (Veroff 1977) having to do with interest in the competent and responsible accomplishment of tasks may be very consistent with some elements of the female role, even though it is clearly contrary to most formulations of the instrumental-expressive distinction.

Facilitating Conditions

Analysis of the effects of the five facilitating variables reveals the now familiar pattern of chance outcomes. Only three of the thirty-five regressions include three-way interaction coefficients more than twice their standard error, one more than would be expected by chance at the .05 level. As in the preceding analyses of life goals and occupational values, the main finding is the absence of facilitation by the selected variables.

Similarly, the pattern of results just slightly hedges the conclusion of chance effects. Girls not reading newspapers decreased their score on content much more than did those reading newspapers, and female newspaper readers increased their score on organization more than nonreaders did, both findings consistent with the idea that media attention facilitates change. On the other hand, decrease in the value of planning was greatest among those girls with many scources of consultation.

These three equations are presented in appendix A, panel 3. All in all, they provide only the slightest support for the facilitation hypothesis.

Academic Achievement

Academic achievement superiority of girls has been discounted and, in some respects, explained away by writers viewing the pattern within the meaning of sex role stereotypes rather than from the perspective of achieving behaviors. On the one hand, the overwhelming female superiority in the attainment of higher academic grades has generally been ignored in discussions and explanations of masculine achievement predominance and of explanations for the failure of females to achieve. On the other hand, when it is considered, feminine academic achievement has often been discounted as another instance of conformity and trying to "please the teacher," as if socially acceptable achieving performances were somehow excluded from the domain of excellence and accomplishment.

As indicated by standardized grade point average, the overall academic achievement of girls is considerably higher than that of boys (table 4.11).[15] This appreciable difference appears in both years and is of the order of .4 of a standard deviation. When it comes to actual achieving performances over the years of high school, girls dramatically outperform boys, for whatever the reason. This substantial achievement superiority should be considered as central evidence in discussions about sex-related achievement patterns, and not discounted as evidence of feminine conformity. Regardless of motives, girls reveal a performance reflecting competence and skill in mastering the varied cognitive tasks underlying graded academic achievement that exceeds the male level appreciably.

The stability of this difference over the time period, when, as we shall see, actual grades increased overall, indicates that sex role processes under-

Table 4.11.

Academic Achievement[a] by Sex and Year

	1964	1975
Males	-.20	-.20
Females	.20	.19
F-Ratio	110.06	112.63
Number	(2685)	(2813)

[a]Overall GPA standardized by school and year.

lying the differences did not change over the period. This is another instance in which general change occurred while sex differences were maintained. In any event, the stability of the difference indicates that female academic superiority is not due to recent emphasis on assertion and achievement training of girls.

Summary and Conclusions

The results of this analysis show girls to have stronger achievement value orientations than boys and to maintain this advantage over the 1964–1975 period, actually increasing it in two cases in findings directly comparable to those of Veroff et al. (1980). These results are directly contrary to expectations about achievement orientations based on general ideas of the significance of ascription in feminine behavior and orientation and specifically to Kluckhohn's formulations of the substitute feminine culture. These data show that girls clearly have higher levels of achievement value orientations than boys do, a finding also observed in other research on college students (Lueptow 1980c). Inclusion of the facilitating variables revealed the now familiar chance pattern bolstered, however, by the meaningfulness of the observed significant relations. It appears that at least two of these value items reflect what we could assume to be the changing message of the media. Finally, we have again observed the very substantial female advantage in achieving academic performance. Contrary to all the discussion about role conflict and fear of success and feminine helplessness and dependence, these girls manifested higher levels of academic performance over the years of high school, in both time periods.

These results and the interpretation of similar findings elsewhere should lead to some rethinking about sex roles and achievement. They suggest that the interpretations up to now may be oversimplifying and misinterpreting the evidence on sex differences in achievement.

The results observed here are consistent with Maccoby and Jacklin's (1974:138) observation that continuing levels of female achievement motivation are higher than those of males and with their finding of no empirical support for commonly accepted assumptions about differential socialization for independence and achievement. The apparent discrepancy between my findings and other evidence on achievement orientations may also be a function of theoretical and measurement issues. The TAT achievement motivation scoring system includes winning in competition with others. This aspect of achievement is not assessed by the achievement value items derived initially from literature reflecting aspects of the Protestant ethic (Strotdbeck 1958). Part of the confusion in this area may arise from neglect of these differences between excellence and accomplishment on the one hand and winning in assertive, aggressive competition on the other. Females may be high achievers but weak competitors.

EDUCATIONAL AND OCCUPATIONAL ASPIRATIONS

Sex difference and change in educational and occupational aspirations are examined in two ways: (1) by considering the effect of sex on the level of educational and occupational aspirations, and (2) by considering the interaction between sex and the determinants of educational and occupational aspiration. The latter analysis involves separate treatments of the aspiration models by sex and year.

As I noted in the preceding chapter, previous work by Sewell and Shah (1968) has demonstrated important sex differences in aspiration and in the pattern of effects in the aspiration model. Rehberg and Rosenthal, whose work is most similar to the analysis of this section, found that sex differences in aspiration that had been observed in research going back to the 1950s still persisted in the 1970s, although these differences were relatively trivial.

Levels of Educational and Occupational Aspiration

Levels of educational and occupational aspiration are examined through the use of several different indicators. Educational aspiration or plan for college is usually based on the student's statement of a college plan. I use that measure but also distinguish between tentative and definite plans and analyze sex differences and change in applications and college acceptances of these pregraduation seniors. This enables us to distinguish between a reported plan and more concrete indicators such as actually making an application and receiving an acceptance from a college. Rehberg and Rosenthal's finding that sex differences persist in stated plans and aspirations but have largely disappeared in attainments may be due to such variation in the realism of the measure. Because of sex differences in confidence and expectancy, boys are more likely to state an unrealized or eventually unatainable goal than girls, who in spite of higher qualifications are less likely to feel confident about success in college. Occupational aspirations are based on expected and ideal responses that have already been described, although in this section I focus on the socioeconomic status level of the occupation. As before, I assume that ideal choices are less constrained by reality considerations, including conscious recognition of sex discrimination and similar related obstacles and should exhibit less sex differentiation than expected choices.

Results

Results of the analysis of educational aspirations are presented in tables 4.12 and 4.13. These tables are based on the total population and include nonresponses among the noncollege bound. The last row of table 4.12 contains the percentages of nonresponse that have been included in the table. It is clear that rates of nonresponse were much greater in 1964, especially for girls, one-third of whom skipped this item. In 1975, nonresponse was negligible and lower for girls than for boys.

The surprisingly high 1964 nonresponse rate of girls is difficult to account for. The possibility that it was an artifact of the differing rates of participation in 1964 and 1975 was considered. As the nonparticipants were disproportionately students with lower grade points, it seemed possible that the 1975 nonresponse rate was low because uncertain people, unlikely to respond to this item about college goals, were not actually in the study as they

Table 4.12.

Percentage ᵃ with Various Formulations of College
Aspiration (Including Missing Data)

Measure of	1964		1975	
College Plan	Males	Females	Males	Females
1. Definite and Tentative Plan	57.2	42.3	49.8	48.2
2. Definite Plan	38.5	28.6	32.4	31.5
3. Applied for Admission	38.0	30.1	32.2	34.2
4. Accepted	29.4	25.2	28.0	29.8
Number	(1393)	(1380)	(1405)	(1422)
% Non Response on Definite and Tentative Plan	10.7	32.5	4.8	3.7

ᵃPercentage in the first four rows of the table are based on total population, including non-respondents.

Table 4.13.

Level of Educational Aspiration by Sex, Year, and Sex by Year

Educational	Metric Coefficients[b]				
Aspiration[a]	Constant	Sex	Year	Interaction	R^2
Tentative or Definite Plan	.57	-.15	-.07	.13	.01
Definite Plan Only	.38	-.10	-.06	.09	.01
Applied for Admission	.38	-.08	-.06	.10	.00
Accepted	.29	-.04		.06	.00

[a]all aspirations coded: 0=not, 1=aspiration.

[b]only coefficients twice the standard error are reported.

were in the 100% participation group of 1964. However, comparative analysis using only the 18-year-old group, whose rate of response in 1975 was much higher than the 17-year-olds, who required parental consent, failed to reveal any important difference in rate of response to this question. The comparative rates of nonresponse in 1975 were 11.6, 32.2, 5.0, 4.0, all within 1% of nonresponse rates for the total population of participants as reported in table 4.12. Thus, the low female nonresponse rate in 1975 could not have been due to nonparticipation in the study. Were that the cause, the rate of nonresponse would have been higher among the higher participation group (now including more of the low grade-point average uncertains) than among the population as a whole. This was clearly not the case.

If we assume that the nonresponses are uncertain and possibly conflicted about their post-high school goals, it seems reasonable to treat them as not having the plans, applications, or acceptances. Students undecided about their plans would seemingly be more likely to avoid answering the question(s) than would those who clearly expected to go on to college or who had been accepted by a college. Nonresponses are coded as not having one of these plans or acceptances.

Table 4.12 shows sex difference, reality effects, and social change. In 1964 substantially higher percentages of boys reported at least tentative plans to attend college. Fifty-seven percent of the boys compared to 42% of the girls had at least tentative college plans, proportions very similar to the 60% and 43% of boys and girls who had made a decision to attend college in Rehberg and Rosenthal's (1978) study of 1970 high school seniors. The decreasing sex difference from tentative plans to acceptance is also consisistent with their finding that while college decisions remained sex differentiated, college entry was not. They found that more boys planned to go to college, but equal proportions of boys and girls actually entered colleges. The analogous pattern in our case shows steadily decreasing sex differences, a pattern mirrored in the declining regression coefficients in table 4.13. These shifts are consistent with observed sex differences in reported self-confidence and anxiety (Maccoby and Jacklin 1974). Male self-confidence, and possibly needs for self-promotion and assertion, may lead to overstatement of goals while female lack of confidence may preclude such display. However, in the final analysis, getting accepted, the attitudinal factors become irrelevant and sex differences diminish, although they do not totally disappear.

These tables (4.12 and 4.13) also show social change and sex role change. Male plans, and to a lesser extent, male acceptances decline over the period while female aspirations increase. These interactions eliminate or reverse the 1964 differences. By 1975 nearly the same proportions of boys and girls had definite plans while slightly higher proportions of girls had applied for admission and been accepted by at least one college.

Similar patterns are observed in level of occupational aspiration (tables 4.14, 4.15). While the differences and effects are trivial in scope, girls had lower occupational aspirations in 1964 and higher aspirations in 1975. Male

Table 4.14.

Average Status of Ideal and Real Occupational Preferences by Sex and Year

Occupational Chair	1964		1975	
	Male	Female	Male	Female
Expected	56.7	52.8	52.6	55.6
Ideal	59.0	54.1	55.6	57.0

Table 4.15.

Level of Occupational Aspiration by Sex, Year, and Year by Sex

Occupation	Metric Coefficients				
	Constant	Sex	Year	Interaction	R^2
Expected	56.7	-3.98	-10.9	6.92	.00
Ideal	59.1	-5.13	-10.0	6.54	.01

level of occupational aspiration declined (recall the shift from white-collar to blue-collar sex-typed jobs previously reported) while female levels increased, creating relatively pronounced interaction effects, although not any appreciable explanation of variance. The coefficients of determination in table 4.15 are nearly zero.

The higher mean status of ideal, compared to expected occupational choices, is consistent with our assumptions that ideal choices are less constrained, although the differences are again very small. However, extending the assumption to female choice again fails to support the commonly held assumption that girls would aspire to higher levels were discrimination and group restraints removed. Girls increased the level of choice from expected to ideal somewhat less than boys did, and this is true for both years. In addition, there is no sense of greater increase between 1964 and 1975 for ideal rather than expected choices. It appears that whatever constraints operate on the choices of these girls, they must be internalized and not consciously perceived as these students consider their vocational futures.

Facilitating Variables

Facilitating variable analysis fails to show any significant effects of intelligence, father's education, mother's work status, number of consultants, or newspaper reading on college plain,[16] ideal occupational aspiration, or expected occupation. Not one of the fifteen three-way interaction coefficients of sex-by-year-by-facilitating variable was larger than two standard errors. The relatively small but consistent changes observed here were not intensified by any of the facilitating variables.

Determinants

This final section reports the sex differences and sex role change in the determinants of educational and occupational aspiration or plan. As in Rehberg and Rosenthal's (1978) analysis, this is accomplished by four separate analyses of aspirations for each sex and year. Interactions are examined by inspection of the differences between relevant partial regression coefficients. Facilitating variable analysis of the model are not attempted as the results to this point do not warrant the complex and costly analysis that would be required.

The model to be studied here is that segment of the general status attainment model having to do with educational and occupational aspirations (Sewell and Shah 1968; Alexander, Eckland, and Griffen 1975; Rehberg and Rosenthal 1978). This model holds that family background factors such as parental education and occupational status and family size, along with intelligence, determine academic performance levels, which in turn affect parental and others' encouragement and level of educational and occupational aspiration.

Parental and others' encouragement are not available in this data set, but I examine the effects of the family background factors of size of family and father's and mother's work status. Mother's work status is treated through dummy variable analysis in which mothers in occupations having Duncan's Socioeconomic Index scores between 40 and 86 are coded 1 on the variable MOHI. Mothers with occupations having SEI scores between 6 and 39 are coded 1 on the variable MOLO. Nonworking, presumably homemaking, mothers consequently are the criterion group. This dummy variable analysis permits observation of effects due to mothers working and also effects due to the level of the mother's occupation.[17] This approach permits a single analysis incorporating both working and nonworking mothers, the later of whom lack occupational status scores.

This analysis also differs by incorporating achievement orientations along with ability. While there is no definite rationale for ordering the achievement-related factors, the substantive and theoretical background work (see Strodtbeck 1958; Rosen 1956, 1959) has treated achievement value orientations as consequences of class-related cultural themes and as antecedent to academic achievement and aspirations. I follow this approach and treat achievement values and intelligence as consequences of the family background factors[18] and as antecedent to grade point and educational and occupational aspiration.

The four separate analyses of educational and occupational aspiration are presented in table 4.16. Pairwise deletion of missing data was used to preserve cases across the substantial missing data for family income and less numerous but still frequent missing data on mother's occupation and intelligence.[19]

As earlier analysis (Lueptow 1975) has shown, family background is more important in determining the 1964 level of achievement value orientations of boys than of girls, although in neither case do these variables account for any appreciable part of the variation in achievement value items. By 1975, female achievement values were slightly more determined than male, although the difference does not reach any accepted level of statistical significance. Intelligence is more determined by family background than the achievement values are, especially for the girls. Grade point is determined about equally for girls and boys, more so in 1964 than in 1975. The sexes

Table 4.16.

Family, Personal, and Educational Determinants of Educational and Occupational Aspiration (Standardized Coefficients)*

(Males – 1964)

Independent Variables	VACH	IQ	GPA	ED ASP	OCC ASP	N
SIBS		-.12	-.08	-.08		(1393)
FED		.17		.14		(1356)
MED	.12	.13				(1368)
FOCC	.07	.11	.07			(1304)
INC				.08		(1089)
MOLO						(1393)
MOHI						(1393)
VACH	–	–	.07	.10	.08	(1331)
IQ	–	–	.60	.12	.16	(1165)
CPA	–	–	–	.40	.47	(1329)
ED ASP	–	–	–	–		(1393)
R²	.04	.12	.48	.46	.44 (1104)	

(Males – 1975)

Independent Variables	VACH	IQ	GPA	ED ASP	OCC	N
SIBS				-.06		(1405)
FED	.14	.18		.14		(1300)
MED						(1316)
FOCC					.16	(1247)
INC	.08	.12				(1050)
MOLO						(1405)
MOHI						(1405)
VACH	–	–	.13	.14		(1317)
IQ	–	–	.53	.10		(1307)
CPA	–	–	–	.31	.12	(1395)
ED ASP	–	–	–	–	.46	(1405)
R²	.04	.08	.38	.32	.40 (1089)	

(Females – 1964)

Independent Variables	VACH	IQ	GPA	ED ASP	OCC ASP	N
SIBS		-.08	-.09			(1380)
FED		.08		.17		(1351)
MED		.16		.11		(1360)
FOCC		.12		.13		(1316)
INC						(850)
MOLO						(1380)
MOHI						(1380)
VACH	–	–		.07	.17	(1327)
IQ	–	–	.66	.10	.20	(1174)
GPA	–	–	–	.30	.33	(1356)
ED ASP	–	–	–	–		(1380)
R²	.03	.09	.52	.38	.30 (1175)	

(Females – 1975)

Independent Variables	VACH	IQ	GPA	ED ASP	OCC ASP	N
SIBS	-.09	-.11				(1372)
FED	.15	.10		.19		(1383)
MED		.10		.14		(1292)
FOCC		.08		.10		(849)
INC		.11				(1422)
MOLO						(1422)
MOHI						(1359)
VACH	–	–				(1347)
IQ	–	–	.59	.12	.15	(1418)
GPA	–	–	–	.10	.14	(1422)
ED ASP	–	–	–	–	.11	
R²	.05	.11	.41	.28	.16 (1117)	

* only coefficients where B is twice the standard error are reported

differ in the effect of achievement values, which are more important to the grades of boys than of girls, and the minor differences in the effect of intelligence. These differences are consistent with the idea that girls' grades are earned by application and effort. These results suggest that boys need to have higher achievement values than girls to realize their potential. Except for slight family effects in 1964, no other factors are important to the determination of grades once intelligence is in the equation.

Turning to the main issues of educational and occupational aspiration, we observe in table 4.16 that male educational aspiration is more determined than female in 1964, although by 1975 this difference is halved. The main effect across the years is the decline in determination of educational aspirations by family, achievement, and aptitude measures. By 1975 only about one-quarter to one-third of the variation in college plan was accounted for by these variables.

The pattern of the partial regression coefficients reveals two sex-differentiated effects. In the first place, and consistent with earlier findings by Sewell and Shah (1968) and Alexander, Eckland, and Griffen (1975), but contrary to Rehberg and Rosenthal's (1978) more recent finding, family background is slightly more important to the 1964 educational aspirations of girls than of boys, while the achievement and ability variables are more important to the aspirations of boys. Directly contrary to Rehberg and Rosenthal's (1978:230) suggestions of trends away from this pattern are the 1975 effects, which reveal an intensification of family influences on the female aspirations and of abilities on the male aspirations. By 1975, parental education and paternal occupation became relatively more important determinants for both girls and boys, but, independent of family background, academic achievement became increasingly unimportant for girls. Finally, contrary to widespread assumptions about the effect of mother's work on sex role change,[20] neither her work status per se nor her level of occupational status result in any significant increment in grades or educational aspiration. These are surprising findings, running counter to various assumptions about changing sex roles.

The failure to observe any effect of mother's work on student, especially female aspiration in this study when the effect of mother's work in sex role socialization and development processes is so widely assumed, may be due to differences in the populations studied. The bulk of the previous work, and the several most significant studies, have been based on college women, in some instances on women in women's colleges who report retrospectively on influences. Few of the studies examine the independent effect of mother's work in equations containing other measures of aptitude, socioeconomic status, and achievement orientations. It may be that in general, more heterogeneous populations like that in my study, mother's work is associated with intelligence and other factors and is not the important instigator of change it is held to be in the sex role literature.[21]

The sharp decline in the importance of grade-point average on college aspiration may be an artifact and possibly reflect a change in teachers' grade-expectancy processes. As we will see in the analysis of academic achievement, there was a substantial increase in the level of grades awarded in 1975 as compared to 1964. With the distribution shifted toward the top of the range, the reduced variance may account for some of the reduction in the association between grades and aspiration. It is also possible that these changing relationships reflect the increasing heterogeneity of college populations and various reasons for college attendance, not all of which have to do with aptitude. The relative increase in the effect of achievement values, less important than intelligence in 1964, but more important in 1975, seems roughly consistent with these ideas.

The relative increase in the importance of family background for girls as compared to boys is hard to explain, especially as father's education is the most important determinant outside of grade-point average for both sexes. This relative increase is also inconsistent with the view expressed by Bandura (1969) and myself (Lueptow 1975) that sources of change in traditional sex roles would most likely be outside the family. However, it is consistent with the general assumption that sex roles are more sharply differentiated at lower socioeconomic status levels. Thus, Sewell and Shah (1968) found that the educational aspirations of girls and boys were relatively similar in college-educated families, but relatively different in families with less than high school education. Perhaps more to the point is the idea that girls are more controlled by families and occupy ascribed roles. These factors make family characteristics more significant for girls than for boys. Thus, as parental socioeconomic status increases, heightened aspirations for children may affect girls in ascribed positions to a greater extent than boys. This would be especially likely if, as Schreiber (1978) argues, education determines the amount of attention given to the media, which carries the message of sex role change. For girls this appears to result in substantial family background effects, which, unlike those of the boys, are on the same order of significance as achievement and aptitude. In any event, whether my speculations are correct or not, table 4.16 reveals a heightened family influence and reduced effect of achievement patterns for girls but not for boys.

We turn finally to occupational aspirations, which are being used in this study for the occupational attainments more commonly presented in the status attainment literature. Research has shown, somewhat unexpectedly, that the effect of education on occupational status attainment is similar for women and men (McClendon 1976; Treiman and Terrell 1975a).

Table 4.16 reveals a sharply sex-differentiated pattern of determinants of occupational aspiration over the time period. For boys, high school grade point and, especially, educational aspiration were the major determinants, although in 1964 achievement values and in 1975 father's occupation were also important. However, the main factor was educational aspiration, and that remained constant for boys. Unlike the boys, female occupational aspiration was affected by intelligence, and to a slightly greater degree than educational aspirations were affected. However, educational aspiration was much less important for girls, declining dramatically between 1964 and 1975 in sharp contrast to the consistency of the pattern among the boys. The result is to reduce considerably the already low female coefficient of determination of occupations. Unlike the findings in the status attainment literature, female educational plan is less strongly related to occupational plan, a relationship that became very low by 1975. Status level of female occupational expectation in 1975 was not strongly related to anticipated college attainment.

This pattern is unexpected and contrary to the findings already discussed that have shown similar patterns of status attainment for women and men (McClendon 1976; Treiman and Terrell 1975a), especially considering the very sharp decline in the effect of education observed in 1975.

In the attempt to account for this unexpected finding, a number of things come to mind. In the first place, it is possible that plans do not stand for attainments, especially for girls, and that the coefficients of concern here are not basically comparable to those reported in prior research. While this is certainly possible, it seems unlikely that such considerable differences could occur given the high correlations between plans and attainment and by the relatively strong and stable educational effects observed among the boys over the two years.

Other possible explanations have to do with the nature of the populations. The typical status attainment study excludes homemakers. In the present case, high school seniors who will become homemakers are included and their occupational aspirations analyzed along with those of seniors who will go into the labor force and would have been included in the typical status attainment study. It is possible that the educational aspirations of the future homemakers may be unrealistic or less meaningful and less related to college plans. For homemakers, college might have more to do with family and social class processes than with status attainment. Unfortunately, this question was not directly put to these respondents. However, a weak test of the proposition can be made using the life goal responses, and assuming that future homemakers will be unlikely to list occupation as their major life goal and more likely to list marriage and the family. The regressions reported in table 4.16 were calculated separately for those listing occupation as most important and for those listing marriage as most important life goal. The preceding explanation leads to the hypothesis that the education-occupation coefficient would be weaker for the girls oriented toward marriage and the family. This turned out not to be the case. The coefficient of occupational determination for the job-oriented was .14, for the family-oriented, .18.

The population of this study also differs from previous work in being a single age cohort, rather than a heterogeneous collection of people in the labor force. The research by Sewell, Hauser, and Wolf (1980) is also of a single age group, the 1957 Wisconsin high school seniors, and they also find education to be a more important determinant of the status of the first job for boys than for girls (regression coefficients 7.215 for boys, 3.783 for girls). Consequently, their observation in explaining this difference would apply here also. At lower educational levels, women are more likely to obtain clerical and other white-collar jobs of higher status than the blue-collar jobs of men. Conversely, at higher levels, men are more likely to obtain higher status professional jobs in engineering, accounting, and law than women are in education, social work, and nursing. In these terms, the decline in the effect of education would suggest a strong increase in the sex typing of status attainment that would substantially mitigate the significance of the higher educational aspiration levels observed in 1975.

Finally, it is possible that these 1975 results reflect real change in the process of status attainment for women in the middle of the 1970s that has not been reported yet, that the advantage that men experience from education in initial job placement observed in Sewell's 1957 cohort has intensified and become the dramatic difference observed here. At present, however, I am aware of no research reporting the late 1970s attainment of a cohort of high school seniors who graduated in the mid-1970s.

Summary and Conclusions

This section has examined sex differences and sex role change in levels of educational and occupational aspiration and in the determinants of educational and occupational aspiration. The results have generally shown sex role change through decreasing male and increasing female aspirations. These changes have been affected by the concreteness of the academic aspirations in that the greatest sex differences occurred through the male advantage in tentative plans, but largely disappeared in the more concrete indicators of making application and being accepted by at least one college. By 1975, higher proportions of girls than of boys had made applications and been accepted by at least one college.

Sex role change was also observed in occupational aspirations. The 1964 male advantage in both ideal and expected occupations gave way to female advantages by 1975 for both categories. These patterns were generally similar for ideal and expected and failed to suggest important differences attributable to contemporary perceptions of obstacles and barriers to occupational attainment.

Finally, none of the five facilitating variables had any significant effect on these changes in educational and occupational aspirations, although it should be recalled that these effects were weak to begin with.

Analysis of the determinants of educational and occupational aspiration within the conceptual frame of the status attainment research showed a number of sex differences, several of which were unexpected. Consistent with earlier research, but inconsistent with more recent research by Rehberg and Rosenthal (1978), social class variables were slightly more important determinants of female aspiration while grades and ability were more important to male aspirations. These patterns sharpened somewhat by 1975, contrary to the idea that achievement principles were replacing family ascription for girls. By 1975, family background factors, with the notable exception of mother's occupational status, were as important to the educational aspirations of girls as were grade point and intelligence, just the opposite of the male pattern, where grade point was by far the most important determinant. However, the notion of ascribed determinants of female aspiration may be mitigated somewhat by the relevance of parental socioeconomic status to the factor of media attention. Family impact may be more due to attention to the women's liberation theme in the media than to traditional ideas of family role ascription.

Occupational aspirations, which, as we have seen, were lower for males in 1975, were more determined by educational aspiration and ability for boys than for girls. This was an appreciable effect in which the male coefficient of determination of expected occupational status was 2.5 times that of the female. As the male coefficients were generally of the same order as those reported in the status attainment literature for occupational status (see McClendon 1976:58), it seemed clear that sex-related differences between aspirations and attainment might be involved.

I have considered several explanations for this unexpected finding but have been unable to satisfactorily explain the effect. It seems likely that sex differences in the link itself are involved and that these differences have to do with the sex typing of work that makes education less important to the occupational status of the female's first job. It is clear that this effect has increased dramatically over the period. If aspirations do stand for attainments, there is a clear suggestion here of markedly increasing sex role differentiation in the status attainment process that should be examined in future research.

CHAPTER 5

SEX TYPING IN ACADEMIC PREFERENCES AND ACHIEVEMENT

Some of the most clearly documented differences between the sexes occur in patterns of academic preference and achievement and in the cognitive skills that underly them. While some of the early interpretations of these differences have more recently come under question, the overal patterns are relatively clear and, as I noted in chapter 3, are roughly consistent with the general outlines of the sex role stereotypes. Women and men exhibit cognitive patterns and intellectual performances that seemingly reflect the main elements of the sex role stereotypes as they appear in the research previously summarized. The female stereotype is categorized by factors emphasizing interpersonal relations, nurturance, and dependence, the male by the factors of aggressiveness and instrumental task orientation.

Bernard (1981:24–30) has used the traditional-modern distinction to distinguish the spheres of women and men, observing that, like traditional cultures, the women's sphere is characterized by ascription, diffuseness, particularism, collectivity orientation, and affectivity (Bernard 1981:24–27). This pattern emphasizes personalized relations in a primary group context or Gemeinschaft, where emotion, feeling, and relationship are more important than understanding, planning, and control of external environments. The male sphere, on the other hand, involves concern with tasks, with external, extrafamilial patterns, and is characterized by achievement, universalism, specificity, affective neutrality, and individualism. In the most general terms, women have been concerned with personal relations, men with comprehension and control of the external environment.[1]

While there are no explicit accepted theoretical statements linking the content of the stereotypes with the empirically derived literature on cognitive differences, it does seem possible that aspects of masculine and feminine culture may reflect conditions and circumstances leading to the development of one or another cognitive pattern. This appears most likely in such areas as the sex typing of work, where women have been heavily concentrated in occupations involving interpersonal relations and service while men have more often held mechanical, technical, and scientific occupations requiring quantitative and spatial skills. There have, of course, been clear execptions to this in such roles as male lawyer and female laboratory assistant.

I have followed Bernard's lead and used distinctive aspects of personalized versus rationalized spheres as background devices for the interpretation of observed differences. While it is well beyond the concerns of this work to attempt theoretical integration of these dimensions, such a framework at least provides the heuristic benefit of an enabling conceptual scheme and points toward the coherence in these divergent representations.

REVIEW OF THE LITERATURE: SEX ROLES AND ACADEMIC PREFERENCES AND PERFORMANCES

The following sections summarize the evidence on sex-related cognitive patterns, taking special note of shifts of interpretation and new evidence that have recently occurred. I give special emphasis to the substantial summaries of Maccoby and Jacklin (1974), notwithstanding the criticisms of the work that raise questions about its authority (Block 1976; Sherman 1975). Whatever the final reckoning may be, it is certainly true that at the present time the Maccoby and Jacklin work is the major summary of empirical literature on sex differences, as recent usage by Seward and Seward (1980) and Wittig and Petersen (1979) attests.

As I have noted, the errors in the work may not be debilitating, for the gist of Block's (1976) detailed critique is that Maccoby and Jacklin's work understates the level of sex difference that actually exists.

Other major sources used in the following review are the works by Sherman (1978), Seward and Seward (1980), and Wittig and Petersen (1979) on cognitive differences and the reports from the National Assessment of Educational Progress.[2] Other more recent individual studies are treated only if they are not subsumed in these major reviews.

Intelligence and Cognitive Style

Overall intelligence and cognitive style appear not to vary between the sexes.

Intelligence

The absence of sex differences in intelligence is partly a function of test standardization, partly a function of differing abilities (Maccoby and Jacklin 1974). Intelligence tests have often been constructed so that overall sets of items produce equivalent scores for males and females, even though the sexes show differentiated abilities in verbal and quantitative subsections.

Maccoby and Jacklin concluded that "the sexes do not differ consistently in tests of total (or composite) abilities through most of the age range studied (1974:65)." However, examination of Maccoby and Jacklin's table 3.1 categorized on age results in the rejection of their contention that test differences are limited to children under 7 years of age. Following Block's (1976) approach, we can see that in the thirty-four studies of children under 7, girls score higher in eight, boys in one (34, F = .24, M = .03), while somewhat higher proportions prevail among children 7 and over (23, F = .30, M = .09). While the differences are not great, they are consistent with Maccoby and Jacklin's conclusion that where differences in mental ability appear, they favor girls, probably because of the importance of verbal items in general tests of mental ability. Jensen (1980) has reached the same conclusion for sex differences in general intelligence. When the sexes do differ, he concludes that the differences reflect the verbal component in tests. Jensen notes that tests are designed to produce equivalent scores for males and females, but even those tests constructed without regard to sex differences, such as Thurstone's Primary Mental Abilities and Raven's Progressive Matrices, fail to show any appreciable difference in overall intelligence between the sexes.

Cognitive Style

One of the most interesting and suggestive ties between sex role stereotypes and cognitive processes lies in the parallels between the characteristics of traditional societies, lower-class populations, and themes in the sex role stereotypes and women's culture as described by Bernard (1971, 1975, 1981). As I have noted, traditional societies, lower classes, and feminine subcultures can be described as ascriptive and particularistic compared to the universalistic-achievement patterns of modern urban-industrial societies, middle classes, and masculine stereotypes and subcultures. In each case, there is a comparison between a relatively circumscribed, personalized, Gemeinschaft way of life and a less restricted, more differentiated, and opportunistic Gesellschaft way of life. In each case, the central feature seems to be person-oriented relations in primary contexts of loyalty and and commitment that are sharply contrasted to the less personalized, more open networks of relationships organized around externalized tasks or purposes that often reflect operations designed to utilize natural laws or principles to control or modify some aspect of nature. The long-term experience of women in all societies has been within households, where personalized relations predominate and universal, nature-based principles are less directly relevant, although by no means absent.

While no one has, to my knowledge, developed the cognitive implications of these distinctions within the context of sex roles, there are some rather direct analogies to work done in social class differences in cognitive development. Of special interest here are the rich theoretical formulations of Bernstein (1971) and their generalization by Cohen (1968).

Bernstein (1971) has drawn cognitive significance from linguistic patterns that are in turn consequences of behavioral demands inherent in status-based and universalistic modes of social relations. The personalized relationships of the Gemeinschaft context occur between persons occupying clear and relatively undifferentiated statuses. In these primary contexts, individuals know each other (or in the family, the statuses involved), comprehend the circumstances of the group's experience and history, and establish emotional commitments to each other. In such a context, the major demands on actors are to show loyalty and relationship. The needs for new information about the situation and the other actors are relatively low. In such a context, demands on language are minimal and result in a simple structure and low level of differentiation, a restricted code. Unmitigated use of a restricted code through socialization and development results in a global orientation toward objects and circumstances. People trained in such contexts are less able to detect and comprehend subtle cues, the significance of parts, or the relations and connections between elements. Viewing the world from the perspective of self through relatively general concepts and meanings results in a global cognitive style more appropriate to diffuse, particularistic relations than to complex universalistic patterns of high discrimination or specificity. Traditional women's roles within the family reflected such a circumstance and are contained within the stereotype of feminine personalization and consequent illogic in the face of universalistic standards.[3]

The Gesellschaft context, on the other hand, places individuals in highly differentiated, often unfamiliar, contexts where meanings and understandings are not obvious reflections of well-known personal or status relations. In such contexts, which typically involve cognitive activity and continuous, affectively neutral treatment of abstractions and models, a greater burden is placed on language. It can no longer convey simply feelings, commitments, and loyalties, it must communicate situationally unique information and meaning. Such a language constitutes an elaborated code, which is the language of the secular institutions in a modern, rationalized, highly complex society. Use of an elaborated code results in a cognitive style involving sensitivity to and perception of parts and the relationships between parts, i.e., an analytic cognitive style. People socialized in contexts with elaborated codes learn to see the elements of objects and events within their own context, independent of the relationship to the observer. This is the mental orientation of the universalistic-achievement system with its emphasis on cognitive over affective components.

Bernstein (1971) and others (Cohen 1968; Hess and Shipman 1969) have asserted that lower-class youth develop in contexts where restricted codes constitute the major carrier of communication. Middle-class youth, on the other hand, develop in contexts that have elaborated as well as restricted codes. Restricted codes are used within routinized family and friendship groupings, elaborated codes in schools, organizations, and associations where cognitive concerns take precedence. As they move between the two contexts, middle-class youth develop an analytic cognitive style and they also develop the ability to take diverse roles. Bernstein held that "the ability to switch codes controls the ability to switch roles" (1971:129). These socially based cognitive differences were seen as underlying the differences in academic performance of youth from different class levels.

The analogy to sex roles is relatively direct. Traditional women's roles have involved particularistic relations within the family as a primary group where ascribed status prevails and personal knowledge of others reduces the need for highly structured communications and information exchanges. Like the middle-class youth, the husband shifts back and forth between the status-based primary relations within the family and the more differentiated and flexible circumstances of the broader, universalistic-achievement society. While the husband shifts roles and codes in this manner, his involvement in the particularistic family roles is considerably less complete than that of his wife. In fact, even when the employed wife shifts roles, she still maintains primary responsibility for family and household matters.

The outcome of these processes would be consistent with the general assumption about sex-related cognitive styles. Women would be seen to be more global, men more analytic. Women, operating within particularistic contexts, would also be more emotional and perhaps impulsive, behaving according to immediate feelings and interpersonal circumstances rather than constant principles or rules based on external arrangements. Men would be more rational, logical, and objective, behaving more often according to the meanings of extended structures of relationships and events and the concepts that describe them.

While not as clearly related to context, ability within particularistic contexts would probably involve perceptual and memory skills while the mental abilities underlying universalistic patterns would necessarily involve the ability to reason and relate to abstract categories and systems of relationship. Such socially based differences in mental ability have been described by Jensen (1974) in accounting for differences in learning between the American middle class and various disadvantaged groups. Disadvantaged children do not differ from advantaged children as much in Type I intelligence, involving repetition and memorization, as they do in Type II intelligence, involving reasoning and abstracting.

Plausible and interesting as some of these formulations are, they are not confirmed by research evidence on sex differences in cognitive style. On the other hand, some of the differences that are observed in cognition and, as we shall see, in mathematics and science, are roughly consistent with these stereotypic distinctions.

According to Maccoby and Jacklin (1974), there is not much evidence on the central issue of analytic cognitive style, and what evidence there is fails to support the proposition. Only one among the six studies of sex differences in analytic-descriptive groupings does in fact show a difference, although that one study shows difference in the male direction.

Evidence on impulsiveness or lack of inhibition, which should be greater in those playing the more affective, particularistic role, runs exactly counter to the proposition. While the differences are few, in the thirty-seven studies reported by Maccoby and Jacklin (1974), plus six more located by Block (1976), males are more impulsive than females. They are less able to defer gratification, less able to inhibit a previously dominant response, and more likely to give a quick, incorrect match of figures differing in small, less apparent details (43, M = .33, F = .07). Similar differences prevail in the six studies of youth aged 11 to 21 reported by Maccoby and Jacklin (6, M = .18, F = .00). Thus, there is no evidence to date supporting the propositions that females are more spontaneous and impulsive than males.

Indirect and somewhat equivocal evidence on expected cognitive differences does appear in restructuring and spatial visualization or perception. This evidence tends to support the proposition but can be interpreted from the perspective of differences in independence, assertion, and self-confidence as well as from a cognitive perspective. In addition, the nature of the evidence provides clearer support for differences along the dimensions of spatial differentiation than for differences in cognitive style.

Differences in spatial abilities are assessed in several ways, some having more relevance to the preceding cognitive distinctions than others, but all reflecting greater male ability to deal with components of configurations, either through identification or the manipulation of elements in space. In analytic tests, males are less field dependent, more able to locate an embedded figure, and more able to perform mental manipulations of spatial relations. As with other sex-related abilities, these differences are absent or minimal in the early years, becoming pronounced only around 10 to 12 years of age. Thus, among children 10 or under, Maccoby and Jacklin (1974) find only a slight masculine advantage (29, M = .21, F = .10), but among youths eleven and over, the differences are obvious in showing a male advantage (35, M = .54, F = .00). They report no studies of spatial analytic abilities for the older group in which females score higher.

Masculine advantage also appears in studies of nonanalytic spatial visualization that involve matching shapes, puzzles, maze performances, and reproduction of spatial relations, none of which requires appreciable internal mediation of the perceived elements. Age is again important, for while there are no sex differences in nonanalytic spatial skills below the age of 11 (24, F = .08, M = .04), above that age the results of the few studies reported by Maccoby and Jacklin (1974) are remarkably consistent (11, M = .73, F = .00). These results are bolstered by the findings obtained in studies of nonanalytic spatial ability since Maccoby and Jacklin's review. Wittig and Petersen (1979) report that six more recent studies generally support the Maccoby and Jacklin conclusions. Only Fennema and Sherman (1977) failed to find significant differences in spatial abilities among adolescent youth. While Sherman (1978) questions the importance of the degree of difference observed here and in other instances of unequivocal findings of sex difference,[4] for whatever reason there do seem to be clearly demonstrated differences between the sexes on spatial skills.

Finally, Maccoby and Jacklin (1974) report sex differences in restructuring tasks involving breaking set, where initial solutions to problems such as Luchin's jar must be exchanged for later solutions, and in anagrams, which involve breaking up the configuration of letters spelling a word in order to reformulate another word. While Maccoby and Jacklin failed to provide their customary tabulation, Block (1976) summarized the fourteen studies on breaking set that involved Luchin's jar or similar problems that were cited by Maccoby and Jacklin. The results of this summary showed a substantial male advantage (14, M = .86, F = .00). Opposite, but less definitive, results were observed with research on anagram solutions. When breaking set consisted of rearranging letters, females did better in four of the studies, males in none (10, F = .40, M = .00). Thus, Maccoby and Jacklin concluded that restructuring ability depended on the task and could not be taken as evidence of general cognitive style or of ability to inhibit response tendencies.

These results have been reinterpreted by Block (1976), who has called attention to the differences in the problems themselves and in so doing illustrated problems of reaching theoretically relevant conclusions from existing data. She notes that problems like the Luchin's jar require insight on the part of the subject, who is not told what type of solution to look for or even that a new solution is required. Consequently, such tests involve insight and independence from the initial patterned approach, elements lacking in anagrams, where the subject is told what solution to seek, i.e., making as many words as possible from the set of letters. Because of this difference, Block claims that the evidence shows male advantage in restructuring.

There apparently are sex-related differences in cognitive functioning, but these differences reflect male independence and spatial skills, the evidence for which is unequivocal.[5] Evidence on cognitive style along a global-analytic dimension is very equivocal, if not absent, resting primarily on male ability to perceive parts within wholes and to perform better when insightful restructuring is required, both results interpretable on the basis of spatial and independence patterns, and both consistent with the Gesellschaft focus of male experience.

Verbal Abilities

Verbal abilities differ in ways consistent with the idea that the particularistic nature of family and related interpersonal relations constitute the important foci for traditional women's roles. Until very recently, women's roles have been defined primarily in terms of the interpersonal nexus involving husband and, especially, children. Even with contemporary emphasis on career, women have established a linkage or bond to children that has been accepted as stronger and more significant than that of men.[6] In all societies women play predominant roles regarding children, and with few exceptions, this occurs within the household. The other key relationship for women has been the husband, which is also related to the household. Female social position and recognition have been largely based on the occupational attainments of the spouse. This particularistic-ascriptive role has placed the woman in an interpersonal nexus more constrained and significant for her than for the man. Under these circumstances it appears possible that women would have stronger orientations toward interpersonal relations and toward other people generally.

As we have seen in preceding chapters, females do have stronger interpersonal orientations, as reflected in life orientations and occupational values as well as in the sex typing of work. Female occupations have tended to be those involving interpersonal relations and services and female occupational values have reflected that orientation.

Considering the importance of communication to individuals whose roles tend to be encapsulated in personalized, particularistic networks, it seems reasonable to expect that such people would in fact place more emphasis on communication skills and would become more adept at their execution.[7] While there is no theory developing these linkages, the empirical evidence on sex differences in verbal ability is clear, for whatever the reason. Maccoby and Jacklin observe that "female superiority on verbal tasks has been one of the more solidly established generalizations in the field of sex differences" (1974:75). While Maccoby and Jacklin equivocate somewhat on this statement in their later explication of the evidence, both Block (1976) and Sherman (1978) conclude that females are superior to males in both verbal precocity and general language skill. Sherman (1978:43) notes that a long history of research evidence prior to 1974 has shown female superiority in verbal skills, as have the studies appearing since the Maccoby and Jacklin review.

Females are more verbally precocious than males in such factors as age at first vocalization, spontaneous vocalization, and early ratings by teachers and mothers. These differences are not great, but the weight of the evidence shows female advantage, especially in the early years. Considering the studies of children under 2 years, Maccoby and Jacklin's (1974) tabulation reveals no study in which boys excelled (13, F = .15, M = .00), although most studies showed no difference. After 2 years of age there are more results in both directions, but the weight of the evidence supports female advantage (16, F = .38, M = .14). Sherman (1978) has reported three additional studies demonstrating female precocity.

Female advantage in tested verbal abilities involving vocabulary, reading, verbal fluency, and anagrams has generally been observed, although the great bulk of the research has returned findings of no difference. Although Maccoby and Jacklin's (1974) textual interpretation states that real difference between the sexes in tested abilities begins to emerge only around ages 10 to 11, their tabulated studies show a more constant pattern. In 131 studies on tested verbal ability, females were found to excel in 28%, males in only 9%. Unlike math, this pattern was roughly constant over the years with results for ages 0 to 4, 4 to 10, and over 10 (27, F = .26, M = .07), (64, F = .25, M = .14), and (40, F = .35, M = .05), respectively. Girls usually show an advantage in verbal skills, although the consistency of results is not as great as those observed on differences in spatial perception.

Sex differences in writing ability were described in the fifth report of the National Assessment of Educational Progress (1971b). Females did better at tests of performance, such as writing a report of self activities and writing a business letter. While the overall differences in the percentages exceeding designated standards were small, they increased across the age groups, reaching a maximum for adults. Thus, the male-female differences in percentage succeeding were −1.3 at age 9, −1.7 at age 13, −3.3 at age 17, and −3.5 for adults. Interestingly enough for the concerns expressed above on parallels between sex role features and cognitive performances, there were no overall sex differences in writing an essay, a task that could be assumed to involve more independent thought and reasoning ability.

Essay writing notwithstanding, the evidence to date reflects a feminine advantage in verbal ability, although the magnitude of the differences is relatively small.

Quantitative Ability

Quantitative ability, like spatial ability, is an area of sex difference that has recently come under critical evaluation and questioning. While Maccoby and Jacklin (1974) concluded that the sex difference in quantitative or mathematical abilities was one of only four clearly established differences between the sexes, recent writing and review on the issue has questioned both the evidence and the interpretation of the differences.

Evidence on Math Achievement

The bulk of the evidence indicates male superiority in quantitative skills, especially in the later years and especially in reasoning and problem solving as compared to relatively simple, repetitive skills. Mullis (1975), summarizing results from some of the early National Assessment of Educational Progress surveys, notes that males scored higher on tests of math in 1972–1973, differences relatively small at ages 9 and 13, but becoming substantial among 17-year-olds and especially among adults. In addition, the differences were initially greater for items testing measurement, geometry, probabilities, and statistics, although by age 17, consumer math items produced the third largest difference, even though this is an area appropriate to the homemaking activities of the majority of adult females. Among 17-year-olds and adults, less than one-third of the females could determine "the lowest price per ounce for a box of rice compared to 40% of the 17-year-old males and 45% of the adult males" (Mullis 1975:10). Her conclusion was that "in the mathematics assessment, the advantage displayed by males, particularly at the older ages, can only be described as overwhelming" (Mullis 1975:7).

Maccoby and Jacklin's (1974) review of research on differences in quantitative ability produced equally conclusive results. Summarizing thirty-five studies using such tests as the WISC arithmetic subtest, STEP, SCAT, and SAT quantitative tests as well as tests of math reasoning, Maccoby and Jacklin found strong but age-related effects. In the eleven studies of youths under 10, females did better more often (11; F = .27, M = .00), but in the twenty-four comparisons of persons 10 years and older, males more often excelled (24, M = .67, F = .00). However, of some significance is the fact that in only one of the studies, the Project Talent comparison, was mathematics experience controlled, a point I will return to.

More recent research fails to produce such definite results and also finds that sex differences in performance levels depend on the type of skill being examined, variations roughly consistent with the idea that males have a more analytic cognitive style and are better at reasoning and working with abstractions and relations, while females are better at repetitive memory tasks. In a 1978 national survey of 13-year-olds and high school seniors, Armstrong (1980) found statistically significant differences in only three of eight comparisons of the two sexes across the two age groups and four measures of ability, two of which favored girls, with girls excelling in computation and spatial visualization. By grade 12, boys excelled on all four dimensions, although the only statistally significant difference was in problem solving, where 72.1% of the senior males and 65.2% of the females achieved correct responses on the test items (Armstrong 1980:11). Similar results for computation, algebra, and application (problem solving) were obtained in the National Assessment of Educational Progress Second Mathematics Assessment, 1977–1978. At age 13, girls excelled in computation and were not significantly different from boys in algebra. However, unlike Armstrong's survey, the NAEP results showed a trivial, but statistically significant, male advantage of 1.6% in the percentage of correct responses on math application items. By grade 12, there were no significant sex differences in computation or algebra, but boys exhibited a more substantial (46.1% versus 41.0%) advantage in application.

Finally, Fennema and Sherman (1977) examined achievement levels, taking into account previous experience by studying only those ninth and twelfth grade math students in four high schools who were "on grade," that is, taking math courses in the typical year as determined by the grade level of the majority of students enrolled in each class. They reported statistically significant male superiority in mathematics achievement in only two of the four high schools, although the level of statistical significance was for all practical purposes at the .05 level[8] in a third. In addition, every single comparison of the sexes within each of the fourteen[9] school-by-class groups showed males to have higher math achievement scores, and the overall sex difference in math achievement in the total population was highly significant. There was also a barely significant school-by-sex interaction, indicating that the difference between the sexes varied somewhat by school. However, contrary to previous research reported by Maccoby and Jacklin and to the national assessment data just described, Fennema and Sherman did not observe significant sex-by-year interactions. When mathematics course taking was controlled, the sex difference was constant over the years.

Questions and Reconsiderations

Sherman (1978) has raised a number of questions about the studies just reviewed and argues that the results should be reconsidered.

In the first place, she points out, the sex differences observed are trivial and unlikely to have any substantive importance in explaining other sex-related behaviors. She observes that sex differences of much less than one standard deviation in average scores are reported in the Maccoby and Jacklin (1974) summary, with the largest differences being in the order of one-half standard deviation. She further notes that the maximum sex-related effect observed in any of the four schools of the Wisconsin study was an omega squared of .06, or 6% of the variation in math achievement levels when course taking was controlled. Whether 2 to 6% of explained variance is important is a matter of judgment. However, Sherman's position reflects a contemporary shift in psychological research interpretation from concern with hypothesis testing to concern with level of effects, a perspective previously more common in survey-based sociological research. Since the great bulk of psychological knowledge is based on simple rejection of the null hypothesis, rather than on "effect parameters" (Cohen 1969), it might be a little stringent to dismiss variables accounting for as much as 6% of the variance or establishing mean differences as large as .5 standard deviation.

A more critical and somewhat more difficult objection to evaluate is the meaning of ability or achievement measures that are applied to populations heterogeneous in training and experience. If males take more math and science than females do, it would not be surprising to find that they had more knowledge and could perform better when given tests of mathematical aptitude, especially tests requiring familiarity with more advanced concepts and approaches. Sherman (1978) argues that the results of the Wisconsin study (Fennema and Sherman 1977) confirm the importance of controlling for course-taking experience. However, plausible as the objection appears, the evidence supporting it is not overwhelming.

In Fennema and Sherman's (1977) research, even when only those students taking the grade-appropriate math courses are included in the research, overall sex differences favoring boys are observed in the total study population and, for all practical purposes, in three of the four schools. Furthermore, in every one of the fourteen school-by-grade comparisons, boys in the same math courses score higher than girls, although the differences in many cases are very small. These patterns make it difficult to accept Sherman's (1978) conclusion that differences between the sexes are due primarily to differences in course taking.

Other evidence also questions this conclusion. Maccoby and Jacklin report that

project Talent analyzed math scores in the senior year of high school, after equating the two sexes on the number of math courses taken. The boys still emerged with substantially higher average scores, a finding that suggests it is not merely the amount of training the two sexes have received that is responsible for the difference in their performance at this age. (1974:85, 89)

While Sherman (1978:57) discounts this matching based only on number of courses, it seems to me a reasonable approach, considering the sequential nature of math and science curriculums. More recent data are reported by Astin (1974), who examined scores in a math and science contest where roughly equal proportions of seventh and eighth grade boys and girls entered the math section. In both grades, boys did substantially better. For example, no girl, but 19% of the boys, scored over 600 on SAT math. These differences among seventh and eighth graders preceded variation in math curriculum, although they do not automatically control for math experience and learning outside of school. Finally, evidence reported by Armstrong (1980) from the NAEP Second Mathematics Assessment indicates that sex differences actually increased with level of course taking. Especially in the higher-level skills involved in application, but also in computation and algebra, male superiority is greatest among the relatively advanced group having taken trigonometry and above, in spite of the fact that the smaller female enrollments would presumably produce a more select population.

Thus, while the final answer is not yet in, it does not appear that consistently observed sex differences in quantitative ability can be accounted for by differences in experience gained by course taking. Furthermore, while there are consistent differences in math courses taken, evidence from the NAEP Second Mathematics Assessment and the Women in Mathematics Survey (Armstrong 1980) indicates that the differences are considerably less than those discussed by Ernest (1976) from Sells' Berkeley data. For the most part, these sex differences in national mathematics enrollments run from 2 to 5%, with only one difference over 6% reported. Such relatively small differences in and of themselves could not introduce important spurious effects into the issue of math achievement.

While course taking does not appear to account for observed differences, changes in patterns over time and in social psychological circumstances may well account for some of the differences. Perhaps, as Sherman suggests, there are increasing female enrollments resulting from redefinition of career and the sex typing of math and science. We will return to those issues later.

Science Achievement

Males are assumed to be interested in science and to be rational and logical in cognitive orientations. This aspect of the stereotype is again consistent with cognitive reflections of differential relations to natural and interpersonal environments and the abilities that may have developed from those differing experiences, both within individual life history and over long periods of biological and cultural evolution.

Evidence on sex differences in scientific achievement is generally consistent with the stereotype.

The 1969–1970 Science National Assessment of Educational Progress Report (1971a) showed typical sex differences. Males scored higher in science, but the differences were greater among 17-year-olds and adults, and they were considerably greater in physical science than in biological science. For example, the mean sex differences in percentages of exercises correct in physical science exercises for 9-, 13-, 17-year-olds, and adults were 0.8, 2.4, 4.2, and 14.2%, respectively. Differences in biological science across the same age groups were only 0.1, 1.5, 1.6, and 2.3%. However, as the report (NAEP 1971:39) observes, these substantial differences in physical science scores could be due to "differential exposure to a physical science curriculum." Similar overall differences for combined physical and biological science exercises in the 1976–1977 assessments, where percentage differences from national norms on the percentage of exercises correct were used to express sex differences for 9-, 13-. and 17-year-olds, were 2.7, 4.5, and 6.0%, respectively.

Finn's (1980) recent analysis of data from the 1970 International Evaluation of Educational Achievement for seventh, eighth, and ninth graders in England, Sweden, and the United States revealed consistent sex differences in science achievement. In each country boys did better than girls in physics and practical science and in all countries except England (where girls in one-sex schools did better than boys in one-sex schools) also did better in biology and chemistry. Except for those three cases, boys did better than girls in science tests in every country and in all four course areas. These findings are interesting because they essentially discount course-taking effects. Among seventh, eighth, and ninth graders, curriculum patterns and course work in science have been generally similar for girls and boys. This would be especially true for Sweden, where deliberate attempts were made to organize the curriculum so that equal opportunities are provided for both sexes. Ironically, sex differences in science tend to be greater in Sweden than in mixed classes in the United States and England.

Finn also observed substantial differences averaging from about .4 standard deviations to .8 standard deviations in liking-disliking science and in participating in scientific activities. Across these societies, the pattern of superior male scientific preference and performance tend to hold and cannot be discounted as an artifact of course taking.

Finally, in a more limited study, Astin (1974) found clear male advantage among 397 seventh and eighth grade boys and girls participating in a math and science contest. Among this group of self-selected students, which should include girls of relatively higher ability, boys received scores on the science tests that exceeded girls' scores by about .6 to 1.0 standard deviations in the eighth grade, although in the seventh grade, male advantage was considerably less. Astin notes that the differences were so substantial that 18% of the boys, but only 3% of the girls, scored above 100, and only five girls scored among the top sixty-four performers.

Studies of representative samples of national student populations, as well as other more selected groups, show clear, although not large, differences in the science performance of girls and boys. These differences appear in early years, well before differences in course taking could have any appreciable effect, and increases over the years of high school to adulthood, a pattern that could of course reflect differential course-taking experience.

Conclusions

The main conclusion from this review is that there is some ambiguity about the evidence on cognitive and academic sex differences and, most especially, some disagreement among authorities about the interpretation of the evidence at hand. In large part this disagreement arises from the heightened interest and more sophisticated critical evaluation developing in sex role research. This is an interesting, if confused, period for students of sex roles, as earlier myths and speculations are laid to rest and new looks taken at the evidence, both old and new. All of this change makes valid conclusions difficult to reach and risky to advance, creating a strong need for the type of evidence generated by this study. For now, however, the preceding review seems to lead to several reasonably clear, but by no means certain, outcomes and interpretations.

In the first place there do seem to be real differences between the sexes in verbal, spatial, and quantitative abilities, and they are generally consistent with the characteristics of stereotypic male and female roles. Women, more often limited to particularistic, ascribed roles enacted within primary contexts of personal orientations, have greater verbal skill than men, although this does not extend to use of language where organization and creative synthesis are required, as in essay writing. Men, oriented toward sex roles with substantial extrafamilial commitments and instrumental, task-oriented themes, appear to have developed spatial and quantitative skills and interests in science that facilitate, if they do not in fact derive from, universalistic-achievement roles that involve interactions with an orderly, predictable environment. The evidence to date supports the proposition of real sex differences in these respects, differences that seem not to be explained away by levels of course taking.

While sex differences in verbal, spatial, quantitative, and scientific achievement levels appear to be real, their scope is relatively small. There is considerable overlap in the distributions of males and females on these dimensions and only small portions of the variance in these abilities are explained by sex. Nevertheless, there are differences of some significance, although the sexes do not constitute discrete categories by any means.

It also seems clear that the scope of these differences, especially those in physical science, increases with age. While there are differences among seventh and eighth graders, the strongest sex differences occur among high school seniors and adults.

Finally, it appears that sex differences are greatest in certain areas that suggest that male intellectual performance differs most where higher order processing and perhaps spatial ability are involved. We have seen that females have better verbal skills and writing abilities, except when writing essays is involved. Similarly, in mathematics, females do better at computations, males do better at problem solving and insight. Stereotypic themes seem to appear in science, where boys do much better at physical science and girls close the gap and in some cases exceed boys in biological science and chemistry.

REVIEW OF THE LITERATURE: CHANGE AND STABILITY IN COGNITIVE PATTERNS

The persistence of sex differences in cognitive functioning will of course depend on the reasons for their existence. If differences rest on relatively arbitrary sex role arrangements, social change, especially that producing masculinization, should eventually eliminate the differences between the sexes. On the other hand, if cognitive differences rest on basic physiological differences between the sexes, change would be less likely, or if enacted, less likely to persist. Thus, the question of biological or environmental causes is relevant to this study.

Alternative Explanations of Cognitive Differences

Alternative explanations of cognitive differences have been advanced for both environmental and biological causes. The use of biological explanations was more common in earlier periods, but the emphasis now is shifting toward environmental explanations. In large part, this is a consequence of the failure to obtain confirming evidence on biological factors and, more recently, the accumulation of negative findings for some of the theories most strongly accepted in earlier periods.

Before turning to the question of empirical evidence on change, I briefly summarize existing biological and environmental theories, drawing especially on Maccoby and Jacklin (1974) Fox, Fennema, and Sherman (1977), Sherman (1978), Wittig and Petersen (1979), and Seward and Seward (1980).

Biological

Biological explanations of sex-related cognitive patterns have received considerable attention at both theoretical and empirical levels. Unfortunately, at the present time this literature is confusing and ambiguous, incorporating both contradictory theories and substantial disagreement regarding the nature of the evidence. Nevertheless, at least three major biological explanations have been advanced. These are (1) the hypothesis of an X-linked recessive gene underlying spatial abilities, and possibly verbal and mathematical abilities; (2) the possible effect of sex hormones on cognitive functioning; and (3) the implications of brain hemispheric lateralization for sex differences in verbal, spatial, and quantitative processes. In all three areas, theoretical development and speculation loom larger than hard empirical support, although there was probably more initial support for the genetic hypothesis than for the other two formulations.

The X-linked hypothesis rests partly on the higher heritability of spatial ability (Maccoby and Jacklin 1974) and on the consistency of early findings and observations with known patterns of genetic transmission. The X-linked hypothesis leads to several predictions based on the sources and distributions of X and Y chromosomes. Because males have only one X chromosome, while females have two, the probability of a female manifesting such a trait is the square of the male probability. Furthermore, because males necessarily receive their single X chromosome from the mother while the female must receive one recessive gene from each parent if the trait is to be manifest, the patterns of parent-child correlations can be predicted, as can the patterns of same- and cross-sex sibling correlations. Finally, the sex-based differences in the likelihood of expressing the recessive trait should result in bimodal distributions in spatial abilities when the sexes are combined.[10]

Early research evidence supported the three major predictions (Vandenberg and Kuse 1979; Sherman 1978). In fact, at the time of their writing, Maccoby and Jacklin (1974) were able to report only supporting evidence for the X-linked hypothesis. Referring to this early evidence, Vandenberg and Kuse note that the distributional predictions appeared in early studies, both in terms of female achievement levels being proportionately the square of the male value and in terms of bimodality of the combined distributions. Similar confirmation appeared in the more definitive pattern of intrafamily correlation. Three early studies observed that the predicted familial correlations of (mother-son, father-daughter) were greater than (mother-daughter), which was greater than (father-son = 0), while one revealed the expected sibling correlation (Vandenberg and Kuse 1979). The change in results of later research is dramatic and at this time seriously questions the validity of the X-linked hypothesis. Seven studies reported between 1976 and 1978 failed to observe the predicted order of correlations within the family, and another failed to observe bimodality in the combined distributions (Vandenberg and Kuse 1979). These results clearly reverse the conclusions in this area since Maccoby and Jacklin's review and cast a different light on the hypothesis itself. Sherman (1978:86) concludes that the X-linked hypothesis has been "disconfirmed."

The second major biological explanation is Broverman's theory of hormone effect on spatial ability. As Maccoby and Jacklin summarize the main effects of that theory, "large amounts of either estrogens or androgens will tip the neural balance toward activating rather than inhibiting functions. . . . [H]owever, estrogens are more powerful, so the balance is tipped further in females than in males" (1974:123).

As I have noted, inhibitory processes are thought essential to cognitive tasks involving complex information processing and restructuring of original stimulus elements. Lack of inhibitory processes would presumably result in immediate action, limiting the person to lower, more repetitive cognitive performances. Thus, girls should do relatively better at word meanings, spelling, computation, and matching, boys at reasoning, analytic approaches, and restructuring.

While scattered findings support those differences, the specific conclusion reached by Maccoby and Jacklin (1974) from their review is that there are no clearly established differences in cognitive style. Nor are the differences in impulsivity consistent with this formulation. Males, not females, turn out to be less able to inhibit response.

The idea that sex hormones produce activating tendencies ironically finds support only for males (Sherman 1978:100–102; Maccoby and Jacklin 1974:123–124). More masculine males are better at repetitive tasks, worse at spatial. Conversely, more masculine (androgenized) females are better at spatial tasks. This produces an anomaly—individual differences run the opposite of group differences. In any event, Maccoby and Jacklin, Sherman, and Vandenberg and Kuse (1979) all agree that any conclusions involving the explanation of sex-related differences in cognitive patterns are premature and unsupported by the evidence.

The third major biological explanation of sex-related cognitive differences draws on the knowledge about brain lateralization—that functions related to speech and analytic thought are believed to be located in the left hemisphere, while those having to do with spatial and global thought are located in the right hemisphere (Bryden 1979). As the verbal-spatial differences parallel the sex-related differences, a voluminous, confusing, and somewhat inconsistent literature has developed on the issue of lateralization processes as explanations for sex differences.[11] In the following review of this literature I draw heavily on Bryden, Sherman (1978), and Seward and Seward (1980).

As Maccoby and Jacklin (1974) noted in their review, two contradictory theories have emerged to explain sex differences in cognition on the basis of brain lateralization. The first of these, advanced by Buffery and Gray, holds that females lateralize earlier and develop left hemisphere specialization in verbal skills. Because of this, they emphasize verbal solutions and are less likely to develop bilateral function in spatial skills. This specialization accounts for their greater verbal skill, while the later, less specialized male development produces greater bilateral spatial functioning (Seward and Seward 1980; Bryden 1979; Sherman 1978). The other theory, advanced by Levy, is that both verbal and spatial hemispheric specializations are evolutionary adaptations to reduce competition between the brain's hemispheres (Seward and Seward), and that, consequently, lateralization of both functions is advantageous. Females, like left-handed people, are thought to have less lateralization, which results in verbal interference with spatial functioning of the right hemisphere. They gain in verbal but lose in spatial skills. Males, exhibiting greater lateralization, have higher spatial scores but somewhat less verbal ability than the bilateral female.

At the present time, the empirical evidence does not clearly support any position. Bryden, in summarizing the overall evidence, asserts that "it is difficult to see any striking patterns emerging. Any conclusions rest upon one's choice of which studies to emphasize, which to ignore" (1979:137).

Bryden does conclude, nevertheless, that the Buffery and Gray theory is clearly not consistent with the evidence, but that there may be some tentative support for Levy's position, a conclusion shared by Sherman (1978). However, Sherman has argued that female verbal preference resulting from verbal precocity and emphasized by sex role distinctions works well for girls, and like a "bent twig" predisposes them toward verbal specialization, even to the point of using the left hemisphere for solving spatial problems.

Plausible as they may have at first appeared, none of the major biological theories currently fares well when faced with empirical testing. In fact, Sherman argues that the major biological determinants are male strength and autonomy. Males have been the hunters, warriors, and sailors and have consequently a long personal as well as evolutionary history working with space, distance, and motion that may account for male spatial skills. Females everywhere have been hearth bound and excluded from external activities such as hunting, where spatial skills are acquired. In short, biology is important primarily as it determines environmental experiences and sex role enactment. We now turn to such environmental explanations.

Environmental

There is a growing and substantial literature emphasizing sex role, rather than biological, explanations for cognitive differences. I draw primarily on Sherman (1978), Fox, Fennema, and Sherman (1977), and Nash (1979) in the following review. By and large, these authorities are representative of contemporary viewpoints in arguing the primacy of environmental explanations over biological. The numerous facets of this argument seem to revolve around two main environmental circumstances: (1) different cognitively relevant experiences of girls and boys, and (2) sex-typed socialization and its consequence for sex-typed perception and orientation of adolescent youth. These formulations are variously supported and questioned by the research evidence, and authorities fail to agree about the weight of the evidence on sex role effects on sex-related cognitive differences.

Sherman concludes: "There is a good deal of evidence to support the theory that sex role directly and indirectly affects sex-related cognitive differences" (1978:171). On the other hand, Nash, reviewing substantially the same evidence, states:

The relationship between sex role and intellectual functioning is a complex one—not subject to simple generalizations. Due to serious flaws in sex-role instruments, confounded cognitive measures, and the limited experimental designs employed, any conclusions or speculations at this time are tentative. (1979:290)

Sex-related experiences have been related to cognitive differences in two ways. Sherman (1977) has called attention to the experiental significance of male and female activities. Male activities involve perception and behavior in an external environment where spatial abilities are critical. As Sherman observes: "All matter of activities involving aiming, visualizing direction, estimating space, and symbolizing space and spatial relations (the essence of mathematics) has been an integral part of male socialization experiences" (1977:187).

Men hunt, sail ships, ride horses, throw spears, wield weapons, and play ball. In addition, activities such as hunting (and one might add warfare) require spatial disembedding. Thus, some of the clearest sex differences appear to have obvious evolutionary or experiential antecedents in sex-typed behavior.[12]

The other major experiential factor is differential course taking. After seventh and eighth grade, boys take more math and science than girls and presumably develop more skills as a consequence. Fennema and Sherman (1977) and Sherman (1978) have concluded that differential course taking may well account for the kind of sex-related differences observed in NAEP and other reports of verbal, spatial, and quantitative aptitudes. However, the evidence is not clearly supportive of this position insofar as sex differences appear even among seventh and eighth grades and among youths with the same number of courses. On the other hand, sex differences in verbal, spatial, and quantitative areas increase during adolescence, perhaps in part because of differential experience.

Differential socialization is almost universally assumed in spite of the absence of support for the proposition in the Maccoby and Jacklin (1974) review. It is generally assumed that the blue-blanket, pink-blanket pattern established in the first few days continues throughout childhood and adolescence, determining appropriate life goals, occupations, and associated behaviors, cognitions, and perceptions. Boys are expected to pursue careers involving science, math, and technology, girls are expected to be less career-oriented, more affiliative and expressive, and less autonomous. In keeping with these expectations, Fox and associates (1977, 1979) assert that parents, teachers, and counselors all pressure boys toward quantitative and scientific curriculum while shunting girls into traditional, nonscientific roles. This shift is facilitated by the supposed conflict between affiliation and achievement (Fox, Fennema, and Sherman 1977) that is embellished by adolescent peer group pressures on stereotyping role performances oriented toward popularity and affiliation.[13]

The result of these patterns is thought to be stereotypic conceptions of cognitive processes. Social and verbal behavior is seen as feminine, spatial, mechanical, and athletic activities are defined as masculine. Thus, girls face the problem of entering study areas defined as inappropriate and peopled with persons having considerably more experience. Math and quantitative subjects are seen as male domains. Females face inappropriate role performances when they chose these areas of study.

Finally, given the tendencies of most students to choose traditional occupations, there are also differences in the perceived usefulness of courses. Males are more likely to think math and science relevant to their career plans, females less so. Consequently, males are more likely to value these areas, choose courses, and acquire more experience.

Generally, then, while the evidence is not conclusive, most authorities writing today attribute differences in environmental effects to experiences that directly provide practice and training in the skill or to differences in course taking and the meaning of courses. These differences in turn follow from socialization differences that direct boys toward spatial, scientific, and quantitative areas while constraining girls to the affiliative, expressive area where verbal skills are the most important cognitive skill.

Evidence on Change and Stability

Turning finally to the central issue, change in sex-related cognitive differences, we can look toward two bodies of evidence, one considerably stronger, but both consistent in their conclusions. These are first, the general change or stability in research findings on cognitive sex differences over the years, and second, longitudinal studies of cognitive differences, which provide especially appropriate evidence for our concern with changing sex roles.

The evidence on sex-related cognitive differences goes back several decades and has been consistent in showing sex differences in cognitive abilities. In fact, Block (1976) noted in her critical review of Maccoby and Jacklin (1974) that from Terman and Tyler's 1959 review to Maccoby's 1966 summary, the evidence consistently showed sex differences in cognitive abilities and performances, among other things. Block concluded that traditional sex differences have persisted and that Maccoby and Jacklin have understated the amount of actual difference between the sexes. She believed that differences observed in the earlier reviews still persisted in all of these areas.

More recent work is less definite, but as I have interpreted it, still supports the idea of sex-related cognitive differences at the end of the 1970s. Fennema and Sherman (1977) found predicted differences in quantitative abilities in every comparison made and in the total population, and in three of four schools, even when course taking was controlled. They found less support for continuing differences in verbal and spatial abilities, suggesting that some change may have occurred in those areas. This suggestion is supported by Armstrong's (1980) analysis of national data, which shows no difference in spatial visualization. However, Armstrong did find sex-related differences in mathematical problem solving, although not in three other quantitative areas. She did observe greater sex differences among those students having the most math background, a finding that questions Sherman's assumption that sex differences in math and science are due mainly to differential course taking. In any event, the pattern of findings in the recent research suggests that some diminution of cognitive differences between the sexes may have occurred in recent years, but that differences still persist.

A more adequate assessment of change is the readministration of the same instruments to comparable populations at different times. For once, such evidence is available. There have been longitudinal studies of cognitive skills in the National Assessments of Educational Progress and in the Project Talent data collections.

The National Assessments of Science (1978) research, based on representative national samples of 9-, 13-, and 17-year-olds, examined change in physical and biological science achievement between 1969 and 1977. One of the dramatic findings of this assessment was the sharp decline in science achievement levels (especially physical science) between the 1969–1970 and 1976–1977 assessments. However, the study showed that sex differences persisted in the face of this general change in achievement levels when the twenty-three items common to all three assessments were considered separately. This stable sex difference occurred across the three age groups. When all the sets of items used in each assessment were compared, sex differences actually increased in each of the age groups from 1969 to 1977, although the level of the sex difference depended quite a bit on the set of items used. Nevertheless, the comparisons show, at the very least, stability in sex difference, if not an actual increase.

The National Assessment of Education Progress (1979) report, *Changes in Mathematical Achievement, 1973–1978,* also revealed consistent patterns in mathematics. Seventeen-year-old males did better in each assessment, although the text interpretation of bar graph differences favoring males indicated that the differences among 9- and 13-year-olds were not statistically significant. As in science achievement, achievement levels declined over the period but, "differences between males' and females' achievement remained constant over the five-year period" (NAEP 1979:21). This held even though the amount of difference was greater among 17-year-olds and in problem-solving applications than in understanding concepts and computations.

Finally, a 1975 replication of ten 1960 Project Talent ability tests in seventeen of the original schools permits analysis of change in sex differences in several cognitive dimensions (Flanagan 1976). As in the NAEP reports, there were substantial declines in tests of vocabulary, English, and mechanical and especially quantitative reasoning. However, Flanagan also observed increased scores in creativity, especially for girls, and in abstract reasoning and mathematics. Unlike the NAEP results, Flanagan observed changes in the sex differences, and the change suggested convergence between the sexes. The amount of difference decreased regardless of which sex had the higher scores. The only important exception to this pattern was the substantial increase in the female advantage in computation.[14]

Of special interest are the shifts in mechanical reasoning and visualization, cognitive skills related to success in mechanical work, according to Flanagan. Flanagan interprets this difference to "reflect a change away from the sex stereotyping that characterized the 1960 group" (1976:11). However, even though some sex role change was observed, traditional sex differences in reasoning and spatial visualization were still observed in 1975. Furthermore, the slight male advantages in quantitative reasoning and mathematics are maintained in 1976. The Flanagan study provides the only clear evidence of change in sex-related cognitive patterns, and that evidence is somewhat tenuous, especially in reasoning and math.

Conclusion

This review of the research evidence, theory, and valuative speculation on cognitive differences indicates that there are real differences between the sexes in verbal, spatial, quantitative, and scientific abilities and that they have not changed markedly in the past decade. On the other hand, the differences are trivial in scope and taken by themselves would not appear to be especially significant in the determination of career potentials or occupational skills.

Biological explanations emphasizing inheritance of a recessive X-linked gene for spatial ability have been disproved by recent research. Evidence for hormone effects has never been very clearly established, nor has the theory itself appeared internally consistent and convincing. The authorities reviewed in the previous summary suggest that brain lateralization might be a valid explanation, although this appears to be primarily in establishing an early preference in females that predisposes certain kinds of learning experiences. About the only persistent basis of support for biological explanations has been the stability of these differences over time. However, the stability of these differences is also consistent with the clearly demarked social roles of women and men observed until the very recent past. Science, math, and spatial experiences have been more directly related to the extra-familial world of men, verbal and empathetic skills more related to interpersonal relations within the household and in the quasimaternal traditional occupational roles women have held.

Unfortunately, evidence does not yet clearly show that socialization and experience produce the small, observed differences. It is not clear that parents deliberately train boys to be quantative and spatial and girls to be verbal. Nor is it clear that girls deliberately do less well in cognitive areas sex typed as male. The perceived usefulness of different cognitive areas and academic subjects to future occupational and life goals appears a reasonable hypothesis not yet adequately tested. Experiential patterns resulting from course taking and other sex-related experiences have been advanced as an explanation for observed differences, but I have questioned the definitiveness of the evidence supporting those assertions, especially that focusing on differential course taking.

Without definitive evidence for either biological or environmental explanations, we must fall back to general concerns and contemporary processes. Given the emphasis on change and the observations of the beginning of change in sex-typed occupational preferences, we might expect consequent change in course preferences and perceived utility of courses as well as shifts in performance in sex-typed content areas.

We now turn to the examination of such evidence, considering stability and change in sex-related differences in valuation of various courses and in the number of sex-related courses taken, as well as in the graded achievement levels within sex-typed courses. Indirect support for socialization or environmental explanations would appear as evidence of change in these orientations and performances.

EMPIRICAL EVIDENCE: SEX ROLES AND ACADEMIC PREFERENCE AND PERFORMANCE

This section considers the evidence on sex role differentiation and change in several aspects of the school's educational program. Sex typing and change appear in course enrollments, in the evaluation of courses, and in the achievement levels attained in various courses.

The preceding review indicates greater female enrollment, evaluation, and achievement in such verbally oriented courses as English, speech, and language, and greater male enrollment, evaluation, and achievement in mathematics and science. The significance of social science courses, music, and art to sex role factors is less clearly elaborated in the literature. The greater interpersonal orientation of women should make social studies slightly more appropriate to females than to males, although at least one study questions that guess.[15] In any event, the main sex-related effects would be expected in the verbal and quantitative-scientific areas. To facilitate observation of possible stereotypic patterns, tables of academic courses are ordered with language and science at the extremes and social studies and art at the center.

While academic courses can be organized in terms of sex-related cognitive distinctions, vocational courses are more related to occupational sex typing and homemaking. Courses directed toward homemaking have been sex-typed as female, as have courses involving office practice and secretarial skills. Training in the skills required for blue-collar crafts and occupations has clearly been oriented toward the male student. Finally, courses having to do with general business skills and bookkeeping do not appear to be clearly related to such traditional sex-typed office positions as secretary and file clerk, but, like social studies, may be equally relevant to either sex. These distinctions are used in the presentation of vocational courses. Office practice, typing, and shorthand are grouped together as vocational courses sex typed as female, while agriculture and the blue-collar crafts are grouped at the other end as male courses. Bookkeeping, general business, and sales are treated as more ambiguous and located at the center of the tables. As with the academic courses, greatest evidence for sex-typed processes is expected at the extremes.

Sex role differences in the sex-typed courses can be expected in several different aspects of course experience. In the first place, sex typing of curriculum should affect enrollment and participation in courses. Such channeling of students into appropriate content areas and their avoidance of inappropriate areas has been assumed by various authorities (see Fox, Tobin, and Brady 1979; Sherman 1978) to be a substantial aspect of experience related to differential achievement, expecially in such sex-typed areas as science and mathematics. While I have questioned the scope of these effects, it is likely that male enrollment would be higher in mathematics and science courses, female enrollment higher in English and language. Considerably stronger sex differences in enrollment in vocational blue-collar craft courses and in secretarial courses should also be observed.

Second, the literature review shows that authorities assume sex differences in orientations toward courses. One such orientation has to do with the perceived value or utility of courses for life goals and occupational plans. It is assumed that boys are more likely to perceive science and mathematics as useful to their future goals and are consequently more likely to enroll in mathematics and science courses than are girls. Generally, we expect to observe that boys rate mathematics and science courses as more helpful to future occupational goals than girls do.

While most of the writing on perceived helpfulness of courses has focused on perceptions of mathematics and science courses, an analogous argument could be made regarding female perceptions of the usefulness of English, speech, and language courses. In addition, vocational specialization makes it likely that girls would perceive the secretarial courses as more helpful than boys would.[16]

Another aspect of course orientations follows from differences in cognitive abilities as well as from sex-typing of courses. Boys might well find mathematics and science more satisfying than girls, both because of greater cognitive ability and also because of sex-typed appropriateness. Similarly, girls might obtain more satisfaction in English and language.

Satisfaction in course content is based on questions about courses the student had "most enjoyed studying." Sex-related differences in cognitive ability should produce greater satisfaction in sex-typed courses where ability can be exercised and where content is sex-appropriate. Boys should enjoy mathematics and science more, girls, language and speech.

Finally, I examine sex-related achievement levels in academic and vocational courses, with special emphasis on the sex-typed academic courses where substantial sex-related differences in ability scores have been attributed to differences in experience and perception. The effects of sex on grades in courses by year of school operate to control the experiential factor, especially in those courses designated as "typical year" courses (see tables 5.1, 5.2). Achievement differences in these courses cannot be attributed to differential experience in the subject matter. Generally, the literature indicates that males should do better in science and mathematics, females in language and possibly in psychology and social science. While vocational courses are not specifically treated in sex role literature, which is more oriented toward college-bound students, it seems reasonable to expect similar differentials in achievement in them, although the lack of female enrollment in blue-collar craft courses precludes a symmetrical analysis across vocational and academic courses.

As in earlier analyses, I consider the evidence in terms of sex differences,

Table 5.1.

Enrollment in Vocational Courses[a]

	Course Year		
Course Title	Sophomore	Junior	Senior
Family		238	669
Home Economics	851	899	1552
Office Practice	41	231	755
Shorthand		955	502
Typing	1773	1664	1171
Bookkeeping	240	465	1030
Business	213	147	307
Sales	60	196	212
Agriculture	362	460	487
Auto Mechanics	81	99	152
Drawing	286	319	349
Electricity	147	163	146
General Shop	329	285	260
Machine Shop	150	342	395
Printing	91	103	119
Sheet Metal	219	233	231
Woodworking	375	424	359

[a]Underlined courses have over 300 students enrolled or constitute the modal year enrollment in that subject. These courses are defined as "typical year" enrollments. Enrollments under 25 are disregarded.

social change, and sex role change. In all three areas (enrollments, perceived utility, and graded achievement), I expect to observe sex differences consistent with the general assumptions about sex typing in education. Boys should be more likely to enroll in mathematics and science, perceive these courses as helpful and enjoyable, and get better grades than girls. Female superiority and preference should appear in language and secretarial courses. As before, these effects appear in the level of the regression coefficient for sex. Social change should appear in ways consistent with the general shift discussed in chapter 4, from institutional commitment to social values of work, patriotism, and success striving, to more individualistic, hedonistic,

Table 5.2.

Enrollment in Academic Courses[a]

Course Title	Course Year		
	Sophomore	Junior	Senior
English	5326	5109	3515
Language	1721	1196	639
Speech	340	457	854
Art	480	618	812
Economics		163	776
History	2052	4715	923
Music	1502	1399	1251
Psychology		102	1487
Social Science	344	326	546
Sociology	31	173	2785
Algebra	1170	728	163
Biology	4678	238	336
Chemistry	92	1737	409
Geometry	2283	710	161
Math	514	764	1255
Natural Science	241	214	305
Physics		123	972

[a]Underlined courses have over 1,000 students enrolled or constitute the modal year enrollment in that subject. These courses are defined as "typical year" enrollments. Enrollments under 25 are disregarded.

less institutional orientations. In the present context this should be reflected in shifts away from difficult, intellectually demanding courses toward more personally relevant, hedonistically directed courses in art, culture, and vocational areas. Social change of this sort should also be related to declining concern about achievement and to lowering performance levels.[17] Finally, sex role change should appear as a reduction in differences in courses taken, perceived utility, enjoyment in studying the course content, and achievement in sex-typed courses. This should be clearest in the areas of mathematics and science, where increasing proportions of girls are expected to enroll, value, and achieve in these traditionally male courses. Female increase would also be expected in previously traditional male vocational courses. This pattern of masculinization might be complemented by reduced emphasis on and performance in courses sex typed as female.

Course Enrollments

Enrollments in this study have been calculated from transcript information rather than from student self-report, which is viewed as an advantage of these data. The baseline used in calculating percentages enrolled in courses is the total population. This includes a small percentage (3.8%) of cases for which transcript information was missing. However, there is no significant sex difference in this missing transcript data.

Enrollments in academic and vocational courses are presented in tables 5.1 and 5.2, where courses are grouped with feminine and masculine sex-typed courses at the extremes and less clearly sex-related courses in the center. Courses with very large enrollments or, in the absence of large enrollments, the modal course year, are underlined as references for later discussions. They are defined as "typical year" enrollments and treated in a manner analogous to the Fennema and Sherman (1977) "on grade" courses. They are used as controls for subject experience due to course taking. It is assumed that students taking specific courses in the "typical year" have comparable background and experience. The large numbers involved in these courses also reduces the possibility that some effects might be due to selection of unique populations in special courses of small enrollment. In all but two of the sex-typed academic courses (table 5.2), there is at least one year in which the course was taken by over 1,000 students. Enrollments in vocational courses sex typed as female (table 5.1) are somewhat lower than enrollments in academic courses, and enrollments in vocational courses sex typed as male are considerably lower, probably because of a more varied and specialized offering within the crafts than within the office skill curriculum. Examination of tables 5.1 and 5.2 reveals considerable variation in the level of enrollment in most subjects across the years. The reader should be mindful of this substantial variation as we proceed to describe the results.

Vocational Courses

Average number of vocational course enrollments by sex and year is presented in table 5.3, along with the regression analysis of difference and change. It is apparent that vocational courses reflect occupational sex typing along the lines observed in the analysis of occupational preferences. Ex-

Table 5.3.

Number of Vocational Courses[a] by Sex and Year

Course	Average Number of Courses				Metric Regression Coefficients[b]			
	1964		1975					
	M	F	M	F	Sex	Year	Inter	R²
Family	.03	.02	.14	.45		.11	.31	.20
Home Economics	.11	.94	.36	.95	.84	.25	-.24	.18
Office Practice	.02	.22	.07	.42	.20	.04	.16	.13
Shorthand	.03	.65	.01	.36	.63		-.27	.22
Typing	.59	1.24	.48	.99	.64	-.11	-.14	.21
Bookkeeping	.22	.48	.17	.37	.26	-.05	-.06	.06
General Business	.12	.19	.09	.08	.07	-.03	-.07	.01
Sales	.02	.02	.14	.15		.13		.03
Agriculture	.36	.01	.48	.08	-.37	.09		.07
Auto Mechanics	.08	.00	.15	.01				
Drawing	.29	.01	.37	.02				
Electricity	.12	.00	.20	.00				
General Shop	.46	.00	.14	.02	(negligible female enrollment)			
Machine Shop	.18	.00	.44	.00				
Printing	.08	.00	.11	.03				
Sheet Metal	.16	.00	.33	.00				
Woodworking	.28	.00	.52	.03				
Number	(1394)	(1379)	(1406)	(1421)	(5600)			

[a]Most courses are year long. Some may be one semester.

[b]Coefficients are from the two variable equations unless the interaction term is larger than two standard errors. Only coefficients larger than two standard errors are reported.

treme sex typing occurs in all of the male crafts and in the secretarial courses, office practice and shorthand. With the possible exception of 1975 male enrollment in office practice, these courses are exclusive to one or the other sex and remain so over the 1964–1975 period.

Sex typing, but not exclusivity, is apparent in the other female courses. In typing, home economics, and family, enrollments are predominatly female, but they also reflect substantial male participation. It turns out that bookkeeping has a substantial female majority, but business and sales show more equal male and female enrollments. These course patterns clearly reflect occupational sex typing, but also show considerable participation of males in female courses, a pattern just the opposite of that expected on the basis of a masculinization hypothesis. Furthermore, these patterns are intensified over the decade. There is increased male, but clearly not female, enrollment in vocational craft courses. In line with shifts in occupational preference already observed, and with the predicted shift toward individually relevant courses, boys increased their enrollment in every blue collar-craft except general shop. Other changes are somewhat course-specific and difficult to generalize, although they do indicate a relative male increase in the traditional female courses.

In vocational courses, then, substantial sex-typing persists, especially across a considerable number of male blue-collar crafts. The sex role change in the female vocational courses is extensive, but varied in outcomes. We have observed substantial sex role change in sex-typed female courses. However, these substantial shifts increased sex typing in two courses and decreased it in three, while the blue-collar crafts remain exclusively male.

Academic Courses

Academic enrollments are analyzed in table 5.4. They show substantial sex typing, but also social change and sex role change.

With a few exceptions, the predicted sex differences in number of courses taken are observed in table 5.4. Girls are more likely to take English, speech, and language, boys are more likely to take math and science. There is less clear-cut difference between the sexes in the social science enrollments, although the greater female enrollment in psychology is consistent with a greater concern for personal relations. Girls are much more likely to take music and somewhat more likely to take art, especially in 1975. Generally, these enrollments differ as expected, but the level of difference is not very great, except for music and language and 1964 enrollments in physics. The substantial sex differences in mathmatics and science enrollment described by some of the writers on sex roles do not materialize in these data. Girls are more similar to boys in mathematics and science enrollments than boys are to girls in language and music. Thus, predicted differences in course taking materialize, but the levels are clearly limited and do not approach the differences in more directly relevant vocational courses.

Change in patterns of course enrollments over the decade are consistent with the idea that the 1960–1970 period involved a marked decline in ado-

Table 5.4.

Number of Academic Courses[a] by Sex and Year

| Course | Average Courses | | | | Metric Regression Coefficients[b] | | | |
| | 1964 | | 1975 | | | | | |
	M	F	M	F	Sex	Year	Inter	R^2
English	2.61	2.70	2.29	2.37	.08	-.32		.05
Language	.59	.92	.36	.67	.32	-.24		.05
Speech	.21	.30	.32	.35	.10	.11	-.07	.01
Art	.25	.30	.31	.50		.07	.13	.02
Economics	.16	.15	.21	.16		.05	-.04	.00
History	1.49	1.45	1.30	1.26		-.19		.03
Music	.51	.98	.54	.93	.43			.03
Psychology	.18	.29	.27	.39	.11	.10		.03
Social Science	.31	.21	.21	.14	-.08	-.09		.02
Sociology	.52	.51	.53	.57		.03		.00
Algebra	.45	.27	.43	.32	-.17		.07	.02
Biology	.92	.98	.91	.94	.05	-.03		.00
Chemistry	.53	.40	.35	.32	-.14	-.19	.11	.02
Geometry	.65	.56	.54	.50	-.06	-.08		.01
Math	.55	.27	.59	.40	-.28	.04	.08	.04
Natural Science	.16	.08	.19	.12	-.08	.04		.01
Physics	.39	.09	.21	.10	-.29	-.17	.18	.08
Number	(1394)	(1374)	(1406)	(1421)	(5600)			

[a]Most courses are year long. Some may be one semester.

[b]Coefficients are from two variable equations unless the interaction term is larger than two standard errors. Only coefficients larger than two standard errors are reported.

lescent acceptance of traditional values of work, citizenship, and success striving. By and large, the students in 1975 less often enrolled in traditional academic subjects like English, language, history, and chemistry. They increased enrollments in speech, psychology, and art, and, as we have just observed, in various vocationally oriented courses. This shift is consistent with the reduction in achievement scores observed in the National Assessments of Educational Progress (1978, 1979).

Of greater concern to this study, however, is that table 5.4 reveals one of the clearest patterns of sex role change yet observed in this study. There is a relative gain in female enrollment in four of the six math and science courses where an increase is realistically possible. Across courses, this increase is variously due either to an actual female increase or to a smaller decline in female than male enrollments over this period. However, in each case the result is a clear convergence in the enrollments of girls and boys, even in such a clearly sex-typed course as senior physics. It is also interesting that a rough equivalence in the enrollments of these sexes has persisted in the three mathematics and science courses for which no interaction is observed. The result of these several patterns in 1975 is a considerably smaller sex difference in average science and mathematics enrollment that has been assumed to exist.

These patterns substantially mitigate the moderate sex typing of science and mathematics that existed in 1964. The overall differences were not overwhelming to begin with and over the decade there was a decided shift toward equivalence in science and math course taking. Even in physics, one-third of the enrollment was female by 1975 compared to one-fifth in 1964. These are encouraging findings for those who have emphasized the importance of quantitative and scientific specialization for later educational, and occupational channeling. If the sex typing of work is a consequence of early preparation in mathematics and science, as Ernest (1976) suggests, these results indicate that an original relatively moderate effect is in the process of being further reduced.

With only one exception, the patterns described in table 5.4 reveal convergence in the enrollment patterns of boys and girls, with the clearest shifts occurring in the highly critical areas of science and mathematics. By 1975 girls had clearly reduced the male advantage in these sex-typed areas. These enrollments represent a substantial sex role change, one that fits the concept of masculinization.

Facilitating Variables

The possibility that observed sex role changes in patterns of course enrollment might be even greater among certain subgroups was examined through the use of the five selected facilitating variables in an analysis limited to the sex-typed courses where the direction of expected change is clearly related to themes in the sex role literature (table 5.5). Table 5.5 summarizes the outcomes of the significant third-order interactions, whether predicted, contrary, or ambiguous. (Regression coefficients for these equations are presented in appendix B, panel 1.)

Table 5.5.

**Direction of Effects[a] of Statistically Significant Third
Order Interactions for Course Enrollments[b]**

Course	Intell.	Father's Educ.	Mother's Work	Numb. Consult.	Read News.
		Facilitating Variables			
Vocational					
Family	+	+		+	
Home Economics		-	-		
Office Practice					
Shorthand		-			
Typing					
Academic					
English				0	
Language					
Speech					
Algebra					
Biology	0	+			
Chemistry					
Geometry					
Mathematics	+	+		+	
Natural Science					
Physics	+			+	0

[a]Signs for direction: (+) = predicted; (0) = ambiguous; (-) = contrary to prediction.

[b]Only the sex-typed courses are reported here. Regression coefficients for the significant interactions are presented in Appendix B, Panel 1.

Table 5.5 shows that fifteen of the seventy-five regressions involving the five facilitating variables and fifteen courses produced significant third-order interaction coefficients. This is four times the number expected by chance at the .05 level and is the strongest support yet for the concept of the facilitating variables. However, the pattern qualifies the conclusion because only in mathematics and science are the results consistently in the predicted direction. Among vocational courses and the academic language courses, only three out of seven results are in the predicted direction.

The pattern of significant interactions of the facilitating variables on the changes in years of mathematics and science enrollments provides evidence that change is occurring where it would be expected, given the assumption of social forces acting on contemporary sex roles. In eight cases out of the thirty-five regressions, the third-order interaction coefficient is greater than two standard errors, over four times the number that would be expected by chance at the .05 level. Furthermore, six of these are in the predicted direction and two are ambiguous. Not a single one of the eight interactions was contrary to prediction. This is one of the few instances in this analysis where the facilitating variables (except mother's work) produce predicted effects. Given the strategic significance of mathematics and science to both personality and social aspects of sex roles, this is a very interesting outcome.

Although the specific patterns of these interactions are consistent with predictions about forces for change, because of the shift away from hard work and achievement, in most cases this means primarily that girls in the high change subgroup merely maintained their positions while other groups declined in their enrollments in sciences and mathematics. Change is thus relative, rather than absolute. In both physics and mathematics, it was the highly intelligent girls with highly educated fathers who increased their enrollments. All other groups declined over the decade. In addition, the effect of consultants in mathematics and physics was consistent with the pattern previously observed, suggesting that consultants were giving sex-typed advice in 1964, liberating advice in 1975. In 1964 the number of consultants was negatively related to female enrollment in physics and mathematics, but in 1975 the number of consultants was positively related to female enrollment in those courses. Thus, while neither the number of effects nor their magnitude was overwhelming, there is evidence here that sex role change in theoretically critical areas of mathematics and science is occurring and to the greatest degree where we might expect them to occur. As before, the only important exception to these patterns is mother's work status, which again fails to produce an effect, contrary to the central importance given this variable in the literature.

Conclusion

Sex differences reflecting academic sex typing in course enrollments have been observed in both academic and vocational courses, although the strongest sex typing of enrollments occurs among vocational courses, especially blue-collar crafts and secretarial courses. Less distinct, but nevertheless predicted, differences were also observed in language, science, and mathematics. However, sex typing in mathematics and science courses was less extreme than some writing in this area would suggest.

Social change was observed in the reduction in the enrollments in traditional academic courses and the increased enrollments in vocational and family courses. These changes were consistent with assumptions about the hedonistic and individualistic nature of social change in the 1970s.

Finally, strong evidence of sex role change was observed in the academic courses where female enrollment in mathematics and science courses increased relative to male enrollments. In the clearest evidence of sex role change observed so far in this study, significant increases in female enrollments relative to male enrollments were observed in four of six courses where such change was possible. In the remaining two courses it turned out that sex differences were not so great to begin with.

For once, the evidence of changing sex roles was further strengthened by the facilitating analysis, which revealed predicted effects in many more of the mathematics and science regressions than could have occurred by chance. It seems clear that an important reflection of burgeoning change in adolescent sex roles has been observed in the increased female participation in mathematics and science.

This picture of change was not observed in the vocational and family courses. Blue-collar shop courses remained totally male, a pattern intensified by the increased male enrollment in the numerous shop courses available to boys. Some reduction in sex typing was observed in shorthand and typing, but this was counteracted by the increased sex typing of family and office practice.

Overall then, the observed change was primarily in academic subjects relevant to college-bound students. Among these students, however, the changes that occurred were clearly in courses of critical theoretical significance.

Course Orientations

As we have seen, attitudinal orientations toward academic courses are presumed to account for observed differences between the sexes, especially in mathematics and science courses. I examine two aspects of these orientations—the perceived helpfulness of the course for future occupational goals and the reported enjoyment in studying courses. The former is related to the sex typing of work and life plans, while enjoyment in studying could reflect either pleasure in performing cognitive tasks the respondent is well equipped to perform or conformity to stereotypic expectations about content area. The idea of mathematics as a male domain has been a central feature of social explanations of sex differences in mathematics enrollment and achievement (Fox, Tobin, and Brady 1979). The principle could also apply to other courses that are clearly sex typed.

Perceived Helpfulness

Perceived helpfulness ratings in this study are based on student responses to a restricted list of courses included in the 1964 questionnaire and necessarily repeated in 1975 (table 5.6).[18] While this list is less inclusive than the transcript-based list used in other analysis, it includes the sex-typed language, science, and vocational courses in which the greatest perceived differences are expected between the sexes and where change is most critical.

The perceived helpfulness of vocational courses varies as expected be-

Table 5.6.

Helpfulness Ratings of Vocational Courses by Sex and Year

Course	Average Helpfulness Rating				Metric Regression Coefficients[a]				Number
	1964		1975						
	M	F	M	F	Sex	Year	Inter	R²	
Home Economics	2.31	2.44	2.26	2.44	.17			.01	(2329)
Office Practice	2.46	2.76	2.18	2.68	.42	-.11		.07	(921)
Shorthand[b]	--	2.31	1.79	2.21	--	--	--	--	(1175)
Typing	2.46	2.71	2.22	2.61	.25	-.23	.13	.09	(4241)
Bookkeeping	2.48	2.43	2.40	2.48			.12	.00	(1938)
Agriculture[b]	2.11	--	2.28	2.33					(655)
Architect Drawing[b]	2.42	--	2.33	--					(433)
Auto Mechanic[b]	2.65	--	2.56	--					(607)
Electricity[b]	2.45	--	2.25	--					(545)
General Shop[b]	2.35	--	2.38	2.29		(negligible female rating)			(1274)
Machine Shop[b]	2.40	--	2.44	--					(827)
Mechanical Drawing[b]	2.32	--	2.44	2.19					(1127)
Printing[b]	2.22	--	2.05	2.33					(418)
Sheet Metal[b]	2.20	--	2.23	--					(679)
Woodworking[b]	2.38	--	2.37	2.00					(1223)

[a]Coefficients are from the two variable equations unless the interaction term is at least two standard errors. Only coefficients larger than two standard errors are reported.

[b]Less than 25 cases in at least one sex by year call. Related means and regressions not computed.

tween the sexes. Office and secretarial courses are rated much higher for girls than for boys. Girls perceive office practice, shorthand, and typing as more helpful than boys do. Furthermore, neither of the significant interactions reflect reduction in sex typing of the office courses, although in the case of bookkeeping these effects are negligible in explaining variation in the ratings. For office practice and typing, however, the sex differences and social change in helpfulness ratings account for meaningful levels of explained variance.

Negligible female enrollment in the traditional male vocational courses precludes comparable analysis, except for five courses in which 1975 female enrollment was at token levels of thirty to ninety respondents. While these levels suggest token process or perhaps even single, special classes, they do provide the basis for some comparison. In three of these courses, expected traditional perceptions prevail, but in agriculture and printing they do not. Printing is especially interesting because the forty-three girls taking this course perceive it as more helpful than boys do. Generally though, in shop, drawing, and woodworking, these courses are perceived as more helpful by boys than by girls.

While the analysis of table 5.6 is unfortunately restricted by enrollment patterns, the limited conclusion is one of continuing sex typing in the perceived utility of these courses. In light of the connections between the vocational offerings in the high schools and traditional sex-typed occupations, this is not a surprising finding. The intensification of the pattern in the two significant interactions is of interest as it suggests continuing sex typing in these courses that parallels the resurgent sex typing of occupational choices already observed.

The differential relevance of the academic courses is apparent in table 5.7. There are statistically significant differences between the ratings of girls and boys in every one of the courses listed, and these differences are without exception in the direction expected from the sex role stereotypes. Girls view English as the most helpful subject, boys view mathematics as the most helpful, a perfect representation of the basic polarity of concerns of the instrumental and expressive orientations. Beyond those prototypic courses, the perceptions remain consistent. Girls see art, language, and psychology as more helpful than boys do, while boys rate biology, chemistry, and physics as more helpful than girls do. The only exception to this pattern is the ambiguous course in social studies, which boys rate as slightly more helpful than girls do.

With the exception of art, all of the coefficients for years are negative and

Table 5.7.

Helpfulness Ratings of Academic Courses by Sex and Year

Courses	Average Helpfulness Rating				Metric Regression Coefficients[a]				
	1964		1975						
	M	F	M	F	Sex	Year	Inter	R^2	Number
English	2.62	2.85	2.32	2.59	.25	-.28		.11	(5354)
Language	1.98	2.08	1.86	1.95	.09	-.12		.01	(2659)
Art	2.04	2.10	2.01	2.16	.11			.00	(2329)
Psychology	2.40	2.53	2.33	2.42	.10	-.09		.01	(1614)
Social Studies	2.36	2.27	2.18	2.15	-.06	-.15		.02	(5201)
Biology	2.14	2.01	2.06	2.05	-.13	-.08	.12	.00	(5207)
Chemistry	2.32	2.19	2.21	2.16	-.09	-.07		.01	(2407)
Mathematics	2.67	2.40	2.51	2.38	-.27	-.16	.14	.04	(5220)
Physics	2.40	2.19	2.32	2.07	-.22	-.08		.03	(1215)

[a]Coefficients are from the two variable equations unless the interaction term is at least two standard errors. Only coefficients larger than two standard errors are reported.

greater than two standard errors. Students were less sanguine about the relevance of the high school courses in 1975 than they were in 1964, again a pattern consistent with the general dissatisfaction with adult norms and institutions. The curriculum in 1975 was perceived as less useful than in 1964.

In contrast to the pattern observed in vocational courses, however, sex role change in the form of masculinization is observed in these ratings. In both biology and mathematics ratings, female perceptions remain constant in the face of the general decrease in perceived helpfulness of courses. In both cases the reduction in perception of helpfulness between 1964 and 1975 is due to male devaluation. Female evaluations hold constant or increase. This constitutes a relative increase and is consistent with the idea that girls in 1975 were beginning to see mathematics and some science as relevant to female as well as male purposes. However, these two courses are only the opening wedge, as the majority of these ratings reflect the traditional stereotypic view of these courses, without change. In most cases, sex differences are maintained in the face of substantial social change in the perceived helpfulness of these courses. If, as the literature suggests, performance differences reflect differential perception of the appropriateness or utility of courses, we are here observing largely, but not completely, unchanging orientations consistent with and probably underlying sex differences in cognitive performance.

Reported Enjoyment

Courses most enjoyed studying provides another view of sex-typed orientations toward vocational and academic courses, again using the restricted listings of courses that was used in the helpfulness ratings. In this case, the base population in each regression consists of those who reported taking the course. The dummy variable scoring of most enjoyed was made if the student reported the named course was "most" or "second most" enjoyed studying.[19] This response probably reflects sex-differentiated cognitive abilities or sex-typed views of appropriateness of the course to the sex of the respondent. Generally, we assume people like what they are good at and, as Kohlberg (1966) and others argue, that values and motives become channeled toward sex-appropriate roles and activities.

The analysis of table 5.8 provides strong support for this conception in the academic courses, and to a more limited degree, among the vocational courses also.

In three of the four vocational courses that can be analyzed, girls more often report the course as one "most enjoyed studying," although the effects are not great and the explained variance negligible. Furthermore, there is no change across the years, nor is there any evidence of convergence. These office and home economics courses are more enjoyed by girls than boys to about the same degree in each year.

With two or three exceptions, reported enjoyment in academic courses is consistent with sex-related differences in cognitive abilities and in sex role aspects of course content. Girls are considerably more likely to enjoy studying English and language, boys are more likely to enjoy studying chemistry, and especially mathematics and physics. Biology is one exception—the sexes do not differ in their enjoyment of studying this science. On the whole, though, these students report enjoying studying course content appropriate to their sex role.

Social change and also sex role change in enjoyment in studying academic courses are clearly evident in the analysis of table 5.8. Consistent with other evidence observed, there is a general decline in the enjoyment of studying academic courses, especially the sciences. While this might reflect in part decreased satisfaction with these specific courses and designation of other academic courses not on this restricted list, it may also reflect shifts toward less demanding, more vocationally oriented course content. Increased satis-

Table 5.8.

Course "Most Enjoyed" Studying by Sex and Year

| Course | Proportion Most Enjoying | | | | Metric Regression Coefficients[a] | | | | |
| | 1964 | | 1975 | | | | | | |
	M	F	M	F	Sex	Year	Inter	R²	Number
Home Economics	.12	.20	.07	.18	.11			.02	(2442)
Office Practice	.00	.12	.08	.15	.09			.01	(1023)
Shorthand[b]	--	.15	.25	.12	--	--	--	--	(1166)
Typing	.02	.09	.02	.09	.07			.02	(4302)
Bookkeeping	.26	.25	.21	.25				.00	(2025)
English	.15	.37	.11	.25	.23	-.03	-.09	.06	(5525)
Language	.05	.18	.06	.12	.12		-.06	.02	(2664)
Art	.14	.17	.19	.21		.05		.02	(1768)
Psychology	.23	.35	.18	.25	.09	-.09		.02	(1664)
Social Studies	.38	.28	.07	.06	-.09	-.30	.08	.12	(5429)
Biology	.16	.16	.12	.12		-.04		.00	(5314)
Chemistry	.20	.12	.09	.10	-.08	-.11	.09	.02	(2394)
Mathematics	.29	.16	.19	.15	-.13	-.10	.10	.02	(5369)
Physics	.22	.05	.11	.02	-.13	-.08		.05	(1205)

[a]Coefficients are from the two variable equations unless the interaction term is at least two standard errors. Only coefficients larger than two standard errors are reported.

[b]Less than 24 cases in at least one sex by year cell. Related means and regressions not computed.

faction with art and the lack of significant change in the listed vocational courses suggests this may be the case.[20]

Of most interest in table 5.8 are the statistically significant interactions showing important sex role change in these subjective orientations toward courses. Significant interactions are observed in five of the nine regressions,[21] in every case reflecting a reduction in sex-related differences in the enjoyment of studying these courses. Female reduction in enjoyment and relative male stability are observed in English and language, resulting in convergence between the sexes in their enjoyment of these courses. Analogous shifts appear in chemistry and mathematics from the male perspective. Male satisfaction drops considerably while female satisfaction remains nearly stable. The result is a relative increase in female satisfaction in these areas, resulting in reduction of the differences in the subjective reactions to these sex-typed courses. Thus, in 1975 sex was less important to the reported subjective reaction to these courses as it was to their perceived utility. It appears that school circumstances at the level of the curriculum and possibly involving advisement of students and perhaps also shifts in the values of the peer subculture have functioned to reduce sex role differentiation and to instigate some of the first major signs of sex role change observed in this research.

Facilitating Variables

In great contrast to the analysis of course enrollments (table 5.5), the facilitating analysis of helpfulness of the sex-typed courses fails to produce any support for the subgroup hypotheses. While four of the forty-five interactions of the five facilitating variables with the nine sex-typed courses (home economics, office practice, typing, English, language, biology, chemistry, mathematics, and physics) are statistically significant, only one is in the predicted direction.

On the other hand, the facilitating analysis of enjoyment comes close to supporting the hypothesis. While only four of the forty-five interactions are again significant, all four of these are in the predicted direction and consistent with the findings that reduction in sex typing of courses is most pronounced among high aptitude, high status students. Highly intelligent girls are most likely to report decreased enjoyment in the traditional course content of English and language, and decreased enjoyment in language is also reported by girls with highly educated fathers. In addition, only those girls with more educated fathers show a relative increase in the enjoyment of studying chemistry. All male groups and girls with fathers limited to high school and grade school education decrease across the period. Thus, while the number of effects could be dismissed as chance, the pattern for course enjoyment provides some borderline support.

Taken overall, however, the facilitating analysis of helpfulness and enjoyment ratings provides little support for the subgroup hypothesis. The equations for the significant interactions are presented in panels 2 and 3 of appendix B.

Conclusion

The analysis of orientations toward vocational and academic course content has shown both tradition and change.

In both the perceived helpfulness of courses and in personal enjoyment in studying courses, these students reveal traditional sex role differentiation consistent with discussions in contemporary literature on social factors underlying sex differences in cognitive performance and achievement. As such writers as Sherman (1978) and Fox, Tobin, and Brady (1979) suggest, boys more often perceive mathematics and science as helpful to their anticipated occupational goals, while girls more often perceive English and language as helpful.

Sex differentiation also appeared in the reported enjoyment in studying course content. Girls more often reported English and language as courses most enjoyed studying while boys more often enjoyed science and mathematics. Whether these differences reflect the outcomes of performances in areas of high competence, or the satisfaction of performing sex-appropriate roles, these students experienced satisfactions where sex role formulations predicted they would occur.

We have also observed social change and, to the greatest degree yet in this research, sex role change. As in the preceding sections on enrollments, we have observed substantial beginnings of change in sex-related orientations toward the curriculum. While these changes do not eliminate sex differences in orientation toward course content, they substantially mitigate them, especially, and significantly, in female satisfaction with mathematics and science. While this is in large part due to the decline in male satisfaction, we have observed near equivalence between the sexes in enjoyment of study in most courses listed. Only in English and physics, the most stereotypic contents, did appreciable sex differences in satisfaction remain in 1975. These are substantial changes consistent with social explanations of cognitive differences.

The facilitating analysis again failed to produce important, consistent effects on these changes—at least for perceived helpfulness. There was some borderline support for change in patterns of enjoyment in that four of forty-five third-order interactions were significant and predicted. They suggested that intelligence and father's education facilitated decreasing sex typing of enjoyment in courses. The latter is interesting, considering the formulations showing that the father is the most important sex-typing agent in girls' orientations toward mathematics and science (see Fox, Tobin, and Brady 1979). Notwithstanding this congruence, there is very little overall support for the idea of the facilitating variables in the two analyses of subjective orientations toward courses.

Course Grades

Course grades are examined for sex difference, social change, and sex role change for all courses in which there are at least twenty-five respondents in each sex-by-year cell. This will mean that some regressions are based on very small, sometimes highly disproportionate, populations of boys and girls. On the other hand, regressions for "typical year" courses are normally based on sizable populations. The reader is reminded of the earlier analysis of course enrollments where "typical year" courses were designated (tables 5.1 and 5.2).

The grade units reflected in the following tables are based on a constant interval scoring system running from 1 to 13 where $F = 1$, $D- = 2$, $D = 3$, etc., and $A+ = 13$. Thus, the qualitatively "average" C would be scored 6.

Sex-related achievement differences in courses are somewhat obscured by the tendency of girls to do better in all courses, whether sex-typed feminine or masculine. Consequently, the effect of sex typing on achievement of boys and girls must be considered in terms of the amount of female superiority, not in the direction of effects as in the achievement measures most commonly reported in the literature. The central issue of my analysis, sex role change, is of course unaffected by this pattern, as the coefficient reflecting the sex-by-year interaction represents relative change in the difference between the sexes over the time period regardless of the original direction of the difference.

Female superiority is expected to be greatest in courses sex-typed as female and least in the mathematics and science courses traditionally defined as masculine.

Vocational Courses

Grades in vocational courses are presented in table 5.9. The strong sex typing of the vocational courses coupled with "typical course" effects severely reduced the number of vocational courses that could be analyzed. Only eleven courses across the three years have distribution adequate for analysis.

Among the handful of vocational courses analyzed in table 5.9, the strength of the regression coefficients and differences between the means reveal that the greatest female superiority occurs in typing, home economics, and family. Smaller differences and one reversal occur in the more general business, bookkeeping, and sales courses. These patterns are consistent with the idea that performance is highest in sex-appropriate courses, whether because of

Table 5.9.

Grades in Vocational Courses[a] by Sex and Year

Year and Course	Average Grades[b]				Metric Regression Coefficients[c]				
	1964		1975						
	M	F	M	F	Sex	Year	Inter	R^2	Number
Sophomore									
Typing	5.87	7.00	6.54	7.50	1.02	.58		.04	(1773)
General Business	4.80	6.14	7.15	7.27	.88	1.68		.06	(213)
Junior									
Typing	6.07	7.08	6.67	8.09	1.17	.88		.05	(1664)
Bookkeeping[d]	7.50	7.18	7.17	7.53					(465)
General Business	5.09	3.97	7.03	7.46		2.70		.18	(147)
Senior									
Family	6.90	8.77	7.08	8.69	1.64	.05		.07	(669)
Home Economics	5.71	7.99	7.76	9.04	2.28	2.05	-1.00	.12	(1552)
Typing	6.02	7.54	7.08	8.63	1.52	1.07		.09	(1171)
Bookkeeping	6.65	7.52	7.55	8.68	.95	1.07		.04	(1030)
General Business	6.20	6.77	8.06	8.79	.62	1.94		.10	(307)
Sales	4.35	4.52	7.95	8.81	.68	3.95		.30	(212)

[a]Courses with fewer than 25 cases in any sex by year cell have been omitted.

[b]Based on a scoring system where (F) = 1; (D-) = 2; (D) = 3 and (A+) = 13.

[c]Coefficients are from the two-variable equation unless the interaction term is at least two standard errors. Only coefficients larger than two standard errors are reported.

[d]Coefficient of determination not significant at .05 level.

underlying differences in aptitudes or because of attitudinal and expectancy effects related to sex-role stereotypes.

Over the decade, grades in most of these vocational courses increase substantially for home economics, general business, and sales. This is surprising in the face of all the previous evidence on declining levels of achievement and commitment. It may reflect better instruction and improved curriculum over the years, or it could reflect the escalation of grades observed in college populations over this period.

Consistent with previous analysis showing continuing sex typing of vocational courses, only one of the eleven interaction coefficients is at least twice its standard error. Girls in senior home economics classes, which are the modal classes, increase their grades over the period relatively less than males do, resulting in a convergence that reduces sex typing in this course. Apart from that single instance, however, table 5.9 shows sex difference, and social change, but very little sex role change. As noted, this is consistent with the lack of change observed in the perceived helpfulness of, and satisfaction with, vocational courses.

Table 5.10.

Grades in Sophomore Academic Courses by Sex and Year

| Course | Average Sophomore Grade[a] | | | | Metric Regression Coefficients[b] | | | | |
| | 1964 | | 1975 | | | | | | |
	M	F	M	F	Sex	Year	Inter	R^2	Number
English	5.96	7.64	7.12	8.55	1.55	1.03		.11	(5326)
Language	7.32	8.09	7.89	8.76	.81	.63		.03	(1721)
Speech	--	--	--	--			-	--	---
Art	6.52	7.74	7.38	8.25	.98	.64		.05	(480)
Economics[c]	--	--	--	--				--	---
History	6.26	7.04	7.08	8.04	.86	.91		.04	(2052)
Music	9.67	9.62	9.71	10.42			.76	.02	(1502)
Psychology[c]	--	--	--	--				--	---
Social Science	5.86	6.06	7.04	7.58		1.28		.05	(344)
Sociology[c]	--	--	--	--				--	---
Algebra	5.96	6.75	6.08	6.50	.57			.01	(1170)
Biology	6.27	6.96	6.91	7.62	.70	.65		.03	(4678)
Chemistry[c]	--	--	--	--				--	---
Geometry	7.20	7.13	7.47	7.80		.47		.01	(2283)
Math	5.96	6.47	8.04	8.45		2.03		.11	(514)
Natural Science	5.95	5.51	6.66	7.31		1.14		.04	(241)
Physics[c]	--	--	--	--				--	---

[a]Based on a scoring system where (F) = 1; (D-) = 2; (D) = 3; and (A+) = 13.

[b]Coefficients are from the two variable equation except where the interaction coefficient is twice the standard error. Only coefficients larger than two standard errors are reported.

[c]Values not reported. Fewer than 25 cases in at least one sex by year all.

Academic Courses

Grades in academic courses over the three years are examined in tables 5.10, 5.11, 5.12, which contain sophomore, junior, and senior grades analyses, respectively.

As we observed in the preceding discussion of achievement motivation, girls are higher achievers than boys in nearly every course they take, mathematics and sciences included.[22] Furthermore, there is no evidence of de-

Table 5.11.

Grades in Junior Academic Courses by Sex and Year

Course	Average Junior Grade[a]				Metric Regression Coefficients[b]				
	1964		1975						
	M	F	M	F	Sex	Year	Inter	R²	Number
English	5.67	7.39	6.96	8.59	1.67	1.24		.12	(5109)
Language	7.32	8.09	7.89	8.76	1.09	1.20		.07	(1196)
Speech[c]	--	--	--	--				--	---
Art	6.65	7.79	7.77	8.62	.97	.95		.07	(618)
Economics[c]	--	--	--	--				--	---
History	6.26	7.04	7.08	8.04	.90	.82		.04	(4715)
Music	10.14	9.92	10.02	10.48			.67	.01	(1399)
Psychology[c]	--	--	--	--				--	---
Social Science[c]	--	--	--	--				--	---
Sociology[c]	--	--	--	--				--	---
Algebra	6.80	.765	7.41	7.75	.63			.01	(728)
Biology	5.26	7.00	7.03	8.19	1.38	1.53		.12	(238)
Chemistry	6.40	6.67	7.79	8.05		1.39		.05	(1737)
Geometry	6.16	6.81	5.94	6.34	.55			.01	(710)
Mth	6.96	7.33	8.07	8.45		1.16		.04	(764)
Natural Science	5.75	5.54	7.49	8.18		2.01		.14	(214)
Physics[c]	--	--	--	--				--	---

[a]Based on a scoring system where $(F) = 1$; $(D-) = 2$; $(D) = 3$; and $(A+) = 13$.

[b]Coefficients are from the two variable equation except where the interaction coefficient is twice the standard error. Only coefficients larger than two standard errors are reported.

[c]Values not reported. Fewer than 25 cases in at least one sex by year all.

Table 5.12.

Grades in Senior Academic Courses by Sex and Year

| Course | Average Senior Grade[a] | | | | Metric Regression Coefficients[b] | | | | |
| | 1964 | | 1975 | | | | | | |
	M	F	M	F	Sex	Year	Inter	R^2	Number
English	6.23	7.75	7.78	9.19	1.47	1.49		.14	(3515)
Language	7.61	8.70	9.45	10.07	.91	1.52		.10	(639)
Speech	7.77	8.82	8.21	9.73	1.22	.70		.06	(854)
Art	7.12	8.24	7.47	8.50	1.07			.04	(812)
Economics	6.34	6.06	9.19	8.00	1.46	.78	-.80	.04	(776)
History	6.26	6.94	7.57	8.32	.71	1.35		.05	(923)
Music	10.17	10.14	10.09	10.62			.53	.01	(1251)
Psychology	6.68	7.80	7.87	9.14	1.20	1.28		.08	(1487)
Social Science	5.29	6.22	7.40	8.89	1.10	2.34		.14	(546)
Sociology	6.21	7.92	7.34	8.72	1.23	1.28		.09	(2785)
Algebra	5.06	6.90	6.21	7.17	1.43			.08	(163)
Biology	7.47	8.96	8.58	9.73	1.26	.92		.06	(336)
Chemistry	6.10	6.76	7.74	7.88		1.36		.05	(409)
Geometry[c]	--	--	--	--				--	---
Math	7.10	7.73	7.81	8.26	.52	.65		.02	(1255)
Natural Science	6.04	6.02	7.44	8.15		1.64		.07	(305)
Physics	7.29	8.99	9.05	9.88	1.70	1.76	-.87	.12	(972)

[a]Based on a scoring system where (F) = 1; (D-) = 2; (D) = 3; and (A+) = 13.

[b]Coefficients are from the two variable equation except where the interaction coefficient is twice the standard error. Only coefficients larger than two standard errors are reported.

[c]Values not reported. Fewer than 25 cases in at least one sex by year all.

cline in this superiority from sophomore to senior years, as some writers on the deleterious consequences of stereotypic feminine dependency assume must occur as adolescent girls increase their concerns about dating and popularity. If anything, tables 5.10, 5.11, and 5.12 show an increase in female achievement advantage in academic courses over the three years of school.

While girls do better in almost every course they take, the strength of the difference is greatest in the verbal skill courses of English, language, and speech. In these courses, sex accounts for about one and a half grade units. The female advantage in English in all three years is larger than all but one other comparison, although that one (physics) is totally unexpected and highly significant. However, with that single exception, this pattern is consistent with the large body of evidence showing female advantage in verbal skills. Also consistent with this is the sex coefficient for speech in the senior, "typical year" class. Except for sophomore language, the sex differences and the time effect account for meaningful amounts of variance in these grades.

Females also do better in mathematics and science, in spite of the assumptions that they are disadvantaged in these areas. Without exception, female grades in mathematics and science are higher than male across the three years of high school. Looking at this overwhelming superiority in achievement, it is puzzling to consider all of the discussion in the sex role literature about male competence and female incapacity. Certainly, the nearly universal experience of all youth and educators must qualify such an assumption. Regardless of anxiety, fear of success, training for dependency, cultural contradictions, and external attributions, the simple fact is that throughout childhood and adolescence, girls outperform boys, as both sexes must obviously observe.

While girls outperform boys in all courses, their relative advantage reflects academic sex typing. They do considerably better than boys in English, language, and speech. In every one of those comparisons the regression coefficient for sex is over two standard errors. On the other hand, almost half of the coefficients in the science and mathematics regressions are under two standard errors. Furthermore, the relative differences are slightly larger for the "typical year" courses than for the smaller, more selective courses. These differences are summarized in the average regression coefficients for sex that are presented in table 5.13.[23] It is obvious the sex differences in the languages are greater than those in the sciences. Considering just the "typical year" courses, it can be seen that the average coefficients for language are over twice those of mathematics and science in the sophomore year and over three times as large in the junior year. The difference in the senior year is somewhat smaller, largely due to the suprising female advantage in physics. The coefficients for the other two senior science and mathematics courses are both less than half those of the language and speech averages.

The somewhat higher sex coefficients in the nontypical year science and mathematics courses appear to be a function of ability selection, resulting in somewhat more intelligent female students. The relatively large female coefficients in these low enrollment science courses are probably due to the

Table 5.13.

Average Sex Regression Coefficients for Grades in Academic Courses[a] by Type of Course

	School Year					
	Sophomore		Junior		Senior	
Type of Course	x_b sex	Numb. of Courses	x_b sex	Numb. of Courses	x_b sex	Numb. of Courses
All Courses						
Languages	1.18	(2)	1.38	(2)	1.20	(3)
Arts and Social Sciences	.58	(4)	.55	(3)	.77	(6)
Math and Science	.41	(5)	.59	(6)	.96	(6)
Typical Year Courses Only						
Language	1.18	(2)	1.38	(2)	1.34	(2)
Arts and Social Sciences	.40	(2)	.34	(2)	1.04	(5)
Math and Science	.47	(3)	.26	(1)	.88	(3)

[a]Including coefficients less than two standard errors not reported in Table 5.11.

presence of better qualified, more intelligent, female students. Of the eleven nontypical year mathematics and science courses, girls have higher intelligence than boys in six.[24] The sex coefficients in these six courses are about twice as strong as those in the remaining courses. Thus, it appears that the large sex coefficients and the apparent increases of the sex coefficients across the years of school are in part due to selective enrollments of more qualified girls in the more specialized courses.

On the other hand, the "typical year" enrollments are, with the exception of physics, largely free of this bias. Of the seven "typical year" courses, girls have higher intelligence in two, boys in two, and there is no important difference in the remaining three. Furthermore, the second lowest and the highest coefficients are found in the only two courses (junior chemistry and senior physics) in which girls have higher intelligence. Only in physics do large important differences in intelligence occur that could account for the coefficient. The average standardized intelligence score of girls in physics is .88, of boys, .62. Senior physics clearly attracts an elite group, but especially an elite group of girls. Thus, within the large enrollment typical courses, girls do better, although except for physics, they are not more intelligent than boys enrolled in the same courses. However, as I have noted, the size of the feminine advantage in mathematics and science is much less than in the language courses. When these selective processes are recognized and when "typical year" courses are considered as the primary evidence, sex typing does appear in the relative, although not in the abosolute, achievement of girls and boys in these courses.

Change in grading patterns across the years is apparent in tables 5.10, 5.11, and 5.12. With only a few scattered exceptions, the data show a marked increase in the level of grades awarded these students over the decade. Students in many courses in 1975 received grades that were around one and a half grading units higher than those received in 1964. Even though achievement scores declined over portions of this period (see National Assessments of Educational Progress 1978, 1979), grades went up in academic courses as they did in the vocational courses. Whether the increase resulted from improved study habits, better developed course content, or teacher leniency is an interesting question that cannot be addressed in this analysis.

Turning finally to the main issue in this study, that of sex role change, we find that tables 5.10, 5.11, and 5.12 are unequivocal about the absence of sex role change in levels of academic achievement. In spite of observations showing fairly substantial sex role changes in enrollments, orientations, and satisfaction, this analysis shows almost no sex role change, and the scattered significant interactions that do occur do not fit any simple conception of changing sex roles.

Of the five significant interactions, only one, senior physics, occurs among the sex-typed language, mathematics, and science courses, and this one shows increasing, rather than decreasing, sex typing. Girls did relatively better than boys in physics in 1964 than they did in 1975, although both sexes improved their grades over the decade. This interaction is due to the relatively larger increase in male grades, which in turn appears to be due to the decreasing male enrollment, resulting in a more selective male physics enrollment with higher intelligence in 1975 than in 1964. In 1964, there were 413 male physics students with an average standardized intelligence score of .57. By 1975 there were only 262 male physics students, but they had an average standardized intelligence score of .71. In the same period, female enrollment increased from 86 to 136, while intelligence scores remained high and essentially constant, .86 in 1964, .88 in 1975. Thus, the unique effect for physics seems largely to be a function of the small, extremely disproportionate enrollments in this "typical year" course. All of the other "typical year" courses had larger, more balanced enrollments, with few differences in the intelligence levels of the sexes, as we have seen.

Two of the remaining three interactions occur in music courses. In both sophomore and junior music courses substantial numbers of girls increased their grades, resulting in the inversion of relative advantages. In both courses, boys did better in 1964, but by 1975 girls received the higher grades. This pattern also appears in senior courses, but the differences are too small to produce a statistically significant interaction coefficient.

It is not clear what this pattern means, nor whether it has any relevance to sex role change. I am unaware of contemporary discussion on this point, although it is clear that musical composition, but not performance, has been in the past a male domain, presumably because of the nature of musical structure and its mathematical foundations. On the other hand, female enrollments are nearly double male enrollments in music courses.[25] Neither is it clear what economics means, nor whether it should be considered more of a male-oriented or female-oriented course. In any event it is a relatively small enrollment course easily affected by ability distribution effects and does not warrant extended interpretation, especially since the introduction of intelligence in supplementary analysis not presented here does reduce the interaction term to less than two standard errors.

Analysis of grades provides no real evidence for changing sex roles. Unlike the patterns of enrollment and orientation, there are sex differences but no comprehensible evidence of change. Whatever produced the sex-typed, differentiated performances in 1964 appeared to be still operating in 1975. This is another case in which substantial change in some social characteristic occurs, but does not affect the differences between the sexes.

Facilitating Variables

Facilitating variables analysis was conducted only for grades in those vocational and academic courses from tables 5.9, 5.10, 5.11, and 5.12 that are clearly sex typed and for which there are adequate enrollments. This amounts to twenty-nine courses, eight sophomore, nine junior, and twelve senior.

This analysis of the effects of relative change in sex-differentiated grades in sex-typed courses returns no support at all for the facilitating proposition. Of the 145 regressions run, only 7 of them resulted in regression coefficients at least twice the standard error. Furthermore, only 4 of these were in the predicted direction, while 3 were contrary to prediction. This is about as close to a chance pattern as one can obtain and does not warrant discussion, although the seven equations are presented in Appendix B, Panel 4.

Conclusions

In the analysis of grades, we have observed stereotypic sex role differences in the form of relative female advantage, greatest in English and language and the female vocational courses, weakest in science and mathematics courses and in the less clearly sex-typed vocational courses. While my interpretation of this relative difference as consistent with sex role patterns is a judgment, the effects, especially in the "typical year" academic courses, seem clear enough to sustain the argument. However, it is obvious that girls do better than boys in practically all courses, even those sex-typed as male. While there seems to be no hard empirically based explanation for this widely recognized pattern (see Dweyer 1979), it probably reflects a consistent sex difference in studentship, albeit with the exact factors unspecified. They may represent greater process achievement motivation or better, more effective patterns of school and work orientation. Whatever they turn out to be, the modification of this pattern of female achievement superiority across the sex-typed courses indicates a composite outcome in which the undetermined female studentship advantage appears to provide a constant level of superiority that sex role processes add to or subtract from.

While evidence is, oddly enough, lacking on the specific sources of such constant advantage, there is abundant evidence on academic sex typing and related cognitive differences, as we have seen. The constant advantage girls appear to have is modified exactly as expected in their performance across languages and sciences, and between clearly feminine vocational courses and those less sex typed. The lack of change in these relative differences and the failure to observe any meaningful facilitating effect indicates that there are important sex role processes continuing through this time period that have stabilized sex differences in course grades. Furthermore, the stability observed in this analysis is as clear as any so far observed in this research to this point. Moreover, it stands in marked contrast to the sex role change found in patterns of enrollment and attitudinal orientations toward courses. We have observed substantial changes in participation and attitude, but not in the relative difference between the sexes in grades.

Hours of Study

Female achievement superiority in academic courses, while not empirically explained, is generally attributed to greater effort and cooperativeness with the purposes of the school. The overwhelming achievement advantage of girls throughout the years of adolescence is discounted by students of achievement processes as consequences of presumably less significant effort rather than of needs to achieve. In any event, there is a supposition that girls try harder, expend more effort, and probably study more.

Self-Reported Hours of Study

A series of questions in the 1964 survey about amount of study in different locations provides us with some rough indication of sex differences in at least the factor of hours of study.

The average number of hours per week these students reported spending in study in different locations is analyzed in table 5.14. These results show that girls do study more, especially at home. Girls report studying about two hours a week more at home than boys.[26] There are no significant sex differences in the time spent studying in school contexts, probably because these hours are more externally controlled and less a function of internal motivation. Evidence of female self-control in studying appears also in the time spent studying while riding the school bus. While the amount of time spent studying on buses is negligible, girls report about twice the amount of time there that boys do. Thus, in the two contexts where internal motivation and

Table 5.14.

Hours of Study Per Week in Various Locations
(N=5600)

Location of Study	Average Hours[a] of Study Per Week				Metric Regressions Coefficients			
	1964		1975					
	M	F	M	F	Sex	Year	Inter.	R2
Library	2.79	2.76	2.63	2.98		-.24	.11	.01
Study Hall	4.98	4.77	2.14	2.07		-1.11		.20
Home	6.29	8.63	5.92	7.31	.50	-.36		.05
Bus	.24	.59	.28	.50	.20		-.09	.02
Classroom	2.14	2.23	3.35	3.25		.24		.01
Other Places	.69	.72	1.52	1.28		.17		.01
Combined Total	17.13	19.71	15.84	17.39	.32	-.48		.04

[a]Scattered and very extreme values have been arbitrarily reduced to 21 for Library, Study Hall and Others, to 31 for Home, 11 for Bus, and 16 for Classroom.

[b]For Regression Analysis, extreme skewdness of all distributions was reduced by using X_i where X_i represents the truncated distributions as described in [a].

self-control seem most important, girls show a clear advantage, consistent with the idea that they outperform boys because they expend more effort on schoolwork.

Over the years, there is a change in the pattern of studying resulting in a substantial net loss of about two hours a week. This appears to reflect curricular or administrative changes that have transferred studying from study halls to classrooms and other places. Nevertheless, there is a real decline in reported time spent studying at home.

Sex role change in study appears, but in opposing directions. Girls report a relative increase over boys in time spent studying in the library while they report a relative decrease in time spent studying on the bus. Of the two, the changing pattern related to library is much stronger and probably more informative. Although it is difficult to be certain about the meaning of the change, it represents a shift by girls from study at home to study in the library, a location less likely to be scheduled than classroom or study hall hours. This increased study in the library may be a function of shifting orientations from family to school and possibly of less stereotypic frames of reference. The shifts could also reflect changing school practices, transportation arrangements, or other background circumstances unrelated to sex role processes.

Facilitating analysis of hours of study was conducted with the five selected variables we have been using throughout preceding analyses. The primary purpose was to scan for possible effects involving sex-related changes in hours of study in the library and at home that might suggest that more nontraditional girls increased study in the library and decreased it at home. However, the facilitating analysis did not reveal any effects at all for study in the library or at home, the two study locations of interest here.

Hours of Study and Academic Achievement

Hours of study are especially interesting for what they may show regarding female effort and preparation as explanations for their academic superiority. While locating the determinants of student grades goes well beyond the concerns of this study, the possibility that the observed female superiority might simply reflect more study and effort is briefly examined.

Table 5.15 shows that hours of study in several of the locations have some effect, but the only appreciable correlations between overall grade point and hours of study occurs for study at home. Hours of study in study hall detracts from overall grade point, possibly because achieving students are less often in study hall. Study in classroom has a minor effect, but this must

Table 5.15.

Correlations Between Overall Grade Point
and Hours of Study[a] at Various Locations

Study Locations	1964		1975	
	Males	Females	Males	Females
Bus	.02	.02	-.03	.02
Classroom	.07***	.09***	.04	.06*
Home	.28***	.27***	.06*	.12***
Library	.03	-.02	.08***	.04*
Study Hall	-.07**	-.16***	-.07**	-.02
Other	.06*	.04	-.07**	.01

[a]Hours of study represent the square root of the truncated distribution.
(See footnote, Table 5.14).

* p < .05
** p < .01
*** p < .001

certainly be a function of class administration rather than of student volition. Consequently, I consider only hours of study at home in the following brief analysis of the several determinants of grades.

In addition to hours of study at home, I will include perceived helpfulness and intelligence in the analysis to see if these variables explain the sex effect.

This analysis is presented in table 5.16, using the "typical year" enrollment classes as dependent variables and conducting the analysis separately for 1964 and 1975 to simplify the interpretation of changes.[27]

The inclusion of intelligence, perceived helpfulness, and hours of study greatly increases the prediction of grades in these courses. The most important factor is intelligence, although perceived helpfulness, especially in mathematics and science, has an appreciable effect, as does hours of study. However, even with these three aspects of course experience controlled, girls still do substantially better than boys. In fact, the metric coefficients for sex presented in table 5.16 are not dramatically affected by the inclusion of these strong predictors, as comparison with the coefficients for sex from tables 5.10, 5.11, and 5.12 reveals. The single-year coefficients for English decrease slightly (about 15%), but those from math and science tend to stay the same while some actually increase. Thus, whatever girls were doing to outperform boys in these courses was relatively independent of such measures of effort as hours of study or of such attitudinal factors as perceived

Table 5.16.

Regression of Sex Typed "Typical Course" Grades Upon Hours of Home Study, Intelligence, Perceived Helpfulness, and Sex (Metric Coefficients)[a]

Typical Year Course	Number	1964 Help	1964 Intell.	1964 Home Study	1964 Sex	1964 R2	Number	1975 Help	1975 Intell.	1975 Home Study	1975 Sex	1975 R2	Sex Coefficient from Table 5.11
Sophomore													
English	(2244)	.54	1.66	.30	1.24	(.48)	(2384)	.50	1.27	.11	1.20	(.32)	1.55
Language	(805)	.66	1.68	.32	.72	(.27)	(673)	.70	1.39	.20	1.05	(.24)	.81
Algebra	(397)	1.11	1.39	.35	.97	(.22)	(634)	.90	1.23		.75	(.18)	.57
Geometry	(953)	.93	1.82	.39		(.30)	(1049)	1.12	1.74		.59	(.30)	
Biology	(2065)	.78	1.65	.35	.33	(.41)	(2096)	.87	1.41	.11	.79	(.31)	.70
Junior													
English	(2227)	.60	1.56	.32	1.34	(.44)	(2199)	.68	1.36	.11	1.36	(.36)	1.67
Language	(605)	.62	1.61	.40	1.20	(.30)	(408)	.75	1.41	.39	1.05	(.27)	1.09
Chemistry	(874)	.88	1.69	.43		(.34)	(665)	1.21	1.41	.26		(.28)	
Senior													
English	(1684)	.56	1.37	.26	1.25	(.36)	(1359)	.60	1.18	.11	1.19	(.29)	1.47
Math	(465)	1.02	1.38	.30	.91	(.31)	(661)	.72	1.26		.72	(.28)	.52
Physics	(465)	1.01	1.55	.46	1.02	(.34)	(376)	.70	1.30	.38	.58	.28	1.70

[a]Only coefficients larger than two standard errors are reported.

helpfulness. Especially noteworthy is the persistence of these differences when intelligence was controlled, a result consistent with my interpretation of sex-typing of the achievement patterns.

This brief analysis indicates that female advantage cannot be dismissed merely as a function of effort (at least as here operationalized) nor as a function of perceived helpfulness of courses nor of selective intelligence. What factors do account for the relative differences in the academic superiority of girls in these two waves is an interesting question that unfortunately cannot be pursued in this analysis. For now we can note that some of the most obvious factors suggested in this report and in the general sex role literature do not account for the difference.

DISCUSSION AND INTERPRETATION

In the preceding analyses we have observed clear sex role change in course enrollments, perceived helpfulness, and satisfaction. Furthermore, in an unusual departure from the customary results in the facilitating analysis, there was some evidence of these sex role changes occurring in the subpopulations where we might expect them to occur.

However, even though these patterns are assumed to be important to sex-differentiated academic achievement, we have observed no sex role change in such achievement itself. Thus, we have found attitudinal, but not behavioral, change in the analysis of academic preference and achievement. Such an inconsistency can be interpreted and explained in two or three different ways.

One possibility is that attitudes and self-reported subjective reactions to course content are more responsive to contemporary social influences in school and society than are graded academic performances. Choices, attitudes, and reported reactions probably reflect determinants emanating at least in part from media formulations and from orientations of counselors and teachers within the school systems themselves during these periods. All of this is probably facilitated by the superiority of girls in academic performances, the long history of liberal education open to both sexes, and the more abstract, less direct relevance of languages and sciences to immediate sex-related concerns and circumstances. The fact is, girls have been taking mathematics and science for some time. The increases we have observed intensify existing patterns, they do not represent dramatic innovations in sex role patterns. Given all of this, it seems likely that we have observed sex role change in areas where such responses can be manifested with minimal disruption of other sex-typed patterns.

The big questions is why the same circumstances failed to generate any change in graded academic performance. If the relative disadvantage in mathematics and science was due to limitations and circumstances based on stereotypic differences, then their presumed reduction should have altered the relative sex role differentiation in grades as in attitudes and enrollments. Why didn't they?

The most obvious explanation is that attitudes and preferences are directly responsive to contemporary social influences, but that academic achievement differences in sex-typed courses more often reflect cognitive differences between the sexes. As we have seen, there is a large body of research and writing developing both biological and social explanations for these cognitive differences.

If the sex differences in verbal, quantitative, and scientific performance are due to biological differences between the sexes, sex differences in performance (in the present case, differences in relative performance) can be expected to continue in the absence of compensating training. From that perspective, this finding must be considered to provide indirect support for biological explanations. The discrepancy in the results between attitudinal and behavioral aspects of experience in sex-typed courses is consistent with the biological explanation, as is the previous research showing no change in the related achievement levels of females and males.

These results are also consistent with social or environmental explanations that focus on early learning and experience in the formulation of cognitive differences. Especially pertinent here are propositions such as Sherman's (1978), emphasizing experiences and advantages. These are also consistent with the differing group contexts previously described. If cognitive differences go back to sex-related childhood learning and experience, involving play in the natural environment, games involving spatial and universalistic skills, and feminine emphasis on interpersonal relations and the early development of verbal skills, such differences would be unaffected by contemporary forces that might well alter attitudes and perceptions. Change in these patterns generating experience and skill might be occuring, but too late to affect the cognitive skills of the 1975 cohort. We might expect such change only after the play patterns and experiences of young girls begin to approximate those of boys.

Other social explanations involving stereotypic effects such as expectancy, mathematics as a male domain, differences in perceived helpfulness, etc., are inconsistent with these results. All of the contemporary explanations involving situational forces emanating from stereotypes would account for change in the behavioral as well as the attitudinal manifestations of these course experiences. Observation of change in one aspect and not the other is inconsistent with such propositions.

These findings on sex differences in academic achievement provide slightly more indirect support for biological explanations than for social or environmental ones, primarily because the bulk of the social explanations emphasizes the significance of contemporary, rather than historical, events. Only future research can answer this question, of course, but continued stability in performance differentials will naturally suggest genetic or biological explanations. The evidence observed here is not inconsistent with such explanations. Nor is it inconsistent with explanations based on early experiential and socialization experiences in different social and physical contexts. This evidence is inconsistent with explanations emphasizing the importance of perceived utility and enjoyment of sex-typed courses. It is certainly inconsistent with propositions explaining sex differences in academic achievement as a function of course-taking experience.

CHAPTER 6

SOCIALIZATION INFLUENCES IN SCHOOL, FAMILY, AND SOCIETY

This final research chapter will focus on student reports of influence and educational circumstances having to do with the process of sex role socialization. The most important contemporary theories of sex role socialization are presented as background for my analysis, as are substantive findings about agencies of socialization. The evidence from this study bears primarily on issues of process, the mechanisms and channels for socialization effects, not on the sex-related effects themselves. Nevertheless, the relevance of the study variables to socialization theories and substantive issues is close enough so that we are informed by the current theories even though direct tests of socialization content are not undertaken in this analysis.

My central purpose is to examine sex differences, social change, and sex role change along a number of dimensions held to be significant in the contemporary literature on sex role socialization. The question is whether some processual aspects of sex role socialization have changed and what the implications are for stability and change in sex-related patterns of influence and experience.

The three major theories of sex role socialization are briefly reviewed, followed by a review of major agencies of socialization. Those sections provide a background and establish the significance for the selected variables to be examined in the final section reporting the results of this analysis.

THEORIES OF SEX ROLE SOCIALIZATION

Not surprisingly, the major explanatory schema for sex role differentiation and acquisition are essentially the major theories of human socialization. However, these theories are approached from the perspective of sex differences and with selective emphasis of those aspects bearing most directly on acquisition of the appropriate sex role.

The three theories most often discussed in conjunction with the acquisition of sex roles are the Freudian, the cognitive developmental, and the social learning. We will also take note of a fourth theory or variant, that having to do with complementary role learning. These theories differ in a number of critical respects that bear upon variables to be examined in this analysis, so that while I can make no direct tests of socialization models, different theories posit alternative hypotheses or predictions that my data can occasionally evaluate.

Freudian Theory

The central feature of the Freudian theory is, of course, energy or motivation (Hall and Lindzey 1970). This energy, which represented the life force, was conceptualized with heavy emphasis on sexual tension release and consequent pleasure, or cathexis. Personality development occurred through a series of stages characterized by the primary source of gratification, first in the membranes of the mouth and lips (oral stage), later in the feelings of pleasure associated with genital manipulation in masturbation. To around four years of age, the process was held to be similar for both sexes, both of whom love the mother for her associations with basic pleasure in these early stages.[1] However, in the phallic stage, Freud held that consequences of sexual differentiation produced differences in the development of the two sexes.

The little boy develops an increasingly sexual attraction to the mother, an orientation that makes him the father's rival. Concern about this danger is intensified by the discovery that little girls lack penises and the assumption that the lack reflects loss, i.e., castration. Castration anxiety causes the boy to repress his feelings for the mother and to identify with the father. This heavily affective process results in the introjection of the paternal image, especially the punishing and rewarding qualities of the father, which become the superego. With this resolution the boy develops masculine sex role characteristics, both in terms of the positive ego ideal and the negative conscience, both aspects of his perceptions of the father. The significant aspects of this development are the suddenness of the transfer, its completeness, and the intensity of the affective components that are involved. In the end, though, the small child can act toward his own urges as the father would. Masculinity depends on identification with the father.

The process for the girl is less clearly developed and is less comprehensible and internally consistent. The girl develops an attachment to the father as she discovers she lacks the penis and is disappointed with and resentful of the mother, who is held responsible and who also shares the inadequacy. Her attachment to the father involves feelings of wanting to have a baby by him, which substitutes for the desired penis. While these orientations are highly charged and affective, they lack the element of fear present in the boy's castration anxiety. Consequently, the girl does not resolve the Oedipal complex suddenly, but gradually over time as she faces the real barriers preventing her from realizing the sexual attachment to the father, and gradually, but never completely, resolves the Oedipal complex. Because of these differences in the process the girl never developes as strong and as independent a superego as does the boy.

These formulations have a number of significant implications for the development of female personality, nearly all of them negative.

In the first place, penis envy establishes a feeling of inferiority on the part of women that runs through all of the relations between the sexes. Second, this sexually based feeling of inadequacy is bolstered by the differing cognitive development in that women lack a strong superego and consequently a strong sense of universalistic justice. Instead of being governed by the general rule-based morality of men, women are governed more by feelings and emotions.[2] Third, these unfortunate circumstances are viewed as permanent because Freud held that the main lines of personality are set in these early psychosexual events and are unchangeable thereafter. Biology is destiny.

Of equal significance to sex role development are the affective orientations that underlie the learning. Freudian identification requires close relations, strong feelings, and family ties. Thus, family socialization is viewed as central, including, of course, the importance of same sex attachments or identification, especially for the boy.

Cognitive Developmental Theory

Like the Freudian theory, Kohlberg's (1966, 1969) theory of cognitive development stresses a single organizing principle. However, in this case the problem the child faces is not the channeling of affective energies, but rather the cognitive organization of the experienced environment. The basic elements of this process are clear-cut and relatively straightforward in their consequences.

According to Kohlberg (1966), the paramount process is the establishment of gender identity as a basic cognitive organizing principle that underlies everything that is to follow. This process begins with the child's early awareness of gender as a basic distinction in the world around him or her, drawing especially on important images of size and form that distinguish women and men. The child labels himself or herself with the appropriate gender label, and from then on cognitive development proceeds in terms of this basic, initial categorization, although at the start, neither the full comprehension of sex roles nor of genital sexuality occurs. The child has a label that, like a name, refers to self but may lack content.

Future learning and cognitive development attaches other meanings and implications to the gender labels and eventually results (around 5 or 6 years of age) in the child's recognition that such a categorization is permanent and unchanging. With that awareness, gender identity is established as a permanent and basic categorical foundation for all later learning and experience. It is locked in the future cognitions for which it provides the basis, as well as in the nature of categories.[3]

Once gender identity is established, future learning takes place in terms of basic, cognitive mechanisms. Thus, (1) the child responds to new elements in a manner consistent with earlier responses (once a girl, always a girl); (2) new objects are evaluated in relation to self and the gender identity, so their meaning depends on gender. For example, sewing might be fun, unless one is a boy, then it is devalued and rejected in favor of building with wood and hard steel tools. Again, being a person who builds with wood but does not sew dresses anchors the gender identity; (3) the cognitive aspect of role patterns results in conformity to normative cultural patterns through principles of consistency and appropriateness, even without actual reinforcements; (4) models are chosen in terms of gender category to be appropriate to self. That is, boys choose fathers to be models, not because of strong affective ties or repressions, but because fathers share the gender category and do things the boy can do and that are interesting to him. Girls model on the mother for the same reasons. Both model on other persons with the same gender category, other nonfamily adults as well as peers.

In all of these cases, the modeling is sharply distinguished from Freudian identification by the sequencing. Whereas Freudian identification preceded the acquisition of superego constructions of gender and sex role, cognitive developmental theory postulates just the reverse. The child acquires gender identity and *then* models on the appropriate parent and peer. Finally, (5) the picture of sexual symmetry is modified by the assumption that both sexes tend to model on persons who have power and prestige. As males are perceived to be stronger, have more power, and be valued more, the orientations of girls bifurcate between the same-sex females and cross-sex males such as the father. In the end, then, the appropriate sex role is constructed by children who sort things out in terms of gender identity and acquire the appropriate characteristics. Once established, the basic sense of gender is stronger and more stable than even physical sexuality, as the literature on transsexuals shows (Money and Tucker 1975).

The cognitive developmental model contains four important features for sex role socialization: (a) With the exception just noted, it, like the Freudian model, emphasizes same-sex socialization—sons should resemble fathers, daughters, mothers; (b) identification follows, rather than precedes acquisition of gender identity; (c) same-sex adults other than parents may have an influence on sex role development, most notably the child's peers; and finally, as in Freudian theory, (d) sex role development is established in the early years and is irreversible after that.

Social Learning Theory

Social learning theory (Bandura 1969; Mischel 1966) differs greatly from the previous two theories. While both psychoanalytic and cognitive developmental theories place great emphasis on internal developments, social learning reflects its behavioristic foundations in emphasizing the role of external events in producing human personality.

The basic proposition is simple—behavior that is reinforced persists, behavior that is punished or not reinforced tends to extinguish. Social learning views sex role behavior as a consequence of the social responses (actual or expected) to appropriate and inappropriate behavior. Boys are rewarded for being aggressive, thus they exhibit more aggressive behavior. Conversely, girls are rewarded for dependency and punished for aggressiveness, thus they become docile and dependent.

The main innovation of social learning theory distinguishing it from more limited behavioristic formulations is the emphasis on observational learning and the distinction between observation and performance. One of the important contributions of the early experimentation (Bandura and Walters 1963; Mischel 1966) was the demonstration that learning occurred without direct reinforcement, that through observation alone, children acquired behavioral repertoires that were later performed in anticipation of reinforcements. Through such learning involving both actual and vicarious reinforcement, children gradually build their sex role capabilities and performances. Observations underlying these capabilities reflect sex appropriate behavior of women and men. Men have learned through observation how to powder their faces and apply lipstick, but they do not carry out the behavior because they would be negatively sanctioned. Similarly, women know how to fight, but generally do not exhibit the behavior because of negative sanctions.

These learning patterns continue through time but are not marked by the highly significant and deterministic events in the early years described in Freudian and cognitive developmental formulations. Rather, development continues through the years and may involve change in later years from patterns acquired earlier. For example, the early pattern of feminine achievement could be altered under the new patterns of dating and popularity that are reinforced in the high school years and explain the assumed decline in female achievement.

Given the ability to acquire behavioral repertoires through observation, the major question is which observations? Out of all the potential models and behavioral sequences that can be observed and imitated, what determines which one will be acquired? The answer to this, as it emerged from experiments, is that the actor who has power to control resources and get rewarded is the one most likely to be imitated (Bandura 1969; Mischel 1966). These powerful, successful models are taken as examples of behavior leading to rewards, and their behavior is consequently performed in anticipation of positive reinforcements.

This aspect of social learning theory has different implications for family sex role socialization than Freudian or cognitive developmental theories. Both of the latter theories describe, for different reasons, same-sex identification. Social learning theory does not. Either parent could be the model for either child, but the powerful parent is seen as the influential parent. While nurturance and warmth between model and child may also have some effect, the parent who has the greatest power is likely to be the determiner of sex-typed behavior. Both children may observe (and learn) the sex-appropriate behavior and attitudes of each parent, but they are more likely to exhibit the behavior of the dominant parent.

This aspect of social learning theory leads to some interesting extensions that link social structure and personality. The power of the model depends on control of resources that would in turn be affected by structural arrangements within and outside of the family. From this perspective, same-sex or cross-sex modeling would depend on the relevant power of the father or mother as perceived by the child. Parental power, in turn, would depend on structural arrangements within and outside of the family.

The classic statement on structural differentiation in the family is the instrumental-expressive formulation of the roles of husband and wife by Parsons et al. (1955). According to Scanzoni (1972), this formulation has important implications for power relations between the parents in that the resources of the instrumental role player are more important than those of the expressive role player. While this imbalance is mitigated by external statuses, the instrumental role nevertheless provides unique access to the opportunity structure not available to the expressive role. The extrafamilial statuses of the spouses, especially those of the husband, are important resources affecting conjugal power balances within the family.

Research evidence supports both the social learning formulations regarding choice of most powerful model and the structural formulations regarding power relations within the family.

Choice of most powerful parent as model or source of perceived influence has been reported in laboratory studies (Hetherington 1964) and in several surveys (Smith 1970, 1976; McDonald 1977), although Bowerman and Bahr (1973) found that girls identified with the mother regardless of power balances within the family.

The consequences of structural arrangements within and outside the family have been described in both general and specific formulations. At the general level, the internal-external relevance of the instrumental-expressive distinction seems pervasive and unchanging. The early findings of Zelditch (1955), as well as the more recent evidence of Poloma and Garland (1971), are consistent with Weitz's conclusion that the basic differentiation still prevails: "The power structure in the society remains male, while the female contribution is private and individual and is often tied to the family" (1977:3).

The primacy of paternal power inherent in this structural arrangement has been consistently observed in family research (Blood and Wolfe 1960; Bahr, Bowerman, and Gecas 1974; Bowerman and Bahr 1973). However, consistent with Scanzoni's (1972) findings and arguments, Hoffman and Nye's (1974) review of research shows that the power of both husband and wife increases with outside employment and status. Even in that respect, Gillespie (1971) argues that the contemporary organization of extrafamilial sex roles results in a relative power advantage for the husband over the wife. The evidence indicates that the father has the greatest power, but it is modified by external statuses of both spouses.

Earlier analysis of the data of this study provided some support for this proposition (Lueptow 1980a). Analysis of the choice of parent reported to be most influential on the student's post-high school plans revealed that choice of father or mother as most influential showed a pronounced same-sex choice pattern, but one that was strongly modified by the various dimensions of social status occupied by the parents. Father's influence increased with his education and occupational status, while mother's influence was unaffected by those factors. However, her influence was increased by her working (but not by the status of her job) and by the size of family. These patterns indicated that it was the father's community status and the mother's internal family status that affected their influence on the child, results viewed as consistent with the basic instrumental-expressive distinctions as well as with the implication of model choice in social learning theory. In combination, structural factors had somewhat more effect than did pressures for same-sex choice. For nonworking mothers with less education than their spouses in families of high socioeconomic status, mother's unilateral influence is negligible—2.3% for males, 7.6% for females. However, at the other extreme, in low SES families in which working mothers have more education than fathers, 24.1% of the males and 50.8% of the females reported mother as most influential. These results are strikingly consistent with social learning formulations on power and control of resources.

Another important implication of social learning theory grows from the principles of observational learning and vicarious reinforcement. Because neither identification nor direct reinforcement is necessary for learning, various social forces and extrafamilial influences may actually constitute the sources of sex-typed behavior. Bandura (1969) notes that as children grow they increasingly turn to peers as models, especially when circumstances of rapid social change create generational gaps and differences. Other sources may involve verbal and pictorial presentations, especially on television and in other media. Social learning is distinctive among these theories in the weight given to media as direct sources of socialization influence.

Another neglected influential source of social learning is the abundant and diverse symbolic modeling provided in television and other audiovisual displays. Since response patterns can be acquired on a purely observational basis, it is not surprising to find in comparative studies that models provided by filmed displays can be as influential as their real-life counterparts in shaping children's behavior. In fact, many of the experiments reviewed earlier, demonstrating extensive modeling effects in both children and adults, utilized pictorially presented models. (Bandura 1969:249)

Finally, the role of extrafamilial influences and social system effects has special significance for issues of social change or sex role change.

In an interesting but generally unrecognized interpretation, Bandura (1969) drew on an unpublished work by Albert Reiss (1966) to interpret the role of

extrafamilial sources of influence. Reiss had suggested that traditional transmission of cultural patterns, including sex roles, through family socialization
necessarily promoted stability, and that social change probably emerged
through other agencies of social organization. Teachers, counselors, peers,
and participants of social movements would all be potential models for socialization into new forms. As assumptions about changing sex roles generally posit masculinization of the woman's role, this influence would necessarily be more critical for girls than for boys. Earlier analysis of the 1964
baseline data of this study produced results consistent with such a formulation (Lueptow 1975:106). Male levels of achievement value orientation were
predicted by family background characteristics as the general theory of the
achievement syndrome predicted, but female levels were not. For girls, the
only family characteristic consistently related to achievement values was income. Furthermore, for girls, the relation between family income and
achievement values was unaffected by measures of paternal and maternal
influence, in contrast to the male pattern. As income is the best single indicator of the family's status, it appeared possible that outside influences such
as counselors or teachers might have reacted to the girl according to the
visible sign of her family status and produced levels of acheivement orientation commensurate with the perceived family status but independent of
other, less visible aspects of family background.

The major aspects of social learning as they pertain to sex role formulation are thus (1) the emphasis on reinforcement, either direct, vicarious, or
inferred, (2) the process of observational learning without the necessarily
direct reinforcement, (3) the distinction between observation and performance, (4) the role of power and success in determining the model, and (5)
the relevance of symbolic models on television and in other media. These
various aspects of the theory make it much more appropriate as a frame of
reference for interpreting change in women's roles than are the other two
major explanations for the acquisition of social roles or sex roles.

Socialization Theories and the Psychology of Sex Differences

The significance of the theories just summarized rests solidly on the widely
accepted assumption in contemporary social science that sex-related personality differences arise through socialization. Therefore it comes as some surprise to realize that neither of the two basic patterns running through these
theories—same-sex identification and differential reinforcement of sex-re-

lated behaviors—is as yet much supported by empirical research. As we have seen, both Freudian and cognitive developmental theories posit same-sex identification, although for sharply different reasons. On the other hand, reinforcement contingencies based on parental ideas about appropriate sex role behavior underlie the social learning theory and its variants. Given the prominence of these theories in the literature, the conclusions of the Maccoby and Jacklin (1974) review of research on sex role socialization are unexpected and controversial.

Parental Models

Maccoby and Jacklin's (1974) review of the literature on modeling fails to support the concept of same-sex identification. While there is ample evidence of sex typing in children's toy and activity preferences, and some evidence that children watch the same-sex model, there is little evidence of same-sex, parent-child similarity. Maccoby and Jacklin (1974:292–294) report that an early review of studies prior to 1950, as well as studies in the 1960s, fails to support either same-sex similarity or imitation, a finding also reported by Barkely et al. (1977) following their review of eighty-one studies. Maccoby and Jacklin conclude, in an opinion that is notable for its nearly universal disregard in the sex role literature,[4] that

our analysis of the arguments concerning the role of modeling in sex typing and our review of the search on selective imitation have led us to a conclusion that is very difficult to accept, namely that modeling plays a minor role in the development of sex-typed behavior.(1974:300)

Differential Reinforcement

Differential reinforcement of sex-appropriate behavior is of course one of the major tenants of the social learning theory and of general descriptions of the acquisition of sex-typed behavior (see Mussen 1969). Generally, it is assumed that boys are rewarded for aggression, independence, and achievement while girls are punished for aggressive behavior and rewarded for dependency (Mischel 1966; Hoffman 1972, 1977).

Maccoby and Jacklin (1974) summarize a broad range of research studies bearing on one or another aspect of these conceptions, and again obtain surprising results.

Consistent with common assumptions, they find that parents interact more with girls under 1 year (20, M= .40, F = .10), although after age 2 the six studies show no sex difference. Boys also receive more stimulation of gross motor behavior than girls (6, M= .67, F = .00) while girls receive more verbal interaction (31, F = .32, M = .06). Older girls, beyond 7 or 8 years of age, receive or report more warmth in relations with parents (15, F = .60, M = .00), but in the early years of 1 to 7, there is essentially no difference in parental warmth (32, F = .22, M = .19).

However, the real surprises come in the training for dependency and assertiveness. Maccoby and Jacklin (1974) found that the research revealed no sex difference in restrictiveness and low independence training (38, M = .26, F = .21), in rewards for dependency (18, F = .22, M = .17), nor in permissiveness or rewards for aggressiveness (28, M = .28, F = .25). Furthermore, there were no significant age effects in these tabulations.

The evidence on the process of socialization also fails to confirm the picture of tightly controlled, phsychologically punished female experience. Boys receive both more physical punishment (21, M = .52, F = .14) and nonphysical punishment (32, M = .32, F = .18) and are more controlled than girls are, contrary to the general sense of the literature. There were also no differences of consequence in the receipt of praise or reward (18, F = .29, M = .22) nor in the important factor of achievement demands (15, M = .33, F = .20).

Except for more early interaction with boys, especially gross muscle interaction, and more verbal interaction with girls, Maccoby and Jacklin report: "Our survey of data has revealed a remarkable degree of uniformity in the socialization of the two sexes. . . . Existing evidence has not revealed any consistent process of 'shaping' boys and girls toward a number of behaviors that are normally part of our stereotypes" (1974:348).

Interestingly enough, Duncan and Duncan (1978) reach an identical conclusion in their analysis of socialization in the Detroit metropolitan area between the 1950s and 1970.

In spite of their apparent plausibility, neither same-sex identification nor differential socialization are supported by the bulk of the evidence on sex role socialization.[5]

Failure to observe interfamilial effects suggests that Bandura may be right in emphasizing such extrafamilial agencies as media, teachers, peers, and schools in the formulation of sex-typed personalities.

Role Learning

Another explanation for the failure to observe same-sex and behavioral reinforcement effects predicted by the identification and social learning theories is that the theories are misdirected. The socialization theories involve identification, modeling, or imitation of parental behavior. An important extension of these models appears in Parsonian (1964:82–92) role theory, which calls attention to the reciprocity inherent in the interactions of parents and children. These interactions involve learning, not only through imitation and modeling, but also by developing an understanding of the intentions and expectations of the significant other.

Whereas the theories reviewed to this point predict that the observer would acquire the *behaviors* of the model, a role-taking perspective emphasizing the importance of reciprocity in social interaction recognizes the possibility that the child might acquire the *attitudes* of the other toward his or her own performance. Since such attitudes would reflect assumptions about both the reciprocal role and the self role, this formulation would account for sex-typed behavior acquired through the influence of the opposite-sex parent as well as from the same-sex parent. It would also explain the surprising failure of research to find relations between same-sex parents and children. It would suggest that masculinity and femininity are acquired through interactions with the cross-sex parent rather than through copying the behaviors of the same-sex parent. In view of the greater concern of the father with sex-typed behavior and his greater power, this formulation suggests the possibility that the father is the key figure in determining sex-typed patterns in both boys and girls (Matteson 1975:59–60).

There is some evidence that the father does have disproportionate influence in the development of sex-typed characteristics. Johnson (1963) concluded, in a review of a number of studies, that the evidence supports the idea that the father differentiates his role toward opposite sex children while the mother does not. Evidence supporting the greater significance of the father's role has been obtained by Rosenberg and Sutton-Smith (1968) and Block (1973).

Indirect evidence for that idea was also obtained in earlier analysis of the baseline data of this study, using occupational value orientations. Boys who were most influenced by the father had stronger instrumental orientations than boys who were most influenced by the mother, a result predicted by both role theory and the identification theories. Of greater interest, however, was the observation that girls influenced by the father had higher expressive orientations than those influenced by the mother. This would not be predicted by identification theories.

The inconclusiveness, confusion, and controversy in the sex role socialization literature may be due to the assumptions underlying research and consequent measurement of key variables. From a role-learning perspective and, especially, from the symbolic interactionist formulations of personality development, the key elements are not individual, sex-typed behavior, but the attitudes and expectations of the significant other as revealed to children in role-related interactions. Taking the attitude of the significant other toward the self, as Mead (1934) argued, may well be the important aspect of sex role socialization that could account for the surprising and controversial research conclusions.

AGENCIES OF SEX ROLE SOCIALIZATION

Traditional treatments of socialization have generally assumed that the family is the primary agency for the transmission of values and behavioral norms from generation to generation. This view has generally been maintained in most traditional psychological theories of socialization and is consistent with the extensive and exclusive control over children maintained by traditional families. However, in recent decades that exclusive control has been partially surrendered to other agencies, such as school and peers, and more recently to media and other social influences. As we have seen, social learning theory provides for such effects through observational learning and vicarious reinforcement. Such an approach also views socialization as a continuing process of learning in which hierarchies of behavioral tendencies are constructed through the life span in response to categories of reinforcers. Such processes do not necessarily involve strong affective attachments to agents and models.

Present formulations of sex role socialization (see Weitzman 1979) must consider the manner in which various agencies, such as family, media, school, and peers contribute to the construction of gender identity and sex-typed personality patterns. While an exhaustive review of these different sources of sex role influence is beyond the scope of this study, I touch on some of the most pertinent features of the various sources as they are emerging in the contemporary literature. The observed or predicted consequences of family, media presentation, peers, and school patterns establish the background reference frame for the variables of this study.

Family

The family has been assumed to be the major source of socialization effects. As the major agency for the transmission of the culture, it has necessarily been a traditional and conservative source of influence. In fact, pressures of social change probably underlie the shift from family to more responsive extrafamilial agencies (Reiss 1966; Bandura 1969).

It is difficult to reach firm conclusions about elements of familial influence, partly because of the inherent ambiguity of much of the evidence and partly because of the controversy surrounding the Maccoby and Jacklin (1974) conclusions. Their exhaustive review finds very little support for either same-sex modeling or sex-differentiated socialization processes. While Block (1976) and L. Hoffman (1977) both disagree with that conclusion, it seems clear that family socialization effects are not as obvious or as strong as might be expected. In that sense the following discussion might be to a large degree moot. On the other hand, all of the evidence is far from in, and two themes are being addressed in the current literature on family socialization: (1) paternal versus maternal influence, and (2) sources of nontraditional orientations within the family.

Paternal Versus Maternal Influence

Paternal versus maternal influence encompasses both the more traditional sex role socialization concerns as well as the more recent consequences of changing women's roles and their effect on family structure. As Lynn (1974) observes, traditional Freudian and Parsonian theories generally held the father to be most important in determining the sex role content, either because of the dynamics of the Oedipal resolution or because of the predominance of the instrumental orientation over the expressive. The mother was the primary influence during the early years when sex role differentiation was less emphasized, while the father became more significant in later years when sex role performances were more clearly expected.

Even under the patterns described by social learning theorists, the father would be expected to have more influence than the mother because of the special advantages of the instrumental role in the broader community and the special limitations on the expressive role in contemporary urban society. As I have already noted and in earlier analysis of the baseline data (Lueptow 1980a), research evidence generally supports that proposition. However, paternal power is affected by the introduction of such resources as paid employment of the wife. Wives who work have relatively more power. Furthermore, there is consistent research evidence showing that children do identify with the more powerful parent. The only exception to this pattern seems to be the tendency of girls to identify with their mothers regardless of power imbalances (Bowerman and Bahr 1973; Curtis 1975). Generally though, identification is to the parent perceived as powerful or, as in my

(1980a) study, the parent who has the structurally based resources underlying power.

Apart from power effects, there does not appear to be extensive evidence refuting the Maccoby and Jacklin (1974) conclusion on lack of same-sex modeling. Even among several recent studies, results are roughly split between same-sex and cross-sex effects.

Orlofsky (1979) found same-sex effects in the relation between parent and child sex-role stereotypic categories. Maternal sex role had more to do with female sex-role characteristics, and the reverse was true for males. However, "neither males nor females were found to differ in sex role as a function of preferring one parent over the other" (1979:500). Meyer (1980) obtained moderately strong mother-daughter correlations on sex role attitudes for 11-year-old girls, but not for 7-year-old girls in a sample of 150 pairs of mothers and daughters. Meyer also found no effect due to mother's working or to her satisfaction with homemaking.

Considered overall, the evidence on same-sex or cross-sex influences remains unconvincing or at least inconclusive. While there is some support for almost any of the formulations reviewed, there is at present no significant accumulation of evidence supporting any of the arrangements derived directly from the three major theories.

Nontraditional Family Influence

Nontraditional family influence within the family is largely perceived as emanating from the consequences of working mothers, although at least two other themes have been advanced. One of these other themes views female nontraditional orientations as consequences of the rejection of the homemaking role by the child after observing maternal dissatisfaction with that role. Lipman-Blumen (1972) and Nagley (1971) found that college women with nontraditional orientations had mothers who were dissatisfied or who were more distant. The other theme suggests that innovation is the result of positive pressures or support for innovation itself, something like Almquist and Angrist's (1979) conclusion about "enrichment" in the experiences of innovating and career-oriented college women. Kelley and Worell (1976) found that androgynous females have parents who encouraged independence and achievement, and Lemkau (1979) and O'Donnell and Anderson (1978) found that innovating females had mothers who were more often college graduates. Not suprisingly, positive socialization by educated, nontraditional parents seems to produce consistent, nontraditional outcomes.

As indicated, however, the great bulk of the evidence reflects the consequences of mother's working status. These studies are generally consistent with L. Hoffman's (1977) argument that change in socialization patterns will follow increased assumptions that women will work after marriage. Working mothers hold such expectations to a greater degree than nonworking mothers (see Bruce 1974). Working mothers also are nontraditional models.

The major authority on the consequences of mother's work is clearly Lois Wladis Hoffman (1979, 1980), and the following summary of the literature on the effects of mother's work draws heavily on her interpretations.

Hoffman's reviews of the effects of mother's work status shows generally that a considerable amount of research on this issue has failed to produce strongly demarked, unequivocal evidence. Although the evidence is not completely clear, there does seem to be some support for the following conclusions. First, mother's work has no harmful effect on children's socialization, although this is clearer for girls than for boys. There is some indication that middle-class boys of working mothers may have depressed academic aptitude compared to middle-class boys with homemaking mothers. Hoffman (1980) suggests that homemaking mothers may socialize too effectively, producing timid, self-controlled, but academically oriented boys with high aptitudes. The presumably less effective socialization of working mothers results in less controlled, more masculine, but less academically proficient boys. It also appears that the lower-class mother's work may cause strain between the father and son because of the father's loss of status. Generally, though, Hoffman concludes that mother's work is more beneficial than harmful.

The most direct effects of mother's working appear to be consequences of the presentation to children (and husbands) of nontraditional models. Working mothers have more actual power within the family and more support from husbands in housekeeping chores and responsibilities. Children in such families acquire less stereotypic conceptions of sex roles, see less difference between the sexes, and view women as more competent. However, in spite of these consequences, there is not much evidence on the effect of mother's work on the children (Hoffman 1980:315).

While the overall sense of the Hoffman reviews is the positive contribution of mother's work, the actual evidence is borderline and subject to alternative interpretations. For example, working women have higher levels of education (U.S. Dept. of Labor 1980) and probably higher levels of intelligence. These variables are not usually controlled in comparisons of working and nonworking mothers.

Recent evidence is not totally consistent with Hoffman's conclusions about the beneficial effects of mother's work. Two recent studies (Lemkau 1979; Van Fossen 1977) do support Tangri's (1972) earlier finding that role innovators have working mothers, especially working mothers in nontraditional occupations, although Van Fossen found that mother's work was important only in egalitarian families. However, in contrast to these studies, a number of recent reports fail to observe the predicted effects. These studies (Seater and Ridgeway 1976; Klecka and Hiller 1977; Macke and Morgan 1978; Rosenfeld 1978; Gold and Andres 1978; Dellas et al. 1979; Sewell, Hauser, and Wolf 1980; Meyer 1980), find that mother's work status has no effect on daughter's attitudes, values, or aspirations, on academic achievement, on preference for mathematics, on stereotypic attitudes, or on occupational mobility.

The results of these studies and the relatively weak support in literature reviewed by Hoffman (1979, 1980) leads to the conclusion that mother's work may have some effect on changiing sex roles, but this is not by any means a certainty. Furthermore, it appears that the relatively neutral effect of work on daughters' achievement patterns may be offset by negative consequences for sons. For now, it appears likely that the main forces for change reside in extrafamilial models and experiences. Maternal employment may be most important because it reduces intrafamilial socialization and increases extrafamilial socialization.

Media

Sex role socialization through observation of same-sex models in magazines, newspapers, and especially in television programming is widely assumed to be occurring (United States Commission on Civil Rights 1977; Butler and Paisley 1980). Such a process is consistent with social learning or cognitive developmental theories, neither of which require strong affectional bonds between model and learner. Bandura (1969:248–250) specifically addresses the significance of media presentations for observational learning in extrafamilial, presumably less traditional, contexts. The portrayal of women and men in magazines, newpapers, television, and movies is seen as an important aspect of sex role socialization.

There are two central empirical issues in media as sources of sex role socialization. One of these is the nature of the portrayal, whether traditional and stereotypic or nontraditional and innovative. The other is the actual effect on observers of the media portrayal. As we shall see, there is considerably more evidence on portrayal than on the socialization effects resulting from observation of media sex role presentations.

Media Portrayal of Sex Roles

Magazine and newspaper articles, stories, and advertisements present women and men in traditional roles (Butler and Paisley 1980).[6] Men are more often shown as employed and employed in higher status jobs. Men in advertisements are more often shown in active participation in recreational roles, women are more often shown in decorative roles. Newspaper articles are written by men, about men who are consistently treated in terms of their own personal history, while women are often featured as wives or are more likely to have their marital status described, along with other personal information less often given for men (Foreit et al. 1980). Generally, newspapers appear to reflect the popular understanding that newsworthy events have been staged more often by men than by women.

Magazines also present stereotypic pictures of women and men (Butler and Paisley 1980), although there is some evidence this presentation is differentiated by social class with more traditional portrayals of women's roles in lower-class than in middle-class magazines. There appears to have been little change over the past decade in these patterns, except for a less sex-typed focus of advertisements in the life style sections of newspapers.

Geise (1979) observed one pattern of change consistent with my previous interpretations of change in values and goals as reflecting liberation and increased feminization, but not masculinization. In an analysis of nonfiction articles in *Ladies Home Journal* and *Redbook* from 1955 to 1976, Geise found declining presentation of traditional sex role perspectives. However, "The change was not so much a case of discarding traditional values and taking on new values as it was questioning of traditions, a careful consideration and open-mindedness to new alternatives, coupled with a tolerance for nontraditional styles" (1979:61). This change in role models was greatest between 1966 and 1976.

The major concern in this literature is with the stereotyped portrayal of women and men on television. In their review of studies on the portrayal of women and men on television, Butler and Paisley (1980) conclude that the evidence shows traditional presentations. Men are seen more often, women less. Men are more often portrayed outside the home in higher status jobs and are most often the authorities in television commercials. Women's activities are more often home bound and carried out for the benefit of men.

Women tend to be younger than men and women's marital status is more often made clear.

Men predominate in television portrayals and women are shown in subordinate, traditional roles, when they are shown. Whether these portrayals reflect real circumstances in the public conception of contemporary sex roles, or essentially exaggerations of basic differences, it is clear that television has not operated as a change agent in showing nonconventional roles for women, as feminists propose it should.[7]

If observational learning does indeed occur, it should result in acquisition of masculine and feminine patterns of the present, not of the future. However, this is complicated further by two features of social learning theory: that children learn the behavior of both sexes, but only exhibit the rewarded sex-appropriate behaviors, and second, that children imitate the most powerful model (Butler and Paisley 1980). Literal application of these two principles would suggest that females might well acquire masculine rather than feminine patterns from the preponderance of dominant male roles portrayed in the media. This of course raises the questions of effects, an issue to which we now turn.

Effects of Sex Role Portrayals

Assessing the causal effects of watching TV portrayals is difficult, if not impossible, because of the intensity and pervasiveness of television viewing by children (Gross and Jeffries-Fox 1978), which may average four or five hours per day. It is impossible to carry out even simple experimental researches because children previously unexposed to television would be too unique to consider. Two alternative approaches have been used, although neither can produce definitive results. They are (1) using analogous results from laboratory experiments and (2) correlating hours of viewing with amount of stereotyping.

Butler and Paisley summarize a number of experiments having indirect relevance to the main issue and find that they support the proposition that television is an agency of sex role socialization (1980:292–296). Female children tried harder after a story with an achieving girl, while children exposed to a videotape showing a female judge were more likely to say that women could be a judge or a doctor. Two or three other studies also showed limited effects following presentation of nontraditional actors or situations. While these studies are suggestive, they naturally raise questions about generalizability, although Butler and Paisley conclude that they do support the proposition about sex role socialization.

The correlation approach provides consistent but causally ambiguous evidence. It turns out that heavy viewers are more stereotypic than light viewers (Butler and Paisley 1980; McGhee and Frueh 1980; Goff, Goff, and Lehrer 1980; Zuckerman 1980). However, it is possible that other factors known to be related to television viewing and stereotyping, such as intelligence and social class, could be creating spurious effects. Not all studies control for intelligence, and none controls for other, currently unrecognized effects. But even if all confounding variables were located, correlational results would still be ambiguous because of directional questions: whether watching television creates stereotypic personalities or whether stereotypic personalities perfer to watch television to a greater extent. Without some unusually ingenious longitudinal design, these questions cannot be easily answered.

Thus, there is abundant evidence that media, especially television, present traditional, stereotypic views of women and men and that these pictures had changed only slightly by the end of the 1970s. It is less evident that these portrayals have definite effects in sex role socialization.

School

The school is viewed as the major extrafamilial agent of socialization, and consequently as "a powerful and limiting influence on the development of sex roles" (Saario, Jacklin, and Tittle 1973:387). With this viewpoint, there is concern about the form and the substance of different aspects of the school experience. Sex role portrayals in children's readers, texts, and tests, sex typing of vocational courses, the historical assymetry of athletic programs, classroom dynamics, and the influence of teachers and counselors are all seen as aspects of the process through which schools socialize children to the basic characteristics of sex roles as traditionally defined (Weitzman 1979).

Texts, Tests, and Readers

Sex-typed portrayals of women and men in school textbooks and readers are an important extension of the general process of media socialization. However, given the importance of the school as agent of socialization, officially selected readers incorporated into classrooms and interpreted by teachers are viewed as even more important than commercial presentations. It is generally assumed that textbooks and readers provide an "anachronistic mirror" of society (Saunders 1975:368), reflecting past sex role arrangements more than future ones. As in the interpretations of commercial media, writers ordinarily assume traditional or even contemporary portrayals to be a cause for concern. For example, Weitzman notes that "rarely are women mentioned in important roles in history, as government leaders, or as great scientists" (1979:36).

Kingston and Lovelace (1977–78) have recently reviewed seventy-eight articles investigating sexism in basal readers and tabulated the criteria used in empirically demonstrating sexism in these seventy-eight studies. They found twelve forms that sexism assumed in reader content, but only four of these appeared in the findings or conclusions of at least ten of these studies. These most common sexist themes are the following:

1. more males than females appeared in the readers in the content, titles, and indices;
2. males were more often presented in a variety of occupations, receiving higher pay and holding more prestigious, albeit dangerous, occupational positions;
3. females and males were presented stereotypically, with girls portrayed as docile, sweet, nice homemakers while boys were more often seen playing outside, very actively playing organized games, while girls emphasized fantasies more;
4. illustrations more often featured males, in some cases by very wide margins,[8] although there was some evidence of change toward equity in illustrations.

While the literature is consistent in reporting replications of findings of sex-typed portrayals, Kingston and Lovelace (1977–78) strongly question the rigor of the research. They conclude that the criteria used are often oversimplified and are seldom specifically and carefully defined, a weakness leading to subjective interpretations and conclusions. They also note the absence of definition of the key terms sexism and stereotype and the confusion of realism and idealism in objecting to the portrayals of representative but traditional role patterns. Similar conclusions followed from Tibbets' (1979) review of a smaller set of five well-known and often cited surveys on sex role portrayal in children's readers. Tibbets questioned the validity of the conclusion reached in those important studies because of the weakness of objective categorization and definition.

An earlier, more carefully designed study by Saario, Jacklin, and Tittle (1973) lends some substance to these arguments. While they report finding evidence of sex role stereotyping in children's readers, this rests largely on ratio of male to female presentations, which range between 1.34 and 2.06 for adults. Of considerable interest, however, is their analysis of sex-typed behavior based on a carefully constructed taxonomy of behaviors and involving interscorer correlations of between .95 and 1.00. On this basis they analyzed four widely used reading textbook series, taking a one-third sample of the 870 stories involved. The results of the behavior analysis (1973:table 3) showed only minimal stereotyping, considerably less than my earlier review of the agreement on the content of stereotypes would suggest. Of the sixteen behaviors tabulated, only six for child and five for adult presentations were significantly more often portrayed for one sex or the other, and these tended to reflect real differences between the sexes.

There were more portrayals of aggressive, physically active behaviors for boys than for girls. Boys were also portrayed more often in problem-solving behaviors. Girls were more often portrayed in fantasy activity, including doll play, and more often presented making statement about self. On the other hand, there were no significant differences in the portrayals of children exhibiting nurturant, directive, expressive, informing, conforming, watching, verbal, routine-repetitive, and constructive-productive behavior. Considering the clarity of stereotypes, the consensus and stability with which they are held, and empirically observed differences between the sexes, it is difficult to view these results as supporting highly stereotyped presentations of girls and boys. These findings, obtained with an unusually rigorous design, suggest that Tibbets may be correct in questioning the conclusions obtained so far.

Finally, it appears that the language of standard tests in school is biased toward males. Saario, Jacklin, and Tittle (1973) found that aptitude tests included much higher proportions of masculine nouns and pronouns, averaging around 2:1 in most tests, but with ratios of 3:1 and 4:1 common. These disproportionate presentations increase in tests over the grades, becoming more masculine in high school than they were in the earlier grades.

Readers and tests are widely seen as portraying a highly sex-typed view of the experiences of males and females, a view leading directly to traditional sex role socialization. However, the basic premises of the discussion emanate more from ideological than from empirical-theoretical positions. Possibly as a result of this stance, the empirical research literature in this area appears particularly susceptible to criticism. While it seems likely that these materials do portray boys and girls somewhat differently, the extent is not accurately delineated, nor are the socialization effects known.

Curriculum and Extracurriculum

Sex role socialization is also affected by the sex typing of patterns within the curriculum and extracurriculum. This is especially true where curriculum organization results in segregation of the sexes, as in vocational training and athletics, although various writers have emphasized the significance of sex typing in academic subjects as well.

As we have seen, male shop and agricultural courses are almost totally segregated. In fact, Saario, Jacklin, and Tittle (1973) point out that in 1972, 95% of the students enrolled in agriculture were males. They see this as the start of a new trend because in 1970 100% of the students in these courses were male! Female vocational courses were somewhat less segregated, but even in office courses 75% of the students are female, as are 85% of the students in home economics. While such patterns are likely to emerge as consequences of general sex role differentiation, and not as independent causes, such segregation must certainly reinforce prevalent distinctions between the sexes.

The other important structural pattern is athletics. Physical education programs have traditionally been segregated and differentially related to interscholastic athletics, which have traditionally been viewed as a male domain (Saario, Jacklin, and Tittle 1973). Male sports have been treated as primary and important representations of the school community. "School spirit" has to a substantial degree meant attention to, and support for, the competitive endeavors of male teams. Even with the introduction of Title IX and its application to athletics, these patterns have not been eliminated (Weitzman 1979).[9]

Differentiation in athletic experience is particularly important because of the increasing importance assigned to organized games in personality development. Students from Piaget (1965) to Lever (1976) have observed differences in the play and games of girls and boys. These differences show girls playing more spontaneously in games with limited organization, less emphasis on winning and on the universalistic rules that establish rights and obligations of players. In this respect, Piaget observed: "We did not succeed in finding a single collective game played by girls in which there were as many rules, and, above all, as fine and consistent an organization and codification of these rules as in the [boys'] game of marbles examined above." (1965:69)

While the difference in the complexity of girls' and boys' games is not limited solely to athletics (Lever 1976), the most popular sports are team sports that involve high levels of complexity in their implementation. While it is not clear that these sex differences in games constitute deliberate socialization processes, nor whether the game preferences are causes or consequences, the experiences themselves can be seen as relating to both universalistic orientations for adjudicating disputes and determining victory and to an emphasis on winning. Sassen (1980) notes that in their play and game activities, girls preserve the personal relationships of the game while boys preserve the rules. There is a potential here for accounting for sex differences along a particularistic-universalistic dimension that makes early and continuous participation in organized sports appear to be a very significant aspect of sex role socialization.

The other aspect of athletics is in heightened levels of aggressive competitiveness, an element of masculine, but not feminine, stereotypes. Rehberg (1969) has speculated that athletics might make a positive contribution to academic programs by providing training in competition and achievement. While earlier analysis of athletic participation of boys using the baseline data of this study produced results counter to the proposition (Lueptow and Kayser 1973–74), analysis of the effect of athletics on aspirations of both sexes in the 1975 wave indicated that sports participation did have an effect on both the levels of educational and occupational aspiration and that the effect was stronger for girls than for boys (Moynihan 1979). While these effects were very weak, they were suggestive of the proposition that increasing feminine participation in athletics may increase the competitive, success orientations of women.

Teachers and Counselors

It is generally assumed that teachers and counselors have reinforced conformity to traditional sex role patterns (Saunders 1975; Weitzman 1979). Reinforcement by teachers is seen as an aspect of the ongoing interactions within the classroom, while counselors' influence has been seen as related to their directing girls into traditional roles.

While sex-differentiated teacher expectancy and response patterns are assumed, it is not clear that the consequences are necessarily disadvantageous to girls. Evidence seems to show that teachers have higher opinions of girls' competence and potential, an orientation recognized by girls who think teachers think they are smarter than boys (Dweck 1978:120). This runs counter to the prevailing assumption of the sex role literature that girls are perceived as less competent than boys. Bank, Biddle, and Good (1980) consider some of these teacher orientations as explanations for boys' disadvantage in reading and suggests that there may be discrimination against boys by teachers who give more negative responses to the same behavior by boys than by girls. Boys also may be penalized by encouragement for extraclass activities and by teachers responding more to boys' rambunctious behavior. Except that such responses may constitute unintended reinforcement for that behavior, there is not much evidence to date indicating exactly how teachers' behavior produces sex role patterns in children, as distinct from providing different responses to the differing behavior of boys and girls.

Traditional orientations in counseling are assumed in at least two regards. One is that counselors rate mental health in terms of sex-appropriate behavior, while also treating masculine characteristics as typical of good personal adjustment (Broverman et al. 1972; Moore and Strickler 1980). The other is that counselors, holding conventional orientations toward sex role differentiation, will advise students in ways that maintain traditional roles by decrying pursuit of innovating patterns.

While there is some evidence that counselors do see traditional roles as most appropriate, they may be less traditional than teachers, and along with teachers may reject the homemaking role as an ideal (Schlossberg and Pietrofesa, 1978). Further, it appears that these attitudes may be changing (Engelhard, Jones, and Stiggens 1976). Finally, several studies found no sex bias in the counseling of either sex (Tanney and Birk 1978), although traditional counseling is more likely to be given by male counselors when it does occur.

The possibility that counselors and teachers may be important sources of nontraditional orientations has been raised by several findings. Bandura (1969) has argued that extrafamilial sources such as teachers and counselors would be especially significant in promoting change in female sex role patterns. There is support for this idea.

Tangri's (1972) finding that influence of faculty was an important determinant of choice of nontraditional courses of college women has received support in studies by Seater and Ridgeway (1976) and Stake and Levitz (1979). The results of the latter study were especially interesting, as they supported Bandura's proposition exactly. There is also a suggestion in these studies that female students are especially affected by male advisors and influences.

Finally, Armor's (1969) analysis of the equality of opportunity data provided support for the beneficial effect of counseling on girls' plans. He found that counseling increased the correlation between educational aspiration and measured ability of high school students, especially among girls and particularly among lower-class girls, the group most likely to be constrained by traditional sex role patterns. His results indicate that counseling frees those girls from traditional sex role constraints and enables them to pursue educational goals commensurate with their abilities.

While this literature on teachers and counselors is extensive, there does not seem to be a substantial body of cumulating results pointing toward the detrimental effects some writers describe. It appears rather that teachers and counselors may well operate as liberating rather than as conservative influences on female sex role socialization.

Peers

The final agency of socialization is the system of peer relations and influence that appears to become especially important in adolescence. During this period, the high school constitutes a central locus for activities and interactions, and the system of relationships and influences that predominates there constitutes what Coleman (1961) called the adolescent society. As the adolescent society exists at a time when youths become sexually mature, interpersonal relations and sex role differentiation become central features of this subculture. In this respect, it is hard to say whether this particular extrafamilial socialization should be initially viewed as a force for change or for stability in sex role socialization.

As the subculture has typically been viewed as a system somewhat independent from and antagonistic to adult cultural goals, it could operate as a liberating force for change. On the other hand, the emergence of sustained, normative, heterosexual dating and social patterns appears to stabilize sex role differentiation, at least in issues of achievement and affiliation.

Affiliation-Achievement Conflict

Various writers have assumed that the conflict between affiliation and achievement constitutes one of the central dimensions of female sex role process and have explored the ramifications (Komorovsky 1946; Hoffman 1972; Horner 1975). These ramifications involve pressure on adolescent girls to hide talent as inappropriate to the feminine role and threatening to boys, fear that unusual success will detract from essential femininity and result in loss of popularity, and a general conflict between achievement and affiliation goals, especially those involving heterosexual attractions. These are all seen as special problems faced by girls more than by boys during their adolescent experience.

The possibility that the affiliation-achievement conflict may reflect a general disjunction in the elemental patterns of these social forms rather than a unique aspect of sex role differentiation has not been treated by others, although evidence has shown that boys also disguise intellectual ability on dates (Dean et al. 1975) and generate negative imagery to a success cue (Levine and Crumrine 1975, Hoffman 1982).

Peer Pressures

The primary source for treatments of the consequences of peer pressure has been Coleman's (1961) *The Adolescent Society*. In this study of ten high schools, Coleman found patterns suggesting independence from parents and emphasis on athletics and popularity to the detriment of student academic achievement. While Coleman showed effects for both sexes, the effect of the peer pressures seemed to determine girls' orientations to a greater degree and to have been used to account for the supposed decline of female academic achievement during high school.[10]

The main lines of Coleman's interpretation were consistent with sex role differentiation and stereotyping. The major sources of peer status appeared to be athletics for boys and popularity for girls, although male status was highest when athletics and scholarship were combined. For girls, scholarship was viewed as less important. Coleman (1961:90) concluded that social success, not academics, was the important achievement area for girls. Interestingly enough, he found that this orientation was stronger in the middle-class schools than in the working-class schools, presumably because in the middle-class schools college-bound boys also seek good grades, a goal placing girls in competition with boys to a greater degree than in lower-class schools, where boys do not seek grades. Sex role effects also appear in the proportions wanting to be remembered as a brilliant student. Over the years of high school this increases among top male students but decreases among female students.

The effects of these orientations on grades was demonstrated indirectly. Female grades did not decline; they were in fact higher than male throughout the school years, but there were differences in the patterns that Coleman (1961) interpreted as consistent with the idea that the adolescent subculture pressured girls somewhat more than boys away from academic goals. Thus, the IQs of girls receiving A's were somewhat lower than the IQs of boys receiving A's or A−'s, indicating to Coleman that boys used their ability more directly than girls did, or that peer pressures diverted female talent to nonacademic areas.[11] Girls' grades were also more homogeneous than boys' grades. This suggested that boys could strive to be a brilliant student or could compensate by rejecting school altogether, but girls sought to be good, though not brilliant, in order not to compete with boys or to lose their feminine image. They became average to balance the adult demands for conforming achievement and stereotypic pressures to be less competent than boys.

Notwithstanding the concern for the deterioration of feminine achievement during the high school years, there is not much actual evidence of the process itself, although one widely cited study (Shaw and McCuen 1960) has been so interpreted. In that research, an examination of the grade history of boys and girls who were overachievers and underachievers in high school revealed an interesting difference. Underachieving and overachieving boys in high school had held these ranks throughout their entire school experience, but underachieving girls did not differ from overachievers until they reached ninth grade. These patterns have been interpreted as evidence that female underachievement was a function of peer pressure intensifying in these years of adolescence.

What is generally overlooked in the Shaw and McCuen (1960) study is that all of the groups *except female overachievers* exhibited a sharp decline in grades around seventh and eighth grades. A more accurate interpretation of their findings, therefore, would be that the depressing effect of school pressures on achievement was *greater for boys than for girls*. These pressures were successfully resisted only by the overachieving girls! Unfortunately, a more recent study replicating these results for girls failed to include boys in the study (Fitzpatrick 1978).

Notwithstanding the assumption of deteriorating feminine achievement under peer pressures for mediocrity (Katz 1979:170; Hunt 1980), there does not appear to be strong evidence, apart from that relating to sex-typed content that may reflect underlying cognitive differences, of a decline in female achievement as a consequence of peer pressures for feminine subordination and popularity.

EMPIRICAL EVIDENCE: SOCIALIZATION INFLUENCES

In this section I examine sex differences and change in several variables whose significance is established by the theoretical and substantive concerns just summarized. While the contemporary literature on sex role socialization is far from coherent or consensual, theoretical and substantive themes most often addressed have implications for several dimensions contained within the data of the present study. Among these are the questions of same-sex versus cross-sex influences; intrafamilial versus extrafamilial influence; the use and evaluation of high school counseling services by the two sexes; the views about appropriate functions or purposes of the high school in educating and training students; participation in extracurricular activities, especially in athletics; and status rating by peers in academic and extracurricular contexts. Each of these areas incorporates several important issues in contemporary discussions of sex role socialization. In each area, predictable sex differences and sex role change would be expected to occur on the basis of arguments and evidence in the sex role literature. As we have seen, these changes are almost universally treated in terms of masculinization. There is an assumption that opportunities and determining experiences available to boys should, and will, become available to girls. This view is most clearly advanced in extrafamilial socialization contexts, but even within the family, there has been concern about the sources of change. This change points toward shifts in the primary sources of socialization themselves.

Sources of Influence

On the basis of theoretical and substantive positions held in the sex role literature, it might be expected that boys would have a broader range of advisement influences, with girls' consultation more limited to family sources. While there are not, to my knowledge, any specific formulations to that effect, the literature describes a more circumscribed, limited environment for girls than for boys and assumes girls to be more closely tied to and dependent on the parental family than boys, who are assumed to have more freedom and independence to range in an extended social environment and to establish more interpersonal relations. In addition, the greater range of vocational options available to males would seem to orient them to a greater variety of potential influence sources.

The major exception to these expectations for greater range of male consultation and influence seems to come from the special significance that extrafamilial sources of influence might have in establishing nontraditional goals for girls. Teachers and counselors appear to be important in this respect, although they are also seen as forces for traditional sex role socialization. However, my conclusion was that compared to the family, teachers and counselors probably represent forces for nontraditional, more than traditional, sex role socialization, although the evidence is very weak on either side of this question. On the whole, we would expect boys to have a broader range of influences, with girls' influences more limited to family. From these perspectives, change in sex roles should produce a shift toward more extrafamilial influence on female socialization across the decade.

Another important question in the literature of sex role socialization is that of same-sex versus cross-sex influences. Identification theories such as the Freudian and cognitive developmental predict same-sex influence, while social learning and role learning theories give more emphasis to paternal influence on both sexes. This pattern is modified by mother's work and other sources of maternal power. On the other hand, literature on nontraditional socialization influence has indicated that male support and encouragement is necessary to female career innovation. Because of these countervailing forces, it is difficult to predict what the pattern of change might actually turn out to be. Changing women's roles and increased maternal employment[12] should make the mother increasingly more influential and especially should bolster the same-sex pattern of influence for the girls.

Results

Analysis of responses to questions about who the student talked to about plans after high school is presented in table 6.1. The proportions and the sex regression coefficients reveal substantial difference between the sexes, but in an unexpected pattern. Contrary to expectations, girls report talking to more different consultants than boys do, with a mean difference of around one-half consultant.

This difference prevails over nearly all possible sources. In all but four cases, higher proportions of girls report the consultation than boys. Three of the exceptions, father, employer, and military recruiter, are highly sex typed, while the pattern in the fourth, college counselor, is not differentiated by sex. In all the others, though, girls report more consultation. Thus, contrary to the limited evidence on friendship networks, girls appear to be involved in a broader range of interpersonal discussion, especially regarding relatives, friends, and high school peers, although also including much heavier reliance (in 1964 at least) on the state employment service. While teachers and counselors are also more often consulted by girls, they are relatively less often consulted than the other major female-oriented sources. The pattern does not suggest that teachers and counselors have a special significance for girls, although that point is more precisely addressed in the following analysis of the most influential consultant.

A slight tendency toward same-sex parental consultation is observed, but it is overwhelmed by the not surprising fact that nearly all children of both sexes report talking to both parents about their post-high school plans. This is basically a universal pattern for girls, and nearly so for boys, especially with regard to the mother. Nearly all adolescents of both sexes discuss their plans with their mothers. A slightly lower proportion, but still an overwhelming majority, also report talking to their fathers.

Changes in the patterns between 1964 and 1975 suggest both social change

Table 6.1.

Persons "Talked To" about Post-Graduate Plans by
Sex, Year, and Sex-by-Year
(N=5600)

Persons talked to about P.G. Plans	Proportion that talked to each of the named persons				Metric Regression Coefficients[a]			
	1964		1975					
	M	F	M	F	Sex	Year	Inter	R2
Family and Friends								
Father	.87	.83	.86	.81	-.05			.00
Mother	.92	.96	.88	.96	.04	-.03	.04	.01
Other Relatives	.61	.73	.57	.68	.12	-.05		.02
Other Adults	.63	.71	.64	.71	.07			.01
Other Friends	.56	.71	.62	.75	.14	.06		.02
School								
Counselors	.82	.87	.72	.74	.03	-.11		.02
Teachers	.59	.64	.56	.55	.05	-.04	-.05	.00
Peers	.83	.94	.82	.92	.10			.02
Community								
State Employ. Serv.	.23	.38	.05	.07	.14	-.18	-.13	.12
Clergymen	.15	.20	.06	.08	.04	-.11		.03
Employers	.32	.31	.40	.35	-.03	.06		.00
College Counselors	.13	.13	.15	.16		.02		.00
Military Recruiters	.24	.03	.19	.07	-.21	-.05	.09	.06
Other	.02	.03	.09	.12	.02	.08		.03
Mean Number	(6.94)	(7.47)	(6.62)	(6.98)	(.44)	(-.41)		(.02)

[a]Coefficients are from the two variable equation unless the interaction regression coefficient
is greater than two errors. Only those coefficients greater than two standard errors are reported.

and limited and selective sex role change. Consistent with my earlier findings about rejection of traditional social institutions and values, there is a substantial decrease in consultation with such representatives of organized adult society as counselors, teachers, and especially, the state employment service and clergy. There is also the suggestion of shifts from ascribed to achieved patterns in the declining consultation with other relatives, but increased consultation with friends, employers, and others. These students increasingly appear to seek advice from individually relevant significant others rather than from formal and traditional others. Peer consultation is very high, especially for girls, and remains essentially stable over the years.

The sex-by-year interactions reveal specific sex-related shifts that do not appear to fit any general pattern of sex role change, certainly not any pattern subsumed under the general concept of masculinization. Contrary to the idea of extrafamilial influences, the decline in consultation with teachers and state employment service is greater for girls than for boys, although in each case the result is convergence from greater female consultation with these sources in 1964 to an equivalent level of consultation between the sexes in 1975. The interaction on use of military recruiters reflects liberalizing sex role change. Consistent with both occupational and labor force changes and the themes of adventure and excitement, girls were twice as likely to talk to military recruiters in 1975 as in 1964. However, this appreciable change occurs on a negligible base since military recruiters are the least likely consultant for girls in both years.

Table 6.1 reveals sex differences in consultation that were not predicted and that indicate a broader female network of interpersonal advisements than males experience. Sex role change was limited and specific, reflecting convergence and, in the one case, liberating changes.

A more precise view of the patterns of influence reported by the sexes can be obtained through analysis of responses to the question about the person having the most influence on post-high school plans. This response reflects a view of consultation and advisement closely related to the concept of identification in socialization literature, and is more appropriate for considering sex differences and change in the reported significance of the several consultants for adolescent socialization.

The major sex differences in table 6.2 are consistent with identification theories of socialization as they reflect patterns of same-sex parental identification. Girls are considerably more likely to report the mother as most influential while boys are more likely to report the father. However, the proportions also show that fathers are more influential than mothers, and this is true for both sexes. Consistent with both social learning and role learning formulations, the more powerful, rewarding, paternal status is associated with considerably more influence on adolescent socialization than is the mother's status. While there is support for same-sex formulations in these responses, there is somewhat stronger support for differential effects, probably reflecting status and power within the family (see also Lueptow 1980a). Fathers are clearly the major perceived influence for both sexes in both years.

Compared to the effects of parental status, the scattered sex differences in

Table 6.2.

Most Influential Consultant

Persons named as "most influential"	Proportion naming Person as "most influential"				Metric Regression Coefficients[a]			
	1964		1975					
	M	F	M	F	Sex	Year	Inter	R^2
Family and Friends								
Father	.39	.29	.40	.28	-.10			.01
Mother	.08	.20	.07	.19	.12			.03
Other Relatives	.05	.04	.05	.05				
Other Adults	.04	.03	.05	.04				
Other Friends	.02	.04	.04	.05	.02	.02		.00
School								
Counselors	.21	.17	.13	.11	-.03	-.06		.01
Teachers	.07	.10	.06	.19	.04			.00
Peers	.03	.04	.05	.07		.03		.00
Community								
State Employ. Serv.	.02	.03	.00	.00	.02	-.02	-.02	.01
Clergymen	.01	.01	.00	.00		-.01		.00
Employers	.02	.02	.05	.02		.02	-.02	.00
College Counselors	.01	.01	.01	.02				
Military Recruiter	.05	.00	.03	.01	-.04	-.01	.02	.01
Other	.01	.02	.05	.07	.01	.04		.02

[a]Regression coefficients are from the two variable model unless the interaction coefficient is larger than two standard errors. No coefficients are reported when R^2 is not significantly different from zero at the .05 level.

designation of other most influential consultants are negligible. While girls are more likely to report talking to high school counselors, they are less likely than males to find counselors most influential. However, it should be noted that both sexes find counselors very influential, second only to parents in exerting influence on post-high school plans. In fact, for boys, counselors are reportedly more influential than mothers. These results indicate that concerns expressed about the roles of counselors in adolescent socialization are well taken. Counselors are perceived as important influences on adolescent socialization or choice and could presumably have a significant impact on either traditional or innovative sex role development.

A reversed sex difference is observed for teachers. Girls are more likely to find teachers influential than boys are, and while the proportions designating teachers as most influential are small, they are higher than any other source except parents and counselors.

The shift between counselors and teachers cannot be explained with these data, but it is consistent with the idea that counselors emphasize traditional roles and that innovating females often draw on the support and encouragement of male professors and teachers.

Other sex differences in reported influence involve negligible proportions of students and are consistent with the overall patterns of consultation. Girls are more likely to be influenced by other friends and boys by military recruiters. In none of these cases, though, are substantial proportions of students involved.

There is a fair amount of shifting in the relative importance of the various influences between 1964 and 1975, mostly consistent with increased personalization. Counselors, state employment service, clergy, and military recruiters became less influential while friends, peers, employers, and others became more influential. These patterns reflect the shift from institutional to personal, individualized, socialization experience also observed in Veroff, Douvan, and Kulka (1981). Interestingly enough, given these shifts, there is no change in the proportions reporting the parents most influential between 1964 and 1975. Whatever else was going on, it appears that the patterned relations between children and parents remained constant and unaffected by these minor, extrafamilial shifts.

Finally, there is little evidence of sex role change in patterns of reported influence, and by inference, in sources of sex role socialization content. Family relations remained constant, notwithstanding the substantial social change and sex role change presumed to have occurred during the period. From this evidence it does not appear that these changes in the pattern of contemporary sex roles, if they did in fact occur, have permeated the structure of relations between parents and children.[13]

Very small percentage changes were involved in the relative decline in influence of state employment service and employers on girls and the increase in reported influence of military recruiters over the period. Except for the real decline in reported influence of state employment service, these interactions involve decline in male as well as increase in patterns of female reported influence. These minor changes, involving almost negligible proportions, do not support conceptions of sex-related change in patterns of adolescent socialization, at least insofar as they are reflected by the structure of relations with influential others. This is especially true for those patterns relating to the most influential agents of socialization.

Facilitating Variables

Facilitating analysis was carried out on responses to most influential consultant only. This analysis was reduced for two reasons. To this point, there has been very little evidence to support the proposition of facilitating variables, and while the issue will be examined in the remaining sections, for purposes of economy the analyses will not be comprehensive.

The results of running the seventy regressions of the fourteen sources of influence with the five selected facilitating variables being used make the preceding discussion substantially moot. Third-order interactions between sex, year, and facilitating variables produce only five third-order interaction regression coefficients that are greater than two standard errors. This is almost exactly the number to be expected by chance at the .05 level. Furthermore, three of these coefficients show that high facilitating females are less likely to be influenced by their mothers, the state employment service, or employers. These results do not warrant discussion, although the regression coefficients for the significant third-order interactions are reported in appendix C, panel 1.

Summary and Conclusions

Results from the analysis of sex differences and change in sources of influence do not support concepts of sex role change or limitations and constraints on female access to a broad range of advisement. Contrary to expectations that girls would experience limited, circumscribed advisement opportunities, girls in this study reported a wider range of consultations both within and outside the family than boys did.

The major change in consultation over the period is in the declining significance of institutional sources of influence and information. Across the decade these students turned from such sources as counselors, clergy, and state employment service in fairly dramatic numbers. These shifts were accompanied by increased influence of such informal sources as friends, peers, and others.

These changes in the pattern of consultation were not accompanied by evidence of sex role change, especially of the sort expected, that would indicate a shift to such extrafamilial influences as teachers and counselors by girls. On the contrary, major declines appeared in girls' use of teachers.

The only evidence of sex role change, and a highly symbolic one at that, was the appreciable increase by girls in use of and influence by military recruiters. While this pattern involved small, almost negligible, numbers of girls, it clearly portends changes in traditional sex role patterns.

Family sources of influence were by far the most frequently used and the most influential. Same-sex influence was observed, although modified considerably by paternal influence. Most students consulted mothers, but fathers were the most influential by a considerable margin for boys and also for girls, although to a lesser degree. A major surprise was the decline in consultation with the mother, although not in her influence. It does not appear that changes in women's roles over this period has any effect on mother's importance as a perceived socialization influence, except, possibly, to decrease her influence for boys.

Analysis of patterns of influence shows sex differences favoring girls, substantial change away from traditional sources, but very little sex role change, at least very little change consistent with a masculinization hypothesis. It appears that the moderately sex-differentiated structure of relationships across a diverse set of potential socialization agents has remained relatively constant over the period.

High School Counseling

The preceding review of the literature indicated that sex-related consequences of counseling are at present unclear. There is argument and evidence that counseling perpetuates traditional roles and there is also argument and evidence indicating that counseling is especially beneficial to the formulation of female aspiration. On the whole, I have concluded that counseling, like the influence of teachers, probably does constitute an innovative rather than a traditional sex role influence. However, that conclusion is not easily substantiated by the evidence with which I am familiar. There is, however, a pervasive assumption that boys are exposed to a broader set of educational and occupational possibilities and that agencies of socialization from the family on place greater emphasis on the achievements and career orientations of boys than of girls, that girls are shunted to a few secretarial and home economics courses while boys are introduced to the broad, full range of adult vocational and career potentials. On that basis we might expect more counseling of boys across a broader content with more success, although sex role change might lead to mitigation of such effects.

Initial examination of the reported number of visits to counselors showed a very skewed distribution. Between 15 and 20% of the students reported having had no visit before or during the senior year, around 40% reported only one or two visits, and a significant minority of students reported as many as twenty or thirty visits. Such range and skewedness indicate that different substantive processes were involved at different points on the scale of visits. Consequently, number of visits has been analyzed with dummy variables reflecting these three separate levels. "No visits" is unequivocal, and students reporting no visits to the counselor were compared to all other students. Among the remainder of students, it was assumed that a few visits would represent advantageous, conventional advisement about colleges, careers, and vocations. Students reporting between one and six visits were compared to the remainder. Finally, it seemed likely that large numbers of reported visits might reflect problem-oriented counseling or therapy. Consequently, students reporting more than six visits were compared to the remainder of students. Sex differences to be described below substantiate these assumptions.

Results

Table 6.3 describes the number of visits to high school counselors reported by students before and during their senior year. Because counseling would seem to have substantially different relevance for college-bound and noncollege-bound students, I present analysis for each group separately.

Among both college-bound and noncollege-bound students, girls are more likely than boys to have received what we have assumed to be a limited number of conventional, probably career- and education-oriented, counseling visits, although the difference results in significant regression coefficients in the senior year only. In addition, the sex difference is greater for noncollege-bound youth, suggesting that contrary to conceptions of female disadvantage, the group most needing extrafamilial support was in fact receiving it. This is consistent with Rehberg's (1978) finding that counseling most improved the ability-performance association for working-class girls.

Boys in both groups are more likely to have had no counseling at all, although the differences are not great. The greatest difference in absence of counseling is between the two postgraduate plan groups in the senior year. Inspection of the proportions in the two panels of table 6.3 reveals that noncollege-bound students are two or three times as likely to have received no counseling during their senior year as the college bound. Again, boys are more likely to have received no counseling during their senior year, although differences are small.

Table 6.3.

Number of Visits to Counselor by Sex, Year, and
Year–by–Sex for College Bound and Non–College Bound

Visits to Counselor	Proportion in Category				Metric Regression Coefficients[a]			
	1964		1975					
	M	F	M	F	Sex	Year	Inter	R^2
College Bound (N=2764)								
Prior to Senior Year								
None	.16	.15	.18	.16				
Moderate (1-6)	.68	.70	.67	.68				
Many (7+)	.16	.15	.15.	.16				
During Senior Year								
None	.08	.04	.12	.10	-.03	.05		.01
Moderate (1-6)	.77	.81	.70	.74	.04	-.07		.01
Many (7+)	.15	.15	.18	.16				
Non–College Bound (N=2120)								
Prior to Senior Year								
None	.25	.19	.23	.22				
Moderate (1-6)	.61	.68	.64	.68				
Many (7+)	.14	.14	.14	.09				
During Senior Year								
None	.19	.13	.26	.22	-.05	.08		.01
Moderate (1-6)	.71	.79	.64	.71	.07	-.08		.01
Many (7+)	.09	.08	.10	.07				

[a]Coefficients are from the two variable equation. Coefficients are not reported when R is not significant. Only those coefficients greater than two standard errors are reported.

There are no changes in the reported number of visits prior to the senior year for either postgraduate group. However, changes do occur in the number of visits during the senior year, and they are essentially down. In line with the preceding analysis on consultants, students report a decline in moderate numbers of visits to counselors during the senior year, a decline of about the same amount for both plan groups. There is also an increase in the proportion who have no visits during the senior year, an increase somewhat greater for the noncollege bound.

While sex differences and change were observed, no interaction appeared that would suggest change in basic sex-related aspects of counseling visits. Both sexes decline in moderate number of visits by about the same amount, maintaining the female advantage in almost the exact degree.

Table 6.4.

Occupational Counseling by Sex, Year, and Year-by-Sex,
for College Bound and Non-College Bound

Aspect of Counseling	Proportion Who Discussed				Metric Regression Coefficients[a]			R2
	1964		1975		Sex	Year	Inter	
	M	F	M	F				
College Bound[b]								
Discussed Vocational Choices	.82	.92	.66	.70	.10	-.16	-.06	.05
If Yes, Discussed:								
Potential Ability	.85	.89	.78	.74	.04	-.06	-.08	.02
Interest	.90	.91	.84	.80		-.09		.02
Test Results	.78	.83	.56	.53	.05	-.22	-.08	.07
Nature of the Vocation	.65	.68	.60	.55			-.09	.00
Non-College Bound[c]								
Discussed Vocational Choices	.71	.87	.55	.61	.16	-.15	-.10	.05
If Yes, Discussed:								
Potential Ability	.90	.90	.75	.76		-.14		.03
Interest	.95	.95	.89	.86		-.08		.02
Test Results	.60	.57	.39	.42		-.18		.03
Nature of the Vocation	.79	.78	.66	.66		-.12		.02

[a]Regression coefficients are from the two variable equation unless the interaction coefficient is larger than two standard errors. Only those coefficients greater than two standard errors are reported.

[b]N ranges between 1995 and 2721.

[c]N ranges between 1210 and 2064.

The frequency and content of occupational counseling is reported in table 6.4, again distinguishing between college-bound and noncollege-bound students. Relatively high proportions of both groups report vocational counseling, although higher proportions of college bound than of noncollege bound received such counseling, notwithstanding the greater immediacy of the concern to noncollege-bound youth. In part, this may involve the differential significance of counseling for hourly jobs or work as compared to career counseling of the college-bound students.

The incidence of occupational counseling runs counter to the assumption of female disadvantage in the receipt of occupational information.[14] In both groups, but especially in the noncollege-bound group, girls are *more* likely than boys to be counseled about occupational choices. While the differences are not great, they are clear-cut, especially for the noncollege bound, the group where female disadvantage and traditional pressures would be most expected.[15]

The decline in high school vocational counseling between 1964 and 1975 is dramatic, especially for the girls. By 1975, the proportion of girls receiving vocational counseling declined by over 20% among both the college-bound and the noncollege-bound groups. For the noncollege-bound group this generates a significant interaction coefficient that, along with sex and year, explains a meaningful proportion of the variance in the amount of vocational counseling this group received. It is clear that these students, and especially the noncollege bound, received less vocational counseling in 1975 and that female utilization declined most of all, in distinct contrast to the expectations about sex role change. During a period when feminist agitation and other social forces increased emphasis on female employment and career achievement, girls in these schools lost a considerable part of their original advantage in amount of vocational counseling.

While the pattern was unexpected, the result of the changes just described resulted in a reduction in sex role differentiation. Both college-bound and noncollege-bound girls became more like boys in experiencing less vocational counseling.

There were few sex differences in the content of counseling, with the exception of test results in 1964, when college-bound girls were more likely than boys to discuss test results and in discussion of potential ability for the occupation. There is no suggestion in these patterns that girls in either group received more limited or circumscribed advisement for work than boys did. If anything, at least among the college-bound girls, there was a slight advantage in content of vocational counseling.

There was substantial change in reported content of counseling between 1964 and 1975, especially for the noncollege bound. Among those students, there is a marked reduction in discussion of test results and to a lesser degree of the nature of the vocation and the potential ability for the occupation. There are not, however, any sex differences in these patterns nor in the reduction of their occurrence between 1964 and 1975.

The pattern for the college-bound students is similar in the decline in discussion of test results, a change that probably reflects educators' concerns about testing and privacy during this period in the mid-1970s. College-bound responses differ greatly, though, in the sex-related declines. In three of the four areas of counseling content, girls reported a greater *decrease* over the period than boys did. In each case, the decrease in content of girls' counseling was great enough to reverse the 1964 advantage to a 1975 disadvantage. In these three content areas, girls received more counseling than boys did in 1964, but less counseling in 1975. This change was especially dramatic in test results, where girls reported a 30% decline in the proportion receiving that type of information. Equally impressive change occurred in discussion of the nature of the vocation. A nearly constant proportion of college-bound boys reported receiving such counseling while girls reporting that content decreased 13%. It appears that the counseling of girls became somewhat more circumscribed or at least limited over the decade, in direct opposition to expectations about liberation and expansion of female opportunities.[16]

The final evidence on counseling involves the evaluation of the helpfulness of counseling to college plans and to post-high school vocational plans (table 6.5). Among the college bound, there are no significant sex differences in evaluation of counseling for either college plans or vocational plans. However, the decline in evaluation of counseling by the college bound between 1964 and 1975 is substantial, running about three-tenths of a scale unit on a response scale running from (not at all helpful) to (very helpful). College-bound students clearly found counseling less useful to their college planning in 1975 than they had in 1964. A similar drop in evaluation occurred regarding the vocational plans of college-bound students. This aspect

Table 6.5.

Evaluation of Counseling by Sex and Year
for College Bound and Non-College Bound

Type of Counseling	Mean Evaluation Scale[a]				Metric Regression Coefficients			
	1964		1975					
	M	F	M	F	Sex	Year	Inter	R^2
			College Bound[b]					
College Plans	2.20	2.21	1.93	1.85		-.31		.04
Vocational Plans	1.85	1.93	1.61	1.60		-.28		.04
			Non-College Bound[c]					
College Plans	1.76	1.91	1.53	1.56	.07	-.28		.04
Vocational Plans	2.01	2.01	1.72	1.71		-.29		.04

[a]Scores represent (1)=not at all; (2)=somewhat; (3)=very helpful. Coefficients are from the two variable equation. Only coefficients greater than two standard errors are reported.

[b]N ranges between 2530 and 2621.

[c]N ranges between 1490 and 1845.

of counseling was rated low, it was lower in 1975, and, again, female ratings declined the most, although not by a significant amount.

Noncollege-bound students exhibited a similar pattern of decline over the period and showed the same tendency to rate the less relevant advisement less highly. Noncollege-bound girls found college plan advisement more helpful than noncollege-bound boys did, although this advantage largely disappeared by 1975. In the more relevant vocational plans, there were no sex differences in the evaluation of noncollege-bound students. Overall, noncollege-bound students found vocational counseling relatively less valuable than the college-bound students found counseling for college.

Facilitating Analysis

Exploratory analysis analogous to that carried out for sources of influence was carried out on the counseling patterns with noncollege-bound and college-bound groups combined.

These analyses continue to show only chance findings. There is only one third-order interaction coefficient larger than two standard errors among the fifteen regression analyses of the five facilitating variables and the three dummy variables of number of visits during the senior year, and that occurs among the high visit problem counseling. There are only two third-order interaction coefficients larger than two standard errors among the twenty-five regressions of the five facilitating variables and the five aspects of occupational counseling. This is only slightly greater than the number expected by chance. Finally, none of the ten regressions of the five facilitating variables and two evaluation items was larger than two standard errors. As these results could easily occur by chance, they will not be discussed here, although the coefficients are again presented in appendix C, panel 2.

Summary and Conclusions

The analysis in this section has been addressed to the question of sex differences in various components of counseling. Generally, the literature on sex differences in education holds that counseling perpetuates traditional patterns. Discussions about greater opportunities, broader choices, and stronger career emphasis for boys than for girls in the sex role literature carry implicit hypotheses about male advantages in the counseling process. While the data of this study cannot examine the direct influence of counseling on boys and girls, it has been used to approach the issue indirectly, through examination of the amount of counseling, emphasis on vocational counseling, and finally, evaluation of the helpfulness of counseling.

The results of this analysis revealed patterns of counseling substantially different from those expected. Separate analysis for college-bound and non-college-bound students shows that the major effects on the counseling process were due to time, not sex. There was a fairly strong reduction in use of counseling over the period, in the number of different aspects of vocational counseling addressed, and in the overall evaluation of the helpfulness of counseling. All of these were consistent with the general theme observed at different places in this analysis, of the rejection of adult institutions and agencies by adolescent students in the 1970s. For the most part, sex did not produce important effects, but where effects were observed, they tended to favor girls rather than boys.

Girls received more counseling during the senior year, at the moderate levels we take to indicate conventional, not problem-oriented counseling. Boys in both postgraduate plans were more likely to receive no counseling. Surprisingly, considering assumptions about schools' limiting vocational opportunities for girls, girls received more vocational counseling than boys did. The only sex differences in the content of counseling occurred among college-bound students and favored girls. The decline in these patterns affected both sexes, although among college-bound students, girls experienced a greater decline than boys in nearly all aspects of occupational counseling.

Ironically, the few interactions that were observed reflected a relative loss of advantage by girls. Thus, the substantial decline in use of and evaluation of counseling involved reversals for college-bound girls that turned their earlier advantage to disadvantage. These results are contrary to the idea that counseling of girls in 1964 would be more limited and that changing sex role patterns would increase counseling opportunities for girls, especially in vocational counseling. In fact, these data show that girls and boys received equivalent counseling in 1964. Where there were differences they favored girls, not boys, but girls lost ground over the decade. While none of these results deals directly with the specific (traditional or nontraditional) content of advisements made by counselors in these schools, it does provide strong indirect evidence questioning the assumption that high school counseling has favored boys, but is responding to forces emphasizing change toward greater female advantage.

Functions of the High School

A series of items about the importance of various listed functions of the high school expressed in terms of "their importance *as tasks of the public high school''* permits examination of sex differences and change in student views about the appropriate role of the high school in their own socialization experience. These items range broadly over the role of the school in traditional cognitive training to less traditional concerns with personal adjustment, social skills, and various practical skills. On the assumption that each sex would prefer socialization experiences appropriate to its anticipated sex roles, we might expect girls to emphasize interpersonal skills while boys could be expected to emphasize occupational, community, and perhaps cognitive skills to a greater degree.

Results

Rating of each of the listed functions (table 6.6) shows that nearly all of the functions are viewed as "fairly important" or "very important." On a scale of 1 to 3, none of the functions was given an average rating under 2, which would be between "unimportant" and "fairly important." Clearly these students accept the view of a broadly diverse, multifunctioned educational-socialization experience within the public high school. This multifunctioned view was held much more strongly by girls than by boys. On all but two of the listed functions, girls rate the factors as more important than boys do, in some cases by substantial margins.

Traditional sex role orientations emerge in these ratings. The greatest sex difference occurs in the much stronger emphasis given the "empathy and social skills" function by girls. On the other hand, substantial difference also appears in the "occupational information" item, which has the second largest sex difference in favor of girls and which cannot be viewed as a traditional difference. However, it is consistent with patterns of counseling differences that showed girls received more vocational counseling and got more information than boys did. Contrary to the sense of much of the writing in the sex role literature, these girls placed more emphasis on the school as a resource for such information than boys did, especially in 1964. In a way, we are observing here a reflection of the national patterns of occupational change without substantial change in sex role patterns, a surprising emphasis on occupational information, but within a context that is otherwise characterized by traditional sex role patterns.

The occupational orientation notwithstanding, the major sex role pattern of table 6.6 is basically in the girls' tendency to rate most of the functions as more important than boys do. Whether this represents their view that the school should be more important in adolescent socialization or simply their more accepting view of the school as an agency of socialization cannot be determined from these differences.

Table 6.6.

Rating of Functions of the High School by
Sex, Year, and Year-by-Sex
(N=5252)

Function	Average Rating				Metric Regression Coefficients[a]			
	1964		1975					
	M	F	M	F	Sex	Year	Inter	R²
Fund of Information	2.52	2.63	2.42	2.55	.12	-.09		.02
Physical Fitness	2.52	2.56	2.36	2.42	.06	-.15		.02
Three R's	2.64	2.78	2.47	2.60	.13	-.18		.04
Emotional Stability	2.65	2.76	2.56	2.70	.13	-.08		.02
Weighing Facts	2.57	2.60	2.52	2.54		-.05		.00
Moral Standards	2.68	2.79	2.50	2.62	.12	-.18		.04
Inquiring Mind	2.63	2.74	2.48	2.59	.11	-.15		.03
Cultural Appreciation	2.17	2.25	2.24	2.24	.07	.07	-.08	.00
Empathy and Social Skills	2.56	2.77	2.52	2.74	.22	-.03		.05
Occupational Information	2.54	2.71	2.40	2.58	.18	-.13		.04
Civic Responsibility	2.48	2.52	2.23	2.22		-.28		.06
Specialized Job Training	2.35	2.48	2.33	2.45	.13	-.03		.01
Patriotism	2.61	2.66	2.10	2.13	.04	-.53		.17
Home Skills	2.16	2.32	2.25	2.35	.16	.09	-.08	.01
World Affairs	2.36	2.50	2.23	2.30	.14	-.14	-.07	.03
Management of Finances	2.41	2.44	2.47	2.55	.06	.09		.01

[a]Coefficients are from the two variable equation unless the interaction coefficient is more than two standard errors. Only those coefficients greater than two standard errors are reported.

The change between 1964 and 1975 is consistent with other changes observed in this study that have reflected deemphasis of social institutions and increased emphasis of individualistic, hedonistic, and interpersonal patterns. This is seen most dramatically in the ratings of "patriotism," which declines by almost one standard deviation over the decade. This item, phrased as "instilling a sense of 'loyalty' to America and the American way of life," was given a medium rating in 1964 as a fairly important function, but by 1975 this was the least important function by a large margin. The only functions even close were "civic responsibility" and "cultural appreciation," although the latter function showed a differentiated increase over the period.

Other substantial declines occurred in the cognitive as well as in the informational aspects of high school. By and large, the 1975 students were much less sanguine about the importance of the school than the 1964 students. The uniqueness of the patriotism factor indicates that this shift was directly related to the social protest and opposition to the war policies of the late 1960s. However, even with the decline, the average ratings of all items, including the patriotism item, are between scale values of 2-"fairly important" and 3-"very important." Thus, the pronounced decline observed in these responses is relative to the higher ratings of 1964 and by no means reflects an absolute rejection of any of the socialization or educational functions of the high school by the 1975 seniors.

There were very few significant interactions. For the most part both sexes expressed declining values to about the same degree, thus preserving the sex differences in the face of general social change, a pattern observed before in this analysis. The interactions that were observed reflected both male increase in the valuation of an item (in two cases) and greater female decrease (in one case). There did not appear to be any interpretable pattern of sex role change in the shifts observed in table 6.6, although the analysis of "most important function" is a more sensitive gauge of such change.

Ratings of the "most important function," presented in table 6.7, permit evaluation of sex differences and change in the relative importance of the functions. Such a selective rating forces choices and emphasizes priorities. It thus has the effect of magnifying small differences and changes.

The most desirable function for the school in the view of these adolescents is "emotional stability." One-fifth of the girls in both years rated this function most important as did over 15% of the boys.[17] "Moral standards" and an "inquiring mind" are also important. Beyond these, however, there is very little consensus about the functions, with only these three being listed by more than 10% of the participants of both sexes. Some of these students see nearly all of these functions as desirable and important. Forced to choose, they scatter their ratings across the full set of tasks. Except for the definite emphasis on character and personality development, a limited number of students find each of the functions to be important.

There are only a few sex differences in the relative importance of these functions, and they are relatively weak. Most notable of these differences is the greater emphasis girls place on "empathy and social skills." Twice the proportion of girls as boys rated this as most important in 1964, and the sex difference increased slightly by 1975. Girls also more often rated "emotional stability" and "moral standards" as most important, thus revealing a traditional sex role pattern, at least in comparison to male ratings. Boys, on the other hand, emphasized "physical fitness," "specialized job training," "cultural appreciation," and "civic responsibility," although negligible

Table 6.7.

Most Important Function of the High School
by Sex, Year, and Year-by-Sex
(N=5140)

Function	Average Rating 1964		1975		Metric Regression Coefficients[a]			
	M	F	M	F	Sex	Year	Inter	R[2]
Fund of Information	.08	.07	.09	.08				
Physical Fitness	.05	.03	.04	.02	-.02			.00
Three R's	.09	.08	.07	.07				
Emotional Stability	.16	.20	.14	.22	.03	-.03	.05	.01
Weighing Facts	.05	.04	.07	.04	-.02			.00
Moral Standards	.12	.15	.08	.10	.02	-.04		.01
Inquiring Mind	.11	.11	.09	.07		-.03		.00
Cultural Appreciation	.00	.00	.03	.01	-.01	.02	-.01	.01
Empathy and Social Skills	.05	.10	.07	.16	.07	.04		.02
Occupational Information	.03	.02	.04	.03				
Civic Responsibility	.04	.02	.03	.01	-.02			.01
Specialized Job Training	.07	.05	.10	.06	-.03	.02		.00
Patriotism	.08	.07	.03	.01		-.05		.02
Home Skills	.01	.02	.03	.03		.02		.00
World Affairs	.01	.01	.02	.01				
Management of Finances	.04	.03	.07	.06		.03		.00

[a]Coefficients from the two variable equation are reported unless the interaction coefficient is over two standard errors. Only coefficients greater than two standard errors are reported. No coefficients are reported when R^2 is not significant.

proportions chose the latter two functions. Thus, while the differences were small, they split between functions roughly characteristic of instrumental and expressive concerns.

Over time there was some shifting of relative importance, but as the coefficients of determination indicate, none of these differences or shifts has any important effects on the choice of functions as most important. We are here examining patterns that are substantially trivial. The strongest regression coefficient indicates a drop of about 5% in the proportion listing "patriotism" as most important and a decline of about 4% in the proportion listing "moral standards" as most important. Very minor increases can be observed in various personal functions, especially empathy and social skills. On the whole, though, while the valuation of the importance of most functions declined noticeably over the decade (table 6.6), the *relative* importance of the different functions observed in table 6.7 remained essentially constant.

Only one important interaction was observed. Girls increased their strong emphasis on "emotional stability" while boys decreased theirs, creating an 8% difference by 1975. This shift adds to the already strong expressive orientations of girls. By 1975, 38% of the girls named either emotional stability or empathy and social skills as most important functions. Adding "moral standards," which taps the characterological aspect of interpersonal relations, accounts for almost half of the girls' choices of "most important" function, compared to less than one-third for the boys. Thus, traditional sex role orientations describing an expressive emphasis characterized the female student's view of the role of the high school, and this traditional orientation strengthened somewhat in 1975.

Analysis of student views of functions of the high school revealed more evidence of social change than of sex role differentiation in emphasis on specific functions. However, the differences that did occur were consistent with traditional sex role formulations. The main differences apart from decline in patriotism were in the female emphasis on social skills, personal adjustment, and moral standards. These are all aspects of successful interpersonal relations. What girls seem to want from the high school is training and experience that will enable them to better cope with challenges of interpersonal relations.

Facilitating Analysis

There was essentially no evidence of a facilitating effect in the analysis of the five selected facilitating variables and the sixteen "most important" functions. Among these eighty regressions, there were only six third-order interactions greater than two standard errors. These six constituted 7.5% of all regressions run, only slightly better than might be expected by chance, and certainly not constituting support for the facilitating effect. Furthermore, these few significant interactions did not exhibit any pattern of special interest and do not warrent discussion. The regression equations for the six significant interactions are presented in appendix c, panel 3.

Summary and Conclusions

This analysis of sex difference and change in adolescent orientations toward high school has shown two or three clear patterns. In the first place, girls rate nearly all of the functions more highly than boys do, suggesting that they view the role of the school as more central to their socialization than boys do, a view much in keeping with the idea that important aspects of contemporary sex role socialization occur outside of the home, in such institutions as schools and workplaces. By and large, girls thought the school should do more different things than boys did.

The other major sex difference was traditional. Girls emphasized the expressive functions of the high school socialization experience much more than boys did. All students gave considerable emphasis to these personal development functions, but in keeping with traditional sex role emphasis on interpersonal relations, girls stressed these factors to a greater degree. However, this traditional feminine view was accompanied by the strong emphasis on occupational training, consistent with the patterns observed in the analysis of counseling. As in the national scene, traditional feminine orientations and occupational interest do not appear contradictory or exclusive. Apart from the emphasis on empathy and social skills and their greater stress of all functions, girls' responses did not differ much from boys'.

There were few interactions in these patterns. While both boys and girls revealed a definite devaluation of the role of the high school between 1964 and 1975 that was consistent with other evidence on adolescent rejection of adult institutions, this devaluation occurred about equally for both sexes. Here as elsewhere, we have observed sex differences that persist in the face of substantial social change. This section shows traditional sex differences and social change but very little sex role change.

Extracurricular Participation

Participation in high school extracurricular activities adds another aspect beyond the formal socialization in the academic curriculum. In the preceding review of literature on sex role socialization, I noted the important potential significance of certain types of adolescent experience in cognitive development and in related orientations toward particularistic versus universalistic modalities. Central among these experiences are the sex differences in athletic participation, which could affect both cognitive and motivational development. Team sports involve a more complex, organized, universalistic context for youth experience than unorganized play or interpersonal association. Lever (1978) finds this to be one of the important demarcations between games played by girls and boys. Athletics could also be an important context for acquiring achievement-related motivations, especially in competitive striving, a pattern I have suggested may differentiate the achievement orientations of males and females.

Other extracurricular participation, especially that having to do with service and leadership, may also mitigate traditional sex role socialization in the family and give the school context a special and significant relevance to girls by providing leadership and independence training not so clearly present in family socialization experience.

In this section I examine sex difference and change in participation in a number of athletic and nonathletic activities that were presented to students in the 1964 survey. This list, which is produced in table 6.8, includes the major sports and activities common in these schools. Unfortunately, the response distributions indicate that the list omits a number of specific other activities that were entered by these students, especially the girls. Thus, in this case, the "others" categories represent a fairly large number of activities, both athletic and nonathletic, that cannot be specified and incorporated into these interpretations. However, the list of major activities that can be interpreted provides us with a reasonably good cross-section of activities to use in evaluating the amount of sex role differentiation and change in the extracurricular activities of these schools during 1964 and 1975.

Results

Table 6.8 presents the proportion of students participating in designated activities and in two undesignated "others" categories. As expected, there are major sex differences in athletic participation, especially in the major interscholastic sports, both contact and noncontact. However, it is interesting and unexpected to note that in three noncontact minor sports, softball, swimming, and tennis, there are negligible differences between the participation levels of girls and boys. While the sex differences in participation in football and wrestling are certainly due to the sex-typed norms that limit contact and power sports to males, the difference between basketball and track on the one hand and the minor sports on the other would appear to be more a function of the status of the sport and its centrality in the interscholastic competitions central to school activities and spirit. If it is an important spectator sport, boys rather than girls are the major participants. However, if it is neither major nor contact the participation levels of the sexes are low but equivalent.

Girls tend to predominate in the nonathletic activities, although not to a degree comparable to the male monopoly in sports. Girls are more likely to be in drama, forensics, glee club, newspaper, and student government, as well as in such specifically female activities as cheerleader and Girls Athletic Association. Girls are also much more likely to have participated in

Table 6.8.

Participation in Extracurricular Activities
by Sex, Year, and Sex-by-Year
(N=5600)

| Activity | Proportion Participating | | | | Metric Regression Coefficients[a] | | | |
| | 1964 | | 1975 | | | | | |
	M	F	M	F	Sex	Year	Inter	R²
Athletics								
Baseball	.19	.03	.14	.03	-.16	-.05	.05	.06
Basketball	.26	.08	.25	.12	-.18		.06	.04
Football[b]	.39	.00	.38	.00				--
Girls Athletic Assoc.[b]	.00	.43	.00	.44				--
Golf	.04	.01	.09	.07	-.04	.04		.02
Softball	.05	.06	.09	.07		.03		.00
Swimming	.02	.03	.04	.04		.02		.00
Tennis	.04	.03	.06	.06		.03		.00
Track	.31	.00	.26	.19	-.31	-.05	.23	.09
Wrestling[b]	.13	.00	.19	.00				--
Non-Athletic								
Cheerleaders	.00	.08	.01	.10	.08	.02		.03
Dramatics	.11	.21	.11	.18	.08	-.02		.01
Forensics	.09	.17	.06	.12	.06	-.04		.02
Glee Club	.16	.42	.10	.33	.25	-.07		.09
Orchestra/Band	.16	.16	.16	.21			.04	.00
Newspaper	.08	.27	.08	.17	.19		-.10	.05
Student Gov't.	.15	.18	.10	.14	.04	-.04		.01
1st Other	.25	.48	.26	.42	.22		-.06	.04
2nd Other	.07	.25	.08	.18	.18		-.07	.05

[a]Two-variable coefficients are reported unless the interaction coefficient is larger than two standard errors. Only coefficients larger than two standard errors are reported.

[b]Participation limited to one sex. Coefficients not calculated.

one of the "other" activities. Thus, there is clearly sex role differentiation in the extracurricular activities.

The change across the years in participation shown in table 6.8 is consistent with the general social changes I have been describing. By and large, there are small but statistically significant changes reflecting the decline in participation in nonathletic activities and an increase in athletic participation. The "other" activities remain constant, although a very slight decline of female participation was observed. This is a fortunate outcome for our interpretation, as it discounts the possibility that sex role change has occurred through increased female participation in the unspecified, uninterpretable "other" activities.

Sex role change was observed in widely varying degrees in athletics. There do appear to be real sex role changes in the incidence of basketball participation and especially in track. From basically no participation in track in 1964, female participation rises in 1975 to nearly approximate that of the males. While this undoubtedly reflects program decisions within these high schools, it does mean that substantial numbers of girls were participating in athletics in 1975 as compared to 1964. Some sex role change was also observed in nonathletic participation, where female participation in the newspaper and in "other" activities declined while male participation continued at the same rate. On the other hand, female participation in orchestra and band increased, consistent with the changes we have observed in the academic music courses.

Generally, table 6.8 shows girls to be well represented in nonathletic extracurricular activities and to be surprisingly equal in those noncontact minor sports that do not carry so much of the esteem of the school. It does not stretch the imagination too much to see that in the very visible, highly emphasized major interscholastic sports, students prefer male rather than female representation. However, the dramatic increase in track and the less dramatic but substantial increase in basketball do reflect sex role change in these central sports, although not so much change that the basic elements of sex-differentiated athletic dominance are eliminated. In the nonathletic activities, girls either hold their own or lose ground. Nevertheless, and insofar as athletic participation does actually produce personality development in motivational and possibly even cognitive components, these changes have to be viewed as signaling important sex role developments.

Ratings of "how helpful the activity will prove to be . . . in later life" are analyzed in table 6.9. While this is an ambiguous response in some regards, it can be used to provide a rough indication of the value of the activity from the students' perspective. We of course cannot know whether the value refers to such concrete things as anticipated athletic scholarships or to less tangible outcomes of training experiences on personality development and later adult success.

Table 6.9 shows that boys see much more value in athletic participation than girls do. These differences are substantial, running between a fifth of a unit score to almost one-half of a unit on a three-point scale. These sex-

Table 6.9.

**Helpfulness Rating of Extracurricular Activities
by Sex, Year, and Sex-by-Year**

Activity[b]	Average Rating 1964		1975		Metric Regression Coefficient[a]			R²	Number
	M	F	M	F	Sex	Year	Inter		
Athletics									
Baseball	2.27	1.87	2.46	2.17	-.35	.20		.04	(528)
Basketball	2.27	1.86	2.37	2.19	-.42		.24	.05	(1005)
Softball	2.31	1.84	2.32	2.18	-.47		.33	.06	(393)
Swimming	2.70	2.41	2.27	2.50	-.28	-.42	.51	.02	(179)
Tennis	2.23	1.85	2.35	2.22	-.21	.24		.04	(263)
Non-Athletic									
Dramatics[c]	2.42	2.27	2.35	2.29					
Forensics[c]	2.61	2.58	2.50	2.57					
Glee Club[c]	2.11	2.05	2.12	2.11					
Orchestra/Band	2.35	2.26	2.32	2.28					
Newspaper[c]	2.17	2.26	2.25	2.24					
Student Gov't[c]	2.41	2.43	2.25	2.29		-.15		.01	(801)

[a]Two variable coefficients are reported unless the interaction coefficient is larger than two standard errors. Only those coefficients larger than two standard errors are reported.

[b]Only those activities with at least 20 students in each sex-by-year cell are reported.

[c]Coefficient of determination is not significantly different from zero. Regression coefficients not reported.

differentiated evaluations do not carry over to the nonathletic activities, however, where there are almost no important differences either between the sexes or across the years. Only student government ratings vary, and they decline over the years, again consistent with the disavowal of adult institutions, in this case the student reflection of a major adult institution.

The changes in ratings of athletics stand in sharp contrast. There is an increased valuation of two of the five sports, made equally by the two sexes. In the other three sports there is a significant interaction reflecting the greater increase in valuation among girls than among boys. While these increases fail to produce equality in the ratings of girls and boys, they nevertheless indicate an important change in the perception of athletics by girls. Such a view should presage increased female participation in athletics, beyond the increases we have observed here.

Facilitating Analysis

In line with the emerging conclusion that the facilitating variables are not important in determining contexts of sex role change, and to reduce the cost of the analysis, I again limit the facilitating analysis to one indicator of extracurricular activity, that of participation itself.

The facilitating analysis of participation results in somewhat equivocal findings. Seven of the seventy regressions of the five selected facilitating variables and eleven activities with enough cases to analyze generate third-order interaction coefficients larger than two standard errors. This is almost three times the number expected by chance. However, examination of the direction of these significant coefficients shows that only three of them manifest the predicted pattern of increased female change in high facilitation contexts. More intelligent girls who read newspapers are more likely to increase participation in orchestra, while girls with more highly educated fathers are more likely to increase participation in tennis. However, three of the other significant interactions involve male, not female effects, while the remaining interaction is in the opposite direction from that predicted. While these outcomes could be seen as borderline support, taken in the broader context of the results of this study, they are not strong enough to constitute important evidence reversing my general conclusions that the facilitating variables do not index circumstances leading to sex role change. As before, the regression coefficients for the significant interactions are reported in appendix C, panel 4.

Summary and Conclusions

As expected, we have observed sex differences in athletic participation, although unexpectedly they were limited to major sports and to contact sports. In the two or three noncontact minor sports, female participation was roughly equivalent to male participation, suggesting that the status recognition awarded school representatives in the major interscholastic competitions may be reserved for boys and have much to do with sex typing in athletic participation. In those noncontact sports where important interscholastic competitions were not involved, girls participated almost as much as boys. Girls were more involved in nonathletic activities than boys were, and to about the same degree. In these regards, my analysis is consistent with Coleman's early research on the adolescent society.

Over the decade, these students decreased their participation in nonathletic and increased participation in athletic activities, a pattern that seems consistent with the general shift toward personalized, hedonistic goals and away from adult achievement and success goals.

Sex role change was observed in two major sports. The most dramatic change was in track, where female participation increased from 0 to 19%. By 1975, female participation in track was only slightly below the 26% participation level of males. In this respect we are observing dramatic change in the high school experience of girls, change that represents masculinization of the feminine role.

Helpfulness ratings were consistent with the participation patterns. There were substantial differences between the sexes in the perceived helpfulness of athletics, with boys viewing athletics as more helpful, but there were few differences in the perceived helpfulness of the other activities. The most striking change over the years was the increased valuation of athletic participation by girls. In one of the clearest sex role changes we have observed, girls have greatly changed their view of the helpfulness of athletics to their later life. These changes reflect a pattern of masculinization. Girls are increasing their participation of and valuation of athletics while generally declining in participation of the other activities. However, the valuation of the nonathletic activities, while constant, is generally as high as for athletics. In athletics, though, girls are clearly moving toward use of socialization experiences previously reserved for boys.

Peer Status

Peer status is an important dimension of the peer subculture assumed to operate within the high schools. In this section I examine sex differences and change in two aspects of peer status: (1) the areas in which students hold high status and (2) the effect of popularity on academic achievement.

As we have seen, Coleman's analysis of the adolescent society was consistent with the views generally held in the sex role literature that boys and girls occupy different, stereotypically appropriate, statuses within the adolescent subculture. The most important status for boys was athletics, while for girls popularity was most important, although girls also received recognition for their extracurricular activities. Further, while neither sex placed the highest emphasis on scholarship, boys valued this particular status more than girls did.

The data of this study include ratings by each respondent of the best athlete, the best student, the most important in extracurricular activities, and the most popular boy and most popular girl. In each case, respondents were asked to list the three top persons in the class. These ratings have been summed within each senior class to produce peer status scores for each student based on the number of choices each student received from classmates divided by the number of students in that senior class.

Traditional sex role differentiation in the adolescent subculture would lead us to expect that boys most often would be named as the best athlete, while girls would more often be named as most important in extracurricular activities. It is difficult to predict what the traditional view of best student might be. Boys value scholarship more and individual achievement is assumed to be a component of the male stereotype, but as we have seen, girls outperform boys by a large margin throughout the years of school. Given the importance of stereotyping, however, it might be expected that boys would more often receive this rating than girls, actual performance differences notwithstanding.

The clearest expression of sex role change would be increased status recognition of girls in athletics and perhaps decreased recognition in activities and popularity, although the latter cannot be effectively analyzed within our model because of the separate ratings of girls and boys.

The other important sex-related aspect of the peer status system has to do with the special significance of popularity for girls. It is generally assumed that girls' needs to be attractive to boys, to date, and to be popular conflict with needs to achieve and succeed, especially when those achievement patterns place them in direct competition with boys for the same goals. As a consequence, it is assumed that female popularity striving reduces effective levels of achievement and success. In the same sense that Coleman has treated the diversion of talent to athletics and popularity, we might expect negative associations between popularity and academic achievement, especially among girls who face problems of role conflict between affiliative and achievement orientations as well as the problem of allocating personal resources to studies or to popularity.

While we cannot examine dating popularity, the general peer ratings of most popular boy and girl must certainly overlap considerably with that general sense of popularity within the adolescent subculture that Coleman was addressing. It seems unlikely that conventional dating popularity within the normative framework of the peer subculture would be independent of the general popularity within the high school class.

Results: Status Ratings

Analysis of peer status ratings in these four dimensions is presented in table 6.10, along with the proportions of students receiving various levels of rec-

Table 6.10.

Peer Status Ratings by Sex, Year, and Year-by-Sex Interaction
(N=5000)

Type of Peer Status	Number of Choices	Proportion Receiving				Metric Regression Coefficients[a]			
		1964		1975					
		M	F	M	F	Sex	Year	Inter	R²
Best Athlete:	0	.80	.98	.81	.95	-1.62	-1.36	1.34	.07
	1-4	.11	.02	.13	.04				
	5+	.09	.00	.06	.01				
Best Student:	0	.80	.79	.81	.80		-.96		.03
	1-4	.14	.13	.14	.15				
	5+	.06	.07	.05	.05				
Most Important:	0	.78	.79	.82	.82	.15	-1.00		.04
	1-4	.16	.12	.14	.12				
	5+	.06	.09	.04	.06				
Most Popular[b]:	0	.65	.69	.70	.72	--	--	--	--
	1-4	.22	.19	.22	.20				
	5+	.13	.12	.08	.08				

[a]Regression coefficients predicting   number of choices/size of school, expressed as an integer. Two variable coefficients reported unless the interaction term is over two standard errors. Only coefficients larger than two standard errors are reported.

[b]Separate responses for "most popular girl," "most popular boy."

ognition. Examination of the proportions shows a somewhat mixed picture. Except for female athletic status, about one-fifth of the students received at least one nomination. However, except for 1964 popularity ratings, considerably less than 10% received more than four choices. Thus, while the recognized status *elite* is limited and fairly broadly known, there is relatively little consensus on the status of the majority of these designated cases. This tendency toward diffuseness in the high status groups is reduced slightly in the regression analysis by scoring only those chosen by at least 1% of their class.[18] This reduced the number of persons scored greater than zero by about 20% in each status category.

As expected, boys are much more likely to be named as best athlete while girls are more often named as most important in extracurricular activities, although the sex difference in athletic status is many times that in extracurricular leadership. There is no important sex difference in the status of best student. Contrary to suggestions in the literature, the students in these schools perceive female academic achievement at about the same level as male achievement, although when the greater actual achievement levels of girls are taken into account it appears that in view of actual accomplishments, boys receive relatively more status recognition than their performance would warrant and girls receive less.

While the nature of the response categories precludes regression analysis of popularity, the proportions named as most popular show that boys are more likely to be viewed as popular than girls are. While this is somewhat contrary to general expectations about the importance of popularity, the proportions probably reflect the significance of athletics, which involves a relatively broad group of boys.

All of the statuses declined over the decade, probably reflecting the reduced response rate in 1975, because some undetermined number of ratings would have been made to seniors who did not participate in our study, thus reducing the proportion receiving one of the three ratings in each group. On the other hand, the very small differences in the face of the substantial number of nonparticipants indicates that high status respondents were more likely to be included in the study than excluded.

Sex role change is clearly observed in one status, that of best athlete. While very small proportions of girls are chosen as best athlete, this proportion more than doubled in 1975. Furthermore, in 1975 there were small but measurable numbers of female students who received more than four choices as one of the three best athletes in the high school. While they represent an almost negligible proportion, they nevertheless constitute a substantial change from the complete absence of such recognition of female athletes in 1964. Overall, then, we do observe sex role change in athletic status commensurate with the changes observed in athletic participation. Girls are participating more in athletics, are perceiving such participation as more helpful, and are beginning to be recognized by their peers for athletic performance.

Apart from athletics, however, no sex role change is observed in table 6.10. Girls continue to be named as most important in extracurricular activities while the sexes are basically equivalent in status as best student in both 1964 and 1975.

Results: Popularity and Achievement

The idea running through the literature that feminine talent is diverted by pressures toward affiliation and away from achievement and excellence leads to the expectation that, among girls at least, more popular students will exhibit lower levels of academic performance. This possibility is examined in table 6.11, where relations between all of the peer status ratings and academic performance are presented.

Table 6.11.

Correlation Between Peer Status Ratings[a]
and Overall GPA by Sex and Year

Status	1964		1975	
	M	F	M	F
Best Athlete	.21	.06	.12	.03[c]
Best Student	.50	.48	.38	.37
Most Important	.35	.37	.24	.21
Most Popular[b]	.29	.28	.14	.14
Number	(1330)	(1355)	(1395)	(1418)

[a]Peer status scores = $\sqrt{x}$ because of highly showed distribution.

[b]Combined responses of most popular boy, most popular girl.

[c]Not significant at the .05 level.

It is obvious that students with high status also obtain higher grades, except for girls receiving recognition as best athletes. While popularity is less highly related than importance in extracurricular activities, the correlation is nevertheless moderate and positive. More popular girls and boys receive higher grades than their less popular peers. It is also obvious that the relation between statuses and grades is almost identical for boys and girls, with the single exception of athletic status. Except for athletics, popularity and recognition appear to impinge on boys and girls in similar fashion, the literature on sex role conflict of girls notwithstanding. Table 6.11 shows a remarkable uniformity of effect between the sexes across the various status levels. What happens to boys seems to happen also to girls, with the notable exception of athletics.

The athletic exception suggests a sex-differentiated pattern of effects in athletic participation and recognition that tends to mitigate the expected benefits of athletic involvement for girls. Whether because of the implications of success in nontraditional areas (Kanter's [1977] tokens?), or because of the diversion of talent and resources into athletic rather than academic achievement, as Coleman (1961) suggested, or possibly because of sex-differentiated patterns of recruitment or selection, it appears the better female students are not disproportionately involved in athletics as the better male students are.[19]

Table 6.11 also reveals a reduction in the size of the correlations in 1975. This may be due to the inflation of grades, possibly also reflecting some changes in the basis of awarding grades. However, a theoretically more interesting possibility is that in 1964 there was a closer integration between the values of the peer subculture and the goals of the educational establishment than there was in 1975. In the earlier year students may have been recognized on the same basis by each reference group, but in the 1970s student recognition and teacher recognition may have rested on different standards applied by peers and adults. While such an interpretation cannot be easily examined here, it is consistent with the theme of social change observed repeatedly in this analysis and interpretation.

While the preceding analysis fails to show any important sex difference in the effects of status (outside of athletics), in some respects it fails to deal adequately with the central issue, which is the diversion of talent. Table 6.11 indicates that the more popular students are also more able students, which is not really a very surprising conclusion. A more direct analysis of the question should take into account the correlation between ability and popularity, for there may be a diversion of female talent even in the face of positive zero-order correlations between popularity and achievement. The test of this is, of course, the examination of the relationship between popularity and grades with intelligence controlled. Such an analysis is presented in table 6.12 for the overall grade point and for each of the typical year courses.

The effect of popularity on the overall grade-point average remains positive and statistically significant even with intelligence in the equation (table 6.12). Furthermore, comparison of the "most popular" coefficients of boys and girls reveals differences just the opposite of what was expected. The only difference between the sexes in the effect of popularity on overall grade point occurs in 1975 and favors girls, not boys. There is no support whatsoever in these coefficients of the independent effect of popularity on overall grade point for the idea that girls must sacrifice academic achievement for general popularity in high school. On the contrary, general popularity appears more advantageous to them than to the boys.

This picture of sex role equivalence or of female advantage is only slightly modified by the analysis of the independent effect of popularity on each of the typical year courses by each sex in each year. A quick scan of the remainder of table 6.12 shows that with only a few exceptions, the positive effect of popularity for each sex prevails across all courses and years. The overwhelming sign of all of these typical year coefficients is positive. In nearly every academic course, being popular is positively related to grades, for both sexes, and with intelligence controlled.

Table 6.12.

**Regression Coefficient for Popularity on Grades
Independent of Ability
(Academic Courses)**

Typical Year Courses	Males 1964 b	N	1975 b	N	Females 1964 b	N	1975 b	N
Overall GPA	.03**	(1160)	.07**	(1303)	.03**	(1170)	.08**	(1345)
Sophomore Courses								
English	.11**	(1159)	.09	(1231)	.05**	(1162)	.08	(1280)
Language	.09**	(342)	.14	(263)	.07**	(491)	.02*	(458)
Algebra	-.04	(253)	-.04	(375)	-.08	(161)	.03	(288)
Geometry	.07**	(487)	.04	(532)	.04	(501)	-.21**	(556)
History	.12**	(541)	.33**	(393)	.05*	(473)	.23*	(415)
Biology	.09**	(1032)	.27**	(1040)	.08**	(1079)	.21**	(11033)
(Mean/Standard Dev.)	(.073/.058)		(.138/.140)		(.035/.058)		(.060/.159)	
Junior Courses								
English	.10**	(1141)	.18**	(1147)	.06**	(1162)	.16*	(1169)
Language	.14**	(246)	.17	(139)	.05	(382)	.18	(288)
History	.10**	(1016)	.12	(1141)	.06**	(967)	.08	(1147)
Chemistry	.08**	(541)	.13	(370)	.06*	(369)	.00	(322)
(Mean/Standard Dev.)	(.105/.025)		(.150/.029)		(.058/.005)		(.105/.082)	
Senior Courses								
English	.07**	(852)	.15	(651)	.08**	(881)	.07	(771)
Speech	.07*	(182)	.06	(139)	.05	(277)	.12	(155)
Mathematics	.08**	(362)	.21	(411)	.05	(112)	.19	(274)
Social Science	.11	(179)	.09	(.92)	-.06	(149)	-.11	(60)
Sociology	.10**	(548)	.20*	(647)	.08**	(579)	.02	(714)
Psychology	.13**	(236)	.04	(328)	.09*	(370)	.20*	(477)
Economics	.09*	(184)	.04*	(242)	.04	(98)	.08	(179)
Natural Science	-.17	(83)	.18	(100)	.40	(35)	.13	(65)
Physics	.04	(413)	.22	(262)	.02	(86)	-.11	(136)
(Mean/Standard Dev.)	(.058/.089)		(.132/.075)		(.083/.127)		(.065/.114)	

More careful scrutiny of the table does produce some extremely weak, borderline evidence for the proposition that popularity is especially detrimental to female achievement. In the first place, among the handful of negative coefficients, those supporting the idea of special female disadvantage in popularity, there are more among the females (five) than among the males (three). However, these negative coefficients are fairly evenly distributed between sophomore and senior years, with none observed for the junior year. Thus, the pattern does not support the idea that feminine popularity-achievement conflicts intensify in the later years of high school.

There is also some very minimal, borderline support in the mean levels of these coefficients in the two sexes. These means, presented after each group of coefficients, are very low and, especially in the low enrollment courses, quite varied in their level. Nevertheless, with only one exception in the six comparisons, the average coefficient is lower for girls than for boys, suggesting that either popularity for boys has more significance in the peer subculture or, and more to the point, female talent is more often diverted from academic achievement by popularity than male talent is. However, given the substantial and highly variable standard deviations, as well as the substantial variation in numbers of students, this interpretation rests on shaky ground. By any reasonably rigorous interpretation, one would be forced to conclude that there is really no important sex difference in table 6.12. There is hardly any support whatsoever for the idea that achieving social goals of popularity results in the diversion of female talent from academic achievement in either 1964 or 1975.

Facilitating Analysis

Use of the five facilitating variables to test for special effects in some subgroups on sex-related changes in peer status produces somewhat equivocal results (table 6.13). In this case there are an unusual number of significant third-order interactions. Almost half of all the tests made resulted in regression coefficients over two standard errors. This is obviously many more

Table 6.13.

Direction of Effects of Statistically Significant
Third Order Interaction for Peer Status[b]

Status[a]	Intell.	Father's Educ.	Mother's Educ.	Numb. Consult.	Read News.
Best Athlete	-			+	+
Best Student					0
Most Important		-		-	+

[a]Sex designated popularity rating precludes regression analogous.

[b]Signs for direction: (+) = predicted; (0) = ambiguous; (-) = contrary to prediction.

than could occur by chance. It is clear that something is going on here; the question is what? The directions of these coefficients in table 6.13 do not convey a convincing picture of greater sex role change in the expected sub-population. Three of the coefficients are in the predicted direction, three are contrary to the prediction, and one is ambiguous. Such an outcome indicates that the interactions reflect something other than sex role change of the sort expected in this study. The significant third-order regression coefficients are presented in appendix B, panel 5.

For those interested in the questionable possibility that this analysis is generating weak but real support for the concept of facilitating conditions, attention is called to the cluster of significant effects involving number of consultations and reading newspaper, three-fifths of which are in the predicted direction with only one of five clearly contrary to the prediction. In these cases there is a reflection of the patterns observed earlier for students who had been most counseled and read newspapers in 1964 to be more traditional (in this case to have relatively lower status), while those most counseled and best read in 1975 had relatively higher status. In preceding sections I have suggested that the message of the media, and probably also of the more traditional institutional consultants, may well have switched between 1964 and 1975 from traditional to nontraditional advisement. The clustering of effects for these two variables in contrast to the reverse effects for intelligence and father's education does suggest this possibility. Nevertheless, the substantial number of nonsupporting effects and the exceptions even among consultants and newspaper reading have to be considered in the face of the lack of support for the facilitating analysis generally.

The analytic approach to the examination of the independent effects of popularity on academic achievement (table 6.12) precludes the usual facilitating regression analysis. However, some sense of the importance of sub-populations can be obtained by using the postgraduate plan groups as representative of broad-ranging distinctions along all of these dimensions. By and large, we can assume college-bound girls to be less traditional and more receptive to innovation than the noncollege-bound girls. Consequently, if there were selective changes in the relative importance of the popularity-achievement pattern, they might be expected to occur to a greater degree among the college-bound youths. Table 6.14 suggests just the opposite. Somewhat larger increases for both sexes occur among noncollege-bound youths of both sexes. This is roughly consistent with Coleman's (1961) finding that feminine achievement is especially conflicted in middle-class schools where college-bound girls compete directly with boys for the same goals.

Table 6.14.

Effect of Popularity upon GPA 2 with Intelligence
Controlled by Post-Graduate Plans

Post Graduate Plan	1964				1975			
	Male		Female		Male		Female	
	b	N	b	N	b	N	b	N
College, Definitely	.02**	(462)	.01*	(344)	.04	(429)	.05*	(426)
College, Tentatively	.01	(220)	.03**	(159)	.08	(229)	.04	(224)
Not College Bound	.01	(361)	.03**	(286)	.07*	(584)	.10**	(648)

* p < .05
** p < .01

However, table 6.14 does not provide any additional support for the idea that popularity in the high school detracts from academic achievement. Nor does it support the idea that popularity-achievement conflicts are especially critical for the achievements of adolescent girls.

Summary and Conclusions

This section has examined some aspects of the idea that sex roles are especially differentiated in the adolescent subculture and that adolescence and especially the later years of high school constitute especially critical periods for girls faced with conflicts between popularity and achievement. Peer status ratings of the best or most important athletes, students and leaders in extracurricular activities, and most popular girl and most popular boy were used in this analysis.

The picture of peer status ratings revealed less sex role differentiation than the literature might lead us to expect, although that which did occur was consistent with the accepted ideas. Boys had higher athletic status, girls had higher extracurricular status, while no difference was observed in student status, a fact perhaps reflecting underrecognition of female scholarship. Except for athletics, however, the sex differences were not very great. Athletics was interesting because female increase in status as best athlete was appreciable over the years, resulting in additional support for the picture of limited change observed in this research. Whereas in 1964 no girls were named as best athlete by more than four peers, by 1975, 1% of the girls were named by five or more students as one of the three best athletes in the school. This is an important change. As we have seen, girls have increased their participation in athletics significantly, and they receive recognition for excellence in this area to a much greater degree.

The other major concern of this section was with the relations between popularity and achievement, assumed to be a major problem facing adolescent girls. My analysis failed to support either the general relation or the specific sex-related significance of the pattern.

Except for athletics, the relations between status and academic achievement were moderately high and almost identical for girls and boys. Except in athletics, where high status males, but not females, get better grades, the sexes appear to have similar experience in their academic performance. All of these correlations drop considerably by 1975, but in almost exact amounts for each sex. Thus, there is no evidence of sex role change in this aspect of the analysis, although there is evidence of social change. Taken at face value, these reductions suggest a more complete integration of school and peer systems in 1964 than in 1975. In 1964, students rewarded by teachers' grades were also esteemed by their peers. In 1975 this was less true. All of these processes and changes were similar for boys and girls, however.

The idea of popularity as an obstacle to achievement or as a diversion of talent was tested by examining the popularity-grade coefficient independent of intelligence. This analysis showed that even with ability controlled, popularity was positively related to achievement for both sexes and to about the same degree, in both 1964 and 1975. Analysis of the effect in all of the typical year academic courses qualified this conclusion only slightly, but did not alter the main finding that popularity was positively related to grades for both sexes in both years. There was not any important support for the idea that popularity and academic achievement were antithetical goals for girls.

None of these conclusions was altered by the limited facilitating analysis undertaken in this section, although there was some ambiguous support for the idea that consultants and media carried a traditional message in 1964, a more liberal and innovative one in 1975.

On the whole, this section has shown less sex role differentiation than the literature would suggest in these aspects of the adolescent experience and almost no evidence of sex role change. Athletics was a clear exception to this. Interestingly enough, however, this represented liberalization and not masculinization, as the change in athletic participation was basically in sports that involved neither contact nor force, nor, for the most part, interscholastic recognition. As in earlier value changes, this seems to describe an extension of female roles rather than an assumption of previously male patterns.

CHAPTER 7

SUMMARY AND CONCLUSIONS

The original point of departure for this study was the question of changing sex roles. The 1964–1975 comparisons were undertaken to generate evidence on the widely held assumption that substantial and dramatic changes were occurring in the roles of women, and to a lesser degree, in the roles of men. This view of changing sex roles is so widely held that it has almost become a truism in the literature, hardly seeming to require any additional empirical verification.

Starting from such a perspective, it has been surprising to discover that the hard empirical evidence has not been totally consistent with that picture of changing sex roles. In fact, my initial appraisal of the existing literature revealed evidence of change on only a limited number of dimensions.

The results of this study have only slightly altered that conclusion. We have observed sex role differentiation in nearly every variable examined and have seen strong evidence of social change over the period, but we have obtained relatively little evidence of change in adolescent sex roles. In nearly every dimension examined, we have observed the perpetuation of the basic lines of sex role differentiation that had existed in 1964.

Considering the differences between the findings of this study and general assumptions about changing sex roles, it may be helpful to consider again the approach of this study.

The basic strategy of this study was to examine change in a whole series of dimensions and variables bearing on one aspect or another of sex role change describing and reported by high school seniors in 1964 and 1975. Lacking theories about sex role differentiation, this study adopted a broadly inclusive formulation that accepted all important differences between the sexes as manifestations of sex role differentiation.[1] Sex role change was then viewed as a relative decline in the extent of such differences across the variables of interest. This broader formulation permitted the inclusion of a large number of variables, giving a more diverse sampling of difference and change than had been previously reported, with the notable exception of the Duncan and Duncan (1978) and Veroff, Douvan, and Kulka (1981) studies, which used similar survey replication strategies to examine a broad range of variables reflecting sex role differentiation within the family and sex differences in subjective aspects of personality.

In this study, this approach has resulted in three characteristics of significance. In the first place, this study is based on a heterogeneous, broadly representative high school population with more variation in personality, experience, and social circumstance than those populations in many studies of attitudes about women's roles that have been based on college women, at times even college women in marriage and the family or sex role courses.[2] Second, the use of a broad range of variables has permitted examination of sex role change across a broader slice of personal experience and character than is generally produced in research on sex role change. While informal, recreational, and sexual aspects of adolescent experience have not been observed here, the data have ranged widely over a large number of variables having to do with family, community, and educational experiences and with relevant personality characteristics. In addition, as these are all manifestations of individual experience and orientation, they have a reality not so clearly present in surveys describing respondent attitudes about appropriate women's roles. These data describe actual persons occupying the same status-role context at these two points in time. Third, the year of the 1964 baseline survey turned out to be especially fortuitous as it occurred at about the latest period possible to still assess the outcomes of traditional feminine socialization. The second survey luckily encompassed the period of turmoil and conflict in the late 1960s and early 1970s.

Throughout the analysis I examined sex role differentiation, social change, and sex role change for each of the variables of the study. In this final summing up, I use the same distinctions in summarizing all of the evidence for each of the three perspectives. I also summarize what seem to have been the major theoretical and substantive positions in other writings that have been reviewed.

SEX DIFFERENCES

From the inclusive approach used in this research, sex roles have been interpreted as including traits or characteristics of personality differentiating the sexes as well as sex-typed features of social roles. Thus, any observed or postulated general difference between males and females was treated as a manifestation of sex role differentiation. While this approach obviously begs many questions about the basic dimensions of sex roles, in the absence of any real theory of sex role differentiation it is a workable approach to the substantive issue, as the summary of results in table 7.1 reveals. In all of the meaningful comparisons in the tables of preceding chapters, sex differ-

Table 7.1.

Summary of Analysis Outcomes

Chapter-Table and Content	Number of Comparisons	Number of Comparisons Showing:				
		Sex Difference[a]	Social Change	Sex Role Change[b]		
				Predicted	Ambiguous	Contrary
Sex Role Change[c]						
4-5 Occ Preferences[d]	2	2	2	2		
4-13 Educ Aspirations	4	4	3	4		
4-15 Occ Aspirations	2	2	2	2		
5-3 Voc Courses-WC	8	6	7	5	1	1
5-4 Acad Courses-Lang	3	3	3	1		
5-4 Acad Courses-Sci	7	7	6	4		
5-8 Course Most Enjoyed	13	10	8	5		
6-4 Occ Counseling	10	4	9	4	1	
6-8 Extracur Partic	19	12	11	6	1	
6-9 Help of Extracur	11	5	4	3		
6-10 Peer Status	3	2	3	1		
Total	82	57	58	37	3	1
Sex Role Stability						
4-2 Life Goals	10	8	10	1		1
4-4 Occ Values	10	10	8	2		1
4-10 Achieve Values	7	5	5			2
4-11 Grade Point[d]	1	1				
5-3 Voc Courses-BC	9	9	8			
5-4 Acad Courses-Misc	7	3	6		2	
5-6 Help of Voc Courses	4	3	2		1	1
5-7 Help of Acad Courses	9	9	8	2		
5-9 Voc Grades	11	9	10	1		
5-10 Acad Grades-Soph	11	6	9		1	
5-11 Acad Grades-Jun	11	7	8		1	
5-12 Acad Grades-Sen	16	13	13		1	2
5-14 Hours of Study	6	2	5	1	1	
6-1 Persons "talked to"	14	13	11	3		1
6-2 Most Influential	14	8	8	2	1	
6-3 Visits to Counselor	12	4	4			
6-5 Evaluation of Couns	4	1	4			
6-6 Function of HS	16	14	16	3		
6-7 Most Import Function	16	8	9			
6-11 Status and Grades	4	1	4			
Total	187	134	148	15	8	8

[a]These include cases where significant interactions may have occurred. In such cases these may be complex differences.

[b]Predicted outcomes reflect previously significant sex differences that become less because of masculinization of the feminine pattern, feminization of the male, or convergency in both patterns. Ambiguous outcomes involve a reduction in sex differences where the original difference was not significant. Contrary involves an interaction that increases the sex difference.

[c]If over 25% of the comparisons in a table show predicted change, that group of comparisons are treated as an instance of sex role change.

[d]No statistical tests made. Outcomes are judgments based upon observation of the results.

ences were widely observed. There were remarkably few areas devoid of sex role differentiation. Only in some of the school processes and outcomes were the experiences of the sexes roughly similar. However, in attitudes, values, and preferences, as well as in behavior, the sexes were sharply distinguished.

Two major bodies of substantive evidence bear upon these questions of sex differences in personality. One reflects evidence about stereotypic conceptions of the nature of women and men, the other involves evidence on actual differences in the personalities of women and men. The evidence on sex role stereotypes is much clearer and more consistent than the evidence on sex differences in personality. There is a remarkable degree of consistency in the content of sex role stereotypes as well as in the self concepts of women and men. The central themes of these differences seem to be strength, assertiveness, objectivity, and reason for men, interpersonal emphasis for women. These differences have been formulated under different rubrics, but the content remains clearly demarked. Furthermore, there is remarkable consensus between the sexes about these characteristics, and there is stability over time. Whether or not these public conceptions reflect actual differences between the sexes or are simply the consequences of institutional arrangements and sex role norms, the personalities of typical women and men are seen as very different by most people.

Evidence on differences in actual personality traits is, for various reasons, much less clear and less consensual. The major source of evidence on such differences is the Maccoby and Jacklin (1974) review of the evidence on sex differences in personality. On the basis of their review, Maccoby and Jacklin concluded that there are only four clearly documented differences in the personalities of the sexes. However, my interpretation, following Block (1976), reached a substantially different conclusion, finding some support for the idea that actual differences prevailed in many more dimensions and were consistent with the main lines of the stereotype, especially regarding male strength and assertiveness and female dependency and interpersonal orientations. Cognitive differences are especially well documented and consistent with the stereotypes. Males have higher quantitative and spatial skills, females have higher verbal skills. However, in spite of some intriguing theoretical implications about social origins of cognitive styles in particularistic versus universalistic contexts, there was little evidence supporting postulated differences in cognitive style.

Another important area of personality difference is that of achievement motivation or orientation. Here most writers emphasize the supposedly greater public recognition of male achievement, argue that women are viewed as less competent and use fear of success, differences in causal attribution and expectancies, and the conflict between achievement and affiliation as explanations for lower female achievement as well as for the greater ambiguity regarding origins and effects of female achievement orientations. This all occurs even though girls outperform boys throughout the years of school. This incongruency leads to suggestions that there may be important differences between achievement described as meeting standards of excellence or accomplishment and achievement viewed as winning out in competition with other persons.

Other basic differences have been observed in the role orientations of women and men. Women have been more oriented toward family and marriage, men more oriented toward occupations and careers. Within occupations women have assumed jobs that are sex-typed in terms of the female stereotype and involve service and support. Occupational values also distinguish the sexes as men are more oriented toward extrinsic aspects of work while women show a much stronger people orientation. Interestingly enough, the sexes do not differ much in orientations toward the intrinsic aspect of work.

The findings of this study supported these general outlines. We have repeatedly observed differences along interpersonal versus individualistic orientations that are consistent with the main elements of the stereotypes and the conceptions of agentic versus communal orientation,[3] and instrumental versus expressive roles.

Thus, the life goals of females reflected family and religious orientations and making a contribution. Males, on the other hand, emphasized luxury, status, success, and security. Similarly, in occupational values, females emphasized helping and working with people while males emphasized money, status, freedom, and adventure. These are almost exact representations of the communal-agentic distinction. Sex-typed differences also appeared in occupational preferences. Over two-thirds of these students expected to enter, and preferred entering, occupations in which over 70% of the occupants were of the same sex. For girls, these were the traditional female helping and serving occupations. While sex typing was reduced among higher status white-collar jobs, it was almost total in the exclusion of females from the blue-collar crafts.

School patterns also showed sex typing consistent with the stereotype. Girls were much more likely to take language courses, to view them as helpful, and to enjoy them. Boys were more likely to enroll in, rate as helpful, and report enjoyment in studying mathematics and science. Furthermore, while girls outperformed boys in all courses, they did relatively less well in science and mathematics courses and relatively much better in languages. All of this strongly supported the general finding described earlier about cognitive differences. It is also consistent with the idea that girls are concerned with interpersonal relations to a greater degree while boys are more concerned with instrumental, problem-solving behavior.

The interpersonal emphasis of females also appeared in the responses about the functions of the high school. Very clear differences emerged in girls' greater emphasis on social skills and personal adjustment as functions the school ought to accomplish.

The achievement patterns observed ran counter to the conventional wisdom in both attitude and behavior. Contrary to conceptions about differences in the cultures of women and men, we observed higher achievement value orientations among females than males, even on items assessing individualistic themes. On these themes, related to important elements of the Protestant ethic, girls were more activistic, future-oriented, and individualistic than boys. However, the most impressive sex difference was in the higher academic achievement of girls. The difference in overall grade-point average approached one-half of a standard deviation. This superiority was maintained in nearly all courses, although mitigated by the sex typing of course content. Finally, these differences were not explained by greater effort, at least not when hours of study were used as the indicator.

With the notable exception of achievement, the evidence of this study showed sex typing of experience and orientation that was generally consistent with the stereotypes and with the idea that females are more oriented toward interpersonal concerns.

SOCIAL CHANGE

Social change has been treated separately in this research to distinguish it from sex role change. It appears that two patterns of change, ideational and structural, were operating over this period.

There is clear evidence of ideational shifts around the end of the 1960s that reflected antiestablishment, antiinstitutional sentiments. These changes probably emanated from civil rights and antiwar agitation and ferment and reflected a clear decline in the acceptance of such traditional values as patriotism and conventional, success oriented striving and commitment. In addition to outright opposition to traditional values, research over this period showed an increased emphasis on hedonistic, individualistic purposes and on interpersonal considerations that seemed to replace institutional arrangements. The women's movement, especially the activist wing, was related to these social events and drew on the liberating, antitraditional purposes. The other dramatic change occurring over this period was the increasing participation of women in the labor force, especially of younger married women with preschool children. This structural change in patterns of employment is probably the clearest and most significant manifestation of sex role change yet observed.

Reflections of the ideological change appear consistently in this analysis and provide good justification for analyzing change in both sexes. For without such comparison, many shifts in female orientation and experience would be attributed to feminine liberation when they are actually aspects of the general shift toward individualistic, hedonistic purposes. Here, as in the Duncan and Duncan (1978) and, especially, in the Veroff, Douvan, and Kulka (1981) studies, there were repeated instances of equivalent social change by each sex that perpetuated the original difference between the sexes.

As summary table 7.1 reveals, there was substantial social change over this period. Significant change was observed in three out of four comparisons examined in this research. For the most part this change was consistent with the idea of antiinstitutional, hedonistic, and personal value shifts.[4]

The 1964–1975 comparisons throughout this analysis revealed a decline in traditional, conventional values about work, success, and patriotism in favor of increased emphasis on comfort and luxury. This was apparent in the life goals analysis, where there was a dramatic decline in valuation of religion and family and in meeting others expectations, making a contribution, and being a success. On the other hand, goals of luxury and adventure were increasingly valued. Similarly, the intrinsic occupational values declined and extrinsic values increased.

Achievement orientations also declined over the period. Every one of the values, except efficacy, declined over the period for both sexes. This was associated with declining educational aspiration levels of males, although not of females. Data from the National Assessment over this period indicated a decline in achievement levels that was consistent with these patterns and with the decline in enrollment in academic courses and the reduced valuation of traditional, basic academic content. Interestingly enough in the face of these trends, we observed a substantial increase in the grades awarded these students over this period, notwithstanding the decrease in reported hours of study between 1964 and 1975.

There was a dramatic decline in use of and evaluation of such institutional sources of influence as counseling, clergy, and state employment service. Students in 1975 saw less value in nearly all of the high school functions or purposes and reduced their participation in extracurricular activities, although both sexes increased participation in athletics. Finally, there was some indication that the integration of the peer subculture and the academic evaluations of the school were closer in 1964 than in 1975. Correlations between peer ratings of status and grades received were considerably higher in the former years.

All in all, there was considerable and consistent evidence of decline in commitment to traditional social values among these students. The effect of this was a decline in emphasis on work and striving and on satisfaction with work, and an increased emphasis on hedonism consistent with evidence from national surveys. There was also marked decline in acceptance of the major adult institutions.

SEX ROLE CHANGE

As we have noted, sex role change in the form of liberation is assumed to emanate from the antiestablishment ferment of the late 1960s and to be a central theme in the women's liberation movement itself. However, many of the purposes of the women's movement reflect long-term trends toward secularization and rationalization. Male roles anchored in technological, occupational spheres have been affected by these processes much earlier and have manifested the patterns of universalistic-achievement that various writers view as central components of male culture and that underlie sex role differences in style and modality, addressed in different ways by writers from Piaget and Freud to Lever and Bernard. At the present time, family-based women's roles centered on ascription and particularism are now being transformed by new concerns about control and recognition. The anomaly of occupying an ascribed status defined particularistically with regard to husband and family in a modern universalistic-achievement society has been clearly recognized by feminists, although as this is written we are observing surprising resistance to some of these trends in the public at large.

At the level of social roles this trend is viewed primarily as a shift from home to work and community through the adjustment of components in the particularistic family sphere to meet the exigencies of the universalistic context. Thus, writers such as L. Hoffman (1977) have argued that sex role change will necessarily be contingent on the recognition by parents that girls will increasingly occupy occupational roles and will need to be trained for such universalistic-achievement roles rather than for particularistic-ascriptive family and household roles.

From this perspective change would involve masculinization as women acquire the options and prerogatives previously held by men alone. While role convergence or even role reversal is a considered possibility, the overwhelming thrust of the writing is that women will become more like men, or at least have the opportunities and options men have had to formulate the characteristics of their achieved roles.

In spite of all the assumptions about the form and the amount of change, actual evidence of change in women's roles is very limited, at least in comparison with the potential change theoretically possible. The major evidence of actual change is in the structured process of labor force participation and in the impact on such family factors as age of marriage, fertility, sexuality, and divorce. More married women with children are working than have ever worked before and more than half of all women are now in the labor force, although it is easily overlooked that almost half of all women are still homemakers.

The other change is perceptual and attitudinal, reflecting the increasing acceptance of nontraditional roles for women. These changes involve acceptance of women working outside of the home, having equal voice within the family, and occupying leadership roles within the community and nation. While changes in the proportions of college and general survey respondents accepting such change are substantial, the overall amount of change is mitigated somewhat by other patterns. For example, the increased employment of women has been somewhat limited to traditional sex-typed occupations, and the amount of occupational segregation has not substantially declined. Furthermore, while the general population has accepted feminine leadership in principle, in practice there has not been very much change in the assumption of national or community leadership by women. Finally, while attitudes about women's social roles have changed dramatically,[5] there has been no change whatsoever in the stereotypes of women and men. From the 1950s to the present time, research evidence shows that the public conception of the personalities of women and men have remained essentially stable, as have the self-conceptions of women and men in my own (1980) research and in Veroff, Douvan, and Kulka (1981).

Finally, the National Assessments of Educational Progress conducted throughout the 1970s have shown relative stability in the sex-typed cognitive differences of males and females both in school and in the general population. Females continued to excel in verbal skills, males in mathematics and science, with the greatest differences occurring in the reasoning and problem-solving aspects of the tests.

Examination of sex role change over the broad range of categories available in this study has resulted in a large number of comparisons over the two time periods. Those comparisons that can be directly evaluated are tallied in table 7.1.[6]

The overall pattern emerging in this research and summarized in table 7.1 is one of very considerable sex role differentiation but not of substantial sex role change. Over and over in this analysis we have observed differences in the attitudes, choices, and experiences of girls and boys. There were very few variables in this study that did not reveal differences between the sexes, differences that were for the most part stereotypic. For example, significant sex differences appeared in 70 percent of the 274 comparisons tabulated in table 7.1. The roles of girls and boys were differentiated across a very wide range of characteristics.

An even more striking theme in this analysis has been the social change revealed in the 1964–1975 comparisons of these variables. Almost nothing stayed the same across this period, neither attitudes, preferences, grades, nor socialization experience. For the most part these changes have reflected the general shift away from traditional, conventional values and commitments toward individualistic, hedonistic patterns. I observed significant evidence of social change in 75% of the 274 interpretable comparisons examined in this study. Thus, whatever sex role change occurred must be interpreted against the general shift from institutional commitment to personal liberation.

Sex role change was relatively rare in this analysis, dramatically less than sex difference or social change. For the most part, sex differences were maintained in the face of substantial social change. Of the 274 comparisons, evidence of differential change appeared in only 74 cases, and about half of these were either ambiguous or contrary to the prediction. In only 19% of the 274 comparisons did we observe change in sex roles resulting in reduced levels of sex role differentiation, in spite of the fact that sex role differentiation was observed in about 70% of the interpretable analyses.

The sex role change that was observed was largely confined to four areas, reflecting (1) occupational and educational preferences and aspirations, (2) course enrollments and evaluations, (3) occupational counseling, and (4) extracurricular participation and status. Predicted sex role change as reflected by interaction terms larger than two standard errors was observed in 45% of all comparisons made in these areas. In these comparisons there were only four interactions larger than two standard errors that were not in the predicted direction. The numbers and names of the specific tables containing these comparisons are presented in the upper panel of table 7.1. Among these tables there was obvious evidence of sex role change, although even here there was slightly more evidence of stability than of change.

The lower panel of table 7.1 shows a considerable amount of stability in sex role differentiation, stability that persists across a broad range of variables, including (1) life goals, (2) occupational values, (3) achievement values, (4) sources of influence on postgraduate plans, (5) amount and evaluation of counseling (apart from vocational counseling), (6) sex-typed views about the functions of the high school, (7) graded academic performance, and (8) relations between peer status ratings and grades. These areas involved many more comparisons than did the areas of change and revealed a profound sense of sex role stability. There were only fifteen predicted interactions among these nearly two hundred comparisons and they were counterbalanced by eight significant interactions in the opposite direction from that predicted. Thus, in all of these areas, a high level of sex role differentiation persisted across the period.

Considering first the areas of stability, it was clear that predicted sex role change did not materialize in personal orientations toward life goals or the meaning of work, areas that manifested some overlap of content. While there was some evidence of liberalization in girls' attitudes and goals, the main components of sex role stereotyping remained unchanged over the decade. This is an important and perplexing result. Notwithstanding the abundant evidence on changing attitudes about women's roles, I failed to observe any important sex-related change in actual orientations and occupational values of high school seniors about to enter the adult world. In the face of substantial social change these students maintained the original differences between the sexes in most of these values, and where change did occur, it reflected liberalization rather than masculinization of personal orientations.

Achievement values also remained relatively stable, although in this case we have observed a reversal of common assumptions about sex differences. Girls have higher levels of achievement value than boys, and they increased this difference over the years. These results seriously question simplistic views of sex differences in achievement orientations. Taken in conjunction with the superiority in academic achievement, these results suggest some needed reappraisal of feminine achievement patterns. It seems unlikely that the portrayal of females as incompetent and passive actually reflects the circumstances experienced by most people in this society. I have suggested that distinctions between competition and accomplishment or impact and process achievement (Veroff 1977) might prove useful in sorting out the confusion in this area.

The stability in sex-related differences in life orientations suggests stability in socialization experience, which is in fact revealed by my analysis. There is almost no change in the patterns of reported influence. The roles of the parents remain remarkably stable, although they do show some degree of same-sex influence. The relative significance of parents, peers, and others has remained, with one or two minor exceptions, quite stable over this period. While I have not assessed content of socialization, there is nothing indicating that marked shifts had in fact occurred in the process of sex role socialization.

This stability also appeared in the number of visits to the counselor and the evaluation of the counselor, although neither of these patterns was strongly sex differentiated in the first place.

There was also no change in the attitudes about the functions that high school should accomplish. While these attitudes revealed stereotypic differences involving greater interpersonal and expressive emphasis by girls, the differences persisted and even intensified over the period. Again, there was no suggestion here that girls in 1975 had relatively different conceptions of high school then they had in 1964.

One of the most remarkable patterns of sex role stability appeared in the grades students received in all courses over the years of high school. Because of female achievement superiority in nearly all courses, it was necessary to interpret these grades in relative, rather than absolute, terms. In relative terms there was very substantial social change and also sex role differentiation in grading patterns that reflected stereotypic cognitive differences. However, notwithstanding change and sex role differentiation, the relative differences between the sexes remained almost completely stable, especially in the sex-typed academic courses. This pattern of stability in sex role differentiation across fifty course-by-year comparisons is one of the most dramatic reflections of continuation of basic elements of sex role differentiation observed in this study. For whatever the reason, biological influences on cognitive processes, student needs to maintain sex role differentiation, or constancy in teacher's expectancies, the sexes maintained their relative position across this period in nearly every single vocational and academic course and in the overall grade-point average. These continuities are the strongest evidence in this research for persistence of adolescent sex roles. The fact that this stability also involves female academic superiority complicates this picture and suggests that achievement orientations and purposes are in fact components of the female rather than the male role.

Finally, the relationships between peer status rating and student grades showed change across the years in all areas, suggesting reduced integration of student and school patterns of evaluation, but, except for athletics, there was neither evidence of sex role differentiation nor sex role change. Concerns about the special effects of peer status pressures on achievement of adolescent girls are not supported by this evidence. The effects are nearly identical for the sexes in both years, with the single important exception of athletics. However, in no case, including athletics, was there greater change over the period in one sex than the other.

Thus, we have observed a substantial level of stability in the extensive patterns of sex role differentiation revealed in this research. There is almost perfect stability across nearly two hundred comparisons even though in nearly all cases there is considerable social change and high levels of sex role differentiation. These results fail to support popular conceptions of dramatic sex role change between the mid-1960s and mid-1970s.

The sex role change we have observed can be largely interpreted as consequences of change in occupational expectations, educational orientations and changing patterns of athletic participation.

Change in occupational preferences and expectations was observed, although limited solely to white-collar jobs. Between 1964 and 1975, girls increasingly indicated preferences for white-collar jobs that had been sex-typed as male. This shift in occupational orientations followed a pattern of masculinization in that there was no comparable shift of males into occupations previously sex-typed as female. The major change in male preferences was from white-collar to blue-collar levels. The shift in female preference was also counterbalanced by the emergence in 1975 of a number of new sex-typed occupations. Overall, however, there was a clear reduction in the sex segregation of student expectations and preferences over the decade. Despite this reduction, there still remained substantial sex typing in occupational preferences.

There were also changes in occupational and educational aspirations consistent with the heightened plans of girls to enter occupations previously sex typed as male. These shifts involved increasing female and decreasing male levels of occupational and educational aspiration. In fact, definite educational plans inverted over the decade, although they were not strongly sex differentiated to begin with.

These changes are generally consistent with evidence from the national scene in these and in preceding years showing the major sex role change to be increased labor force participation of younger married women. This major change in female employment has been remarked on but has not been accompanied by major changes in sex roles beyond those directly involved in the occupational participation itself, although L. Hoffman (1977) and others have argued that change in sex role socialization content will follow, but not precede, increasing parental expectations about future labor force, as compared to homemaking, roles for their daughters. In this analysis we have observed change in occupational and educational aspirations but not in life goals, work values, or patterns of socialization that would indicate that change in the content of sex role socialization had begun.

The changes in course enrollments and orientations that were observed here are consistent with the idea expressed by Fox, Tobin, and Brady (1979) and others that sex typing of academic courses is related to sex typing of occupation, that females do not take mathematics and science courses because they do not expect to enter occupations requiring those skills and they consequently see those courses as masculine areas. We have observed sex typing in course enrollments, orientations, and relative achievement that was consistent with such formulations, although the strength of sex role differentiation in these areas was considerably less than that described in the literature. The changes observed involved relative increase in female enrollment in some previously male courses in mathematics and science and relative decrease in enrollment in languages and in the courses teaching traditional secretarial and office practice. Girls also increased their valuation of mathematics and science courses and, in a very suggestive sex role shift, reported increased enjoyment in studying mathematics and science. They also reported increased helpfulness of mathematics and biology, although overall changes in perceived helpfulness were not as numerous as changes in enrollment and enjoyment. However, while numerically limited, the substantive significance of these shifts made them among the most important changes observed in this study.

This picture of important change in some of the most clearly documented aspects of sex roles was sharply qualified by the surprising absence of change in the relative difference in achievement within these sex-typed course areas. As I have noted, relative sex differences in grades were maintained with remarkable consistency over all of the comparisons made. There was not a single instance of change in sex role differentiation in any of the sex-typed academic courses over this period.

The discrepancy between change in course enrollments and orientations and stability in grades has implications for the interpretation of these effects. The changes in enrollments and orientations are consistent with the changes in occupational expectations and with unobserved but possible school-based changes in conceptions about sex typing of courses. However, stability in the relative performance differences is puzzling and suggests biological explanations for these cognitive patterns. It seems possible that while occupational and course orientations may reflect decision processes based on social circumstances within the school and community, behavioral differences indexed by grades may well reflect biologically based differences in cognitive functioning. They may also reflect needs to maintain sex differences on the part of these adolescents, although as we have seen, there are few sex-differentiated links between facets of peer recognition and academic grades.

Sex role change was also observed in occupational counseling, especially for college-bound youths. However, the nature of the sex difference was unexpected and the change a little difficult to interpret. Girls had received more occupational counseling in 1964 than boys did, in both plan groups. However, this changed drastically by 1975. Frequency of occupational counseling was generally reduced for both sexes, but the effects were substantially greater for girls than for boys. These results are not easily interpreted within our model of sex role change. They essentially represent the loss of an advantage girls had earlier, a loss that makes their experience more consistent with that of boys, which represents sex role change as we have defined it. However, as I have suggested that occupational counseling could be viewed as a force for sex role change, it seems wrong to view this shift as an aspect of masculinization of the female role. Basically, girls received relatively more counseling and valued it more in 1964 than in 1975. It is of course possible that these patterns represent negative reactions to traditionalistic sex-typed counseling, that my interpretation is wrong and that more liberated, nontraditional girls in 1975 rejected the traditionalistic counseling that was more appropriate and acceptable in 1964. While this possibility cannot be dismissed, it does not appear likely in view of the general absence of evidence that these traditional attitudes and values have changed over the decade. In addition, the more extensive female counseling observed in 1964 would not seem necessary if counselors were making advisements to traditional sex-typed roles. Clearly a major change has occurred with respect to sex differentiated counseling experience but it is hard to determine exactly what it means in our present frame of reference.

The final major change observed in this study is also related to school experience and is probably a consequence of change in school programs and encouragement. By 1975 girls had increased participation in athletics and had received increased recognition from peers for athletic excellence. While these shifts were limited to one or two sports and involved almost negligible numbers, they are of course highly suggestive and connotative of change in basic socialization experience. As competitive, organized athletics have been so highly sex typed as masculine within the high schools, even the limited changes observed here represent substantial attacks on the sterotype. Furthermore, given the theoretical and substantive ideas about the importance of organized sports for the development of universalistic, rule-based behavior as well as for competitive orientations and purposes, these shifts can be seen as consequential. They do appear, however, with evidence that athletic participation of girls in minor, noncontact sports was nearly the equivalent of boys in 1964.

It appears that we have observed more stability than change across the full range of characteristics studied in this research. Contrary to the general assumptions of academic writers and possibly of the general public, the examination of sex role change over the full range of these variables shows that more remains the same than actually changes.

The changes observed were related to change in occupational orientation and possible reflections of such shifts in course experience. Female occupational orientations (but not the sex-typed meaning of work) seem to be changing, probably reflecting real changes in labor force participation of women. It also appears that patterns within the school are also changing, possibly reflecting students' and teachers' recognition of these shifts. That this may not be an unmitigated advantage is revealed by the reduction of the female advantage in occupational counseling. The change in athletic participation, evaluation, and status of girls probably reflects school as well as student response to contemporary efforts to equalize athletic programs. In this we are probably observing a singularly clear instance of sex role change.

FACILITATING ANALYSIS

The absence of effects from the facilitating analysis has been consistently observed in this research. While there was some scattered support having to do with patterns of effects here and there, the overall analysis failed to support the idea that sex role change was more advanced among students of higher intelligence, with more highly educated fathers, with mothers who work, who consult more people about post-high school plans, and who read newspapers. Plausible as these formulations appeared at the start of this research, the extensive search for third-order interactions resulted in what must be viewed as essentially chance findings. Out of some 685 regressions run with each facilitating variable, there were only 19 significant third-order interactions when intelligence was used, 15 when father's education was used, 4 for mother's work, 12 for number of consultants, and 15 for reading newspaper. None of these exceeds 3% of the total tests made, and all could easily have occurred by chance. Consequently, I am forced to conclude that none of these had any real effect on the limited amount of sex role change observed in this study.[7]

The absence of facilitating effects has been mitigated here and there by patterns of results that were consistent with the propositions and probably could not have occurred by chance. However, these were too scattered and in some cases were too ambiguous to the interpretation to warrant consideration here. Furthermore, in many other cases the effects in the significant interactions ran in the opposite direction from that expected. Taken overall, there has been little support generated for this concept.

The nearly complete failure of these facilitating variables to produce an effect must be considered as further indirect support for the idea that the school and not the family or the community has been the primary agent of the limited change observed. The facilitating variables tapped important and varied aspects of family and community experience. Their irrelevance to the limited changes actually observed indicate that the source of the change, such as it was, did not lie in the family or in the community or general media. The failure of these variables to have any effect has to be considered as support for the role of the school in producing the changes we have observed.

Another interpretation is that no sex role change of any consequence has in fact been observed in this study outside of changes directly related to academic experience and advisement. If there is no change, it is not surprising that the agents and facilitators of change have no effect.

CONCLUSIONS AND SPECULATIONS

The results of this research have revealed general stability in sex roles between 1964 and 1975, results consistent with other research terminating at roughly the same time (Duncan and Duncan 1978; Veroff, Douvan, and Kulka 1981). In the face of pervasive (but not especially large) sex differences across nearly all variables examined in this study and in the face of extensive social change in orientations reflecting anti-establishment sentiments (patterns also observed by the Duncans and especially by Veroff, Douvan, and Kulka), we have observed only a limited amount of sex role change. As in the research now being reported by Herzog and her colleagues (Herzog 1982; Herzog, Bachman, and Johnston 1983), this change is generally related to increasing occupational opportunity and, in this study, to analogous broadening of female experience in the school curriculum and extracurriculum. But, except for these inherently important shifts in work and school, basic sex role parameters reflecting instrumental and expressive differences and basic family role division seem to be persisting into the 1980s.

The picture that is emerging from this and other research is one of increasing female opportunity for occupational and educational experience along with traditional sex role differentiation within and outside the family. Females continue to value interpersonal relations, marriage, and family while also expecting to realize opportunities and satisfactions in occupational and community roles. As we have seen, while females value work as much or more than males, they also seek different satisfactions from work, differences relating to communal and agentic distinctions. Similarly, as this is written, Herzog, Bachman, and Johnston (1983) report that while high school students increasingly accept working mothers, they much prefer working fathers and continue unchanged in their preferences for traditional housework and child care arrangements, results quite consistent with Thornton, Alwin, and Camburn's (1983) recent panel study showing continuing shift toward egalitarian and liberating attitudes, but persistence, even retrogression, in attitudes about sex role specialization along an instrumental-expressive dimension.[8] Thus, it appears that liberation rather than masculinization is the best way to characterize the results that have been observed in this study and which are accumulating in other research as well. Limitations and restrictions, especially in work and education, are falling in the face of the drive for equal opportunity, but there is little evidence that women and men seek identical roles, either in the family or outside. While their magnitude is modest, sex differences persist through a wide range of factors in this and in other research. There is even evidence that the changes in values about women's role have stabilized in the later half of the 1970s (Cherlin and Walters 1981; Lueptow and Clough n.d.), while perceptions of sex role stereotypes remain both pervasive and stable through the end of the 1970s (Lueptow and Clough n.d.; Williams and Best 1982; Ruble 1983).

These results necessarily qualify some of our conventional assumptions about changing sex roles.

In the first place, it does not appear that changing attitudes about women's role have had marked effects upon real life goals and experiences of adolescents in the mid 1970s, even though the message of the counter culture did have clear and pervasive effects upon the values and experiences of these students. This suggests that scholarly reactions in the early 1970s may have overstated the public acceptance and involvement in changing sex roles. It is also possible these changes have always had more to do with the liberation of the housewife and her equity in work and community affairs than with major challenges to the basic relations between the sexes and the alterations of sex-differentiated personality. Except for the liberating shifts in occupational and academic preferences and experiences, there are no strong indicators in this research or in other accumulating research of changes in the basic sex role parameters. Whether for cultural, interpersonal, or biological reasons, the main lines of differentiation between the sexes are persisting into the 1980s.[9]

Given these considerations and the surprisingly limited evidence of sex role change in this and other researches through the 1970s, it seems possible that sex role change in the coming decades might be less extensive than expected, even in the face of the substantial female occupational participation.[10] Surprising as it seems to me now, recalling the anticipation of the discovery of change when I began planning this research in the early 1970s, I am actually less sanguine about change in the coming decades than I was then. It now appears to me that while change in sex roles will certainly occur, the basic parameters of contemporary sex roles may be unaffected, that the increasing opportunities realized by today's women will result in liberation and freedom, but will not necessarily lead to revolutionary alterations across the full range of sex role patterns.

While these conclusions seem reasonable to me at this time on the bases of the research as I know it, it is important to recognize that we are currently looking at the first, preliminary evidence of a social process just now commencing. While this preliminary evidence from the present study and from other research indicates less, more limited change than the literature suggests is occurring, the final determination of the scope, nature, and speed of change in sex roles will necessarily rest upon evidence that will emerge in the coming decades. Given the complexity and ambiguity of some of the changes observed in this research, along with the significance of the social issues involved, the need for careful and extensive study of change and stability in all facets of contemporary sex roles is very apparent.

For now, I must conclude that while some change in sex roles has been observed in this and in other research through the 1970s, there has been less change and more stability than I had expected to observe.

APPENDIX A.

Metric Regression Coefficients for Significant Third Order Interactions of Goals and Values on Sex, Year, and Facilitating Variables

Dependent Variable	Facilit. Variable	Cons	Sex	Year	FAC	YRSX	YRFC	SXFC	SXYFRC	R²	N
Panel 1. LIFE GOALS											
Security	MED	2.76	-.19	-.12	-.05	.17	.03	.02	-.06	.02	(5290)
Occup	MWORK	2.84	.00	.00	.00	-.21	-.04	.00	-.11	.01	(5314)
Contrib	MWORK	2.49	.09	-.24	-.06	.22	.11	.08	-.16	.03	(5314)
Luxury	TCHCON	1.79	-.20	.22	.00	-.24	-.07	-.06	.13	.07	(5420)
Family	TCHCON	2.57	-.17	-.21	.04	.14	.04	-.04	-.10	.03	(5420)
Security	Urban	2.69	-.14	-.18	-.02	.18	.03	.00	-.04	.02	(5250)
Luxury	News	1.73	-.11	.20	.04	-.34	-.04	-.12	.19	.07	(5345)
Status	News	2.04	.14	.00	.10	-.36	-.04	-.15	.19	.02	(5345)
Panel 2. OCCUPATIONAL VALUES											
Leadshp	Intell	2.08	-.09	.11	.04	-.15	-.07	-.02	.11	.02	(4913)
Adventure	News	2.07	.08	.37	-.04	-.23	-.13	-.14	.27	.04	(5435)
Panel 3. ACHIEVEMENT VALUE-ORIENTATIONS											
Planning	CONS	3.10	-.12	-.35	.02	.36	.02	.03	-.04	.04	(5334)
Content	News	2.51	.24	-.08	.14	-.42	-.09	-.13	.24	.00	(5257)
Organ	News	2.41	.25	.24	.12	-.20	-.16	-.18	.21	.00	(5257)

APPENDIX B.

Metric Regression Coefficients for Significant Third Order Interactions of Enrollment, Orientation and Grades on Sex, Year, and Facilitating Variables

Dependent Variable	Facilit. Variable	Cons	Sex	Year	FAC	SXFAC	YRFAC	YRSX	SXYRFC	R²	N
Panel 1. AVERAGE ENROLLMENT											
Family	Intell	.03	-.01	.12	-.01	.01	-.04	.31	-.09	.23	(4993)
Family	FED	.05	-.03	.17	-.01	.01	-.02	.43	-.04	.21	(5379)
Family	Conslt	.03	-.01	.16	.00	.00	-.01	.44	-.02	.20	(5600)
Home Ec	FED	.11	1.38	.42	-.00	-.21	-.05	-.48	.11	.23	(5379)
Home Ec	MWORK	.02	1.14	.33	.06	-.21	-.06	-.49	.18	.18	(5450)
Shorthand	FED	.01	.87	.00	.04	-.10	-.01	-.34	.40	.24	(5379)
English	Conslt	2.30	.12	-.02	-.02	-.01	-.04	-.26	.04	.06	(5600)
Biology	Intell	.92	.06	-.01	-.00	.05	.09	-.03	-.08	.01	(4993)
Biology	FED	.92	.04	-.23	-.00	.07	.07	.07	-.04	.02	(5379)
Math	Intell	.55	-.30	-.04	.20	-.19	-.08	.09	.16	.06	(4993)
Math	FED	.28	-.06	.07	.10	-.08	-.02	-.06	.06	.06	(5379)
Math	Conslt	.47	-.08	.16	.01	-.03	-.02	-.24	.45	.04	(5600)
Physics	Intell	.42	-.32	-.20	.24	-.18	-.09	.22	.14	.22	(4993)
Physics	Conslt	.18	-.08	-.09	.03	-.03	-.01	-.04	.03	.09	(5600)
Physics	News	.13	-.03	.03	.15	-.15	-.12	-.06	.14	.09	(5509)
Panel 2. PERCEIVED HELPFULNESS											
Office Pr	MWORK	1.86	1.68	.80	.49	-.90	-.56	-1.45	.84	.17	(956)
Typing	News	2.16	.58	.07	.18	-.17	-.13	.35	.22	.09	(4187)
Chemistry	Intell	2.35	-.14	-.13	.25	-.29	-.18	.10	.24	.04	(2173)
Math	FED	2.65	-.17	-.15	.01	-.04	-.00	-.02	.06	.04	(5025)
Panel 3. MOST ENJOYED STUDYING											
English	Intell	.15	.23	-.03	.00	.06	.02	-.09	-.05	.06	(4934)
English	FED	.14	.14	-.11	.00	.04	.02	.02	-.05	.07	(5316)
Language	Intell	.06	-.13	.01	-.02	.10	.01	-.08	-.09	.04	(2379)
Soc Stu	FED	.08	.02	.00	-.01	.04	.00	.04	-.04	.03	(2598)
Chemistry	FED	.12	.02	-.03	.04	-.04	-.04	-.07	.06	.03	(2338)

APPENDIX B. (continued)

Dependent Variable	Facilit. Variable	Cons	Sex	Year	FAC	SXFAC	YRFAC	YRSX	SXYRFC	R²	N
Panel 4. Grades											
Sophomore Courses											
Typing	FED	5.04	.99	-.03	.36	.06	.18	1.16	-.46	.06	(1707)
Geometry	News	7.23	.84	1.94	.00	-.54	-.97	-2.37	1.62	.01	(2256)
Junior Courses											
Typing	FED	5.27	1.41	1.37	.38	-.20	-.34	-1.07	.54	.07	(1619)
Biology	Intell	5.65	1.18	1.38	.94	.87	.30	-.00	-1.37	.29	(212)
Geometry	Intell	6.01	-.03	.01	1.59	.79	.31	.22	-1.32	.24	(649)
Senior Courses											
Typing	Conslt	5.50	.24	-.43	.07	.17	.22	3.65	-.51	.11	(1171)
Speech	Intell	7.78	.72	.57	1.04	.54	.24	.77	-1.02	.29	(753)

APPENDIX C.

Metric Regression Coefficients for Significant Third Order Interactions of School Factors on Sex, Year, and Facilitating Variables

Dependent Variable	Facilit. Variable	Cons	Sex	Year	FAC	SXFAC	YRFAC	YRSX	SXYRFC	R2	N
Panel 1. MOST INFLUENTIAL CONSULTANT											
Mother	Intell	.08	.13	-.01	-.01	.01	.02	-.01	-.05	.03	(4537)
Other Adults	Conslt	.11	-.05	-.07	-.01	.00	.01	.08	-.01	.00	(5071)
St Emp Service	FED	.03	.03	-.01	-.00	-.01	.00	-.04	-.01	.02	(4912)
Employers	Conslt	.02	-.03	-.01	.00	.00	.00	.00	-.01	.00	(5071)
Other	MWORK	.01	.01	.04	.00	-.00	.00	-.06	-.04	.01	(4969)
Panel 2. COUNSELING											
Senior Vis. ?	Intell	.12	-.03	.01	.05	-.02	-.04	.01	.04	.01	(4993)
Dis Voc Choice	Intell	.76	.09	-.15	.07	-.02	-.02	-.06	.06	.06	(4889)
Nat of Occup	Fed	.79	.03	-.11	-.04	.00	.02	.08	-.04	.03	(3605)
Panel 3. MOST IMPORTANT FUNCTIONS OF HIGH SCHOOL											
Inquiring Mind	Intell	.11	-.00	-.02	.07	-.01	-.04	-.02	.04	.04	(4597)
Inquiring Mind	FED	.03	.06	.01	.03	-.02	-.02	-.10	.03	.01	(5016)
Wgh&Appl Facts	News	.11	-.05	-.11	-.03	.02	.07	.12	-.08	.00	(5068)
Spec Job Train	Intell	.07	-.03	.02	-.04	.04	.01	-.01	-.03	.02	(4597)
Patriotism	MWORK	.13	-.10	-.10	-.04	.07	.04	.08	-.06	.02	(5073)
World Affairs	News	-.02	.02	.09	.02	-.02	-.05	-.08	.05	.00	(5068)
Panel 4. EXTRACURRICULAR PARTICIPATION											
Baseball	Intell	.19	-.02	-.05	.01	-.04	-.03	.04	.04	.06	(4993)
Orchestra	Intell	.17	-.00	-.00	.06	-.02	-.01	.05	.05	.03	(4993)
Tennis	FED	-.01	.03	.03	.02	-.02	-.01	-.03	.02	.01	(5379)
Softball	Conslt	.05	-.03	.01	.00	.00	.00	.08	-.01	.00	(5600)
Glee Club	News	.07	.46	.02	.05	-.12	-.04	-.19	.10	.09	(5509)
Orchestra	News	.04	.15	.12	.07	-.09	-.07	-.16	.13	.00	(5509)
Student Govt	News	.01	.19	.06	.08	-.10	-.06	-.16	.10	.01	(5509)

APPENDIX C. (continued)

Dependent Variable	Facilit. Variable	Cons	Sex	Year	FAC	SXFAC	YRFAC	YR3X	SXYRFC	R²	N
Panel 5. PEER STATUS											
Best Athlete	Intell	1.79	-1.73	-1.46	.72	-.71	-.62	1.44	.62	.09	(4993)
Most Imp	FED	.52	-.34	-.43	.23	.25	-.19	.38	-.25	.07	(5379)
Best Athlete	Conslt	.56	-.55	-.43	.16	-.15	-.13	.44	.13	.07	(5600)
Most Imp	Conslt	.09	-1.02	-.10	.14	.16	-.11	.89	-.14	.07	(5600)
Best Athlete	News	.66	-.46	-.38	.60	-.68	-.57	.25	.64	.07	(5509)
Best Student	News	.27	1.75	-.13	.51	-.96	-.47	-1.50	.83	.04	(5509)
Most Imp	News	.31	1.96	-.15	.46	-1.02	-.44	-1.80	.95	.05	(5509)

NOTES

1. SOCIAL CHANGE AND SEX ROLE CHANGE: AN OVERVIEW

1. With regard to scope and reality aspects of the data, the only comparable reports, to my knowledge, are the researches by Duncan and Duncan (1978) on changing sex roles within the family and Veroff, Douvan, and Kulka (1981) on personality changes between 1955 and 1976.

2. For an interesting interpretation of the relevance of ascribed status to feminine characteristics, see Darley (1976).

3. The assumptions in this paragraph are based in large part on opinions expressed in the move to change the name of the American Sociological Association, Section on Sex Roles to Section on Sex and Gender. Other views of the problem appear in Lipman-Blumen and Tica-mye's (1975) formulation of these distinctions and those of Spence and Helmreich (1978), who argue against using sex role to include both sex-related personality and role aspects, as I do in this study.

4. The difficulty of defining women as a social category is addressed by Chafe (1977) in his discussion of inequality and change.

5. Current legal cases having to do with the economic rights of roommates who have shared domiciles and sex and with the issue of marital rape begin to open some of these doors, of course, as do increased public interest in child care and welfare of battered wives. All of these issues had been unrecognized in the traditional social arrangement. One of the interesting anomalies resulting from the current juxtapositioning of modern and traditional patterns is the lack of qualification for motherhood and parenthood. While performance of most roles in a modern universalistic-achievement society requires some demonstration, often certification, of competence to exhibit the performances of achieved roles, traditional values, buttressed by religious systems, assume nearly all biologically capable adults are qualified parents. It is interesting to note the different approaches society takes to parenting by adopted or substitute parents. In her argument for women's equality, Rossi (1964) felt it necessary, when advocating surrogate parents for working mothers, to tie the suggestion to formal training in child rearing that the full-time mother had not herself been required to obtain. Again, we see the differences between ascription and achievement, the sacred and the secular.

6. Discussion of the apparent disarray in the organizational aspects of the women's movement (Freeman 1979) and in the countermovements on abortion and the Equal Rights Amendment goes beyond the already broad concerns of this chapter. It is likely that the goals of the movement articulated around secular, rationalistic themes are increasingly viewed by many women, and rightly so, as striking at the fundamental nature of traditional family and sexual relations. The women's movement may founder on this issue and lose support it may otherwise have maintained related to correcting basic injustices in the society, as Freidan has now realized (Freidan, 1981). It is interesting that in my study of change in women's role attitudes between 1974 and 1980, the ERA was the only item from a set of twenty on which college students

revealed an increasing conservatism, a tendency that dramatically increased between 1977 and 1980.

2. THE 1964–1975 SURVEYS: DATA AND ANALYSIS

1. The original plan had called for a study over the period of the decade 1964–1974, but initial funding problems delayed the start one year. University procedures precluded a local grant for the project that would include money for expenses of necessary field liaison persons. The willingness of Larry Masters and other colleagues in the research area to assume personal expenses in preparation for the survey saved the project, as did the support of the dean of the College of Education of the state university located in the survey area.

2. One of the few sex-related patterns of interest in the 1964 noncollege-bound study was the recognition that, given the vocational plans of that period, girls' high school and post-high school technical education provided a more adequate preparation than did the boys'. This difference, especially at college level training, is now viewed as an aspect of sex-typed work, that is, women being trained for jobs prior to entrance, men trained on the job.

3. In 1964, each of the twenty systems had a single senior high school. By 1975, two of the participating systems had added an additional high school, so there were nineteen high schools participating on the 1975 survey from seventeen of the original 1964 systems. Data from one of these schools were not prepared in time to be included in this part of the analysis.

4. As the percentage nonwhite in this study area is negligible, neither race nor ethnicity is considered in this research. While this limits the representativeness of the research it simplifies the interpretation and relevance of my findings to contemporary sex role change, for black and white women differ in their occupational experience and change (Treiman and Terrell 1975a) and in their stance toward the predominantly white women's movement (Chafe 1977).

5. This final proportion is larger than that in the analysis reported in this chapter because it includes cases added after the analysis described in this chapter was completed. These cases involved a redefinition of participation in two of the schools and further file development and cleaning of the data. This resulted in negligible changes in response rates that would not affect any of the interpretations or conclusions reached in the analysis reported here. Correlation between the response rates reported in this chapter and those finally used in the analysis reported in the following chapters is .96.

6. Data on nonparticipants was collected "blind" from records of nonparticipants selected by counselors or by the researchers or from copies of records made with names blanked out.

7. These interactions were examined more directly in regression analysis not reported here. Probably because of the substantial colinearity between intelligence and grades, this analysis was difficult to interpret. It generally supported the text interpretation of table 2.1, however.

8. Both the linear and the quadratic terms in the polynomial regression equation given on the graph in figure 2.1 are significant, but no terms of power greater than 2 were significant.

In the markedly discrepant school, officials combined the survey administration with an effort to obtain signed consent forms for the school's local use of student records and transcripts. In accomplishing this, the school administered attendance forms signed by the students in the assembly and retained by the school administration. All of the school counselors assisted the two research professors in administering the questionnaires in this assembly. The result of these factors was a student rate of consent considerably above the level predicted. Statistical analysis indicates that this school is in fact an outlier. A t test for the difference between school H's participation rate of 80.2% and its regression estimate of 53.0% (Walker and Lev 1953:400ff), where the regression estimate is based on the second-degree equation for the other seventeen schools, yielded a t value of 3.01 with 14 df ($p = .01$).

9. Consistent with treatments by Cochran (1963), Rosenthal and Rosnow (1975), and Sewell and Hauser (1975), bias is formally defined as the departure of an estimate based on the sample

of participants from the population value. This is distinct from a simple difference between participants and nonparticipants.

10. See Cohen and Cohen (1975) for discussions of this application of regression.

11. This research on the effect of the working mother is summarized by Hoffman and Nye (1974). Many of the earlier studies, such as Almquist and Angrist (1970) and Tangri (1972) were based on analysis of college students. Recent research by Macke and Morgan (1978) on high school students fails to obtain support for the idea that daughter's work orientations are significantly affected by mother's work status. As we shall see below, mother's family power (Bahr, Bowerman, and Gecas 1974) and influence (Lueptow, 1980a) are affected by her work status.

3. PERSONALITY, SEX DIFFERENCES, AND CHANGE: REVIEW OF THE EVIDENCE

1. Money and Tucker (1975) except only lactation, impregnation, ovulation, and menstruation. They assert that all other sex distributions overlap, a position advanced by most writers (See Chafetz 1978 for illustrations of different distributions).

2. One of the best illustrations of these differing approaches occurs in the critique of Maccoby and Jacklin (1974) by Block (1976). Maccoby and Jacklin conclude that their comprehensive review shows many fewer clear differences (four out of nineteen) than popular conceptions lead us to expect. In fact, most writers cite Maccoby and Jacklin as the authoritative source for demonstrating the relative absence of important sex differences, in spite of the extensive evidence of difference they summarize. Block reaches different conclusions, arguing that Maccoby and Jacklin's evidence documents substantial sex differences, an interpretation shared by L. Hoffman (1977). While a substantial part of this difference goes to errors and omissions in scholarship, there is also a fundamental conceptual, interpretive difference. Maccoby and Jacklin place considerable weight on the proportion of studies showing no difference between the sexes on the various traits being assessed while Block, arguing that Maccoby and Jacklin's methodology increases the likelihood of observing no difference, focuses on the proportion of studies showing differences in favor of males or females. From this perspective (plus adjustments for scholarship and method), there are substantial sex differences.

3. Obviously, these generalizations have never been totally true in any society, although the division describes basic characteristics of marital role differentiation in Western society. Of considerable significance for the issues of change is the fact that the asymmetry of this arrangement first exposed men to the profound changes of rationalization and secularization accompanying the development of science and technology in Western culture. Thus, men increasingly became involved in achieved, instrumental roles operating through universalistic principles, while women remained relatively more involved in ascribed roles manifested in particularistic relations. From these perspectives, the interpersonal nexus within which expressive values are enacted is generally more characterized by the pattern variables of affectivity, collectivity orientations, and diffuseness as well as ascription and particularism, while the task-oriented nexus of the instrumental roles is characterized by affective neutrality, individualism, and specificity as well as achievement and universalism. These are the patterns that also distinguish primary and secondary groups and traditional versus modern societies. Bernard (1981:24–30) has used these and other elements of the modernization process to delineate the central feature of the female world. This world is of course the Gemeinschaft.

4. See Lerner (1958), Kahl (1968), and Inkeles and Smith (1974) for explications of the content and causes of modernity and the parallels in conceptions of modernity and individualistic achievement orientations. Both Kluckhohn (1969) and Rossi (1965) have called attention to the significance of individualism and autonomy as explanations for male achievements and

advantages in contemporary society and science. The fact that the interpersonal and communicative skills attributed to women are exactly the characteristics required in information- and service-oriented postmodern or postindustrial society (Bell 1973) has not been generally recognized by students of sex roles who deemphasize sex differences and advocate and predict convergence and masculinization. Bernard (1975, 1981) is of course one important exception.

5. The reader is reminded that the content presented in tables 3.1 and 3.2 was generated deliberately to reflect the stereotypic attributes of male and female personality. Characteristics that fail to differentiate the typical personalities of women and men naturally do not work their way to these lists. Furthermore, the internal consistency is in part artifactual in that two or three studies use similar sources. On the other hand, Williams and Bennett (1975) found that the majority of traits on the Adjective Check List were assigned by college students to one or the other sex.

6. Ashmore and Del Boca (1979) take issue with this assumption, but recent research by Williams and Best (1982), reported since this was written, strongly supports this picture of the consistency and pervasiveness of sex role stereotypes, even across thirty contemporary societies.

7. This is the notation, following Block (1976), that I use to provide a shorthand description of the outcomes of the extended tabulations reported by Maccoby and Jacklin. The first value in the parentheses refers to the number of comparisons, the male and female proportions refer to the proportion of studies showing each sex higher on the characteristics.

8. This is one of the points of difference between Maccoby and Jacklin's and Block's (1976) interpretation. Maccoby and Jacklin consider the studies showing no statistically significant difference while Block's approach emphasizes the direction and strength of the effect in only those studies that do show significant differences.

9. Darley (1976) has used this distinction in a provocative, but apparently untested, formulation to explain sex differences in anxiety and confidence. She suggests that both sexes become sensitized to the appropriate type of sanctions. Women in ascribed roles become sensitive to and consequently more often perceive negative sanctions and thus become anxious and expect failure. Men in achieved roles become sensitive to positive sanctions, develop self-confidence, and expect success.

10. In modern societies these are occupations. The stability of the occupational prestige ratings over time and between cultures attests to the importance of this pattern of universalistic achievement. Housewives and members of the "culture of poverty" (Lewis 1966) are uniquely disadvantaged in this respect. They are literally outside the main status system, as Harrington (1962) noted earlier regarding poverty and as today's feminists fully realize regarding housewifing. Treating housewifing as an occupation, or at least recognizing its cash value, moves it from what Bernard (1975) refers to as the "status" system into the "cash nexus" system, which constitutes the social basis of status recognition in a modern society.

11. Some writers interpret this to mean that men have *become* more conflicted about achievement, although Hoffman's findings (1982) have suggested this may in large part be a function of sex-differentiated shifts in decisions and practices in coding fear of success. Generally, writers such as Deaux (1976) and Spence and Helmreich (1978) conclude that the observed effects probably have more to do with realistic outcomes of perceived role circumstances than with a psychological motive related to success.

12. Both psychology (McClelland 1953) and sociology (Blau and Duncan 1967) have provided classic illustrations of this omission.

13. This can be seen in the work of sociologists Rosen (1956, 1959) and Strodtbeck (1958) and in the social psychological treatments of Atkinson (1958) and McClelland (1961).

14. There is an interesting and generally overlooked overlay between these psychological treatments and sociological work on powerlessness by Seeman and his colleagues (Seeman and Evans 1962; Seeman 1963; Neal and Seeman 1964). People who think they have more control

over their own circumstances are more likely to obtain information and be informed along personally relevant dimensions than those who feel they do not have control. Similar effects appeared in Coleman's study of equality of educational opportunity.

15. Most of the early research on the antecedents of achievement motivation focused on sons only.

16. Bernard's (1981) work overlaps this focus, but is not as directly focused on the dimensions underlying the achievement value orientations being discussed here.

17. The status attainment research is primarily addressed to the issue of social mobility along a vertical dimension. Educational attainment is measured in years of education; occupational status based on the importance of the occupation in the eyes of the public has most often been measured by the Duncan Socioeconomic Index (Duncan 1961).

18. Analysis of this process within a single cohort (Sewell, Hauser, and Wolf 1980) reveals important exceptions to the equivalence. Women receive an initially higher status, although education is more important to the initial occupational attainment of men. Over time, however, men have a more vertical career pattern and eventually exceed women of the same age, while education becomes more important to the status attainment of women who have faced broken career patterns men have not experienced. All of this tends to produce similarity in occupational statuses between the sexes in populations of diverse ages.

19. Veroff (1977) has formulated a similar but more elaborate taxonomy of achievement motivation types, arguing that men may be more concerned with the impact of their achievement in terms of evidencing power and competitive success, while women may be more concerned with responsible and autonomous accomplishment of the task, i.e., with the process, not the impact of achievement.

20. The conflict posed for women by role innovation must be especially salient for college students, especially for those at colleges such as Douglas College, which, "as a women's college. . . . was especially sensitive to the Women's Liberation Movement, offering numerous courses and activities related to women's issues" (Parelius 1975b:146). The majority of these students preferred to combine family and career, as did those in Bronzaft's (1974) analysis. However, in evaluating work and setting priorities, the students in Parelius' study acknowledged attitudinal positions they believed would be unacceptable to prospective spouses. For example, 81% of the students in 1973 agreed that a wife's career is of equal importance to her husbands, but only 31% believed men would "want to marry a woman holding that view" (Parelius 1975b:147).

21. Veroff, Douvan, and Kulka (1981) did observe differences in achievement, but this may have been partly a function of the coding categories they used. These involved intrinsic satisfactions inherent in such factors as responsibility, complexity, and use of abilities, but also such extrinsic status factors as recognition and feelings of importance. On the clearly intrinsic factor, interesting work, there were no substantial differences, and by far the greatest differences were on the people-oriented, or affiliative, items.

22. Part of the sex-related difference in values in this and probably in other similar instances actually reflects occupational variation. Thus, in Auster's (1978) study, the specialties of men and women differed along sex-typed lines. The number-one choice of men was administration, ranked twelfth by female nursing students. The number-one choice of women was obstetrics, ranked ninth by male nursing students.

23. The apparent contradiction in these two interpretations is in part a statistical artifact generally unrecognized in studies like Williams et al. (1977). When one compares average scores of the sexes *across* all items, the base variance includes sex *and* item differences. As it happens, there is more difference in the overall rating of the items than between the sexes. As Duncan and Duncan (1978) observe, both sexes live in the same society. Few of these men or women conceived of themselves as cynical, jealous, or timid, but many of both sexes saw themselves as friendly, ambitious, and responsible. When compared on single items, item variance

was of course elimited and sex differences appeared, almost without exception in the stereotypic direction.

24. The central purpose of *The Inner American* was to determine whether there had been changes in subjective mental health and coping with problems between 1957 and 1975.

25. Even among those committed women who would work even if they did not need the money, only 23% gave intrinsic work satisfaction as the reason they would continue. The most common reasons (34%) had to do with avoiding boredom and being with people (Veroff, Douvan, and Kulka 1981).

26. Veroff, Douvan, and Kulka (1981), dealing with more subjective aspects of parenting also find a decline in institutional aspects and an increase in the interpersonal. However, they also observe small, but ubiquitous sex differences supporting the instrumental-expressive division in the family.

4. SOCIAL CHANGE AND SEX ROLE CHANGE IN ORIENTATIONS TOWARD LIFE, WORK, AND ACHIEVEMENT

1. These items were constructed from a content analysis of responses to an open-ended question about life goals originally given to entering college freshmen living in the same general area as the high school students of this study.

2. These interpretations are based on the coefficients for sex. When there are statistically significant interactions such comparisons must be qualified depending on the relative strength of the three coefficients. A very strong interaction could mean that the sex effect is true for only one of the two years.

3. This is one illustration of a theme that reappears in diverse contexts—that change occurs but the sex difference is maintained. Such a process suggests the possibility that for some reason, women and men find it important to maintain sex-related distinctiveness, regardless of actual role content.

4. The variables used in this analysis and the hierarchy of regressions that were examined are summarized below.

X_1 Sex   (males = 0, females = 1)
X_2 Year   (1964 = 0, 1975 = 1)
X_3 Facilitator (actual value or category)
X_4 Sex by year
X_5 Sex by facilitator
X_6 Year by facilitator
X_7 Sex by year by facilitator
$Y_1 = a + b_1 x_1 + b_2 x_2 + b_3 x_3$
$Y_2 = a + b_1 x_1 + b_2 x_2 + b_3 x_3 + b_4 x_4 \, b_5 x_5 + b_6 x_6$
$Y_3 = a + b_1 x_1 + b_2 x_2 + b_3 x_3 + b_4 x_4 + b_5 x_b + b_6 x_6 + b_7 x_7$

While the interaction terms in each equation were examined, the important term is, of course B_7, and it is this coefficient being discussed in the text at this point.

5. As I have noted, the interpretations of sex differences and social change are qualified by the presence of an interaction. When substantial interactions are observed, differences between the sexes are greater for one year than another. As my major interest is in the interaction itself, this is not a serious problem and does not warrant extended analysis of sex differences in values by year.

6. The rationale for continuing the facilitating analysis with this reduced set of variables is essentially a combination of economy in reducing the massive computer analysis resulting from calculating sixteen regressions for each dependent variable and expediency in continuing the analysis in the event some facilitating pattern may emerge. The five variables chosen reflect personality, social structure, intrafamilial and extrafamilial socialization, and media attention. It is assumed that they stand as reasonable proxies to the remainder.

7. The index of dissimilarity is a simple, direct, easily interpreted measure of difference in the percentage distributions of members of two groups over a fixed number of categories. Its value is one-half the sum of the absolute differences in percentages of the groups across all categories.

A sex-typed occupation is an occupation chosen by at least five respondents, with one sex constituting at least 70% of those choosing the occupation.

8. It is possible that the major constraints on female preference are enacted through sex role socialization. These internalized constraints would of course be incorporated into the ideal preferences and would not, consequently, appear in the ideal-expected discrepancy. However, the consciously perceived obstacles limiting ideal choices are the most important category, as they reflect frustration and constraint experienced in the contemporary situation. Obviously, much of the writing about equal opportunity is directed to this issue of women being denied occupations they subjectively prefer to attain. Thus, we will assume the consciously perceived discrepancy between ideals and expectations is the more direct manifestation of sex discrimination and constraint, and examine that process in its own terms while acknowledging the substantial human issue involved in the institutionalized limitation of opportunity through socialization.

9. These occupations, the number of females choosing and the percentage female are: social scientist (21/80.8), technician (92/92.1), waitress, stewardess (46/79.3), and attendant (41/95.3).

10. This shift included the emergence of new male sex-typed occupations. These occupations, the number of males choosing and the percentage male, are athletic (11/78.6), firefighter (7/100.0), cabinet maker (10/100.00), printer (15/100.0), plumber (6/100.00) welder (21/100.00), and truck driver (25/92.3).

11. As late as 1973, only a scattering of women were enrolled in apprenticeship and training programs for predominantly male occupations in Wisconsin (U.S. Department of Labor 1974). Of the 382 women enrolled in 1973, 89.5% were in five essentially sex-typed occupations: cosmetologist, barber, day care teacher, home health aide, and cook.

12. Academic achievement in specific courses will be examined in chapter 6, where I consider sex-typed differences in performance relevant to the important literature on sex differences in cognitive functioning.

13. Inclusion of the generic "man" in the first two items raises the possibility that female responses were attributional to an ideal male, rather than self-relevant. This possibility was considered in data analysis and interpretation (Lueptow 1975) and in an experiment designed to test the proposition (Lueptow 1980b). Both results indicated that female responses were self-relevant and unaffected by the use of generic "man."

14. While not quite as strong, these differences also appear in my (1980b) study of college students.

15. The standardization of grade-point average within each school and year precludes the analysis of change over the years. Later analysis of specific course grades in metric code reveals substantial increases in grades awarded between 1964 and 1975.

16. The total consistency of this pattern indicated that the expense of running ten more regressions for college application and acceptance was not warranted.

17. I am indebted to McKee McClendon for introducing me to this approach to the difficult analytic problem created by study of occupational status effects in populations that include nonworking mothers. McClendon is obviously not responsible for my present usage and interpretation.

18. See Kerckhoff (1974:56–57) for a different interpretation of this sequence. However, as Kerckhoff notes, this is not a critically important issue, as our major concerns are with the determinants of educational aspiration, not with the exact ordering of the intervening variables.

19. Analysis based on listwise exclusion of cases did not differ in any important manner from this analysis.

20. See Hoffman and Nye (1974) for one review of these papers.

21. Mother's work was also unimportant in Sewell, Hauser, and Wolf's (1980) study of the status attainment process of the 1957 Wisconsin high school seniors.

5. SEX TYPING IN ACADEMIC PREFERENCES AND ACHIEVEMENT

1. As Bernard (1981) notes, this basic distinction has been made by various sociologists using different terms, but in each case describing a world of personalized relationships versus a world of impersonal instrumentalities. Bernard has used Tonnies' distinction between *Gemeinschaft* and *Gesellschaft* to refer to the central concern of these distinctions. Here and elsewhere, we use Parsons' (1951) pattern variables to refer to essentially the same circumstances.

2. These studies are currently being reported by the Education Commission of the States, 1860 Lincoln St., Suite 700, Denver, Colorado 80295.

3. Bernard reports an illustration of this conjunction taken from Spaack and having to do with the inability of "modal" woman to accept universalistic principles when they lead to particularistic suffering or injustice. Thus,

Her husband says, "Don't you see that the law *has* to take this position, even if it occasionally causes injustice?" The feminine modal personality does not. That is not the logic of her (particularistic) world. Her perch is in a particularistic world, his in a universalistic one. *They do not see the same things.* (Emphasis mine) (1971:27)

4. Sherman (1978) discounts many of the Maccoby and Jacklin conclusions and generally argues that there are no important sex differences in cognitive performances. She appears to base this assertion on three circumstances. First, she calls attention to the general inadequacy of existing research as a basis for any clear-cut conclusion at the present time. Second, she stresses the more recent results of her Wisconsin research on large samples that fail to confirm important intellectual and sex differences. Finally, she notes that even if one accepts the results as real, they are trivial in their degree, generally involving relationships in which sex accounts for at best 1 or 2% of the variance in the variable of interest.

5. The strength and consistency of the evidence on spatial skills led earlier scholars to posit biological explanations for the sex differences. I will return to this question subsequently.

6. Rossi (1977) has recently argued that this bond rests on biological processes emerging from evolutionary prehistory. The concept is also consistent with the general reproductive strategies that make the family group more important to women than to men (Daly and Wilson 1978).

7. This line of speculation is not inconsistent with Sherman's "bent twig" hypothesis that early verbalization in girls makes it possible "that more girls than boys might establish verbal communication as a preferred mode of interacting with the environment" (1978:43).

8. The F ratio reported for sex differences in mathematics in the third school was 3.80 (Fennema and Sherman 1977:table 4.). This is for all practical purposes nearly 3.84, which is the F ratio at the .05 level with degrees of freedom one and infinity. Sherman's interpretation is especially stringent considering that the real issue is the hypothesis of male superiority, which would justify a one-tailed test. Observing statistically significant sex differences in three out of four schools among students with exactly the same course experience would cast a different light on these results than Sherman's (1978) own interpretation.

9. Only grades 9 to 11 were included in two of the four schools.

10. See Vandenberg and Kuse (1979) for more detailed descriptions of these predictions and evaluation of the evidence to date.

11. See especially Bryden (1979) and Sherman (1978) for comprehensive and critical reviews of this literature. Among the inconsistencies is the fact that the right (spatially oriented)

hemisphere is also known to be the location of more global, gestalt processes, cognitive patterns attributed to feminine cognitive style.

12. Contemporary evidence for these distinctions appear in Lever's (1978) report of differences in children's games. Boys' games are more structured and complex, organized around rules and leading to clearly defined goals. Such universalistic-achievement contexts would appear relevant to these general sex-related experiences and development of cognitive differences.

13. The feminine conflict between achievement and affiliation is widely assumed but weakly documented, as I have noted.

14. While the evidence is neither extensive nor definitive, the observed differences suggest that traditional sex differences persist in mathematical reasoning, although they appear to be disappearing in computation and comprehension. Such a difference is consistent with the concept of sex differences in cognitive style.

15. Simpson (1974) found that high school teachers perceive science and mathematics as more appropriate for male teachers and English and foreign language as more appropriate for female teachers. However, they failed to perceive any important sex typing for social studies, which was viewed as appropriate for either sex.

16. Lack of female enrollment in blue-collar craft courses precludes analogous examination of male-oriented vocational courses.

17. Veroff et al. (1980) have observed stability in achievement motivation scores of males, but increase in those of females, between 1957 and 1976. I, have observed a decline in achievement value orientations but about equally for both sexes (see table 4.10).

Reductions in performance were reported in the National Assessments of Educational Progress (1978, 1979) in science and mathematics.

18. Comparisons of the numbers rating the helpfulness of courses with the enrollments calculated from the transcript information revealed that with one exception (English), more students rated the helpfulness of courses than were actually credited with taking them. These discrepancies ranged from a difference of 34 cases for psychology to 483 for language. The single exception, English, was rated by 5,354 students, while transcript data show 5,397 were enrolled in at least one English course. The possibility of general errors in transcript coding was checked by verifying the detailed course information on the analysis file against the transcripts for a 3.5% random sample. The error in coding courses was under 1%. Thus it appears that the discrepancy was due to the fact that students may have taken the subject before tenth grade. In some cases the respondents seemed to be confused, as when they apparently viewed English as a language. In any event, the self-reported perceptions reflect the student's own view of his or her course taking and its value.

19. This results is a dichotomous dependent variable. Predicted values and coefficients refer to the proportion of students taking the course. While dichotomous dependent variables violate some of the assumptions of the linear model, they can be used effectively, according to Cohen and Cohen (1975).

20. Supplementary analysis supports this idea. Whereas in 1964 about 70% of both boys and girls named one of the listed academic courses as most enjoyable, by 1975, only 44% of the responding boys and 48% of the responding girls designated one of these academic courses as most enjoyable. Thus, there was a substantial shift toward courses coded "other." Because social change is a less central concern in this study, I have not carried out the additional recoding necessary to incorporate these "other" responses. As the shift is essentially identical for girls and boys, even through the "second most enjoyed" response, it cannot affect either the sex difference or the important third-order interaction indicating sex role change.

21. A *nearly* significant interaction is also observed for physics, where the interaction coefficient is 1.85 times the standard error and is positive like the other critical coefficients.

22. The apparent inconsistency between the pattern of feminine superiority across all courses in these data and the common finding of greater male aptitude in science and mathematics is

probably due to the difference between achievement measured by aptitude scores and that measured by class grades. While Dwyer (1979) concludes that the anomaly has not yet been explained by empirical evidence, it seems likely that some combination of effort and application, perhaps higher levels of task-oriented achievement motivation, and a more organized approach to schoolwork generally may account for it. Rehberg and Rosenthal (1978) think the effect is due to girls' greater "effort" or "cooperation." While this is an intriguing issue, it goes beyond the purposes of the present discussion, although I will return briefly to the question of effort as indicated by hours of study in following sections.

23. This summary necessarily discounts the effect of interactions in the few cases in which they are important. In these cases there is of course no meaningful single difference between the sexes; rather, the difference depends on the year. In most cases, however, the coefficient approximates the average sex difference across the two years.

24. These six courses are junior algebra, biology, and geometry, and senior algebra, biology, and chemistry.

25. Because music and chorus were not included in the list of courses rated for helpfulness and enjoyment of study, orientations toward the content are unavailable and cannot be used to provide possible clues to the meaning of these effects. While it appeared that intelligence or enrollment patterns might account for this interaction, introducing intelligence into the analysis left the results essentially unchanged.

26. This difference appears in the means of table 5.15, not the regression coefficients, which are based on transformed values in this table only.

27. The "typical year" courses senior speech and natural science were not rated on "helpfulness" and consequently were excluded from this analysis.

6. SOCIALIZATION INFLUENCES IN SCHOOL, FAMILY, AND SOCIETY

1. This summary draws heavily upon those in Frieze et al. (1978) and Rohrbaugh (1979).

2. This may be an instance where Freud the observer has awareness that Freud the psychoanalyst confuses. The senses of superego differences described here are similar to the differences that I have suggested may result from socialization and experience in personalized, as contrasted to impersonal, universalistic contexts. See Douvan (1970) for another interpretation of the consequences of the different physiological experiences of the sexes during adolescence. She argues that the greater uncertainty surrounding the female experience and the less objective, quantifiable feedback of girls' activities result in a greater dependence on others for the determination of self structure.

3. As various writers have noted, one of the major problems with Kohlberg's formulation is that developmental stages involving stable, unchanging categories occur some time after gender identity has been observed in children (Maccoby and Jacklin 1974; Frieze et al. 1978).

4. Fox (1979) is one exception to this.

5. This evidence of course leaves much to be desired, as Maccoby and Jacklin (1974) point out again and again and as Block (1976) asserts in her critique. We have disregarded those evaluations in the interest of summarizing the unequivocal overall outcomes.

6. This section draws heavily on the Butler and Paisley (1980) review.

7. The confusion and difficulty with interpreting these findings are illustrated in the discussion of sex-related occupational portrayals on television in the report on Women and Minorities in Television by the United States Commission on Civil Rights (1977). That report states: "The presentation of women as wives and mothers is reinforced in the data on occupational portrayals. Over half of the white (57.0 percent) and nonwhite (53.4 percent) female characters could

not be identified in an occupational role whereas 69 percent of the white males and 60 percent of the nonwhite males could be so identified.''

While it is true that women's labor force participation is underrepresented (43% in occupational roles on TV, 55% in American labor force in 1975), it is even more true for men (69% on TV, 84% in American labor force in 1975). It is hard to know what to make of such numbers when they in fact understate the real sex role differentiation. TV has more often failed to portray an occupational role for women, even though that corresponds to reality. Similar patterns appeared in occupational distributions, also treated as evidence of sex differences. The proportions of TV portrayals of women as professionals, managers, and officials were almost exactly the same as the U.S. Census for 1973, while clerical occupations of women were portrayed in only 19% of the roles even though 34% of women in the labor force were in clerical occupations in 1973. Except for low status underrepresentation in both sexes, TV during that period fairly accurately represented women's occupational status, according to the data presented in the United States Commission on Civil Rights Report (1977:35).

8. Science textbooks are expecially guilty of this. Heikkinen (1978) found that in seventeen chemistry textbooks from the 1940s to the 1970s, pictures were overwhelmingly male, generally above 80% and reaching 100% in many books, including two published in the 1970s.

9. See *Harvard Educational Review* (1979) for an informed interview on some of these issues.

10. That this relative decline in female achievement superiority has been primarily limited to sex-related achievement tests and courses rather than to overall graded performance has been generally overlooked. Discussions of the supposed female decline generally treat it as pervasive rather than specific to sex-typed content and perhaps experience (see Hunt 1980).

11. Coleman (1961) failed to observe any sex difference in the correlation between aptitude and grades for total classes, nor any school difference in the correlations according to the emphasis on grades in the school. He argued that the effect could only be expected among students who had high enough ability to actually get the rewards of good grades.

12. In this population, up from 40.8% in 1964 to 52.2% in 1975.

13. The parental consent requirement under the informed consent requirements of the 1975 survey administration could have produced a disproportionate number of participants having closer rather than distant relations with at least one parent, thus overstating the parental consultation in 1975. This possibility was examined by analyzing persons "talked to" separately for students 17 and under and those 18 and over. There was a slightly greater tendency for 17-year-olds to report talking to parents than for the 18-year-olds, but the difference was too small to be a factor, averaging only 2.6% over the eight sex-by-year cells.

14. Unfortunately, these data do not permit testing the more direct issue of whether counselors advise girls to consider only traditional, sex-typed occupations. Indirectly, of course, the greater incidence of female counseling runs counter to the concept that counselors limit female choice and advise the pursuit of traditional occupations. It would not appear necessary for girls to have *more* counseling to choose traditional, conventionally sex-typed roles, nor to anticipate homemaking responsibilities.

15. This bears on one of the concerns behind the Fox Valley Curriculum Study Council's 1964 survey, that noncollege-bound boys were disadvantaged compared to noncollege-bound girls. While viewpoints have now changed, in 1964 the secretarial and office skills available to noncollege-bound girls were seen as more directly beneficial in post-high school job seeking than the skills available to noncollege-bound boys.

16. The survey data do not provide clues to the reasons for these dramatic declines in use and significance of counseling. Again, it is possible that these changes reflect liberated females' rejection of traditional sex-typed counseling. It is also possible that conscientious counselors were attempting to avoid counseling input that might reflect sex typing in their advisement.

17. Interestingly enough, other analysis of this data shows that while these students think their personal development should be the most important purpose of the high school, they think it is among the least well-performed functions of the school (Hammes and Lueptow 1980).

18. This was a result of a fortuitous coding error. In the calculations of scores based on (number of choices/size of school */100), the decimal fractions were dropped and only integer values retained, thus giving those with less than 1% a zero status score even though they may have had one or two choices. Considering the ambiguity of peer status scores based on only one or two choices, especially in the very large schools, this seemed like a good correction to apply and the scores were not recalculated.

19. The marked skewedness and substantial differences in the proportion of each sex recognized as best athlete raise the possibility that part of the difference in these correlations might be due to distribution effects.

7. SUMMARY AND CONCLUSIONS

1. In specific sections of the analysis it seemed desirable to modify this rule to take into account such important substantive issues as sex typing in language, science, and mathematics. In such analysis, some sex differences were ignored to maintain the focus of substantive and empirical sex role differentiation.

2. While the study population is locally representative and heterogeneous, it lacks national representation. I have suggested that Wisconsin may be reasonably representative of the nation as a whole, however, with the exception of nonwhite groups.

3. Very similar results were obtained by Veroff, Douvan, and Kulka (1981) in their national samples. They found support for the traditional instrumental-expressive distinction in orientations and parenting, greater interpersonal emphasis of females in work and in life adjustment and stereotypic differences in anxiety and control, among other things. Overall, they found that the sexes differed on most of the dimensions examined, although as in this research, these pervasive differences were generally small in magnitutude.

4. Again, similar results were obtained by Veroff, Douvan, and Kulka (1981). They found evidence of more personalized, individualized experience, a decline in the importance of institutions and roles and an increased emphasis on informal, interpersonal support between 1957 and 1976.

5. As I have noted, even as this was written evidence of stabilizing, even reversal, of these attitudes has been reported (Cherlin and Walters 1981).

6. Some comparisons such as the analysis of popularity and grades reported in table 6.12 could not be formulated within this conception, could not be easily summarized, and were excluded from the tally in table 7.1.

7. As the summary count indicates, mother's work was unique in producing almost no effect whatsoever, with only 4 of the 685 regressions producing a significant third-order interaction. This necessarily questions an assumption in the contemporary literature that working mothers constitute important sources of sex role change.

8. While 65 to 78% of the women in their 18-year panel study held nontraditional attitudes about working mothers, power, and extra-familial roles in 1980, 45% nevertheless agreed that "It is more important for a wife to help her husband's career than to have one herself," while 60% agreed that "It is much better for everyone if the man earns the main living and the woman takes care of the home and family" (Thornton, Alwin, and Camburn 1983:213). On the other hand, these proportions represented about a 6% decline in agreement from 1977. Except for the increase in agreement from 23% to 33% that "There is some work that is men's and some work that is women's and they should not be doing each others," all women's role items became more nontraditional between 1977 and 1980 in this panel of mothers.

9. After observing remarkable consistency in sex role stereotyping in thirty contemporary societies, Williams and Best :1982) now come to conclude that sterotypes reflect real behavioral differences that probably rest upon biological factors, a position contrary to their initial beliefs. With equality of opportunity to remove stereotypic restraints inappropriate to individual personalities, they suggest value and satisfaction prevails in the experience of sex differences.

10. It is possible, however, that such limited changes may have substantial social consequences. For, the emerging picture seems to be that women will increasingly be involved in occupations and careers and in other nonfamily community roles, but may also maintain traditional prerogatives in motherhood and family and may continue to hold many traditional feminine values pertaining to interpersonal relations, nurturance, service and achievement. It seems likely the combination of traditional feminine purposes interlaced with the increased power and control inherent in the status and income of occupational roles will introduce new and important themes into the social fabric. Given the nature of contemporary problems and the central characteristics of the sex role stereotypes, it would appear such an outcome could only be beneficial.

REFERENCES

Albrecht, Stan L., Howard M. Bahr, and Bruce A. Chadwick. 1977. "Public Stereotyping of Sex Roles, Personality Characteristics, and Occupations." *Sociology and Social Research* 61:223–240.

Alexander, Karl L., Bruce K. Eckland, and Larry J. Griffen. 1975. "The Wisconsin Model of Socioeconomic Achievement: A Replication." *American Journal of Sociology* 81:324–342.

Almquist, Elizabeth M. and Shirley S. Angrist. 1970. "Career Salience and Atypicality of Occupational Choice Among College Women." *Journal of Marriage and the Family* 32:242–249.

Anderson, James G. and Francis B. Evans. 1976. "Family Socialization and Educational Achievement in Two Cultures: Mexican-American and Anglo-America." *Sociometry* 39:209–222.

Armor, David J. 1969. *The American School Counselor: A Case Study in the Sociology of Professions*. New York: Russell Sage.

Armstrong, Jane M. 1980. *Achievement and Participation of Women in Mathematics: An Overview*. Denver: Education Commission of the State.

Ashmore, Richard D. and Frances K. Del Boca. 1979. "Sex Stereotypes and Implicit Personality Theory: Toward a Cognitive-Social Psychological Conceptualization." *Sex Roles* 5:219–248.

Astin, Helen S. 1974. "Sex Differences in Mathematical and Scientific Precocity." In J. C. Stanley, D. P. Keating, and L. H. Fox eds., *Mathematical Talent: Discovery, Description, and Development*, pp. 81– . Baltimore: Johns Hopkins University Press.

Astin, Helen S. and Alan E. Bayer. 1975. "Sex Discrimination in Academe." In M. T. Mednick et al., eds., *Women and Achievement*, pp. 372–395. Washington, D.C.: Hemisphere.

Atkinson, John W., ed. 1964. *An Introduction to Motivation*. Princeton: Van Nostrand.

—— 1958. *Motives in Fantasy, Action, and Society*. New York: Van Nostrand.

Auster, Donald. 1978. "Occupational Values of Male and Female Nursing Students." *Sociology of Work and Occupations* 5:209–233.

Bahr, S. J., C. Bowerman, and V. Gecas. 1974. "Adolescent Perceptions of Conjugal Power." *Social Forces* 52:237–367.

Bandura, Albert. 1969. "Social-Learning Theory of Identificatory Processes." In David A. Goslin, ed., *Handbook of Socialization Theory and Research*, pp. 213–262. Chicago: Rand McNally.

Bandura, Albert and Richard H. Walters. 1963. *Social Learning and Personality Development*. New York: Holt, Rinehart, and Winston.

Bank, Barbara, J., Bruce J. Biddle, and Thomas L. Good. 1980. "Sex Roles, Classroom Instruction, and Reading Achievement." *Journal of Educational Psychology* 72:119–132.

Barkley, Russel A., Douglas G. Ullman, Lori Otto, and Jan M. Brecht. 1977. "The Effects of Sex Typing and Sex Appropriateness of Modeled Behavior on Children's Imitation." *Child Development* 48:721–725.

Bayer, Alan E. 1975. "Sexist Students in American Colleges: A Descriptive Note." *Journal of Marriage and the Family* 37:391–399.

Bednarzik, Robert W. and Deborah P. Klein. 1977. *Labor Force Trends: A Synthesis and Analysis.* Special Labor Force Report 208. Washington, D.C.: U.S. Department of Labor, Bureau of Labor Statistics.

Bell, Daniel. 1973. *The Coming of Post-Industrial Society.* New York: Basic Books.

Bem, Sandra L. 1974. "The Measurement of Psychological Androgyny." *Journal of Consulting and Clinical Psychology* 42:155–162.

—— 1977. "On the Utility of Alternative Procedures for Assessing Psychological Androgyny." *Journal of Consulting and Clinical Psychology* 45:196–205.

Bem, Sandra L., Wendy Martyna, and Carol Watson. 1976. "Sex Typing and Androgyny: Further Explorations of the Expressive Domain." *Journal of Personality and Social Psychology* 34:1016–1023.

Berger, Peter I. 1973. "Religious Institutions." In Neil J. Smelser, ed., *Sociology: An Introduction,* pp. 303–346. 2d ed. New York: Wiley.

Bernard, Jessie. 1971. *Women and the Public Interest.* Chicago: Aldine-Atherton.

—— 1975. *Women, Wives, Mothers: Values and Options.* Chicago: Aldine.

—— 1981. *The Female World.* Riverside, N.J.: Free Press.

Berndt, Thomas J. 1979. "Developmental Changes in Conformity to Peers and Parents." *Developmental Psychology* 15:608–616.

Bernstein, Basil. 1971. *Class, Codes, and Control.* Vol. I: *Theoretical Studies Toward a Sociology of Language.* London: Routledge and Kegan Paul.

Blau, Peter M. and Otis D. Duncan. 1967. *The American Occupational Structure.* New York: John Wiley.

Block, Jeanne H. 1973. "Conceptions of Sex Role: Some Cross-Cultural and Longitudinal Perspectives." *American Psychologist* 28:512–526.

—— 1976. "Issues, Problems and Pitfalls in Assessing Sex Differences: A Critical Review of 'The Psychology of Sex Differences.' " *Merrill-Palmer Quarterly* 22:283–308.

Blood, Robert O., Jr. and Donald M. Wolfe. 1969. *Husbands and Wives.* New York: Free Press.

Bowerman, C. E. and S. Bahr. 1973. "Conjugal Power and Adolescent Identification with Parents." *Sociometry* 36:366–377.

Boyd, Monica. 1974. "Equality Between the Sexes: The Results of Canadian Gallup Polls, 1953–1973." Paper presented at the annual meeting of the Canadian Sociology and Antropology Association.

Boyle, Richard P. 1969. "Functional Dilemmas in the Development of Learning." *Sociology of Education* 42:71–90.

Brim, Orville G., Jr. 1958. "Family Structure and Sex Role Learning by Children: A Further Analysis of Helen Koch's Data." *Sociometry* 21:1–16.

—— 1960. "Personality Development as Role Learning." In Ira Iscoe and Harold W. Stevenson, eds., *Personality Development in Children,* pp. 127–159. Austin: University of Texas Press.

Bronfenbrenner, Urie. 1958. "Socialization and Social Class Through Time and Space." In Eleanor Maccoby, T. M. Newcomb, and E. L. Hartly, eds., *Readings in Social Psychology,* pp. 400–425. New York: Holt, Rinehart and Winston.

Bronzaft, Arline I. 1974. "College Women Want a Career, Marriage and Children." *Psychological Reports* 35:1031–1034.

Brookover, Wilber B. and Edsel L. Erickson. 1969. *Society, Schools, and Learning.* Boston: Allyn and Bacon.

Broverman, Inge K., Susan R. Vogel, Donald R. Broverman, Frank E. Clarkson, and Paul S.

Rosenberg. 1972. "Sex Role Sterotypes: A Current Appraisal." *Journal of Social Issues* 28:59–78.

Bruce, John Allen. 1974. "The Role of Mothers in the Social Placement of Daughters: Marriage or Work?" *Journal of Marriage and the Family* 36:492–497.

Bryden, M. P. 1979. "Evidence for Sex-Related Differences in Cerebral Organization." In Michele A. Wittig and Anne C. Petersen, eds., *Sex Related Differences in Cognitive Functioning*, pp. 121–143. New York: Academic Press.

Butler, Matilda and William Paisley. 1980. *Women and the Mass Media: Sourcebook for Research and Action*. New York: Human Sciences Press.

Centers, Richard and D. E. Bugental. 1966. "Intrinsic and Extrinsic Job Motivations Among Different Segments of the Working Population." *Journal of Applied Psychology* 50:193–197.

Chafe, William H. 1977. *Women and Inequality: Changing Patterns in American Culture*. New York: Oxford University Press.

Chafetz, Janet Saltsman. 1978. *Masculine, Feminine, or Human? An Overview of the Sociology of Gender Roles*. 2d ed. Itasca, Ill.: Peacock.

Chase, D. 1975. "No More 'Brat' or 'Bastards.' " *Nations Schools and Colleges* 2:27–32.

Cherline, Andrew and Pamela Barnhouse Walters. 1981. "Trends in United States Men's and Women's Sex-Role Attitudes: 1972 to 1978." *American Sociological Review* 46:453–460.

Cochran, W. G. 1963. *Sampling Techniques*. New York: Wiley.

Cohen, Jacob. 1969. *Statistical Power Analysis for the Behavioral Sciences*. New York: Academic Press.

Cohen, Jacob and Patricia Cohen. 1975. *Applied Multiple Regression Correlation Analysis for the Behavioral Sciences*. New York: Wiley.

Cohen, Rosalie. 1968. "The Relations Between Socio-Conceptual Styles and Orientations to School Requirements." *Sociology of Education* 41:201–220.

Coleman, James. 1961. *The Adolescent Society*. New York: Free Press.

—— 1966. *Equality of Educational Opportunity*. Washington, D.C.: GPO.

Cross, Patricia. 1971. *Beyond the Open Door*. San Francisco: Jossey-Bass.

Curtis, Russell L. 1975. "Adolescent Orientation Toward Parents and Peers: Variations by Sex, Age, and Socioeconomic Status." *Adolescence* 10:483–494.

Cutler, M. 1975. "If the New Student Privacy Law Has You Confused, Perhaps That's Because You're Sane." *American School Board Journal* 169:44–49.

Daly, Martin and Margo Wilson. 1978. *Sex, Evolution, and Behavior: Adaptations for Reproduction*. North Scituate, Mass.: Duxbury.

Darley, Susan A. 1976. "Big-Time Careers for the Little Woman: A Dual-Role Dilemma." *Journal of Social Issues* 32:85–98.

Davis, D. 1975. "The Buckley Regulations: Rights and Restraints." *Educational Researcher* 4:11–13.

Dean, Dwight G., Edward A. Powers, Rita Braito, and Brent Burton. 1975. "Cultural Contradictions and Sex Roles Revisited: A Replication and a Reassessment." *Sociological Quarterly* 16:207–215.

Deaux, Kay. 1976. "Sex: A Perspective on the Attribution Process." In John H. Harvey, William J. Ickes, and Robert F. Kidd, eds., *New Directions in Attribution Research*, pp. 335–352. Hillsdale, N.J.: L. Erlbaum Associates.

—— 1979. "Self-Evaluations of Male and Female Managers." *Sex Roles* 5:571–580.

Deaux, Kay, Leonard White, and Elizabeth Farris. 1975. "Skill vs. Luck: Field and Laboratory Studies of Male and Female Preferences." *Journal of Personality and Social Psychology* 4:629–636.

Dellas, Marie, Eugene L. Gaier, and Catherine A. Emihovich. 1979. "Maternal Employment and Selected Behaviors and Attitudes of Preadolescents and Adolescents." *Adolescence* 55:579–589.

Douvan, Elizabeth. 1970. "New Sources of Conflict in Females at Adolescence and Early Adulthood." In Judith Bardwick, Elizabeth Douvan, and David Guttman, *Feminine Personality and Conflict*, pp. 31–43. Belmont, Calif.: Brooks/Cole.

Duncan, Berverly, and Otis Dudley Duncan, with the collaboration of James A. McRae. 1978. *Sex Typing and Social Roles: A Research Report*. New York: Academic Press.

Duncan, Otis Dudley. 1961. "A Socioeconomic Index for All Occupations." In Albert J. Reiss, Jr., *Occupations and Social Status*, pp. 109–138. Glencoe, Ill.: Free Press.

Duncan, Otis Dudley, Howard Schuman, and Beverly Duncan. 1973. *Social Change in a Metropolitan Community*. New York: Russell Sage.

Durkheim, Emile. 1949. *The Division of Labor in Society*. George Simpson, translator. Glencoe, Ill.: Free Press.

Dweck, Carol S. 1978. "Achievement." In Michael E. Lamb, ed., *Social and Personality Development*, pp. 114–130. New York: Holt, Rinehart and Winston.

Dwyer, Carol A. 1979. "The Role of Tests and Their Construction in Producing Sex-Related Differences." In Michael A. Witting and Anne C. Peterson, eds., *Sex-Related Differences in Cognitive Functioning*, pp. 335–353. New York: Academic Press.

Engelhard, Patricia Ann, Kathryn Otts Jones, and Richard J. Stiggens. 1976. "Trends in Counselor Attitudes About Women's Roles." *Journal of Counseling Psychology* 23:365–372.

Ernest, John. 1976. *Mathematics and Sex*. Santa Barbara: University of California.

Farley, Jennie, June Ha Brewer, and Susan W. Fine. 1977. "Women's Values: Changing Faster than Men's?" *Sociology of Education* 50:151.

Feather N. T. and J. G. Simon. 1975. "Reactions to Male and Female Success and Failure in Sex-Linked Occupations: Impressions of Personality, Causal Attributions, and Perceived Likelihood of Different Consequences." *Journal of Personality and Social Psychology* 31:20–31.

Feldman, Saul D. 1973. "Impediment or Simulant? Marital Status and Graduate Education." In Joan Huber, eds., *Changing Women in a Changing Society*, pp. 220–232. Chicago: University of Chicago Press.

Fennema, Elizabeth and Julia Sherman. 1977. "Sex-Related Differences in Mathematics Achievement, Spatial Visualization and Affective Factors." *American Educational Research Journal* 14:51–71.

Ferree, Myra Marx. 1974. "A Woman for President? Changing Responses: 1958–1972." *Public Opinion Quarterly* 38:390–399.

—— 1976. "Working Class Jobs: Housework and Paid Work as Sources of Satisfaction." *Social Problems* 23:431–441.

Finn, Jeremy D. 1980. "Sex Differences in Educational Outcomes: A Cross-National Study." *Sex Roles* 6:9–26.

Fitzpatrick, Jody L. 1978. "Academic Achievement, Other Direction, and Attitudes Toward Women's Roles in Bright Adolescent Females." *Journal of Educational Psychology* 70:645–650.

Flanagan, J. C. 1976. "Changes in School Levels of Achievement: Project Talent Ten and Fifteen Year Retests." *Educational Researcher* 5:9–12.

Flanagan, John C. and Steven M. Jung. 1971. *Progress in Education: A Sample Survey (1960–1970)*. Palo Alto, Calif.: American Institute for Research.

Floyd, H. H. and D. R. South. 1972. "Dilemma of Youth: The Choice of Parents or Peers as a Frame of Reference for Behavior." *Journal of Marriage and the Family* 34:627–634.

Foreit, Karen G., Terna Agos, Johnny Byers, John Loris, Helen Lakey, Michael Palozzini, Michel Patterson, and Lillian Smith. 1980. "Sex Bias in the Newspaper Treatment of Male-Centered and Female-Centered News Stories." *Sex Roles* 61:475–481.

Fox, L. H., E. Fennema, and J. Sherman. 1977. *Women and Mathematics: Research Perspectives for Change*. Washington, D.C.: GPO.

Fox, Lynn H., Dianne Tobin, and Linda Brady. 1979. "Sex Role Socialization and Achievement in Mathematics." In Michele A. Wittig and Anne C. Petersen, eds., *Sex Related Differences in Cognitive Functioning: Developmental Issues*, pp. 303–332. New York: Academic Press.

Freeman, Jo. 1973. "The Origins of the Women's Liberation Movement." *American Journal of Sociology* 78:792–811.

—— 1979. "The Women's Liberation Movement: Its Origins, Organizations, Activities, and Ideas." In Jo Freeman, ed., *Women: A Feminist Perspective*, pp. 557–574. 2d ed.

Freidan, Betty. 1963. *The Feminine Mystique*. New York: Dell.

—— 1981. *The Second Stage*. New York: Summit Books.

French, Elizabeth and G. S. Lesser. 1964. "Some Characteristics of the Achievement Motive in Women." *Journal of Abnormal and Social Psychology* 68:119–128.

Frieze, Irene H. 1975. "Women's Expectations for and Causal Attributions of Success and Failure." In M. T. Mednick et al., eds., *Women and Achievement*, pp. 158–171. Washington, D.C.: Hemisphere.

Frieze, Irene H., Jacquelynne E. Parsons, Paula B. Johnson, Diana N. Ruble, and Gail L. Zellman. 1978. *Women and Sex Roles: A Social Psychological Perspective*. New York: Norton.

Fullan, Michael and Jan Loubser. 1972. "Education and Adaptive Capacity." *Sociology of Education* 45:271–287.

Garrison, H. H. 1979. "Gender Differences in the Career Aspirations of Recent Cohorts of High School Seniors." *Social Problems* 27:170–185.

Geise, L. Ann. 1979. "The Female Role in Middle Class Women's Magazines from 1955 to 1976: A Content Analysis of Nonfiction Selections." *Sex Roles* 5:61–62.

Giele, Janet Zollinger. 1978. *Women and the Future: Changing Sex Roles in Modern America*. New York: Free Press.

Gillespie, Dair L. 1971. "Who Has the Power? The Marital Struggle." *Journal of Marriage and the Family* 33:445–458.

Gjesme, Torquin. 1975. "Achievement-Related Motives and School Performance for Girls." *Journal of Personality and Social Psychology* 37:629–636.

Goertzel, Ted. 1972. "Changes in the Values of College Students 1958 to 1970–71." *Pacific Sociological Review* 15:235–244.

Goff, David H., Lynda Dysart Goff, and Sara Kay Lehrer. 1980. "Sex-Role Portrayals of Selected Female Television Characters." *Journal of Broadcasting* 24:467–478.

Gold, D. and D. Andres. 1978. "Developmental Comparisons Between Ten-Year-Old Children with Employed and Nonemployed Mothers." *Child Development* 49:75–84.

Gove, Walter and Jeannette F. Tudor. 1973. "Adult Sex Roles and Mental Illness." *American Journal of Sociology* 78:812–835.

Gross, E. 1968. "Plus ca Change? . . . The Sexual Structure of Occupations Over Time." *Social Problems* 16:198–208.

Gross, Larry and Suzanne Jeffries-Fox. 1978. "What Do You Want to Be When You Grow Up, Little Girl?" In Gary Tuchman, Arlene Kaplan Daniels, and James Benit, eds., *Hearth and Home: Image of Women in the Mass Media*, pp. 240–265. New York: Oxford University Press.

Hall, Calvin S. and Gardner Lindzey. 1970. *Theories of Personality*. New York: Wiley.

Hammes, Richard R. and Lloyd Lueptow. 1980. "What Are School's Functions and How Do They Perform?" *National Association of Secondary School Principals Bulletin* 64:87–92.

Harrington, Michael. 1962. *The Other America: Poverty in the United States*. New York: Macmillan.

Harvard Educational Review. 1979. "Women and Education I." Vol. 49.

Heikkinen, H. 1978. "Sex Bias in Chemistry Texts: Where Is a Woman's Place?" *Science Teacher* 45:16–21.

Herzberg, F., B. Mausner, R. O. Peterson, and D. F. Capwell. 1957. *Job Attitudes: Review of Research and Opinion.* Pittsburgh: Psychological Service of Pittsburgh.

Herzog, A. Regula. 1982. "High School Seniors' Occupational Plans and Values: Trends in Sex Differences 1976 Through 1980." *Sociology of Education* 55:1–13.

Herzog, A. Regula, Jerald G. Bachman, and Lloyd D. Johnston. 1983. "Paid Work, Child Care, and Housework: A National Survey of High School Seniors' Preferences for Sharing Responsibilities Between Husband and Wife." *Sex Roles* 9:109–135.

Hess, Robert D. and Virginia C. Shipman. 1969. "Early Experiences and the Socialization of Cognitive Models in Children." In Bernard C. Rosen, H. J. Crockett, and C. Z. Nunn, eds., *Achievement in American Society,* pp. 193–211. Cambridge, Mass.: Schenkman.

Hetherington, E. Mavis. 1964. "A Developmental Study of the Effects of Sex of the Dominant Parent on Sex-Role Preference, Identification, and Imitation in Children." *Journal of Personality and Social Psychology* 2:188–194.

Hochschild, A. R. 1973. "A Review of Sex Role Research." *American Journal of Sociology* 78:1011–1029.

Hoffman, Lois Wladis. 1972. "Early Childhood Experiences and Women's Achievement Motives." *Journal of Social Issues* 28:129–155.

—— 1977. "Changes in Family Roles, Socialization, and Sex Differences." *American Psychologist* 32:644–657.

—— 1979. "Maternal Employment: 1979." *American Psychologist* 34:859–865.

—— 1980. "The Effects of Maternal Employment on the Academic Attitudes and Performance of School Aged Children." *School Psychology Review* 9:319–335.

—— 1982. "Methodological Issues in Follow-Up and Replication Studies." *Journal of Social Issues* 38:53–64.

Hoffman, Lois Wladis and F. Ivan Nye. 1974. *Working Mothers.* San Francisco: Jossey-Bass.

Hoffman, Martin L. 1977. "Social and Personality Development." *Annual Review of Psychology* 28:295–321.

Horner, Matina S. 1975. "Toward an Understanding of Achievement-Related Conflicts in Women." In Martha T. S. Mednick et al., eds., *Women and Achievement,* pp. 206–220. Washington, D.C.: Hemishpere.

Hunt, Janet G. 1980. "Sex Stratification and Male Biography: From Deprivation to Abundance." *The Sociological Quarterly* 21:143–156.

Hyman, Herbert H., Charles R. Wright, and John Shelton Reed. 1975. *The Enduring Effects of Education.* Chicago: University of Chicago Press.

Inkeles, Alex and David H. Smith. 1974. *Becoming Modern: Individual Change in Six Developing Countries.* Cambridge, Mass.: Harvard University Press.

Jensen, Arthur. 1974. "Interaction of Level I and Level II Abilities with Race and Socioeconomic Status." *Journal of Educational Psychology* 66:99–111.

Jensen, Arthur R. 1980. *Bias in Mental Testing.* New York: Free Press.

Johnson, Miriam M. 1963. "Sex-Role Learning in the Nuclear Family." *Child Development* 34:319–333.

Johnson, Richard W. 1977. "Relationships Between Female and Male Interest Scales for the Same Occupations." *Journal of Vocational Behavior* 11:239–252.

Kahl, Joseph A. 1968. *The Measurement of Modernism: A Study of Values in Brazil and Mexico.* Austin: University of Texas Press.

Kanter, Rosabeth Moss. 1976. "The Impact of Hierarchical Structures on the Work Behavior of Woman and Men." *Social Problems* 24::415–430.

—— 1977. "Some Effects of Proportions on Group Life: Skewed Sex Ratios and Responses to Token Women." *American Journal of Sociology* 82:965–990.

Katz, J. 1972. *Experimentation with Human Beings*. New York: Russell Sage.

Katz, Phyllis A. 1979. "The Development of Female Identity." *Sex Roles* 5:155–178.

Kelley, Jeffrey A. and Leonard Worell. 1976. "Parent Behaviors Related to Masculine, Feminine, and Androgynous Sex Role Orientation." *Journal of Consulting and Clinical Psychology* 44:843–851.

Kerckhoff, Alan C. 1974. *Ambition and Attainment: A Study of Four Samples of American Boys*. Washington, D.C.: American Sociological Association Rose Monograph Series.

Kingston, A. J. and T. Lovelace. 1977–78. "Sexism and Reading: A Critical Review of the Literature." *Reading Research Quarterly*, 13:133–161.

Kirschner, Betty F. 1973. "Introducing Students to Women's Place in Society." *American Journal of Sociology* 78:1051–1054.

Klecka, Carol O. and Dana V. Hiller. 1977. "Impact of Mother's Life Style on Adolescent Gender-Role Socialization." *Sex Roles* 3:241–255.

Klinger, Eric. 1966. "Fantasy Need Achievement as a Motivational Construct." *Psychological Bulletin* 66:291–308.

Kluckhohn, Florence. 1969. "American Women and American Values." In B. C. Rosen et al., eds., *Achievement in American Society*, pp. 453–469. Cambridge, Mass.: Schenkman. (Originally published 1953.)

Kohlberg, Lawrence. 1966. "A Cognitive-Developmental Analysis of Children's Sex-Role Concepts and Attitudes." In Eleanor Maccoby, ed., *The Development of Sex Differences*, pp. 82–173. Stanford: Stanford University Press.

—— 1969. "Stage and Sequences: The Cognitive-Developmental Approach to Socialization." In David A. Goslin, ed., *Handbook of Socialization Theory and Research*, pp. 347–480. Chicago: Rand McNally.

Kohn, Melvin and Carmi Schooler. 1978. "The Reciprocal Effects of the Substantive Complexity of Work and Intellectual Flexibility: A Longitudinal Assessment." *American Journal of Sociology* 84:24–52.

Komorovsky, Mirra. 1946. "Cultural Contradictions and Sex Roles." *American Journal of Sociology* 52:184–189.

Lemkau, Jeanne Parr. 1979. "Personality and Background Characteristics of Women in Male-Dominated Occupations: A Review." *Psychology of Women Quarterly* 4:221–239.

Lerner, Daniel. 1958. *The Passing of Traditional Society: Modernizing the Middle East*. Glencoe, Ill.: Free Press.

Lerner, Gerda. 1975. "Placing Women in History: Definitions and Challenges." *Feminist Studies* 3:5–14.

Lever, Janet. 1976. "Sex Differences in the Games Children Play." *Social Problems* 4:478–487.

—— 1978. "Sex Differences in the Complexity of Children's Play and Games." *American Sociological Review* 43:471–483.

Levine, Adeline and Janice Crumrine. 1975. "Women and the Fear of Success: A Problem in Replication." *American Journal of Sociology* 80:964–974.

Lewis, Oscar. 1966. "The Culture of Poverty." *Scientific American* 215:19–25.

Lipman-Blumen, Jean. 1972. "How Ideology Shapes Women's Lives." *Scientific American* 226:34–42.

Lipman-Blumen, Jean and Harold J. Leavitt. 1976. "Vicarious and Direct Achievement Patterns in Adulthood." *The Counseling Psychologist* 6:26–32.

Lipman-Blumen, Jean and Ann R. Ticamyer. 1975. "Sex Roles in Transition." In Alex Inkeles et al., eds., *Annual Review of Sociology* 1:297–337.

Lueptow, Lloyd B. 1973. "Need for Achievement and Continuation in College." *Psychological Reports* 33:455–458.

—— 1975. "Parental Status and Influence and the Achievement Orientations of High School Seniors." *Sociology of Education* 48:91–110.

—— 1980a. "Social Structure, Social Change, and Parental Influence in Adolescent Sex Role Socialization: 1964–1975." *Journal of Marriage and the Family* 42:93–103.

—— 1980b. "Gender Wording, Sex, and Response to Achievement Value Items." *Psychological Reports* 46:140–142.

—— 1980c. "Consensus, Change, and Stability in Sex Role Orientations, 1974–1977." *Sociological Focus* 13:125–141.

Lueptow, Lloyd B. and Lynn Clough. n.d. "Consensus and Stability in Sex Role Orientations: 1974–1980." Manuscript.

Lueptow, Lloyd B. and Brian D. Kayser. 1973–74. "Athletic Involvement, Academic Achievement, and Aspiration." *Sociological Focus* 7:24–36.

Lueptow, Lloyd B., McKee J. McClendon, and John W. McKeon. 1979. "Father's Occupation and Son's Personality: Findings and Questions for the Emerging Linkage Hypothesis." *Sociological Quarterly* 20:465–475.

Lynn, David B. 1974. *The Father: His Role in Child Development*. Monterey, Calif.: Brooks/Cole.

McClelland, David C., John W. Atkinson, Russell A. Clark, and Edgar L. Lowell. 1953. *The Achievement Motive*. New York: Appleton-Century-Crofts.

—— 1961. *The Achieving Society*. Princeton: Van Nostrand.

McClendon, McKee J. 1976. "The Occupational Status Attainment Processes of Males and Females." *American Sociological Review* 41:52–64.

Maccoby, Eleanor Emmons and Carol Nagy Jacklin. 1974. *The Psychology of Sex Differences*. Stanford: Stanford University Press.

McDonald, Gerald W. 1977. "Parental Identification by the Adolescent: A Social Power Approach." *Journal of Marriage and the Family* 39:705–719.

McGhee, Paul E. and Terry Frueh. 1980. "Television Viewing and the Learning of Sex-Role Stereotypes." *Sex Roles* 6:179–188.

Macke, Anne Stathams and William R. Morgan. 1978. "Maternal Employment, Race, and Work Orientations of High School Girls." *Social Forces* 57:187–204.

McKee, J. P. and A. C. Sherriffs. 1959. "Men's and Women's Beliefs, Ideals, and Self-Concepts." *American Journal of Sociology* 64:356–363.

Mackie, Marlene. 1977. "On Congenial Truths: A Perspective on Women's Studies." *Canadian Review of Sociology and Anthropology* 14:117–128.

McLaughlin, Steven D. 1978. "Sex Differences in the Determinants of Status." *Sociology of Work and Occupations* 5:5–31.

Mandle, Joan D. 1979. *Women and Social Change in America*. Princeton: Princeton Book Co.

Manhardt, P. J. 1972. *"Job Orientation of Male and Female College Graduates in Business."* *Personnel Psychology* 25:361–368.

Marini, Margaret M. and Ellen Greenberger. 1978. "Sex Differences in Occupational Aspirations and Expectations." *Sociology of Work and Occupations* 5:147–178.

Mason, Karen Oppenheimer, John L. Czajka, and Sara Arber. 1976. "Change in U.S. Women's Sex-Role Attitudes, 1974–1974." *American Sociological Review* 41:573–396.

Matteson, David R. 1975. *Adolescence Today: Sex Roles and Search for Identity*. Homewood, Ill.: Dorsey Press.

Mead, Geroge Herbert. 1934. *Mind, Self, and Society: From the Standpoint of a Social Behaviorist*. C. W. Manis, ed. Chicago: University of Chicago Press.

Meyer, Buf. 1980. "The Development of Girl's Sex-Role Attitudes." *Child Development* 51:508–514.

Miller, Ann P. 1978. "Changing Work Life Patterns: A Twenty-Five Year Review." *Annals* 435:83–101.

Miller, Joanne, Carmi Schooler, Melvin L. Kohn, and Karen Miller. 1979. "Women and Work: The Psychological Effects of Occupational Conditions." *American Journal of Sociology* 85:66–94.

Mischel, Walter. 1966. "A Social-Learning View of Sex Differences in Behavior." In Eleanor Maccoby, ed., *The Development of Sex Differences*, pp. 56–81. Stanford: Stanford University Press.

Money, John and Patricia Tucker. 1975. *Sexual Signatures: On Being a Man or a Woman*. Boston: Little, Brown.

Monteiro, Lois A. 1978. "Change and Stability: Attitudes Toward Women's Role and Abortion: 1970 to 1975." Paper presented at the annual meeting of the Population Association of America.

Moore, Helen and Catherine Strickler. 1980. "The Counseling Profession's Response to Sex-Biased Counseling: An Update." *Personnel and Guidance Journal* 59:84–87.

Morris, Charles and Linwood Small. 1971. "Changes in the Conceptions of the Good Life by American College Students from 1950 to 1970." *Journal of Personality and Social Psychology* 20:254–260.

Morris, Richard T. and Raymond J. Murphy. 1959. "The Situs Dimension in Occupational Structure." *American Sociological Review* 24:231–234.

Moynihan, Mary Minard. 1979. "Extracurricular Activities, Maternal Employment, and the Educational and Occupational Aspirations of Females and Males." Ph.D. dissertation, University of Akron.

Mullis, Ina V. S. 1975. *Educational Achievement and Sex Discrimination*. Denver: Education Commission of the States.

Mussen, Paul H. 1969. "Early Sex-Role Development." In David A. Goslin, ed., *Handbook of Socialization, Theory and Research*, pp. 707–732. Chicago: Rand McNally.

Nagely, D. L. 1971. "Traditional and Pioneer Working Mothers." *Journal of Vocational Behavior* 1:331–341.

Nash, Sharon Churnin. 1979. "Sex Role as a Mediator of Intellectual Functioning." In Michele A. Wittig and Anne C. Petersen eds., *Sex Related Differences in Cognitive Functioning*, pp. 263–302. New York: Academic Press.

National Assessment of Educational Progress (NAEP). 1971a. National Assessment Report 4. 1969–1970 Science: Group Results for Sex, Region, and Size of Community. Washington, D.C.: GPO.

—— 1971b. *National Assessment Report 5. 1969–Writing: Group Results for Sex, Region and Size of Community*. Washington, D.C.: GPO.

—— 1978. *Three National Assessments of Science: Changes in Achievement, 1969–1977*. Denver: Education Commission of the States.

—— 1979. *Changes in Mathematical Achievement, 1973–1978. Results from the Second Assessment of Mathematics*. Denver: Education Commission of the States.

Neal, Arthur and Melvin Seeman. 1964. "Organization and Powerlessness: A Test of the Mediation Hypothesis." *American Sociological Review* 29:216–226.

Neufeld, E., D. Langmeyer, and W. Seeman. 1974. "Some Sex-Role Stereotypes and Personal Preferences, 1950 and 1970." *Journal of Personality Assessment* 38:247–254.

Niles, F. S. 1979. "The Adolescent Girls' Perception of Parents and Peers." *Adolescence* 55:591–597.

O'Donnell, Jo Anne and Dale G. Anderson. 1978. "Factors Influencing Choice of Major and Career of Capable Women." *Vocational Guidance Quarterly* 26:214–221.

Oppenheimer, Valerie Kincade. 1968. "The Sex-Labeling of Jobs." *Industrial Relations* 7:219–234.

—— 1973. "Demographic Influence on Female Employment and the Status of Women." *American Journal of Sociology* 78:946–961.

Orlofsky, Jacob L. 1979. "Parental Antecedents of Sex-Role Orientation in College Men and Women." *Sex Roles* 5:495–512.

Parelius, Ann P. 1975a. "Change and Stability in College Women's Orientations Toward Education, Family and Work." *Social Problems* 22:420–432.

—— 1975b. "Emerging Sex-Role Attitudes, Expectations, and Strains among College Women." *Journal of Marriage and the Family* 37:146–153.

Parsons, Talcott. 1951. *The Social System.* Glencoe, Ill.: Free Press.

—— 1959. "The School Class as a Social System: Some of Its Functions in American Society." *Harvard Educational Review* 29:297–318.

—— 1964. *Social Structure and Personality.* New York: Free Press.

Parsons, Talcott, Robert Bales, and James Olds. 1955. *Family, Socialization, and Interaction Process.* Glencoe, Ill.: Free Press.

Piaget, J. 1965. *The Moral Judgment of the Child.* New York: Free Press.

Poloma, Margaret M. and T. Neal Garland. 1971. "The Myth of the Egalitarian Family: Familial Roles and the Professionally Employed Wife." In Athena Theodore, ed., *The Professional Woman,* pp. 741–761. Cambridge, Mass.: Schenkman.

Rehberg, Richard A. 1969. "Behavioral and Attitudinal Consequences of High School Interscholastic Sports: A Speculative Consideration." *Adolescence* 4:69–88.

Rehberg, Richard A. and Evelyn R. Rosenthal. 1978. *Class and Merit in the American High School.* New York: Longman.

Rehberg, Richard W. and Judie Sinclair. 1970. "Adolescent Achievement Behavior: Family Authority Structure and Parental Socialization Practices." *American Journal of Sociology* 75:1012–1034.

Reiss, Albert J., Jr. 1966. "Social Organization and Socialization: Variations on a Theme about Generations." Manuscript, University of Michigan.

Riessman, David. 1950. *The Lonely Crowd: A Study of the Changing American Character.* New Haven: Yale University Press.

Rohrbaugh, Joanna Bunker. 1979. *Women: Psychology's Puzzle.* New York: Basic Books.

Rosen, Bernard C. 1956. "The Achievement Syndrome." *American Sociological Review* 21:203–211.

—— 1959. "Race, Ethnicity, and the Achievement Syndrome." *American Sociological Review* 24:47–60.

—— 1973. "Social Change, Migration, and Family Interaction in Brazil." *American Sociological Review* 38:198–212.

Rosen, Bernard C. and Carol S. Aneshensel. 1978. "Sex Differences in the Educational-Occupational Expectation Process." *Social Forces* 57:164–186.

Rosen, Bernard C. and R. G. D'Andrade. 1959. "The Psychosocial Origins of Achievement Motivation." *Sociometry* 22:185–218.

Rosenberg, Bernard G. and B. Sutton-Smith. 1968. "Family Interaction Effects on Masculinity-Femininity." *Journal of Personality and Social Psychology* 8:117–120.

Rosenberg, Morris. 1957. *Occupations and Values.* New York: Free Press.

Rosenfeld, Rachel. 1978. "Women's Intergenerational Occupational Mobility." *American Sociological Review* 43:36–46.

Rosenkrantz, Paul, Susan Vogel, Helen Bee, Inge Broverman, and Donald M. Broverman. 1968. "Sex-Role Stereotypes and Self-Concepts in College Students." *Journal of Consulting and Clinical Psychology* 32:287–295.

Rosenthal, R. and R. L. Rosnow. 1975. *The Volunteer Subject.* New York: Wiley.

Rossi, Alice S. 1964. "Equality Between the Sexes: An Immodest Proposal." *Daedalus* 93:607–652.

—— 1965. "Women in Science: Why so Few?" *Science* 148:1196–1202.

—— 1977. "A Bio-Social Perspective on Parenting." *Daedalus* 106:1–33.

Ruble, Thomas L. 1983. "Sex Stereotypes: Issues of Change in the 1970s." *Sex Roles* 9:397–402.

Saario, Terry N., Carol Nagy Jacklin, and Carol Kehr Tittle. 1973. "Sex Role Stereotyping in the Public Schools." *Harvard Educational Review* 43:386–416.

Safilios-Rothschild, Constantine. 1979. *Sex Role Socialization and Sex Discrimination: A Synthesis and Critique of the Literature.* Washington, D.C.: U.S. Department of Health, Education and Welfare.

Sassen, Georgia. 1980. "Success Anxiety in Women: A Constructivist Interpretation of Its Source and Its Significance." *Harvard Educational Review* 50:13–24.

Saunders, Fay. 1975. "Sex Roles and the School." *Prospects* 5:362–371.

Scanzoni, John. 1972. *Sexual Bargaining.* Englewood Cliffs, N.J.: Prentice Hall.

—— 1976. "Sex Role Change and Influence on Birth Intentions." *Journal of Marriage and the Family* 38:43–58.

Schlossberg, Nancy K. and John J. Pietrofesa. 1978. "Perspectives on Counseling Bias: Implications for Counselor Education." In Lenore W. Harmon, Janice M. Birk, Laurine E. Fitzgerald, and Mary Faith Tanney, eds., *Counseling Women,* pp. 59–74. Monterey, Calif.: Brooks/Cole.

Schmidt, Gunter and Volkmar Sigusch. 1972. "Changes in Sexual Behavior Among Young Males and Females Between 1960–1970." *Archives of Sexual Behavior* 2:27–45.

Schooler, Carmi. 1972. "Social Antecedents of Adult Psychological Functioning." *American Journal of Sociology* 78:299–322.

Schreiber, E. M. 1978. "Education and Change in American Opinions on a Woman for President." *Public Opinion Quarterly* 42:171–182.

Schuler, Randall S. 1975. "Sex, Organizational Level, and Outcome Importance: Where the Differences Are." *Personnel Psychology* 28:365–375.

Schwartz, Audrey J. 1971. "A Comparative Study of Values and Achievement: Mexican-American and Anglo Youth." *Sociology of Education* 44:438–462.

Seater, Barbara B. and Cecilia L. Ridgeway. 1976. "Role Models, Significant Others, and the Importance of Male Influence on College Women." *Sociological Symposium* 15:49–64.

Seeman, Melvin. 1863. "Alienation and Social Learning in a Reformatory." *American Journal of Sociology* 69:270–284.

Seeman, Melvin and J. W. Evans. 1962. "Alienation and Learning in a Hospital Setting." *American Sociological Review* 27:772–782.

Seward, John P. and Georgene H. Seward. 1980. *Sex Differences: Mental and Temperamental.* Lexington, Mass.: Lexington Books.

Sewell, William H. 1965. "Community of Residence and Occupational Choice." *American Journal of Sociology* 70:551–563.

—— 1971. "Inequality of Opportunity for Higher Education." *American Sociological Review* 36:793–809.

Sewell, William H. and Robert M. Hauser. 1975. *Education, Occupation, and Earnings: Achievement in the Early Career.* New York: Academic Press.

Sewell, William H., Robert M. Hauser, and Wendy C. Wolf. 1980. "Sex, Schooling, and Occupational Status." *American Journal of Sociology* 86:551–583.

Sewell, William H. and Vimal P. Shah. 1968. "Parent's Education and Children's Educational Aspirations and Achievement." *American Sociological Review* 33:191–209.

Shaw, Merville C. and John T. McCuen. 1960. "The Onset of Academic Underachievement in Bright Children." *Journal of Educational Psychology* 51:103–108.

Sherman, Julia A. 1975. "Review of the *Psychology of Sex Differences* by Maccoby, E. E. and Jacklin, C. N." *Sex Roles* 1:297–301.

—— 1977. "Effects of Biological Factors on Sex-Related Differences in Mathematics Achievement." In Lynn H. Fox, Elizabeth Fennema, and Julia Sherman, *Women and Mathematics: Research Perspectives for Change*, pp. 137–206. Washington, D.C.: GPO.

—— 1978. *Sex-Related Cognitive Differences: An Essay on Theory and Evidence.* Springfield, Ill.: Charles C. Thomas.

Sherriffs, A. C. and J. P. McKee. 1957. "Qualitative Aspects of Beliefs about Men and Women." *Journal of Personality* 25:451–464.

Simpson, Richard L. 1974. "Sex Stereotypes of Secondary School Teaching Subjects: Male and Female Status Gains and Losses." *Sociology of Education* 47:388–398.

Smith, Thomas Ervin. 1970. "Foundations of Parental Influence upon Adolescents: An Application of Social Power Theory." *American Sociological Review* 35:860–872.

—— 1976. "Push Versus Pull: Intra-Family Versus Peer-Group Variables as Possible Determinants of Adolescent Orientations Toward Parents." *Youth and Society* 8:5–26.

Smuts, Robert W. 1971. *Women and Work in America.* New York: Schocken Books. (Originally published in 1959 by Columbia University Press.)

Spence, Janet T. and Robert L. Helmreich. 1978. *Masculinity and Femininity: Their Psychological Dimensions, Correlates and Antecedents.* Austin: University of Texas Press.

Spitz, Glenna and Joan Huber. 1980. "Changing Attitudes Toward Women's Nonfamily Roles:1938–1978." *Sociology of Work and Occupations* 7:317–335.

Stake, Jayne E. and Ellen Levitz. 1979. "Career Goals of College Women and Men and Perceived Achievement-Related Encouragement." *Psychology of Women Quarterly* 4:151–159.

Stein, Aletha H. and Margaret M. Bailey. 1975. "The Socialization of Achievement Motivation in Females." In Martha T. S. Mednick, Sandra Schwartz Tangri, and Lois Wladis Hoffman, eds., *Women and Achievement*, pp. 151–157. Washington, D.C.: Hemisphere.

Strodtbeck, Fred. 1958. "Family Interaction, Values, and Achievement." In David C. McClelland et al., eds., *Talent and Society*, pp. 135–158. New York: Van Nostrand.

Tangri, Sandra Schwartz. 1972. "Determinants of Occupational Role Innovation Among College Women." *Journal of Social Issues* 28:177–199.

Tanney, Mary F. and Janice M. Birk. 1978. "Women Counselors for Women Clients? A Review of the Research." In Lenore W. Harmon, Janice M. Brik, Laurine E. Fitzgerald, and Mary Faith Tanney, eds., *Counseling Women*, pp. 108–217. Monterey, Calif.: Brooks/Cole.

Thornton, Arland and Deborah Freedman. 1979. "Changes in the Sex Role Attitudes of Women, 1962–1977: Evidence from a Panel Study." *American Sociological Review* 44:831–842.

Thornton, Arland, Duane F. Alwin, and Donald Camburn. 1983. "Causes and Consequences of Sex-Role Attitudes and Attitude Change." *American Sociological Review* 48:211–227.

Tibbets, Sylvia Lee. 1979. "Research in Sexism: Some Studies of Children's Reading Material Revisited." *Educational Research Quarterly* 4:34–39.

Tönnies, Ferdinand. 1940. *Fundamental Concepts of Sociology.* Charles P. Loomis, translator. New York: American Book Co.

Treiman, Donald J. and Kermit Terrell. 1975a. "Sex and the Process of Status Attainment: A Comparison of Working Women and Men." *American Sociological Review* 40:174–200.

—— 197b. "Women, Work, and Wages—Trends in the Female Occupation Structure." In Kenneth Land and Seymour Spilerman, eds., *Social Indicator Models*, pp. 157–199. New York: Russell Sage.

Turner, Ralph. 1964. "Some Aspects of Women's Ambition." *The American Journal of Sociology* 70:271–285.

Tyree, Andrea and Judith Treas. 1974. "The Occupational and Marital Ability of Women." *American Sociological Review* 39:293–302.

United States Commission on Civil Rights. 1977. *Window Dressing on the Set: Women and Minorities in Television.* Washington, D.C.: U.S. Commission on Civil Rights.

—— 1978. *Social Indicators of Equality for Minorities and Women.* Washington, D.C.: GPO.

United States Department of Labor. 1980. *Perspectives on Working Women: a Databook.* Washington, D.C.: GPO.

Vandenberg, Steven G. and Allan R. Kuse. 1979. "Spatial Ability: A Critical Review of the Sex-Linked Major Gene Hypothesis." In Michele Andrisin Wittig and Anne C. Petersen, eds., *Sex-Related Differences in Cognitive Functioning,* pp. 67–95. New York: Academic Press.

Van Fossen, Beth Ensminger. 1977. "Sexual Stratification and Sex-Role Socialization." *Journal of Marriage and the Family* 39:503–574.

Veroff, Joseph. 1977. "Process vs. Impact in Men's and Women's Achievement Motivation." *Psychology of Women Quarterly* 1:283–293.

Veroff, Joseph, Charlene Depner, Richard Kulka, and Elizabeth Douvan. 1980. "Comparison of American Motives: 1957 versus 1976." *Journal of Personality and Social Psychology* 39:1249–1262.

Veroff, Joseph, Elizabeth Douvan, and Richard A. Kulka. 1981. *The Inner American. A Self-Protrait from 1957 to 1976.* New York: Basic Books.

Waite, Linda. 1976. "Working Wives: 1940–1960." *American Sociological Review* 41:65–80.

Walker, H. and J. Lev. 1953. *Statistical Inference.* New York: Holt.

Ward, Dawn and Jack Balswick. 1978. "Strong Men and Virtuous Women: A Content Analysis of Sex Roles Stereotypes." *Pacific Sociological Review* 21:45–53.

Weiner, Bernard. 1972. *Theories of Motivation: From Mechanism to Cognition.* Chicago: Markham.

Weitz, Shirley. 1977. *Sex Roles: Biological, Psychological, and Social Foundations.* New York: Oxford University Press.

Weitzman, Lenore J. 1979. *Sex Role Socialization.* Palo Alto, Calif.: Mayfield.

Wesley, Frank and Claire Wesley. 1977. *Sex-Role Psychology.* New York: Human Sciences Press.

Wicker, W. E. 1968. "Requirements for Protecting Privacy of Human Subjects: Some Implications for Generalization of Research Findings." *American Psychologist* 23:70–72.

Williams, Gregory. 1976. "Trends in Occupational Differentiation by Sex." *Sociology of Work and Occupations* 3:38–62.

Williams, John E. and Susan M. Bennett. 1975. "The Definition of Sex Stereotypes Via the Adjective Check List." *Sex Roles* 1:327–337.

Williams, John E. and Deborah Best. 1977. "Sex Stereotypes and Trait Favorability on the Adjective Check List." *Educational and Psychological Measurement* 37:101–110.

—— 1982. *Measuring Sex Stereotypes: A Thirty-Nation Study.* Beverly Hills: Sage Publications.

Williams, John E., Howard Giles, John R. Edwards, Deborah L. Best, and John T. Daws. 1977. "Sex-Trait Stereotypes in England, Ireland, and the United States." *British Journal of Social and Clinical Psychology* 16:303–309.

Winterbottom, Marion R. 1958. "The Relation of Need for Achievement to Learning Experiences in Independence and Mastery." In John W. Atkinson, ed., *Motives in Fantasy, Action, and Society,* pp. 453–378. New York: Van Nostrand.

Wirth, Louis. 1938. "Urbanism as a Way of Life." *American Journal of Sociology* 44:3–24.

Wittig, Michele A. and Anne C. Petersen. 1979. *Sex-Related Differences in Cognitive Functioning.* New York: Academic Press.

Wolf, Wendy C. and Rachel Rosenfeld. 1978. "Sex Structure of Occupations and Job Mobility." *Social Forces* 56:823–844.

Wright, James D. 1978. "Are Working Women *Really* More Satisfied? Evidence from Several National Surveys." *Journal of Marriage and the Family* 40:301–313.

Yankelovich, Daniel. 1974. *The New Morality: A Profile of American Youth in the 1970's.* New York: McGraw Hill.

Zeldich, Morris, Jr. 1955. "Role Differentiation in the Nuclear Family: A Comparative Study." In Talcott Parsons et al., eds., *Family, Socialization, and Interaction Process,* pp. 307–351. Glencoe, Ill.: Free Press.

Zuckerman, Diana, Dorothy G. Singer, and Jerome L. Singer. 1980. "Children's Television Viewing, Racial, and Sex-Role Attitudes." *Journal of Applied Social Psychology* 10:281–294.

NAME INDEX

SUBJECT INDEX

Academic achievement: female advantage in, 125-26; sex role stereotypes and, 141

Academic preferences and sex role stereotypes, 141

Achieved status, 2, 10-11

Achievement motivation: explaining sex differences in, 64-67; process versus impact, 124, 280, 299n19

Achievement orientations: accomplishment versus competition, 272-73; cultural foundations, 60-61; female advantage in, 274; personality dimensions, 62-63; social foundations, 61-62

Achievement syndrome, 62-63, 70

Achievement values: described, 23-24; female advantage in, 122-23; sex differences in origins, 211; social class and, 67-68

Adolescent society, 228-29, 257

Agencies of sex role socialization: athletics, 225; counseling, 238-45, curriculum and extra-curriculum, 224-26; family, 215-19; media, 219-22; peers, 228-30; teachers and counselors, 226-28, 235-36; texts, tests and readers, 222-24; see also Sex role socialization

Agentic-communal distinction, 53-54; see also Sex role stereotypes

Androgyny, 8-9, 53-54

Ascribed status, 2, 10-11, 13; negative sanctions and anxiety and, 298

Athletics: competitiveness and, 226; increased female evaluation of, 254-55; increased female involvement in, 284; increased female participation in, 254; increased female recognition in, 260; sex differences in grades of 'best athlete,' 261; universalism and, 225-26, 251

Attitudes about women's role: change in, 15-16, 277; equal pay for equal work, 85; persistence of traditional views, 286-87; sex differences in, 76-77, 93; stabilizing in late 1970s?, 85-86; woman for president, 85

"Bent twig" hypothesis, 302n7

Bias, 37-39

Biological explanations: of cognitive patterns, 157-61, 283; Freudian, 205; of persistence and consistency of stereotypes, 307n9; stability of achievement differences and, 201-2

Brain lateralization and sex differences in cognition, 160-61

Career and family roles: conflict between, 74-76, 82-84; male advantage, female disadvantage, 74-75; mother's work and child care, 74-75; status ambiguity of homemaking, 75-76; women choose both, 84-85, 91-93; work as liberating, 75-76

Civil Rights movement, 11, 26

Cognitive developmental theory, 205-7

Conditions facilitating change, 42-47

"Congenial truths," 50-51

Counseling, 23; change in use and evaluation of, 243-44, 283; decline in female advantage, 242-43, 245; influence on post-graduate plans, 235; social change reflected in, 245

Course enrollments, 20-21, 171-74

Empirical findings indexed here include both results obtained in this study and those described in the background reviews of the literature throughout the book.